2025
신경향

심슨 전략서

구문·문법·독해·생활영어
All in One 전략서

커넥츠 공단기 gong.conects.com 심슨영어연구소 카페 cafe.naver.com/shimson2000

| 심우철 지음 |

이 책의 구성과 특징

1 한 권으로 완벽 마스터하는 공시 영어 압축 요약서

심슨 전략서 한 권으로 구문·문법·독해·생활영어 전 영역 완벽 대비,
공시생들의 재도전, 초시생들의 기본서 복습 요약을 위한 압축서

2 심슨쌤만의 유일무이한 문제 풀이 전략

28년의 강의 노하우를 응축시킨 총 59가지 핵심 전략을 통해 심슨쌤만의
특별한 문제 풀이 비법과 스킬 전수

3 신경향, 신유형 완벽 반영

2025 출제 기조 전환 예시 문제를 철저하게 분석하여 교재에 완벽 반영,
새로운 경향에 맞추어 시험에 나오는 포인트들만을 엄선

4 풍부한 연습 문제

전략을 적용해 볼 수 있는 풍부한 연습 문제와 더불어 실전 감각까지 늘릴 수 있는 실전 모의고사 1회분 수록

5 상세한 해설

별도의 책으로 구성된 정답 및 해설서로 빠르게 정오답 확인 및 상세한 해설 파악

6 암기 노트

문법·어휘·생활영어 추가 학습을 위해 핸드북 형태로 암기 노트를 구성하여 시험 직전까지 핵심 문법 포인트/실무 핵심 어휘/생활영어 표현 회독 연습 가능

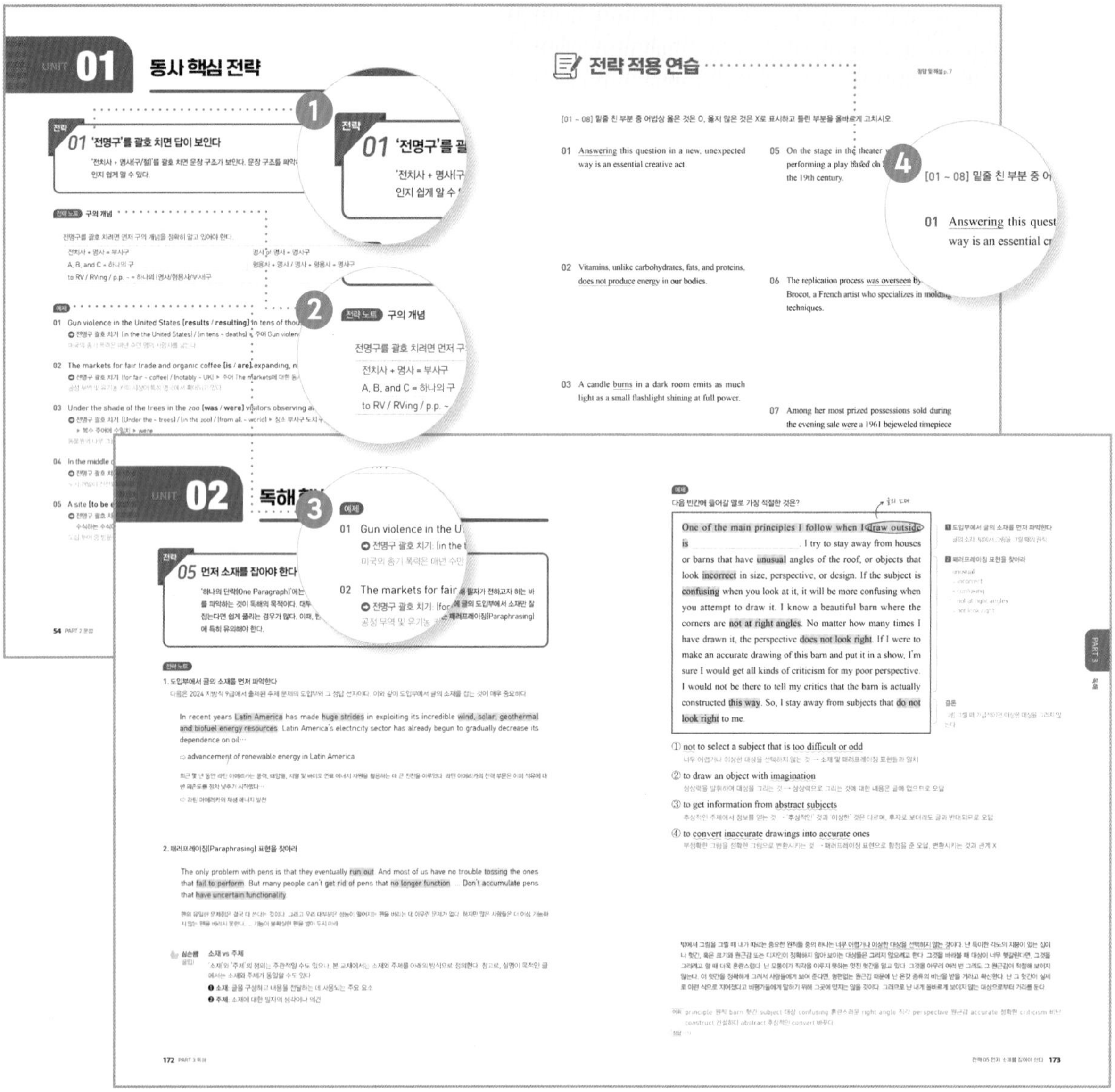

① PART별 핵심 전략

심슨쌤의 구문·문법·독해·생활영어 문제 풀이 핵심 전략을 단순 명료하게 제시

② 전략 노트

각 전략의 개념 및 이론 요약 수록

③ 예제

전략에 특화된 대표 예제 문제 풀이를 통한 전략 적용 warm-up

④ 전략 적용 연습

전략 학습 후 바로 풀어보는 연습 문제로 실력 up

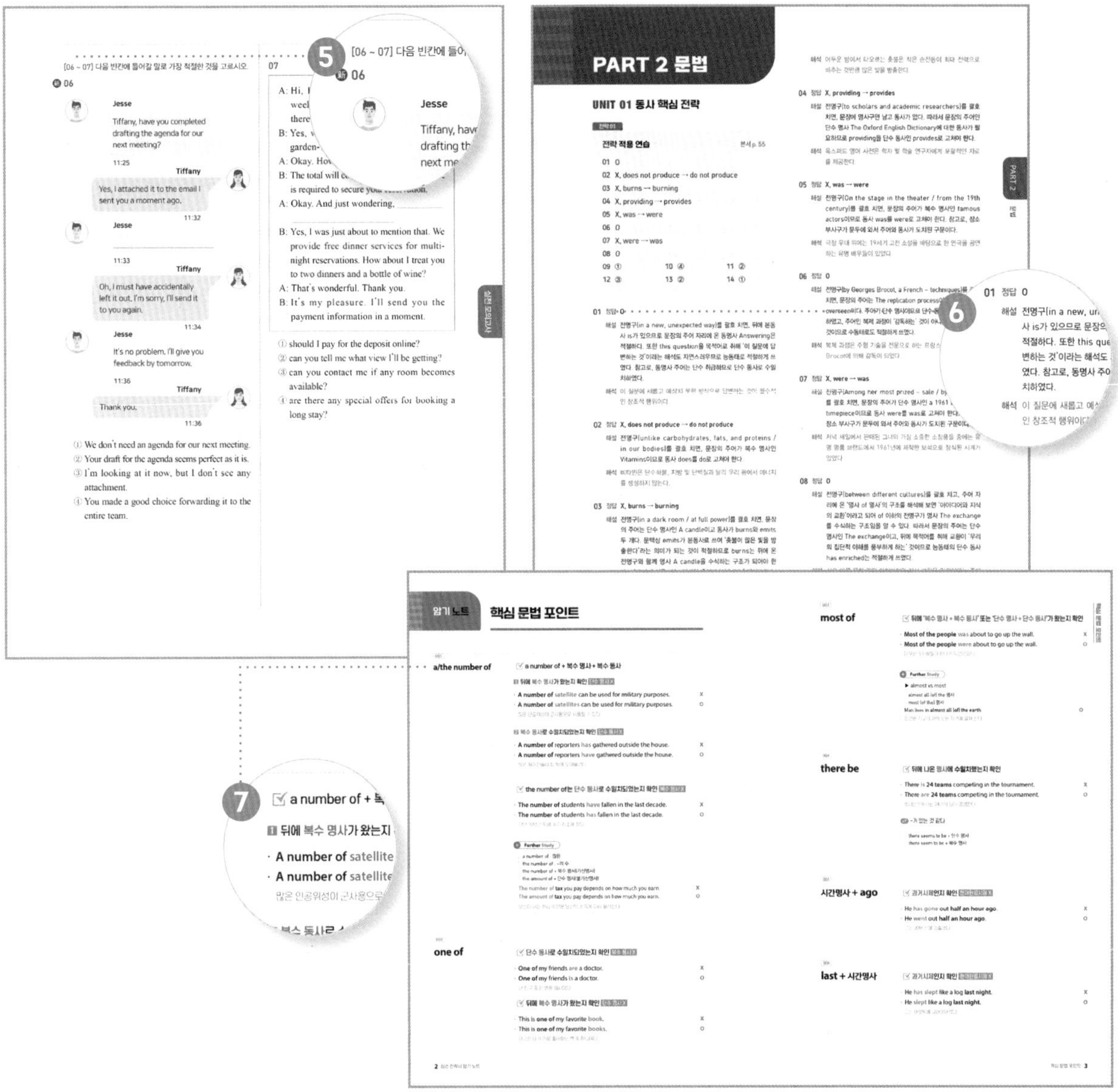

5 실전 모의고사

전략을 실전으로 적용해 볼 수 있는 실전 모의고사 1회분 수록

6 정답 및 해설

연습 문제의 정답 및 상세한 해설 제공

7 암기 노트

어휘처럼 접근하는 핵심 문법 포인트 120개, 출제 기조 전환에 맞추어 선별한 실무 핵심 어휘 200개, 주제별/상황별 생활영어 표현까지 추가 학습

목차

2025 공무원 영어, 이렇게 바뀐다

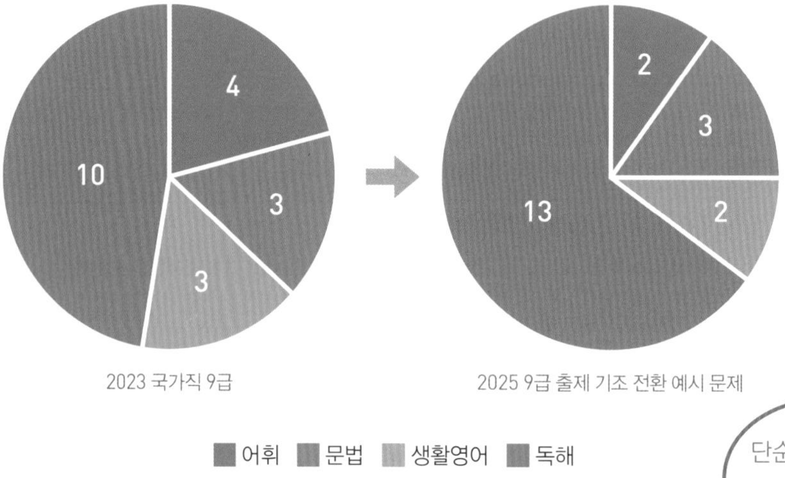

단순 암기 지양
+
독해 비중 증가

Part	2023 국가직 9급			2025 9급 출제 기조 전환 예시 문제 (2023년 11월 인사혁신처 발표)		
	문제 유형	문항 수		문제 유형	문항 수	
어휘	동의어	2문항	4문항	빈칸형	2문항	2문항
	이디엄 동의어	2문항				
문법	문장형	1문항	3문항	新 빈칸형	1문항	3문항
	영작형	1문항				
	단락형(밑줄형)	1문항		단락형(밑줄형)	2문항	
생활영어	대면형 빈칸	2문항	3문항	대면형 빈칸	1문항	2문항
	어색한 대화	1문항		新 비대면형 빈칸 (문자메시지)	1문항	
독해	제목/주제/요지/빈칸완성2/일관성/문장삽입/순서배열	10문항	10문항	新 신유형 (이메일/안내문/웹페이지)	6문항	13문항
				기존 유형 (주제/요지/일관성/문장삽입/순서배열/빈칸완성 2)	7문항	
계	20문항			20문항		

I. 어휘

문제 유형	문항 수
빈칸이 포함된 짧은 문장을 주고 선지 4개 중 의미상 가장 적절한 것을 고르는 문제	2문항

II. 문법

문제 유형	문항 수
新 빈칸형 문제 빈칸이 포함된 짧은 문장을 주고 선지 4개 중 빈칸에 들어갈 알맞은 품사나 형태를 고르거나, 문장 구조를 파악하여 어법상 가장 적절한 것을 고르는 문제	1문항
단락형(밑줄형) 문제 2 문장 이상으로 구성된 단락을 주고 밑줄 친 선지 4개 중 어법상 옳지 않은 것을 고르는 문제	2문항

출제 기조 맛보기

[1 ~ 3] 밑줄 친 부분에 들어갈 말로 가장 적절한 것을 고르시오.

1. Recently, increasingly ________ weather patterns, often referred to as "abnormal climate," have been observed around the world.

① irregular
② consistent
③ predictable
④ ineffective

2. Most economic theories assume that people act on a _________ basis; however, this doesn't account for the fact that they often rely on their emotions instead.

① temporary
② rational
③ voluntary
④ commercial

新 3. By the time she ___________ her degree, she will have acquired valuable knowledge on her field of study.

① will have finished
② is finishing
③ will finish
④ finishes

[4 ~ 5] 밑줄 친 부분 중 어법상 옳지 않은 것을 고르시오.

4. You may conclude that knowledge of the sound systems, word patterns, and sentence structures ① are sufficient to help a student ② become competent in a language. Yet we have ③ all worked with language learners who understand English structurally but still have difficulty ④ communicating.

III. 생활영어

문제 유형	문항 수
대면형 빈칸 문제 두 명이 주고받는 대화문에서 맥락상 빈칸에 들어갈 가장 적절한 표현을 고르는 문제	1문항
新 비대면형 빈칸 문제 두 명이 주고받는 문자 메시지에서 맥락상 빈칸에 들어갈 가장 적절한 표현을 고르는 문제	1문항

[6 ~ 7] 밑줄 친 부분에 들어갈 말로 가장 적절한 것을 고르시오.

6.

A: Hello. I'd like to book a flight from Seoul to Oakland.
B: Okay. Do you have any specific dates in mind?
A: Yes. I am planning to leave on May 2nd and return on May 14th.
B: Okay, I found one that fits your schedule. What class would you like to book?
A: Economy class is good enough for me.
B: Any preference on your seating?
A: ______________________________
B: Great. Your flight is now booked.

① Yes. I'd like to upgrade to business class.
② No. I'd like to buy a one-way ticket.
③ No. I don't have any luggage.
④ Yes. I want an aisle seat.

新 7.

Kate Anderson
Are you coming to the workshop next Friday?
10:42

Jim Henson
I'm not sure. I have a doctor's appointment that day.
10:42

Kate Anderson
You should come! The workshop is about A.I. tools that can improve our work efficiency.
10:43

Jim Henson
Wow, the topic sounds really interesting!
10:44

Kate Anderson
Exactly. But don't forget to reserve a seat if you want to attend the workshop.
10:45

Jim Henson
How do I do that?
10:45

Kate Anderson
____
10:46

① You need to bring your own laptop.
② I already have a reservation.
③ Follow the instructions on the bulletin board.
④ You should call the doctor's office for an appointment.

IV. 독해

문제 유형	문항 수
新 유형 • **이메일**: 민원 관련 이슈, 업무 관련 내용 등 (목적/동의어 문제 출제) • **안내문**: 행사 안내문(정부 및 지자체 연계 행사)(제목/불일치 문제 출제) • **웹페이지 글**: 공공업무/정부 및 지자체 업무 또는 관련 사업(일치/불일치 문제 출제)	총 6문항 (지문당 1~2문항)
기존 유형	총 7문항

▶ 문제 유형 소개

- **주제·제목·목적**: 지문에서 글의 핵심 내용을 묻는 문항으로 주제·제목·목적으로 가장 적절한 것을 고르는 문제
- **요지·주장**: 지문에서 필자가 강조하거나 필자의 견해를 뒷받침하는 내용으로 가장 적절한 것을 고르는 문제
- **일관성**: 지문 내에 4개의 밑줄 친 문장 중 주제와 연관성이 없거나 문장 간의 논리적 흐름이 가장 어색한 문장을 고르는 문제
- **문장 삽입**: 1~2 문장의 별도로 주어진 글이 있고, 4개의 선지가 지문 문장 사이사이에 위치하여 주어진 글이 위치할 자리로 가장 알맞은 것을 고르는 문제
- **순서 배열**: 1~2 문장의 별도로 주어진 글 뒤로 각 문장의 지시사, 대명사, 연결어 등의 세부적인 연결고리를 찾아 가장 알맞게 이어질 (A)~(C)의 문단 순서를 고르는 문제
- **빈칸 추론**: 지문에서 밑줄 친 자리에 들어갈 내용으로 가장 알맞은 것을 고르는 문제
- **일치·불일치**: 지문과 일치하거나 일치하지 않는 선지를 고르는 문제 (영문/한글 선지 혼용)

[8 ~ 9] 다음 글을 읽고 물음에 답하시오.

新

Send Preview Save

To	Clifton District Office
From	Rachael Beasley
Date	June 7
Subject	Excessive Noise in the Neighborhood

My PC Browse

To whom it may concern,

I hope this email finds you well. I am writing to express my concern and frustration regarding the excessive noise levels in our neighborhood, specifically coming from the new sports field.

As a resident of Clifton district, I have always appreciated the peace of our community. However, the ongoing noise disturbances have significantly impacted my family's well-being and our overall quality of life. The sources of the noise include crowds cheering, players shouting, whistles, and ball impacts.

I kindly request that you look into this matter and take appropriate <u>steps</u> to address the noise disturbances. Thank you for your attention to this matter, and I appreciate your prompt response to help restore the tranquility in our neighborhood.

Sincerely,
Rachael Beasley

8. 윗글의 목적으로 가장 적절한 것은?
   ① 체육대회 소음에 대해 주민들의 양해를 구하려고
   ② 새로 이사 온 이웃 주민의 소음에 대해 항의하려고
   ③ 인근 스포츠 시설의 소음에 대한 조치를 요청하려고
   ④ 밤시간 악기 연주와 같은 소음의 차단을 부탁하려고

9. 밑줄 친 "steps"의 의미와 가장 가까운 것은?
   ① movements
   ② actions
   ③ levels
   ④ stairs

新 [10 ~ 11] 다음 글을 읽고 물음에 답하시오.

(A)

We're pleased to announce the upcoming City Harbour Festival, an annual event that brings our diverse community together to celebrate our shared heritage, culture, and local talent. Mark your calendars and join us for an exciting weekend!

Details

- **Dates:** Friday, June 16 – Sunday, June 18
- **Times:** 10 : 00 a.m. – 8 : 00 p.m. (Friday & Saturday)
  10 : 00 a.m. – 6 : 00 p.m. (Sunday)
- **Location:** City Harbour Park, Main Street, and surrounding areas

Highlights

- **Live Performances**
  Enjoy a variety of live music, dance, and theatrical performances on multiple stages throughout the festival grounds.
- **Food Trucks**
  Have a feast with a wide selection of food trucks offering diverse and delicious cuisines, as well as free sample tastings.

For the full schedule of events and activities, please visit our website at www.cityharbourfestival.org or contact the Festival Office at (552) 234-5678.

10. (A)에 들어갈 윗글의 제목으로 가장 적절한 것은?
① Make Safety Regulations for Your Community
② Celebrate Our Vibrant Community Events
③ Plan Your Exciting Maritime Experience
④ Recreate Our City's Heritage

11. City Harbour Festival에 관한 윗글의 내용과 일치하지 않는 것은?
① 일 년에 한 번 개최된다.
② 일요일에는 오후 6시까지 열린다.
③ 주요 행사로 무료 요리 강습이 진행된다.
④ 웹사이트나 전화 문의를 통해 행사 일정을 알 수 있다.

新 12. Enter-K 앱에 관한 다음 글의 내용과 일치하지 않는 것은?

Enter-K
https://enter-k.org
MENU

Use the new **Enter-K** app for your customs declaration.

Use the new Enter-K app upon your arrival at the airport. One notable feature offered by Enter-K is the Advance Declaration, which allows travellers the option to submit their customs declaration in advance, enabling them to save time at all our international airports. As part of the ongoing Traveller Modernization initiative, Enter-K will continue to introduce additional border-related features in the future, further improving the overall border experience. Simply download the latest version of the app from the online store before your arrival. There is also a web version of the app for those who are not comfortable using mobile devices.

① It allows travellers to declare customs in advance.
② More features will be added later.
③ Travellers can download it from the online store.
④ It only works on personal mobile devices.

新 13. Office of the Labor Commissioner에 관한 다음 글의 내용과 일치하는 것은?

office of labor
https://olc.gov.org/introduction
Office of the Labor Commissioner
INTRODUCTION POLICY ISSUES DATA SERVICES NEWS SEARCH
HOME > INTRODUCTION

Office of the Labor Commissioner (OLC) Responsibilities

The OLC is the principal labor regulatory agency for the state. The OLC is responsible for ensuring that minimum wage, prevailing wage, and overtime are paid to employees, and that employee break and lunch periods are provided. In addition, the OLC has authority over the employment of minors. It is the vision and mission of this office to resolve labor-related problems in an efficient, professional, and effective manner. This includes educating employers and employees regarding their rights and responsibilities under the law. The OLC takes enforcement action when necessary to ensure that workers are treated fairly and compensated for all time worked.

① It ensures that employees pay taxes properly.
② It has authority over employment of adult workers only.
③ It promotes employers' business opportunities.
④ It takes action when employees are unfairly treated.

17. 주어진 문장이 들어갈 위치로 가장 적절한 것은?

> In particular, in many urban counties, air pollution, as measured by the amount of total suspended particles, had reached dangerous levels.

> Economists Chay and Greenstone evaluated the value of cleaning up of air pollution after the Clean Air Act of 1970. (①) Before 1970, there was little federal regulation of air pollution, and the issue was not high on the agenda of state legislators. (②) As a result, many counties allowed factories to operate without any regulation on their pollution, and in several heavily industrialized counties, pollution had reached very high levels. (③) The Clean Air Act established guidelines for what constituted excessively high levels of five particularly dangerous pollutants. (④) Following the Act in 1970 and the 1977 amendment, there were improvements in air quality.

18. 주어진 글 다음에 이어질 글의 순서로 가장 적절한 것은?

> Before anyone could witness what had happened, I shoved the loaves of bread up under my shirt, wrapped the hunting jacket tightly about me, and walked swiftly away.

> (A) When I dropped them on the table, my sister's hands reached to tear off a chunk, but I made her sit, forced my mother to join us at the table, and poured warm tea.
>
> (B) The heat of the bread burned into my skin, but I clutched it tighter, clinging to life. By the time I reached home, the loaves had cooled somewhat, but the insides were still warm.
>
> (C) I sliced the bread. We ate an entire loaf, slice by slice. It was good hearty bread, filled with raisins and nuts.

① (A) – (B) – (C)
② (B) – (A) – (C)
③ (B) – (C) – (A)
④ (C) – (A) – (B)

[19 ~ 20] **밑줄 친 부분에 들어갈 말로 가장 적절한 것을 고르시오.**

19.

> Falling fertility rates are projected to result in shrinking populations for nearly every country by the end of the century. The global fertility rate was 4.7 in 1950, but it dropped by nearly half to 2.4 in 2017. It is expected to fall below 1.7 by 2100. As a result, some researchers predict that the number of people on the planet would peak at 9.7 billion around 2064 before falling down to 8.8 billion by the century's end. This transition will also lead to a significant aging of populations, with as many people reaching 80 years old as there are being born. Such a demographic shift ______________, including taxation, healthcare for the elderly, caregiving responsibilities, and retirement. To ensure a "soft landing" into a new demographic landscape, researchers emphasize the need for careful management of the transition.

① raises concerns about future challenges
② mitigates the inverted age structure phenomenon
③ compensates for the reduced marriage rate issue
④ provides immediate solutions to resolve the problems

PART 1

구문

구문(문장 해석) 핵심 공략법

1 2025 공무원 영어 시험 출제 기조 전환

구분	출제 기조 전환 전	출제 기조 전환 후
어휘	동의어 찾기 문제	빈칸형 문제 ▶ 문장 해석이 중요해짐
문법	짧은 문장의 단편적 문법 지식을 묻는 문제	단락형 문제 ▶ 긴 문장의 해석이 필요해짐
독해	9~10 문항	13문항 ▶ 독해 문항 비중이 높아짐

2 구문 학습의 중요성

2025 출제 기조 전환 예시를 살펴보면 토익형 문법 문제(빈칸형)와 생활영어 문제를 제외하고 모든 지표가 '정확한 해석 능력 강화'를 가리키고 있다. 문장을 정확하고 빠르게 해석하기 위해서는 무엇보다도 구문 학습이 선행되어야 한다. 문장의 구조를 파악할 수 있어야 문장 해석이 가능하며, 해석이 되어야 글을 읽고 문제를 정확하게 풀 수 있기 때문이다. 구문 파트에서는 최신 경향에 맞추어 반드시 알아야 할 핵심적인 12가지 구문 해석 전략을 한데 모아 소개한다. 이 전략들로 대부분의 영어 문장을 해석할 수 있다고 자신한다.

UNIT 01

문장 해석 핵심 전략

전략 01 '전명구'만 괄호 쳐도 해석이 보인다

전략 노트

1. 전치사 + 명사 = 부사구[부가 정보]

[전치사 + 명사]는 부가 정보를 나타내므로 괄호 치고 없는 셈한다.

- The baby (on the sofa) (in the living room) saw her parents.
  거실에서 소파 위의 아기가 부모를 보았다.

2. 명사 of 명사 = 명사구

① ~의 ② ~중에 ③ ⤺ ④ 동격

- the development of science 과학의 발전
- one of his friends 그의 친구들 중에 한 명
- a cup of milk 한 잔의 우유
- the city of Seoul 서울이라는 도시

3. A, (B,) and/or C = 하나의 단위(구)

① 명사, 명사, and/or 명사 = 명사구
② 형용사, 형용사, and/or 형용사 = 형용사구
cf. 전치사 + 명사구 → 부사구

- emotions like grief, guilt, resentment, and anger
  슬픔, 죄책감, 분노, 그리고 노여움과 같은 감정들
- The color of the T-shirt must be red, yellow, or blue.
  티셔츠의 색은 빨강, 노랑, 또는 파랑이어야 한다.

4. 형용사 + 명사 / 명사 + 형용사 = 명사구

① 형용사 + 명사/명사 + 형용사 = 명사구
② 명사 + to RV/RVing/p.p./관계사절 = 명사구

- the single picture 단 하나의 그림
- a book written in English 영어로 쓰인 책
- the ability to move goods, people, and information safely
  물건들, 사람들, 그리고 정보를 안전하게 이동시키는 능력

전략 적용 연습

정답 및 해설 p. 2

[01 ~ 20] 다음을 해석하시오.

01 the purpose of your letter

02 one of the greatest baseball players

03 one of the most popular and enduring toys

04 the democratic ideals of the young country

05 over half of the world's millions of species of plants and animals

06 the principle of 'equality of opportunity' fundamental to the individual

07 one of the important changes from a traditional society to a modern society

03
enduring 오래가는

04
democratic 민주(주의)적인

05
millions of 수백만의

06
fundamental 중요한, 근본적인

08 an efficient way to socialize with other students

08
socialize with ~와 어울리다

09 the decline of socialism and the emergence of capitalism in the twentieth century

09
decline 쇠퇴, 감소
emergence 등장

10 a blended characteristic of emotional, intellectual, and behavioral talents

10
blended 혼합된

11 The development of sports into the forms of the present day began in late 17th century England.

12 One of the most peculiar public health problems in post-Presley America is mass fainting at pop music concerts.

12
peculiar 특이한, 독특한
fainting 실신

13 With the rapid spread of railways and the increase in ocean transport, long distance traveling became more common.

13
spread 확산

14 Schools also try to teach the important value of life such as honesty, good manners, teamwork, and cooperation.

14
cooperation 협동

15 The economic changes in East Asia are one of the most significant developments in the world in the second half of the 20th century.

15
significant 중요한
the second half 후반(기)

16 Apart from these two basic relationships, the animal may be affected directly or indirectly in countless different ways by other plants and animals around it.

16
apart from ~외에도
countless 셀 수 없이 많은

17 The greatest of all the accomplishments of 20th-century science is the discovery of the structure of DNA by James Watson and Francis Crick in 1953.

17
accomplishment 업적
structure 구조(물)

18 Rigorous consideration and reconsideration of customer needs is critical to any process for developing and launching new or improved products and services.

18
rigorous 엄격한
critical 중요한, 비판적인
launch 출시하다

19 The development of the first laptop computers in 1986 was accelerated by the creation of CPUs around the mid-1980s or computer central processing units.

19
accelerate 가속화하다

20 The different races of mankind have a sufficient sexual attraction for each other so that in the absence of any geographical or cultural obstacles to genetic mixture it is highly probable that in the course of a few thousand years the human race would become racially uniform.

20
sufficient 충분한
attraction 매력
absence 없음, 부재
probable (어떤 일이) 있을 것 같은
uniform 단일한, 획일적인

전략

02 해석이 복잡하면 동사를 잡아라

전략 노트

1. 동사에 따라 결정되는 문장의 5형식과 해석법

1형식(완전 자동사)	S + V	S가 V하다
2형식(불완전 자동사)	S + V + SC	S는 SC이다
3형식(완전 타동사)	S + V + O	S는 O를 V하다
4형식(수여 동사)	S + V + IO + DO	S는 IO에게 DO를 V하다
5형식(불완전 타동사)	S + V + O + OC	S는 O가 OC하도록/하는 것을 V하다

- The accident happened yesterday. 그 사고는 어제 발생했다.
- She is an English teacher. 그녀는 영어 선생님이다.
- The early bird catches the worm. 일찍 일어나는 새가 벌레를 잡는다.
- He gave me a birthday present. 그는 나에게 생일 선물을 주었다.
- You always make me happy. 너는 언제나 날 행복하게 만든다.

2. CIPARST 동사: 직접목적어에 주로 명사절을 취하는 4형식 동사

convince
inform
promise
ask
remind
show
tell
teach

\+

O(사람)
O에게

\+

that절
what절
if[whether]절
to RV
~라고 / ~라는 것을 / ~하도록

▶

확신시켜 주다
알려 주다
약속하다
묻다
상기시키다
보여 주다
말하다
가르쳐 주다

- Cindy convinced me that she could make it on time.
  Cindy는 나에게 자신이 제시간에 도착할 수 있다고 확신시켜 주었다.
- The doctor informed her that her baby had a rare disease.
  의사는 그녀에게 그녀의 아기가 희귀병을 가졌다는 것을 알려 주었다.
- John reminded Mary that she should get there early.
  John은 Mary에게 그녀가 그곳에 일찍 도착해야 한다고 상기시켰다.

3. 지각동사

see / watch / observe hear / listen to notice feel	+	O	+	OC(RV/RVing/p.p.)	▶	보다 듣다 알아채다 느끼다
		O가		OC하도록/하는 것을		

• I saw him enter the room. 나는 그가 방에 들어가는 것을 보았다.

• She felt the raindrops fall[falling] on her face. 그녀는 얼굴에 빗방울이 떨어지는 것을 느꼈다.

4. 사역동사

let have make	+	O	+	OC(RV/p.p.)	▶	시키다·허락하다 시키다·요청하다 시키다·강요하다
		O가		OC하도록/하는 것을		

❶ 사역동사 let은 목적어와 목적격 보어의 관계가 수동일 때 목적격 보어로 반드시 be p.p.를 써야 한다.

• They won't let him leave the country. 그들은 그가 나라를 떠나지 못하게 할 것이다.

• My boss had me bring the document. 나의 상사는 내가 그 서류를 가져오게 했다.

• My mother made me clean my room. 엄마는 내가 내 방을 청소하게 했다.

5. 준사역동사

help	+	(O)	+	(to) RV	▶	돕다
		(O가)		(to) RV하는 것을		

get	+	O	+	OC(to RV/p.p.)	▶	시키다
		O가		to RV하도록/p.p.되도록		

• My wife helped me (to) make breakfast. 내 아내는 내가 아침을 만드는 것을 도와주었다.

• Many people got us to put out the fire. 많은 사람들이 우리가 불을 끄도록 했다.

6. COREAF/P 동사: 목적격 보어에 to 부정사를 사용하는 동사

동사	+ O + to RV	뜻
cause		야기하다
compel		강요하다
order		명령하다
require		요구하다
enable		할 수 있게 하다
expect		예상[기대]하다
encourage		격려[장려]하다
ask		요청[요구]하다
allow		허락[허가]하다
advise		조언[충고]하다
force		강제[강요]하다
permit		허락하다

+ O (O가) + to RV (to RV하도록/하는 것을)

- The poor harvest caused prices to rise sharply. 흉작은 급격한 가격 상승을 야기시켰다.
- I won't enable him to behave like that. 나는 그가 그렇게 행동할 수 있게 두지 않을 것이다.
- The company forced its employees to work overtime. 회사는 직원들이 야근하는 것을 강요했다.

전략 적용 연습

정답 및 해설 p. 2

[01 ~ 19] 다음을 해석하시오.

01 The letters from my boyfriend and lots of pencils were on the desk in my room.

02 The pleasures of contact with the natural world are not reserved just for the artists.

02
reserved 예약된, 지정된, 제한된

03 One of the most remarkable communication systems found in the world of animals is that of the European honeybee.

03
remarkable 놀랄 만한, 주목할 만한

04 Comfortable living conditions include not only chemical and physical cleanliness, but also privacy, space, and quietness.

04
comfortable 편안한, 쾌적한

05 Implementing strict cybersecurity protocols at your workplace can prevent unauthorized access and the inadvertent disclosure of confidential information.

05
implement 시행하다
unauthorized 공인[승인]되지 않은
inadvertent 부주의한
disclosure 공개
confidential 기밀의

06 The combination of wide-ranging knowledge and technical expertise gave him a unique preparation for addressing complex challenges in the field of artificial intelligence.

06
wide-ranging 폭넓은
address 해결하다

07 When giving performance feedback, you should consider the recipient's past performance and your estimate of his or her future potential in designing its frequency, amount, and content.

07
recipient 받는 사람
estimate 평가, 추정(치)

08 The division of Europe into a number of independent states, connected, however, with each other by the general resemblance of religion, language, and manners, is productive of the most beneficial consequences to the liberty of mankind.

08
division 분할
productive ~을 가져오는
beneficial 유익한
consequence 결과, 중요성

09 The constant noises of electronic devices like computers, mobile phones, fax machines, stereos, and home appliances will drown out the sounds of the birds singing in the morning, the wind blowing through the trees, or a pencil drawing on rough paper.

09
constant 끊임없는
appliance 가전제품
drown out (소음이) ~을 들리지 않게 하다
rough 거칠거칠한

10 They should remind passengers to keep buses clean through the use of the signs.

11 The women's hormones also help the body keep itself against some kinds of illnesses.

12 There is no doubt that allowing children to see any movies may do harm to them.

13 The strategic use of strong brand image and brand power allows companies to expand their business.

13
strategic 전략적인
expand 확장시키다

14 Many bosses tell people what to do and how and when to do it, without explaining the reasons for their rules.

15 Consequently, doctors advise people to eat more grains, fruit and vegetables, and eat less meat and fewer dairy products.

15
consequently 그 결과
dairy product 유제품

16 Richardson promised us that he would prioritize consistent and transparent communication at every stage of the project's timeline.

16
prioritize 우선시키다
consistent 일관된
transparent 투명한

17 Let children look at their fingers through a magnifying glass, and they'll understand why mothers want them to wash before dinner.

17
magnifying glass 돋보기

18 The teacher had the students submit their essays by Friday without any exception, emphasizing the importance of meeting the deadline for thorough feedback and constructive revisions.

18
emphasize 강조하다
thorough 철저한
revision 수정

19 Growing concern about global climate change has caused activists to organize not only campaigns against fossil fuel extraction consumption, but also campaigns to support renewable energy.

19
concern 우려
extraction 추출

전략

03 동사 뒤를 예상하는 힘을 길러라

전략 노트

1. 분리·박탈 동사

동사		O(사람)		of	명사		의미
rob deprive clear relieve cure	+	O(사람) ~에게서	+	of	명사 ~을/를	▶	빼앗다 빼앗다 제거하다, 치우다 완화하다, 덜어 주다 치료하다, 없애다

- He tried to rob her of her share of her father's estate.
  그는 그녀에게서 아버지의 재산 중 그녀의 몫을 빼앗으려고 애썼다.
- The accident deprived me of the pleasure of baseball.
  그 사건이 나에게서 야구의 즐거움을 빼앗았다.
- This medicine will relieve you of your pain.
  이 약은 당신의 통증을 가라앉힐 겁니다.

2. 인지 동사

동사		O(사람)		of	명사		의미
convince inform remind assure warn notify	+	O(사람) ~에게	+	of	명사 ~을/를	▶	확신시키다 알리다 상기시키다 보증하다 경고하다 통보하다

- You'll need to convince them of your enthusiasm for the job.
  당신은 그 직무에 대한 당신의 열정을 그들에게 확신시킬 필요가 있을 겁니다.
- She informed them of the news about the strong typhoon.
  그녀는 그들에게 강력한 태풍에 대한 소식을 알렸다.
- It reminds me of the memories of the past 24 years.
  그것은 내게 지난 24년간의 기억을 상기시켜 준다.

3. 제공 동사

동사		목적어					의미
provide / supply / furnish / present	+	O(사람)	+	with	명사	▶	제공하다
endow		~에게		~을/를			부여하다
equip							갖추게 하다

- Many public universities in Europe provide students with an excellent free education.
  유럽의 많은 공립 대학들은 학생들에게 뛰어난 무상 교육을 제공한다.
- Foreign governments supplied the rebels with weapons.
  외국 정부들이 그 반군들에게 무기를 공급했다.

4. 금지·억제 동사

동사		목적어					의미
keep / prevent / stop / discourage / hinder / prohibit	+	O(사람)	+	from	(동)명사	▶	방해하다, 막다
deter / dissuade		~이/가		~하지 못하도록			단념하게 하다
ban							금지하다

- The extremely cold weather kept the football club from practicing outside.
  너무 추운 날씨는 축구팀이 밖에서 연습하는 것을 못 하게 했다.
- The school prohibits students from using cell phones in class.
  학교는 학생들이 수업 시간에 휴대전화를 사용하는 것을 금지한다.
- Failure didn't deter him from trying again.
  실패는 그가 다시 도전하는 것을 단념시키지 못했다.

전략 적용 연습

정답 및 해설 p. 3

[01 ~ 06] 다음을 해석하시오.

01 We have to provide children with an opportunity to learn to get along with one another.

01
get along with ~와 잘 지내다

02 The tour guide informed the tourists of the itinerary changes due to unexpected road closures caused by a local festival.

02
itinerary 여행 일정표
closure 폐쇄

03 The supervisor reminded the staff of the importance of punctuality for the upcoming staff meeting scheduled for tomorrow morning.

03
supervisor 감독관
punctuality 시간 엄수
upcoming 다가오는

04 The unexpected betrayal by his closest friend deprived Peter of his trust in others, leading him to become cautious and careful in his relationships.

04
betrayal 배신
cautious 조심하는

05 Installing smoke detectors in your home can prevent fires from spreading silently and causing extensive damage before they escalate into major emergencies.

05
escalate 확대되다
major 심각한, 중대한

06 The economic crisis robbed many families of their ability to afford essential items like food, housing, and medical care, leaving them struggling to make ends meet and facing increased financial stress.

06
struggling 어려움을 겪고 있는
make ends meet 생계를 꾸려나가다
face 직면하다

UNIT 02 절 해석 핵심 전략

전략 04 문장에 'that'이 나오면 앞에서 끊는다

전략 노트

1.

동사/형용사 + that + S + V

접속사: ~것/사실

that 앞에 동사나 형용사가 나오면, that은 명사절을 이끄는 접속사이다. 해석은 '~것, ~사실'로 해석한다.

- He realized that he had made a terrible mistake.
  그는 자신이 엄청난 실수를 저질렀다는 사실을 깨달았다.
- Experts believe that the coming drought will be more intense.
  전문가들은 다가오는 가뭄이 더 극심해질 것이라고 믿고 있다.
- He is afraid that she will forget to bring the toy back.
  그는 그녀가 장난감을 돌려주는 걸 잊어버릴까 봐[잊을 것이라는 사실이] 두렵다.

2.

명사 + that + ① (S) + V / ② S + V

① 관계대명사: 그런데 그 명사
② 동격: ~라는

that 앞에 명사가 나오면, that은 ① 관계대명사(그런데 그 명사)나 ② 동격(~라는)으로 쓰인다. 특히 that 앞에 idea, belief, thought, news, rumor, fact, truth, possibility, evidence와 같은 단어가 나오면 that 이하는 앞의 명사에 대한 동격의 that일 수 있다.

- Mark has a book that is very interesting.
  Mark는 책을 한 권 가지고 있다. 그런데 그 책은 매우 재미있다. = Mark는 매우 재미있는 책을 한 권 가지고 있다.
- I enjoyed the movie that we watched together last weekend.
  나는 영화를 즐겼다. 그런데 그 영화는 우리가 지난 주말에 함께 봤던 것이다. = 나는 지난 주말에 우리가 함께 봤던 영화를 즐겼다.
- The fact that he passed away makes me sad.
  그분이 돌아가셨다는 사실은 나를 슬프게 한다.
- The truth that honesty is the best policy is widely accepted.
  정직이 최선의 정책이라는 진실은 널리 받아들여진다.

전략 적용 연습

정답 및 해설 p. 3

[01 ~ 10] 다음을 해석하시오.

01 Television has high-quality programs that help us understand many fields of study like science, medicine, the arts, and so on.

02 Traffic jams that might be caused by poor road conditions slow the delivery of goods and services and often prevent people from getting to work on time.

02
traffic jam 교통 체증

03 Hurricanes bring winds and slashing rains that flood streets, flatten homes, and leave survivors struggling to pick up the pieces.

03
slashing 세찬, 맹렬한
flood 물에 잠기게 하다
flatten (건물 등)을 무너뜨리다, ~을 납작하게 만들다
pick up the pieces 사태를 수습하다

04 At your age, your great-grandparents never dreamed that personal computers would receive e-mail letters from anywhere in the world.

05 More and more studies are finding that certain foods and spices can provide effective relief from common health problems.

05
relief 경감, 제거

06 An important belief of the religion was that the gods would give magical powers to those who offered them payment in the form of a food or animal sacrifice.

06
sacrifice (신에게 바치는) 제물, 희생

07 Some people have found that certain colors on the package of an attractive product will cause people to reach out and take that product instead of buying another product of the same kind with different colors.

08 He was incredibly proud that she had overcome her stage fright and delivered a flawless performance.

09 The possibility that life exists on other planets and that we might one day communicate with extraterrestrial beings inspires scientific exploration.

10 The evidence that smoking is linked to lung cancer and that quitting can significantly reduce health risks underscores the importance of public health campaigns.

07
attractive 마음을 끄는
reach out (손 등을) 뻗다

08
fright 공포
flawless 완벽한, 흠 없는

09
extraterrestrial 지구 밖의, 외계의
inspire 자극하다, 고무하다

10
underscore 강조하다

전략

05 문장 중간에 'S + V'가 나오면 that이 생략되었다

전략 노트

1.

동사	+	(that)	+	S + V
		접속사: ~것/~사실		

문장 중간에 'S + V'가 나오고 그 앞에 동사가 나오면 명사절을 이끄는 접속사 that이 생략되었다.

- She believes Tom will succeed in his new job.
  그녀는 Tom이 그의 새 직장에서 성공할 것이라고 믿는다.
- The environment ministry said only 26 percent of the country was below sea level.
  환경부는 나라의 오직 26%만이 해수면 아래에 있다고[있다는 사실을] 말했다.

2.

명사	+	(that)	+	S + V
		목적격 관계대명사		

문장 중간에 'S + V'가 나오고 그 앞에 명사가 나오면 목적격 관계대명사가 생략되었다.

- A true friend is a person you can trust.
  진정한 친구는 당신이 신뢰할 수 있는 사람이다.
- Tension is the most widespread complaint people bring to their physicians.
  긴장은 사람들이 의사에게 가져오는 가장 널리 퍼진 불평이다.

전략 적용 연습

정답 및 해설 p. 3

[01 ~ 07] 다음을 해석하시오.

01 Recently, however, there has been a lot of research that proves our mind affects illness and healing.

02 They really insist their company should use only one specific method or technology to improve efficiency.

03 I think people are free to do anything they want, so long as it does not violate law and public morality.

04 Sometimes little children are so 'sold' by commercials that they really believe their family must eat only one kind of cream or use a certain brand of soap.

05 Listening to somebody else's ideas is the one way to know whether the story you believe about the world — as well as about yourself and your place in it — remains accurate or requires adjustment.

06 Although it is hard to accept that this person doesn't return your feelings, it may help you to know that the pain you now feel will be erased from your heart when you find someone who does love you back.

07 A mouse potato is the computer equivalent of television's couch potato; someone who tends to spend a great deal of leisure time in front of the computer in much the same way the couch potato does in front of the television.

03
violate (법 등을) 어기다
public morality 공중도덕

04
sell 설득하다
commercial 광고 (방송); 상업의

05
adjustment 조정

06
erase 지워 버리다

07
mouse potato (일·오락을 위해) 컴퓨터 앞에서 시간을 많이 보내는 사람
equivalent (가치·크기 등에서) 대응어구, 동등한 것
couch potato 오랫동안 가만히 앉아 텔레비전만 보는 사람

전략

06 맨 앞에 '명사 + 관계사'가 나오면 두 번째 동사가 진짜 동사다

전략 노트

명사	+	관계사	+	(S) + V1 ~	+	V2
S						진짜 V

문장 맨 앞에 「명사(S) + 관계대명사/관계부사」가 나오면, 두 번째 동사가 진짜 동사가 된다.

- The book which is on the desk belongs to me.
  책상 위에 있는 책은 내 것이다.
- The consumers who use home shopping are now trendier than in the past.
  홈쇼핑을 이용하는 소비자들은 과거보다 지금 더 유행에 민감하다.
- In reality, the people who are most different from us probably have the most to teach us.
  실은, 우리와 가장 다른 사람들이 아마도 우리에게 가르칠 것이 가장 많을 것이다.
- In mature markets, breakthroughs that lead to a major change in competitive positions and to the growth of the market are rare.
  충분히 발달한 시장에서는 경쟁적 지위들에서의 중요한 변화와 시장의 성장을 가져오는 획기적인 발전이 드물다.

전략 적용 연습

정답 및 해설 p. 4

[01 ~ 06] 다음을 해석하시오.

01 Many old people who have watched TV for a long time think that watching TV for hours makes people foolish.

02 Young people who are armed with a strong sense of ethics and morals will not be affected by those harmful websites.

02
armed 무장한
ethic 윤리

03 The final impression you make to prospective employers, colleagues, or clients can be just as important as the initial impression you made.

03
prospective 미래의, 장래의
initial 처음의

04 A meta-analysis of numerous studies on childhood development concluded that children who develop a love for reading at a young age tend to perform better academically throughout their lives.

04
numerous 수많은

05 The scientist who had dedicated his entire career to researching a cure for a rare disease finally made a medical breakthrough that could save millions of lives.

05
dedicate 바치다, 전념하다
breakthrough 획기적[비약적] 발전

06 The children who listened to the radio produced more imaginative responses, whereas the children who watched the television produced more words that repeated the original story.

06
imaginative 창의적인
whereas 반면에

전략

07 맨 앞에 접속사가 나오면 콤마에서 끊는다

전략 노트

접속사	+	S + V ~,	/ +	S + V
S + V ~	/ +	접속사	+	S + V

문장 맨 앞에 접속사가 나오면 콤마(,)에서 끊고, 문장 중간에 접속사가 나오면 접속사 앞에서 끊어 해석한다.

- When the sun comes out, / flowers bloom.
  해가 뜨면 꽃이 핀다.
- Because you are a hard worker, / I will nominate you for the promotion.
  당신이 열심히 일하는 사람이기 때문에, 나는 당신을 승진에 후보로 지명할 것이다.
- Since Thomas Edison first made moving pictures, / movies have been very popular.
  Thomas Edison이 처음으로 영화를 제작한 이래로 영화는 매우 인기가 있어 왔다.
- As long as you follow the recipe, / the cake will turn out delicious.
  네가 레시피를 따르는 한 케이크는 맛있게 나올 것이다.
- Most cats will not scratch / unless you touch them.
  대부분의 고양이들은 만지지 않으면 할퀴지 않을 것이다.
- Driving is strictly prohibited / while you use this medicine.
  당신이 이 약을 사용하는 동안에는 운전이 엄격히 금지되어 있다.
- You can go home early / once you finish the work.
  일단 당신이 일을 끝내기만 하면 집에 일찍 갈 수 있다.
- The audience applauded her / as she walked on stage.
  그녀가 무대 위로 걸어갈 때, 청중들은 그녀에게 박수를 보냈다.

전략 적용 연습

정답 및 해설 p. 4

[01 ~ 06] 다음을 해석하시오.

01 When you are online, there is a great temptation to use bad language because you don't know the person you are speaking to.

01
temptation 유혹

02 Whenever he encountered obstacles on his journey, he reflected on whether they're opportunities for growth and strove to overcome them with perseverance.

02
encounter (우연히) 만나다
reflect on 되돌아보다
strive 노력하다
perseverance 인내(심)

03 Their parents may not be aware of the danger of excessive screen time, because it has not attracted the attention of modern science, though many children have been experiencing negative effects on their health and development.

03
excessive 과도한
attract attention 관심을 끌다

04 People feel excited and happy when their favorite team wins, and they feel sad and disappointed when their favorite team loses.

05 Once you hit on something you find interesting, keep asking questions in order to get the other person engaged in the conversation and deepen your understanding of the topic.

05
hit on (방법·계획 등)을 갑자기 떠올리다
engage in ~에 참여하다
deepen 심화시키다

06 The visitor to the Himalayas will seldom meet anybody who has actually seen the elusive snow leopard with his own eyes, although everyone says that they have a brother or a cousin or a friend who has seen one.

06
elusive 눈에 잘 띄지 않는, 파악하기 어려운
snow leopard 눈 표범

전략

08 '관계사 vs 의문사'는 앞에 명사의 유무를 본다

전략 노트

1. 관계대명사

명사	+	who(m) / which / that / whose+명사	+	(S) + V

① ~하는 ② 그런데 그 명사

who(m)/which/that/whose 앞에 명사가 있으면 관계대명사로, 해석은 '그런데 그 명사'로 해석하면 직독직해가 가능해진다.

- I have a sister who is a writer.
  나는 여동생이 있다. 그런데 그 여동생은 작가이다. = 나는 작가인 여동생이 있다.
- He is a teacher whom[that] we admire.
  그는 선생님이다. 그런데 그 선생님을 우리가 존경한다. = 그는 우리가 존경하는 선생님이다.

2. 관계부사

명사	+	when / where / why / how	+	S + V

① ~하는 ② 그런데 그 명사에서(는)

when/where/why/how 앞에 명사가 있으면 관계부사로, 해석은 '그런데 그 명사에서(는)'로 해석하면 직독직해가 가능해진다.

- He lives near the Han River where many Koreans enjoy their leisure time.
  그는 한강 근처에서 산다. 그런데 그 한강에서 많은 한국인들이 그들의 여가 시간을 즐긴다.
  = 그는 많은 한국인들이 그들의 여가 시간을 즐기는 한강 근처에 산다.

3. 의문사

who	whose + 명사	which	which + 명사	what	what + 명사	+	(S) + V
누가·누구	누구의 명사	어느 것	어느·어떤 명사	무엇·것	무슨·어떤 명사		

when	where	why	how	how + 형·부	+	S + V
언제	어디서	왜	어떻게 ~하는 방법	얼마나 형·부하는지		

who/whose/which/what/when/where/why/how 앞에 명사가 안 나오면, 의문사로 사용되었다.

- Everybody knows who gave the money to Shimson.
  누가 그 돈을 Shimson에게 주었는지를 모두가 알고 있다.
- There are many theories about why the dinosaurs went extinct.
  공룡이 왜 멸종되었는지에 대한 많은 이론들이 있다.

전략 적용 연습

정답 및 해설 p. 4

[01 ~ 14] 다음을 해석하시오.

01 Biologists and researchers will be provided with DNA information that will be key to understanding the structure, organization, and function of DNA.

02 They do their best to create enjoyable and protective environments in which the children feel comfortable and safe.

03 The person to whom I offered a helping hand during their darkest moments eventually became my closest confidant and lifelong friend.

04 The requirements of fashion have dictated some curious designs, not all of which made walking easy.

05 This is probably why these treatments, most of which are now deemed to be completely ineffective, usually appeared to "cure" the problem.

06 The coach appointed as team captain the person who he knew had earned the respect and admiration of their teammates through their hard work and dedication.

01
key 핵심적인; 열쇠

03
helping hand 도움
confidant (비밀도 털어놓는 절친한) 친구

04
dictate 지정하다

05
deem ~라고 여기다

06
appoint 임명하다
admiration 칭찬
dedication 헌신

07 She couldn't help but wonder who might have left the anonymous note on her desk, filled with cryptic messages and clues.

07
anonymous 익명의
cryptic 수수께끼 같은, 비밀의
clue 단서

08 She was deeply intrigued by the rumors about who might have discovered the hidden treasure buried deep within the ancient cemetery.

08
intrigue 흥미를 끌다
cemetery 묘지

09 The team members were discussing whom they should appoint as the new team leader for the project and which criteria they should prioritize in their decision-making process.

09
criteria 기준(criterion의 복수형)
prioritize 우선순위를 매기다

10 They debated for days about where to go for dinner and finally decided which restaurant they would choose for their anniversary celebration.

10
debate 의논하다
anniversary 기념일

11 We also have a message board area where young people can freely communicate about their problems.

11
message board 게시판

12 After hours of searching, they finally found where the hidden treasure was buried, deep beneath the ancient oak tree in the forest clearing.

12
ancient 아주 오래된, 고대의
oak tree 오크 나무
clearing 개간지

13 He explained how physical activity positively influences cognitive processes, emphasizing a multitude of benefits that regular exercise brings to overall brain health.

13
cognitive 인지의
a multitude of 아주 많은
overall 전반적인

14 Every parent knows how crucial the choice of friends is for every child. Childhood friendships tell parents which ways their children are tending.

14
crucial 매우 중요한
tend (어떤 방향으로) 나아가다

전략

09 복합관계사는 '모든'의 의미를 갖는다

전략 노트

PART 1 구문

1. who(m)ever / whichever / whatever ⊕ (S) + V

~하는 사람이면 누구든(지 간에) / ~하는 것이면 어느 것이든 / 무엇이든(지 간에)

- Whoever finds the coin in the bread will have good luck for the coming year.
  그 빵에서 동전을 발견하는 사람이면 누구든지 내년에 행운을 갖게 될 것이다.
- Whichever they choose, we must accept their decision.
  그들이 선택하는 것이면 어느 것이든지, 우리는 그들의 결정을 수락해야만 한다.

2. whichever / whosever / whatever + 명사 ⊕ (S) + V

~하는 어느 명사든 / 누구의 명사든 / 어떤[무슨] 명사든

- Whichever side they choose, we must respect their decision.
  그들이 선택하는 어느 쪽이든, 우리는 그들의 결정을 존중해야만 한다.
- I can give you whatever book you want.
  나는 네가 원하는 어떤 책이든 너에게 줄 수 있다.

3. whenever(= no matter when) / wherever(= no matter where) ⊕ S + V

~할 때마다 / ~하는 곳마다

- Whenever you come, she will meet you.
  네가 올 때마다, 그녀는 너를 만날 것이다.
- I observe the moon wherever I go.
  나는 가는 곳마다 달을 관찰한다.

4. however(= no matter how) + 형·부 ⊕ S + V

아무리 형·부해도

- However hard you try, you cannot win the race.
  네가 아무리 열심히 노력할지라도, 너는 그 경주에서 이길 수 없다.

5. no matter who / no matter which / no matter what ⊕ (S) + V

~하는 사람이면 누구든지 간에 / ~하는 것이면 어느 것이든지 간에 / 무엇이든지 간에

- I will not give up on my dream, no matter what they say.
  그들이 말하는 게 무엇이든지 간에 나는 내 꿈을 포기하지 않을 것이다.

전략 적용 연습

정답 및 해설 p. 5

[01 ~ 07] 다음을 해석하시오.

01 Whichever path you choose to follow, make sure it leads you towards fulfillment and happiness.

01
fulfillment 성취(감)

02 Whoever stands by your side during tough times, you should express your gratitude and appreciation for their resolute loyalty and care.

02
tough 힘든
gratitude 고마움
appreciation 감사
resolute 굳건한

03 Whoever takes the time to listen to others with empathy and understanding fosters deeper connections and stronger relationships.

03
take the time to RV 시간을 들여 ~하다
empathy 공감
foster 조성하다

04 Whatever steps one takes to support their friends during challenging times strengthen their friendships and foster a sense of unity and solidarity.

04
take step(s) 조치를 취하다
challenging 힘든, 도전적인
strengthen 강화하다
unity 일치단결
solidarity 연대

05 Whatever doubts may cloud your thoughts, remember that you are capable of achieving greatness, and trust in your abilities to reach new heights.

05
cloud 흐리게 하다
height 단계, 높이

06 No matter how many setbacks you face, remember that each one is a stepping stone towards success.

06
setback 좌절
stepping stone 디딤돌

07 No matter where your journey takes you, remember that every destination holds its own lessons and adventures.

07
lesson 교훈

UNIT 03 준동사 해석 핵심 전략

전략 10 문장 맨 앞에 준동사가 나오면 콤마를 찾아라

전략 노트

1.

To RV ~ , ⊕ S + V

to RV하기 위해

문장 맨 앞에 「To RV ~ , S + V」가 나오면, 목적을 나타내는 부사적 용법으로 'to RV하기 위해'로 해석한다.

• To appreciate this film, we should understand its historical background.
이 영화를 감상하기 위해서는, 우리는 그것의 역사적 배경을 이해해야 한다.

2.

To RV ~ ⊕ V

to RV하는 것은

문장 맨 앞에 「To RV ~ + V」가 나오면, 주어로 쓰여서 'to RV하는 것은'이라고 해석한다. 이때 to RV는 명사적 용법이다.

• To save enough money to buy a house is very important to married couples.
집을 살 정도의 충분한 돈을 저축하는 것은 부부들에게 매우 중요하다.

3.

RVing / p.p. ~ , ⊕ S + V

RV하다 / p.p.되다 | 그런 S가

문장 맨 앞에 「RVing / p.p. ~, S + V」가 나오면 분사구문이다. 이때 주어(S) 앞에 '그런'을 붙여서 해석한다.

• Written in plain English, the book has been read by many people.
쉬운 영어로 쓰였다. 그런 그 책은 많은 사람들에 의해 읽혔다. → 쉬운 영어로 쓰인 그 책은 많은 사람들에 의해 읽혔다.

4.

RVing ~ ⊕ V

RVing하는 것은

문장 맨 앞에 「RVing ~ + V」가 나오면, 주어로 쓰여서 'RVing은' 또는 'RVing하는 것은'이라고 해석한다. 이때의 RVing은 동명사이다.

• Taking in lots of water before you go to sleep will help you wake up in a good mood.
잠자리에 들기 전에 물을 많이 마시는 것은 네가 기분 좋게 일어나도록 도와줄 것이다.

전략 적용 연습

정답 및 해설 p. 5

[01 ~ 11] 다음을 해석하시오.

01 To determine what should and should not be retouched is extremely difficult.

01
retouch 수정하다

02 To make them feel more comfortable during their travels, some members of the tour group advised, "When in Rome, do as the Romans do."

03 To read a good national daily or to watch the news on TV is one of the quickest ways to keep abreast of the day's events.

03
keep abreast of ~을 놓치지 않다, ~에 뒤처지지 않게 하다

04 To provide training and job placement assistance for unemployed individuals, the government implemented various programs aimed at enhancing employability skills.

04
job placement 취업 알선[배치]
enhance 향상시키다
employability 취직 능력

05 Working in the dairy, he learned that no matter what the size of the bottle, the cream always came to the top.

05
dairy 낙농장

06 Experiencing an extremely shocking event, some people continue to re-experience it through dreams and recollections.

06
recollection 회상

07 Becoming a good conversationalist requires knowing how to start a conversation, how to keep it going, and how to end a conversation.

07
conversationalist 달변가, 이야기를 잘하는 사람

08 Asked if he could come to the party that night, he eagerly accepted the invitation and promised to bring a gift for the host.

08
eagerly 열렬히

09 Discovering a hidden waterfall deep in the forest during our hiking expedition, we were enchanted by its majestic beauty and tranquil surroundings.

09
expedition (탐험 등의) 여행
enchant 매료시키다
majestic 장엄한
tranquil 고요한

10 Coupled with the free flow of information which is a natural result of free trade, a prosperous middle class will eventually demand political change and this will ultimately lead to a gradual democratization of the country and an improvement in its human rights records.

10
prosperous 부유한
gradual 점진적인

11 Ensuring the protection of students from cyberbullying necessitates the implementation of comprehensive educational programs that promote responsible digital citizenship and foster a culture of respect and empathy in virtual spaces.

11
ensure 보장하다
cyberbullying 사이버 폭력
necessitate 필요로 하다
comprehensive 종합적인
responsible 책임이 따르는

전략

11 문장 중간에 준동사가 나오면 앞에 무엇이 왔는지를 봐라

전략 노트

1.

be ⊕ to RV

① to RV하는 것이다 (90%)
② be to 용법 (10%)

to RV 앞에 be동사가 나온 경우, ① 'to RV하는 것이다' 또는 'be to 용법(예정· 의무·의도·가능·운명)'으로 해석한다.

• The key is to find a form of exercise that you enjoy.
핵심은 당신이 좋아하는 형태의 운동을 찾는 것이다.

• He is to arrive here this evening. [be to 용법: 예정]
그는 오늘 저녁에 여기에 도착할 것이다.

2.

명사 ⊕ to RV

① 앞 명사 수식
② to RV하기 위해

to RV 앞에 명사가 나온 경우, ① 앞 명사 수식(to RV하는/to RV할) 또는 ② 'to RV하기 위해(목적)'로 해석한다. 특히 명사가 way, effort, ability, time, possibility, opportunity, tendency, right이면 to RV는 주로 앞 명사를 수식한다.

• We have the right to express our thoughts.
우리는 우리의 생각을 표현할 권리가 있다.

• The way to learn a language is to practice speaking it as often as possible.
언어를 배우는 방법은 가능한 한 자주 그 언어로 말하는 것을 연습하는 것이다.

• She bought some eggs to make scrambled eggs.
그녀는 스크램블드 에그를 만들기 위해 달걀을 조금 샀다.

3.

감정·판단의 표현 ⊕ to RV — 이유·원인 | ~~~ to RV — 목적 or 결과

to RV 앞에 감정·판단의 표현이 나온 경우, 이유·원인(to RV하게 되어서)으로 해석한다. 나머지의 경우는 목적(to RV하기 위해) 혹은 결과(그 결과 to RV하다)로 해석한다.

• I am happy to help you with your report.
나는 너의 보고서를 도와줘서 기쁘다.

• She exercised hard to lose weight.
그녀는 몸무게를 줄이기 위해서 열심히 운동했다.

4.

명사 ⊕ RVing / p.p. : 앞에 명사를 수식

RVing하는 / p.p.된

RVing / p.p. 앞에 명사가 나온 경우 명사를 수식하는 분사로, RVing은 현재분사로 'RVing하는 명사'로 해석하고, p.p.는 과거분사로 'p.p.된 명사'라고 해석한다.

- The person standing across the street is my brother.
  길 건너에 서 있는 사람이 내 동생이다.
- The package delivered to the wrong address can be returned.
  잘못된 주소로 배달된 소포는 반송될 수 있다.

5.

전치사 / 동사 ⊕ RVing : 동명사로 해석

RVing하는 것

RVing 앞에 전치사나 동사가 나온 경우, 동명사로서 'RVing하는 것'으로 해석한다.

- She left here without saying a good-bye to us.
  그녀는 우리에게 작별 인사를 하는 것 없이 이곳을 떠났다.
- We all enjoy watching movies together on weekends.
  우리는 모두 주말에 함께 영화를 보는 것을 즐긴다.

6.

콤마(,) ⊕ RVing / p.p. : 분사구문으로 앞에 '그러면서'를 붙여서 해석

그러면서 RVing / p.p.하다

RVing / p.p. 앞에 콤마(,)가 나온 경우, 분사구문으로서 앞에 '그러면서'라는 말을 붙이고 RVing / p.p.를 쭉 이어서 해석한다.

- He sat confidently, answering all of the questions.
  그는 자신감 있게 앉아 있었다. 그러면서 모든 질문에 답했다.
  = 그는 모든 질문에 답하면서 자신감 있게 앉아 있었다.
- He practiced basketball every day, improving his skills significantly.
  그는 매일 농구 연습을 했다. 그러면서 그의 기술을 상당히 향상시켰다.
  = 그는 그의 기술을 상당히 향상시키면서 매일 농구 연습을 했다.

전략 적용 연습

정답 및 해설 p. 5

[01 ~ 12] 다음을 해석하시오.

01 The best way to treat a cold or a mild fever is to make the sufferer as comfortable as possible.

01
mild 가벼운

02 Supermarket managers employ a diverse array of strategies and techniques to encourage customers to spend more money on their shopping excursions.

02
employ 사용하다
diverse 다양한
excursion (보통 단체로 짧게 하는) 여행

03 To deprive students of access to quality education is to hinder their ability to acquire the necessary knowledge, skills, and opportunities essential for unlocking their full potential and achieving success in various aspects of life.

03
quality 양질의
hinder 저해하다
acquire 습득하다
unlock (재능·잠재력 등)을 끌어내다

04 Because of the power of humor to boost creative thinking, many companies have adopted the strategy of opening the meetings with a joke or other form of humor to loosen people up and get the creative juices flowing.

04
boost 촉진하다
loosen up 긴장을 풀다
juice (美구어) 힘

05 Cloning is one of the scientific achievements including heart transplants and test-tube babies.

05
cloning 생물 복제
transplant 이식
test-tube 시험관 안에서 만들어 낸

06 The herd of cattle passing along the same routes every year influenced the life and industries of the land they crossed.

06
herd (가축의) 떼
cross 가로지르다

07 Fainting is a temporary loss of consciousness caused by insufficient oxygen to the brain, and can be brought on by various reasons.

07
temporary 일시적인
consciousness 의식
insufficient 부족한

08 Brushing your teeth is essential for removing the remaining food on your teeth and keeping your mouth clean and healthy.

09 By improving your English skills in this age of information, you will be able to experience a larger world and broaden your horizons.

09
broaden 넓히다
horizon (욕구·지식·흥미의 범위를 나타내는) 시야

10 Computerization and mechanization of production lines have lessened the need for manual labor, resulting in increased efficiency and productivity across industries.

10
lessen 줄이다
manual labor 수작업
productivity 생산성

11 Nobody can ever accomplish anything by worrying, and worry itself can easily lead to a number of problems, including fatigue, loss of sleep, overeating, and an overall loss of concentration.

11
accomplish 이루다
fatigue 피로
concentration 집중(력)

12 We were grateful to be invited to the prestigious conference, where we had the chance to network with industry leaders and gain valuable insights into emerging trends.

12
grateful 감사하는
prestigious 권위 있는, 일류의
conference 회의, 회담
network 네트워크를 구축하다
insight 통찰력
emerging 떠오르는

UNIT **04**

기타 구문 해석 핵심 전략

전략 12 It is로 시작하는 문장은 '가주어-진주어'거나 '강조 구문'이다

전략 노트

1. 가주어-진주어

It + be동사 + 형·명 + to RV / that절

(It: 가주어 / to RV / that절: 진주어)

문장 맨 앞에 'It + be동사 + 형용사·명사'의 형태가 나오면, 「가주어-진주어」 구문일 확률이 높다. 직독직해는 '그것(it)은 형·명이다 〈뭐가?〉 to RV / that절 이하가'로, to RV / that절 앞에서 〈뭐가?〉라는 추임새를 붙여 주면 된다.

- It is true that mental skills become increasingly important at high levels of competition.
  높은 경쟁 수준에서 정신 능력이 점점 더 중요해지고 있다는 것은 사실이다.

2. 강조 구문

It + be동사 + 강조 내용(명사 / 부사(구)(절)) + that절

'It + be동사'와 that절 사이에 강조할 내용을 넣어 의미를 강조하는 구문을 「It ~ that 강조 구문」이라 한다. 강조 구문의 that절에는 강조 내용이 빠진 문장이 이어진다.

- It was her that I saw in front of the library. [명사 강조]
  내가 도서관 앞에서 본 것은 바로 그녀였다.
- It is in the leisure or sports clothes that the greatest revolution has taken place. [부사구 강조]
  가장 큰 혁명이 일어난 곳은 바로 레저나 스포츠 의류(부분)이다.

3. 가목적어-진목적어

S + make / find / think / keep + it + 형·명 + to RV / that절

(it: 가목적어 / 형·명: 목적격 보어 / to RV / that절: 진목적어)

「가목적어-진목적어」 구문에서는 'S가 V한다 그것이 형·명하도록 〈뭐가?〉 to RV가 / that절 이하가'로, to RV / that절 앞에서 〈뭐가?〉라는 추임새를 붙여 주면 된다.

- He found it impossible to meet the deadline.
  그는 마감 기한을 맞추는 것이 불가능하다는 것을 알았다.

전략 적용 연습

정답 및 해설 p. 6

[01 ~ 07] 다음을 해석하시오.

01 It is important to take into consideration absent-mindedness or poor eyesight before believing that a friend is actually disregarding you.

01
take into consideration 고려하다
absent-mindedness 멍함
disregard 무시하다

02 It's also true that we kids don't have to do a lot of boring chores that our parents had to do.

02
chore 허드렛일

03 Some writers on Britain have talked about the British desire to belong, and it is certainly true that the pub, or the working man's club, or the numerous other clubs play a very important part in many people's lives.

03
belong 소속감을 느끼다

04 In my opinion as a musician, the Internet has made it possible for me to share my music with people that have never been reached by conventional methods.

04
conventional 전통적인

05 Many students find it difficult to comprehend complex scientific theories and principles, especially without adequate explanation from teachers.

05
comprehend 이해하다
adequate 적절한

06 It is compassion that all of the greatest and highest ideals of human spirit, including forgiveness, acceptance, trust and hope, are based on.

06
compassion 연민
acceptance 수용

07 It was when I completed the marathon, despite all the obstacles and moments of doubt throughout the training process, that I understood the true meaning of perseverance and personal achievement.

07
obstacle 장애물
perseverance 인내(력)

PART 2

문법

문법 핵심 공략법

1 단락형 문제

문제를 풀기 전 먼저 선택지를 쭉 훑어보며 어디에 밑줄이 쳐져 있는지를 보도록 한다. 단락형 문제에서는 동사나 준동사에 밑줄이 있는 경우가 많다.

동사나 준동사에 밑줄이 쳐진 경우

문장 구조 분석을 통해 밑줄이 동사 자리인지 준동사 자리인지 먼저 파악한다.

- ▶ 동사 자리인데 실제 동사에 밑줄이 쳐진 경우, 그 동사의 수일치와 능·수동이 맞는지를 파악한다. 단, 동사가 완료시제(have/had p.p.)라면 시제까지 고려해야 한다.
- ▶ 준동사 자리인데 실제 준동사에 밑줄이 쳐진 경우, 그 준동사의 능·수동을 파악한다. 단, 준동사가 완료형(to have p.p.나 having p.p.)이라면 시제까지 고려해야 한다.

관계대명사에 밑줄이 쳐진 경우

관계대명사는 격이나 완전/불완전을 묻는다. 앞의 선행사는 물론, 뒤에 오는 절의 빠진 문장 성분을 확인하도록 한다.

형용사나 부사에 밑줄이 쳐진 경우

해석을 통해서 그 밑줄이 명사를 수식하거나 주격/목적격 보어로 쓰였는지(형용사) vs 동사를 수식하는지(부사)를 파악한다.

You may conclude that knowledge of the sound systems, word patterns, and sentence structures ① are sufficient to help a student ② become competent in a language. Yet we have ③ all worked with language learners who understand English structurally but still have difficulty ④ communicating.

▸ 정답은 ① are이다. 문장의 주어가 단수 명사 knowledge이므로 이에 수일치하여 복수 동사 are를 단수 동사 is로 고쳐야 한다.

2 빈칸형 문제

선택지를 보고 단순히 품사나 어형을 묻는 문제인지 두 개 이상의 절로 구성되어 용법과 해석까지 필요한 문제인지 파악한다.

품사나 어형을 묻는 문제

한 단어의 네 가지 형태가 선택지로 나오는 문제이다. 빈칸이 주어, 동사, 목적어, 보어, 수식어 중에 어떤 자리인지를 파악해서 선택지 중 알맞은 품사나 형태를 고른다.

The time needed to prepare for the exam ________ based on individual study habits.

① vary ② varies ③ varying ④ to vary

▸ 빈칸은 문장의 주어 The time에 대한 동사 자리이다. 따라서 준동사인 ③과 ④는 답이 될 수 없고, 나머지 선택지 중 단수 주어에 수일치한 ② varies가 답이 된다. 참고로, needed ~ exam은 앞에 나온 명사 The time을 수식하는 분사구이며, based on ~ habits 또한 독립분사구문(혹은 전명구)이다.

용법과 해석까지 묻는 문제

가산/불가산 명사의 구분, 자/타동사의 구분, 동사의 능·수동 및 시제 구분, 접속사/전치사의 구분 등 문장 구조 파악뿐만 아니라 단어의 용법과 해석까지 필요로 하는 문제이다.

To better assist you, please specify your preferred arrival time ________ we can prepare accordingly.

① so that ② still ③ or ④ for example

▸ 빈칸은 두 개의 절을 연결하는 접속사 자리이다. 따라서 부사인 ②와 ④는 답이 될 수 없고, 나머지 선택지 중 문맥상 '원하는 도착 시간을 명확히 알려주면 그에 맞춰 준비할 수 있다'라는 의미가 자연스러우므로 부사절 접속사 ① so that이 답이 된다.

UNIT 01

동사 핵심 전략

전략 01 '전명구'를 괄호 치면 답이 보인다

'전치사 + 명사(구/절)'를 괄호 치면 문장 구조가 보인다. 문장 구조를 파악해야 동사 자리인지 준동사 또는 다른 품사 자리인지 쉽게 알 수 있다.

전략 노트 구의 개념

전명구를 괄호 치려면 먼저 구의 개념을 정확히 알고 있어야 한다.

전치사 + 명사 = 부사구	명사 of 명사 = 명사구
A, B, and C = 하나의 구	형용사 + 명사 / 명사 + 형용사 = 명사구
to RV / RVing / p.p. ~ = 하나의 (명사/형용사/부사)구	

예제

01 Gun violence in the United States **[results / resulting]** in tens of thousands of deaths annually.
➲ 전명구 괄호 치기: (in the United States) / (in tens ~ deaths) ▶ 주어 Gun violence에 대한 동사 자리 ▶ results
미국의 총기 폭력은 매년 수만 명의 사망자를 낳는다.

02 The markets for fair trade and organic coffee **[is / are]** expanding, notably in the UK.
➲ 전명구 괄호 치기: (for fair ~ coffee) / (notably ~ UK) ▶ 주어 The markets에 대한 동사 자리 ▶ 복수 주어에 수일치 ▶ are
공정 무역 및 유기농 커피 시장이 특히 영국에서 확대되고 있다.

03 Under the shade of the trees in the zoo **[was / were]** visitors observing animals from all over the world.
➲ 전명구 괄호 치기: (Under the ~ trees) / (in the zoo) / (from all ~ world) ▶ 장소 부사구 도치 구문 ▶ 주어 visitors에 대한 동사 자리 ▶ 복수 주어에 수일치 ▶ were
동물원의 나무 그늘 아래에는 세계 각지에서 온 동물들을 관찰하는 관람객들이 있었다.

04 In the middle of progress in urban development, there is **[concern / concerned]** over the depletion of natural resources.
➲ 전명구 괄호 치기: (In the middle ~ development) / (over the ~ resources) ▶ there 도치 구문 ▶ 동사 is에 대한 주어 자리 ▶ 명사 concern
도시 개발이 진전되는 가운데 천연자원 고갈에 대한 우려가 있다.

05 A site **[to be explored / was explored]** during the city tour is Windsor Castle by the River Thames.
➲ 전명구 괄호 치기: (during the city tour) / (by the River Thames) ▶ 주어 A site, 동사 is, 주격 보어 Windsor Castle인 구조 ▶ 주어 A site를 수식하는 수식어구 자리 ▶ to 부정사의 형용사적 용법 ▶ to be explored
도심 투어 중 방문할 장소는 Thames 강변의 Windsor 성이다.

전략 적용 연습

정답 및 해설 p. 7

[01 ~ 08] 밑줄 친 부분 중 어법상 옳은 것은 O, 옳지 않은 것은 X로 표시하고 틀린 부분을 올바르게 고치시오.

01 Answering this question in a new, unexpected way is an essential creative act.

02 Vitamins, unlike carbohydrates, fats, and proteins, does not produce energy in our bodies.

03 A candle burns in a dark room emits as much light as a small flashlight shining at full power.

04 The Oxford English Dictionary providing a comprehensive resource to scholars and academic researchers.

05 On the stage in the theater was famous actors performing a play based on a classic novel from the 19th century.

06 The replication process was overseen by Georges Brocot, a French artist who specializes in molding techniques.

07 Among her most prized possessions sold during the evening sale were a 1961 bejeweled timepiece by a renowned luxury brand.

08 The exchange of ideas and knowledge between different cultures has enriched our collective understanding of what it means to be human.

新 [09 ~ 14] 밑줄 친 부분에 들어갈 말로 가장 적절한 것을 고르시오.

09 Most people in Korean society ______ education as the main propeller of social mobility.

① view
② views
③ viewing
④ to view

10 Elements of income in a cash forecast ________ according to the company's circumstances.

① variable
② variation
③ is varied
④ will vary

11 According to Statistics Korea's data, buying a median-priced home in Seoul __________ 9.2 years.

① require
② requires
③ requiring
④ to be required

12 Like many smartphone owners, the students in the class _________ too much time in looking at the screen.

① spending
② to spend
③ were spending
④ will be spent

13 The local community center across from the elementary school has __________ its operating hours to provide more services.

① extensively
② extended
③ extends
④ extend

14 Despite advancements in scientific knowledge and tools, there are __________ in predicting weather patterns, mainly due to technological limitations.

① restrictions
② restricted
③ restrictive
④ restricting

전략

02 접속사가 1개 나오면 동사는 2개가 된다

문장에 접속사/관계사/의문사가 몇 개 있는지 파악하고 그 '접속사의 개수 + 1'을 하면 동사의 개수를 알 수 있다. 반대로 말해, 동사가 2개이면 접속사/관계사/의문사가 하나 있어야 한다. 결국 동사의 개수를 알면, 전치사구나 수식어구가 포함된 문장인지, 접속사나 관계사로 두 문장이 연결된 한 문장인지 구별할 수 있다.

Tip! 접속사/관계사/의문사가 나온 절(접속사/관계사/의문사 + S + V)을 하나로 묶으면 진짜 주어, 동사가 나오는 주절을 파악하기가 훨씬 쉬어진다.

PART 2 문법

전략 노트 전치사 vs 접속사 vs 관계사 vs 접속부사

1. 전치사(+ 명사(구)) vs 접속사(+ S + V)

~ 동안	㉺ during	㉾ while
~ 때문에	㉺ because of	㉾ because
~에도 불구하고	㉺ in spite of, despite	㉾ (al)though, even though, even if

* p. 87 〈주의해야 하는 전치사 및 접속사〉 참고

2. 전치사와 접속사 둘 다 쓰이는 단어

before	㉺㉾ ~ 전에	than	㉺㉾ ~보다
after	㉺㉾ ~ 후에	like	㉺㉾ ~처럼[같이]
until	㉺㉾ ~까지	as	㉺ ~처럼[같이]; ~로서 ㉾ ~ 때문에; ~ 동안; ~대로; ~하듯이
since	㉺ ~ 이래로 ㉾ ~ 이래로; ~ 때문에		
considering (that)	㉺㉾ ~에 관하여	for	㉺ ~을 위해; ~에 대해 ㉾ 왜냐하면 ~이니까
given (that)	㉺㉾ ~을 고려해 보면		

3. 접속부사

대조	however, yet, still, nevertheless, nonetheless
부연	besides, furthermore, moreover, also, then, likewise
결과	therefore, hence, thus, afterwards

❶ 접속부사는 접속사가 아니라 부사다. ('S + V + **접속사 + 접속부사**, + S + V' / 'S + V. **접속부사**, S + V' / 'S + V; **접속부사**, S + V')

4. '________ + 명사(구), 완전한 문장' / '완전한 문장, ________ + 명사(구)'

완전한 문장 앞이나 뒤에 명사(구)만 남아 있으면 전치사가 답이다.

5. '~ 명사, 부정대명사 + of + ________ + V'

'부정대명사 + of + 목적격 관계대명사'이므로 관계대명사 whom 또는 which가 답이다.

예제

01 **[Because / Because of]** the cold weather, I stayed at home all day long.

➲ 동사 1개(stayed) ▶ '______ + 명사(구), 완전한 문장' 구조 ▶ 전치사 자리 ▶ Because of

추운 날씨 때문에, 나는 하루 종일 집에 있었다.

02 **[Because / Because of]** it was cold, I stayed at home all day long.

➲ 동사 2개(was / stayed) ▶ '______ + S + V, S + V' 구조 ▶ 접속사 자리 ▶ Because

날씨가 추웠기 때문에, 나는 하루 종일 집에 있었다.

전략 적용 연습

정답 및 해설 p. 8

[01 ~ 07] 밑줄 친 부분 중 어법상 옳은 것은 O, 옳지 않은 것은 X로 표시하고 틀린 부분을 올바르게 고치시오.

01 The treasure for which she was grasping was a bag of pearls.

02 The number of students enrolled in the online course is over 10,000, many of them are from India.

03 Coffee has a bitter and slightly acidic flavor has a stimulating effect on humans.

04 Living for a time in a foreign country makes us aware of the merits in which our own country is deficient.

05 Persons who are daring in taking a wholehearted stand for truth often achieving results that surpass their expectations.

06 Despite these similarities with other creatures, however, the evolution of mankind differs from that of other species.

07 This literal meaning of the word 'beach,' furthermore, doesn't capture individual responses to the word because of every individual has a different association with the word.

新 [08 ~ 13] 밑줄 친 부분에 들어갈 말로 가장 적절한 것을 고르시오.

08 An American teenager __________ Singapore who had vandalized property was sentenced to a traditional Singaporean punishment of caning.

① living in
② to be lived in
③ lived in
④ was lived in

09 The belief that we have to study English hard for our future ________ us to stay motivated.

① to cause
② to be caused
③ causes
④ is caused

10 In the evening we went to a party at the home of one of Diana's friends, ____________ are connected with the movie industry.

① some of who
② some of they
③ most of whom
④ most of them

11 The idea that justice in allocating access to a university has something to do with the good that universities properly pursue ___________ why selling admission is unjust.

① to explain
② to be explained
③ explain
④ explains

12 Korean kites, __________ with those in other countries, are based on scientific principles, especially in their shapes which make good use of the wind.

① compare
② compared
③ comparing
④ to compare

13 Clovis Chappel wrote _______ the Roman city of Pompeii was being excavated, the body of a woman was found mummified by the volcanic ashes of Mount Vesuvius.

① that
② therefore
③ that when
④ during

전략 03 결국 '문장 중간의 S + V'가 중요하다

'접속사의 개수 + 1 = 동사의 개수'에는 2가지 예외가 있다. ① 분사구문에서 접속사가 생략되지 않은 경우와 ② 목적격 관계대명사나 접속사 that이 생략된 경우이다. 이는 문장 구조 파악을 어렵게 만드는데, 동사의 과거형과 과거분사형 모두 Ved 형태인 경우도 마찬가지다. Ved가 동사(과거형)인지 과거분사인지는 문장 구조와 능·수동을 통해서 파악하도록 하자.

전략 노트 '접속사의 개수 + 1 = 동사의 개수'의 2가지 예외

1. 분사구문의 경우, 접속사가 있지만 동사는 하나만 온다.
접속사 + RVing/p.p./형용사 ~, S + V: 접속사가 생략되지 않은 분사구문

2. 문장 중간에 'S + V'가 나온 경우, 앞에 that이 생략되었다.
명사 + (that) + S + V: 목적격 관계대명사 that 생략
동사 + (that) + S + V: 접속사 that 생략

예제

01 When **[take / taking]** a short walk, I met a classmate in high school.
➲ 접속사 1개(When), 동사 1개(met) ▶ 접속사가 생략되지 않은 분사구문 ▶ 현재분사 또는 과거분사 자리 ▶ 분사의 의미상 주어인 내가 '산책하는' 것 ▶ 능동의 현재분사 taking
나는 잠시 산책을 하다가 고등학교 때 반 친구를 만났다.

02 The Internet class I took yesterday **[was / to be]** "Shimson Grammar."
➲ 접속사 X, 동사 1개(took) ▶ 문장 중간에 온 '명사 + (that) + S + V' 구조 ▶ 형용사절의 명사 수식 ▶ 주어 The Internet class에 대한 본동사 자리 ▶ was
내가 어제 들었던 인터넷 수업은 "Shimson Grammar"였다.

전략 04 주어, 목적어, 보어 자리에는 명사가 들어간다

주어, 목적어, 보어, 전치사의 목적어 자리에는 반드시 명사가 들어가야 한다. 따라서 동사 앞이나 동사 뒤 또는 전치사의 뒤에 오는 자리라면 명사가 답이다.

전략 노트 문장 내 각 품사의 자리

명사 자리	S(명사) + V + O(명사) + C(명사/형용사) / 전치사 + O(명사) / 한정사 + 명사
부사/전명구 자리	S / V / O / C 이외의 자리
부사의 다양한 위치	S + (부사) + V / S + V + (부사) / be/have + (부사) + p.p. / to + (부사) + RV / (부사) + RVing

예제

01 Regular exercise offers numerous **[benefits / beneficial]** for physical and mental health.
➲ 타동사 offers의 목적어 역할 & 형용사 numerous의 뒤 ▶ 명사 자리 ▶ benefits
규칙적인 운동은 신체적, 정신적 건강에 많은 이점을 제공한다.

02 The **[conclusion / conclusive]** of the report emphasized the need for immediate action to address the issue.
➲ 문장의 주어 역할 & 정관사 The의 뒤 ▶ 명사 자리 ▶ conclusion
보고서의 결론은 그 문제를 해결하기 위해 즉각적인 조치가 필요하다고 강조했다.

전략 적용 연습

정답 및 해설 p. 10

[01 ~ 07] 밑줄 친 부분 중 어법상 옳은 것은 O, 옳지 않은 것은 X로 표시하고 틀린 부분을 올바르게 고치시오.

01 Many things we now throw away to be valuable resources.

02 When to give a blood transfusion, doctors must be very careful.

03 One more thing you need to do is to join a club devoted to mathematics.

04 The sudden drop in temperature is like due to the arrival of a cold front.

05 Travelers keen on exploring ancient ruins must obtain proper permits before entrance restricted archaeological sites.

06 Because the work scientists do in Greenland, people all over the world are learning more about the weather and the environment.

07 Outside, she would tend a small flower garden, which was the envy of the neighborhood. With Mom, everything she touched turned to gold.

新 [08 ~ 15] 밑줄 친 부분에 들어갈 말로 가장 적절한 것을 고르시오.

08 The budget is about 25% higher than originally ________.

① expecting
② expected
③ expectations
④ we are expected

09 Persistence and resilience are key qualities needed for ________ in overcoming challenges.

① success
② successive
③ succeed
④ to succeed

10 One of the major problems we faced both as individuals and as a society ________ through our patient efforts.

① solving
② solved
③ was solved
④ were solved

11 The teacher's ________ of the scientific concept was clear and concise, making it easy for the students to understand.

① explain
② explained
③ explanation
④ explainable

12 The complexity of human nature is ________ shown in the play through the characters' different wants and motivations.

① to interest
② interesting
③ interested
④ interestingly

13 Continuous ________ for personal growth is critical for long-term fulfillment in every aspect of life and career development.

① improve
② improved
③ improvement
④ improvable

14 Although the camping gear ________ selected is heavy for backpacking, we have lightweight alternatives perfect for long hikes.

① that
② you
③ was
④ have

15 When faced with obstacles, showing ________ means refusing to give up, persisting in your efforts, and maintaining a positive attitude despite setbacks.

① persevere
② persevered
③ perseverance
④ perseverant

전략

05 수일치는 진짜 주어를 잡는 것이 핵심이다

수일치 문제는 주어와 동사 사이에 다양한 형태의 수식어구를 넣어 복잡한 구조로 제시하거나, 도치 구문으로 주어가 뒤에 위치하는 경우 등으로 출제되므로 진짜 주어를 잡아 동사의 수를 일치시키는 것이 중요하다. 하지만 단순한 구조 파악으로 해결되지 않는 '명사 of 명사' 형태의 주어처럼 해석을 통해 주어를 파악해야 하는 경우도 있다는 점을 유념해 두도록 하자.

PART 2 문법

전략 노트 수일치 문제로 나오는 대표적인 세 가지 경우

1. 주어와 동사 사이에 '수식어구'가 있는 경우

주어(S)	[전치사 + 명사]	동사(V)
	[부정사]	
	[형용사]	
	[분사]	
	[관계사]	
	[동격]	

2. 주어와 동사가 도치된 경우

부정어 / Only + 부사(구/절)	+ V + S
장소·방향·위치의 부사구 / 유도부사[There/Here]	+ V + S(일반명사) + S(대명사) + V

3. '명사 of 명사'가 주어인 경우

the number of + 복수 명사 + 단수 동사	a number of + 복수 명사 + 복수 동사
the amount of + 단수 명사 + 단수 동사	an amount of + 단수 명사 + 단수 동사

예제

01 People living in the country **[seems / seem]** simple.

➲ 수식어구 괄호 치기: (living ~ country) ▶ 주어 People에 대한 동사 자리 ▶ 복수 주어에 수일치 ▶ seem

시골에 사는 사람들은 소박한 듯하다.

02 In some of the boxes **[was / were]** a huge amount of paper.

➲ 수식어구 괄호 치기: (In ~ boxes) ▶ 장소 부사구 도치 구문 ▶ 주어 a huge amount of paper에 대한 동사 자리 ▶ 'an amount of + 단수 명사 + 단수 동사' 구조 ▶ was

몇몇 상자 안에는 거대한 양의 종이가 들어 있었다.

03 The number of smoking people **[has / have]** decreased.

➲ 주어 The number of smoking people에 대한 동사 자리 ▶ 'the number of + 복수 명사 + 단수 동사' 구조 ▶ has

흡연자의 수가 줄었다.

전략 적용 연습

정답 및 해설 p. 12

[01 ~ 09] 밑줄 친 부분 중 어법상 옳은 것은 O, 옳지 않은 것은 X로 표시하고 틀린 부분을 올바르게 고치시오.

01 The amount of work I had to do were too much for me.

02 Government controls on pesticide use prevents this natural disaster.

03 The climbers on the sheer face of the mountain need to be rescued.

04 At the next stage in the food chain is the animals that eat the plant eaters.

05 Our efforts to conserve energy lead the company to create new sustainable products.

06 The number of children attending school has more than doubled during the last half-century.

07 The fact that someone is interested enough to give help to poor villagers often work wonders.

08 Similar to beetles, which have hard wing covers for protection, cuckoo bees, despite their compact body shape, relies on deception to reproduce.

09 While the point of cleaning your house is to make it cleaner, the process of cleaning your house actually make things worse.

新 [10 ~ 15] 밑줄 친 부분에 들어갈 말로 가장 적절한 것을 고르시오.

10 The project conducted by experienced experts ________ to progress smoothly, ensuring client satisfaction.

① continue
② continues
③ continuing
④ continuation

11 _________ doctors study hard in order that they can keep abreast of all the latest developments in medicine.

① A number of
② The number of
③ One of
④ An amount of

12 Many people who live in this part of the world ________ likely to be worried again with the beginning of the cold weather.

① to be
② being
③ is
④ are

13 Only recently _______ electric vehicles become a viable alternative to gasoline-powered cars, thanks in part to government incentives.

① has
② have
③ does
④ being

14 Each year, as many as two hundred towns in the United States just __________ from the map as far as the Postal Service is concerned.

① to disappear
② disappearing
③ disappears
④ disappear

15 One company developed what it called a 'technology shelf,' on which ___________ possible technical solutions that other teams might use in the future.

① to place
② placing
③ was placed
④ were placed

PART 2

문법

전략

06 주어에 'one of'나 'most of'가 나온 경우, 뒤의 명사에 유의하라

아무리 주어를 잡아서 문장 구조 분석과 해석을 해도 내가 생각한 수일치와 다를 때가 있다. 따라서 수일치의 특이 사항은 따로 익혀두도록 하자.

전략 노트 주의해야 하는 수일치

1. one of 명사

one/either/each/neither	+ of + 복수 명사 + 단수 동사

2. 부분명사 of 전체명사

부분명사 (some, any, most, all, a lot, part, portion, half, the rest, one-third, 30 percent)	+ of + 복수 명사 + 복수 동사 + of + 단수 명사 + 단수 동사

3. to 부정사, 동명사, 명사절은 셀 수 없으므로 단수 취급한다.

4. 상관접속사

Both A and B	+ 복수 동사
Either A or B / Neither A nor B / Not A but B / Not only A but also B / B as well as A	+ V(B에 수일치)

5. 'There + be동사' 구문

There	is	+ 단수 명사
There	are	+ 복수 명사

예제

01 Nearly three-fourths of the earth **[consists / consist]** of water.

➲ 주어인 '부분명사(three-fourths) + of + 전체명사'에 대한 동사 자리 ▶ of 뒤 단수 명사 the earth에 수일치 ▶ consists
지구의 거의 4분의 3이 물로 이루어져 있다.

02 Using smartphones properly **[is / are]** a way of saving phone bills.

➲ 주어인 동명사구 Using smartphones properly에 대한 동사 자리 ▶ 동명사구 주어는 단수 취급 ▶ is
스마트폰을 올바르게 사용하는 것이 전화 요금을 절약하는 한 가지 방법이다.

03 There **[was / were]** few visitors to the Leaning Tower of Pisa because of the bad weather.

➲ 유도부사 'There + be동사 + 주어' 구문의 동사 자리 ▶ 복수 주어 few visitors에 수일치 ▶ were
궂은 날씨 때문에 피사의 사탑을 찾는 방문객은 거의 없었다.

04 Neither Congress nor state legislatures **[has / have]** authorized the development of such a system.

➲ 주어인 상관접속사 'Neither A nor B'에 대한 동사 자리 ▶ B에 해당하는 복수 명사 state legislatures에 수일치 ▶ have
의회와 주 입법부 모두 그러한 시스템의 개발을 승인하지 않았다.

전략 적용 연습

정답 및 해설 p. 13

[01 ~ 08] 밑줄 친 부분 중 어법상 옳은 것은 O, 옳지 않은 것은 X로 표시하고 틀린 부분을 올바르게 고치시오.

01 I was sure that all of the questions on the test was correct.

02 Watching fireflies is one of the nicest things about summer evenings.

03 One of the reasons some birds migrate are to find food sources in warmer climates.

04 Regretting all your petty mistakes only worsen the situation you are currently facing.

05 A large portion of their patients in the hospital was people who did not have an organic disease.

06 More than three-fourths of knowledge acquired in school are applicable in real-life situations.

07 Major League Baseball spokesman Pat Courtney said there have been discussions on the topic but nothing has been advanced.

08 What's surprising about the research findings are that they suggest a previously unknown link between genetics and behavior.

新 [09 ~ 14] 밑줄 친 부분에 들어갈 말로 가장 적절한 것을 고르시오.

09 Extensive search capabilities as well as a user-friendly interface ________ the search engine.

① distinguishes
② distinguish
③ distinguishable
④ distinguishing

10 That there is a hidden fee in their monthly phone bill ________ several customers feeling cheated.

① leave
② has left
③ have left
④ is left

11 Born in Genoa, Italy, Piccolo Paganini was ________ the greatest composers of the nineteenth century.

① a number of
② the number of
③ an amount of
④ one of

12 The negotiations broke down since ________ of the diplomats' peace offers was accepted by the opposing party.

① most
② both
③ either
④ neither

13 A recent study finds that listening to music before and after surgery ________ patients cope with related stress.

① to help
② helping
③ helps
④ help

14 Many factories are rapidly adopting automation, even though there are still 30 percent of ________ being done manually.

① tasking
② tasked
③ task
④ tasks

전략

07 능·수동은 '주어와 동사의 해석'을 통해서 해결하라

일반적으로 능·수동은 'S가 V하다'의 해석이 자연스러우면 능동, 'S가 V되어지다'의 해석이 자연스러우면 수동이 답이다. 하지만 그렇게 안 풀리는 문제가 많다. 그럴 때는 'S가 V하다(능동) vs S를 V하다(수동)'의 정확한 해석을 기반으로 문제에 접근해 보자.

전략 노트 '능동 vs 수동' 구별법

❶ 동사의 주어(S)를 찾아라.

❷ 'S와 V의 해석'을 통해서 능·수동을 따져라.

'S가 V하다'로 해서 말이 되면 → 능동 vs ┌ 'S가 V되어지다'로 해서 말이 되면 → 수동
└ 'S를 V하다'로 해서 말이 되면 → 수동

❗ 완전자동사(1형식)와 불완전자동사(2형식)는 수동태로 쓸 수 없다.

❸ 동사 뒤 목적어의 유무를 확인하라. (단, 예외가 있으니 조심할 것)

목적어가 있으면 → 능동 vs 목적어가 없으면 → 수동

❹ 감정이나 희로애락 동사는 그 감정을 주어가 주는 건지 당하는 건지를 따져라.

주어가 감정을 주면 → 능동 vs 주어가 감정을 느끼면(당하면) → 수동

감정이나 희로애락을 나타내는 동사					
interest	흥미를 끌다	disappoint	실망시키다	surprise	놀라게 하다
excite	흥미를 일으키다	frustrate	좌절시키다	amaze	놀라게 하다
please	기쁘게 하다	depress	우울하게 하다	astonish	놀라게 하다
amuse	즐겁게 하다	bore	지루하게 하다	frighten	놀라게 하다
satisfy	만족시키다	tire	지치게 하다	embarrass	당황하게 하다
impress	감명을 주다	exhaust	지치게 하다	confuse	당황하게 하다

예제

01 The monument **[destroyed / was destroyed]** in the war.
➡ 주어인 The monument에 대한 동사 자리 ▶ 기념비가 '파괴한' 것이 아니라 '파괴된' 것 ▶ 수동태 was destroyed
그 기념비는 전쟁 중에 파괴되었다.

02 Barbara **[traveled / was traveled]** to Uganda last year.
➡ 주어인 Barbara에 대한 동사 자리 ▶ Barbara가 '여행하여진' 것이 아니라 '여행 간' 것 ▶ 능동태 traveled
Barbara는 작년에 우간다를 여행했다.

03 Gustave Eiffel **[built / was built]** the Eiffel Tower in 1889.
➡ 주어인 Gustave Eiffel에 대한 동사 자리 ▶ 목적어(the Eiffel Tower) 있음 ▶ Gustave Eiffel이 에펠탑을 '짓는' 것 ▶ 능동태 built
Gustave Eiffel은 1889년에 에펠탑을 지었다.

04 The whole family **[is suffering / is suffered]** from the flu.
➡ 주어인 The whole family에 대한 동사 자리 ▶ 온 가족이 '경험되는' 것이 아니라 '경험하는' 것 ▶ 능동태 is suffering
온 가족이 독감에 걸렸다.

05 The city **[is situating / is situated]** at an elevation of 1,350m.
➡ 주어인 The city에 대한 동사 자리 ▶ 완전타동사 situate의 목적어 없음 ▶ 주어인 도시가 '위치시킨[놓은]' 것이 아니라 '위치된[놓인]' 것 ▶ 수동태 is situated
그 도시는 해발 1,350미터에 위치해 있다.

06 The game **[wins / is won]** with 11 players on the team over 90 minutes.
➡ 주어인 The game에 대한 동사 자리 ▶ 경기가 '이기는' 것이 아니라 '이겨지는' 것 ▶ 수동태 is won
90분 동안 팀에 11명의 선수들이 참여해야 경기에서 이긴다.

전략 적용 연습

정답 및 해설 p. 15

[01 ~ 09] 밑줄 친 부분 중 어법상 옳은 것은 O, 옳지 않은 것은 X로 표시하고 틀린 부분을 올바르게 고치시오.

01 That wonderful thought was suddenly occurred after I came to Jeju.

02 The novel was so excited that I lost track of time and missed the bus.

03 Everyone encouraged to grow his or her own vegetables in those days.

04 Educational problems should solve upon the agreement of the society members.

05 This belief may reflect the way amnesia is usually portrayed in movies, television, and literature.

06 Advertising dollars have simply been following the migration trail across to these new technologies.

07 The students pleased to see that a mysterious black substance made a dark and dry line when it was rubbed over paper.

08 Recently, I narrowly escaped a head-on collision when a driver who was used his phone became distracted and crossed the centerline.

09 I still remember the awesome feeling I had on that day in May when my little feet were carried me up the stairs into the grandstands at the car racing stadium.

新 [10 ~ 15] 밑줄 친 부분에 들어갈 말로 가장 적절한 것을 고르시오.

10 She ______________ primarily as a political cartoonist throughout her career.

① has known
② has been known
③ had known to
④ is known to

11 The Aswan High Dam __________ Egypt from the famines of its neighboring countries.

① protecting
② to be protected
③ has protected
④ has been protected

12 The attorney explained to the client that without signing the contract, the legal transaction ___________________ complete.

① could not consider
② could not be considered
③ has not been considering
④ should not have considered

13 The following is a list of recommendations that ___________ by environmentalists for reducing your daily carbon footprint.

① are suggesting
② have suggested
③ were suggested
④ has been suggesting

14 According to the report, based on thorough data analysis, crime rates ______________ stable in urban areas over the past decade.

① is remaining
② have remained
③ to remain
④ were remained

15 Teenagers overwhelmed by unrealistic standards of success are commonly __________ by the constant pressure to conform to unattainable ideals.

① depress
② depressed
③ depression
④ depressing

전략

08 동사는 결국 '수일치'와 '능·수동'을 묻는다

문법은 동사를 가장 많이 묻는다. 동사는 일단 수일치와 능·수동이 적절한지를 우선하여 판단해야 하는데, 둘 다 결국 주어와 동사의 관계가 핵심이기 때문에 주어를 먼저 잡고 동사의 수와 태를 따진다. 특히 능·수동의 경우, 구문적으로 조심해야 할 동사들이 있으니 숙지해 두도록 하자.

전략 노트 능·수동 구별 시 주의해야 하는 동사

1. 뒤에 명사가 와도 수동일 수 있는 동사(4·5형식 동사의 수동태)

4형식 동사	be [given/offered/taught/told/shown]	+ 명사
5형식 동사	be [called/named/elected/considered/made]	+ 명사

2. 뒤에 명사가 없어도 능동일 수 있는 동사(자동사)

appear	나타나다	disappear	사라지다
happen, occur, take place	발생하다	come	오다
arrive	도착하다	vary	다르다

* p. 88 〈자동사 vs 타동사〉 참고

3. be p.p. 뒤에 전치사가 오는 동사('자동사 + 전치사' 타동사구의 수동태)

be referred to as	~라고 불리다	be thought of as	~로 간주되다
be laughed at	비웃음을 받다	be looked at	보여지다, 검토되다
be listened to	듣게 되다	be spoken to	이야기되다
be agreed on	합의되다	be dealt with	처리되다
be run over	치이다	be disposed of	처분되다

4. 구문을 잘 이해해야 하는 동사(분리·박탈/인지/제공/금지·억제 동사의 수동태)

분리·박탈	be [robbed/deprived/relieved]	+ of + 명사
인지	be [convinced/informed/reminded/assured]	+ of + 명사
제공	be [provided/supplied/presented/equipped]	+ with + 명사
금지·억제	be [prevented/prohibited/stopped/kept]	+ from + 명사

* p. 90 〈분리·박탈/인지/제공/금지·억제 동사〉 참고

예제

01 This story was about the incidents that **[happened / were happened]** in the 1920s.

➡ 복수 명사 the incidents를 선행사로 받는 that 관계사절 내 동사 자리 ▶ '발생하다'라는 뜻의 happen은 완전자동사 ▶ 능동태만 가능(수동태 불가능) ▶ 능동태 happened

이 이야기는 1920년대에 일어났던 사건들에 관한 것이었다.

02 Our school's basketball team can **[be referred to / be referred to as]** the "Eagles" due to our mascot.

➡ 조동사 can 뒤 동사원형 자리 ▶ 'A를 B라고 부르다'라는 뜻의 'refer to A as B' 구문 ▶ 주어인 우리 학교 농구팀이 '"이글스"라고 불리는' 것 ▶ 수동태 be referred to as

우리 학교 농구팀은 마스코트 때문에 "이글스"라고 불릴 수 있다.

전략 적용 연습

정답 및 해설 p. 16

[01 ~ 10] 밑줄 친 부분 중 어법상 옳은 것은 O, 옳지 않은 것은 X로 표시하고 틀린 부분을 올바르게 고치시오.

01 The traffic lights were turned green, and I pulled away.

02 The issue of climate change must be dealt through immediate action and global collaboration.

03 I was reminded precious memories and the passage of time when looking at old photographs.

04 Problems in society should be looked at from different perspectives to find effective solutions.

05 The renovated park in the neighborhood is named "Green Haven Park" to celebrate its natural beauty.

06 The talented musician was offering a recording contract after impressing the judges at the competition.

07 The students who missed the deadline was required to hand in their assignments by the end of the week.

08 For decades, child-rearing advice from experts has encouraged the nighttime separation of baby from parent.

09 Architects designing modern buildings create innovative blueprints that review and approve before construction begins.

10 The website with its wide-ranging collection of educational materials provides valuable resources for students to enhance their learning experience at home.

新 [11 ~ 16] 밑줄 친 부분에 들어갈 말로 가장 적절한 것을 고르시오.

11 Severe acute respiratory syndrome (SARS) is caused by a virus that __________ in 2003.

① identified
② was identified
③ were identified
④ identifying

12 Shimson was unfortunate to have a serious injury after he ______________ by a distracted motorist.

① run
② has been run
③ were running over
④ was run over

13 I came to understand there was too much work that consistently _____________ my time and energy.

① demanded
② demanding
③ was demanded
④ were demanded

14 The *Iliad* and the *Odyssey*, the Koran, and the Old and New Testaments can all ___________ myths.

① referring to
② refer to as
③ be referred to
④ be referred to as

15 The combustion of oxygen that keeps us alive and active ___________ out by-products called oxygen free radicals.

① have been sending
② sending
③ sends
④ were sent

16 Many children living in poverty, especially in developing countries, _____________ proper nutrition, healthcare, and education.

① are deprived of
② have deprived
③ were depriving of
④ has been deprived

전략

09 시제는 signal을 찾아라

시제의 경우, yesterday나 ago와 같은 과거시제를 나타내는, 또는 since와 같은 현재완료시제를 알려주는 명백한 signal이 있으므로 먼저 주변에서 이런 단서를 포착해야 한다.

전략 노트 특정 시제를 나타내는 signal

명백한 과거시제를 나타내는 signal	시간 + ago ~ 전에 last + 시점 지난 ~에	in + 과거 연도 ~년에 yesterday 어제
현재완료시제를 나타내는 signal	since + 과거 시점 ~ 이래로 until now / so far 지금까지	for/over the last/past + 기간 지난 ~동안
과거완료시제를 나타내는 signal	시간 표현 + before ~ 전에	by the time + 과거 시점 ~했을 무렵

❶ since라고 해서 다 같은 since가 아니다. '~ 때문에'라는 뜻의 이유 접속사일 때는 다른 시제와 함께 쓰일 수 있다.

예제

01 Peter **[came / has come]** here two months ago.

➲ 주어인 Peter에 대한 동사 자리 ▶ two months ago는 과거시제를 나타내는 signal ▶ 과거시제 came

Peter는 두 달 전에 이곳에 왔다.

02 I **[didn't attend / haven't attended]** any parties since I came here.

➲ 주어인 I에 대한 동사 자리 ▶ 시간 부사절 since I came(과거시제)은 주절이 현재완료시제라는 signal ▶ 현재완료시제 haven't attended

나는 이곳에 온 이후로 어떤 파티에도 참석하지 않았다.

03 The extent of deforestation in tropical regions **[worsened / has worsened]** markedly over the past fifty years.

➲ 주어인 명사구 The extent of deforestation에 대한 동사 자리 ▶ over the past fifty years는 현재완료시제를 나타내는 signal ▶ 현재완료시제 has worsened

열대 지역에서의 삼림 벌채 정도는 지난 50년 동안 현저하게 악화되었다.

04 The couple **[have dated / had dated]** for ten years before they finally tied the knot.

➲ 주어인 명사구 The couple에 대한 동사 자리 ▶ 'for ten years before + 과거시제절'은 과거완료시제를 나타내는 signal ▶ 과거완료시제 had dated

그 커플은 마침내 결혼에 골인하기 전까지 10년 동안 교제했다.

전략

10 동사가 'have/had p.p.'이거나 '종속절의 미래시제'이면 시제에 주목하라

동사 자리라면 대개 수일치와 능·수동을 먼저 확인한다. 하지만 주어진 동사가 'have/had p.p.'이거나 종속절에 'will/shall RV'가 나온 경우, 반드시 시제까지 잘 따져 보아야 한다. 시제 관련 문제 중 출제 빈도수가 높은 것이 바로 완료시제와 시간·조건의 부사절 내 시제 문제이기 때문이다.

전략 노트 주의해야 하는 시제

1. 시간·조건의 부사절에서는 현재시제가 미래시제를 대신한다. 단, 명사절이나 형용사절의 경우, 내용상 미래시제라면 미래시제로 쓴다.

- 부사절: If/when S + V(현재시제), S + V(미래시제)
- 명사절: 타동사 + if/when S + V(미래시제)
- 형용사절: 시간 명사 + when S + V(미래시제)

시간 접속사	when ~할 때, ~하면 until/till ~할 때까지 as ~할 때	while ~하는 동안에 after ~한 후에 by the time ~할 때쯤이면	before ~하기 전에 as soon as ~하자마자
조건 접속사	if 만약 ~라면 in case ~인 경우에	once 일단 ~하면 only if ~해야만	unless 만약 ~이 아니라면 as long as ~하는 한

cf. 명사절 접속사: that, whether, if, what, 의문사, 복합관계대명사

2. 'By the time + S + V(현재시제), S + ________'에서는 will have p.p.(미래완료시제)가 답이 된다.

예제

01 When he **[responds / will respond]** to my email, he will provide the information we need.

➲ when 시간 부사절 내 동사 자리 ▶ 주절은 미래시제(will provide) ▶ 시간 부사절에서는 현재시제가 미래시제를 대신함 ▶ 현재시제 responds

그가 내 이메일에 응답할 때, 그는 우리가 필요로 하는 정보를 제공할 것이다.

02 I don't know when he **[responds / will respond]** to my email next week.

➲ 동사 know의 목적어 역할인 when 명사절 내 동사 자리 ▶ next week은 미래시제를 나타내는 signal ▶ 미래시제 will respond

나는 다음 주에 그가 내 이메일에 언제 답장할지 모른다.

03 I can't predict the time when he **[responds / will respond]** to my email next week.

➲ 시간 명사 the time을 선행사로 받는 when 형용사절(관계사절) 내 동사 자리 ▶ next week은 미래시제를 나타내는 signal ▶ 미래시제 will respond

나는 다음 주에 그가 내 이메일에 답장할 때를 예측할 수 없다.

04 Many people **[had made / will have made]** resolutions for self-improvement by the time the new year arrives.

➲ 주절 내 동사 자리 ▶ 시간 부사절 'by the time + S + 현재시제(arrives)' ▶ 미래완료시제 will have made

새해가 다가올 무렵에는 많은 사람들이 자기 계발을 위한 결심을 했을 것이다.

전략 적용 연습

정답 및 해설 p. 18

[01 ~ 11] 밑줄 친 부분 중 어법상 옳은 것은 O, 옳지 않은 것은 X로 표시하고 틀린 부분을 올바르게 고치시오.

01 I wonder if she will finish the work by tonight.

02 I was born in Taiwan, but I have lived in Korea since I started work.

03 It was very unusual that he hasn't shown up for the class yesterday.

04 I was just going to clean the office, but someone had already done it.

05 I'll think of you when I will be lying on the beach on my next vacation.

06 Until 1920, women's events have become very important and popular.

07 This book is on the bestseller list for months by the end of next month.

08 When the concert tour will start tomorrow, the fans of the group will be excited.

09 By the time Mr. Clark became the CEO, he has worked in the tech industry for over 24 years.

10 All you have to do is to boil broccoli in water just until it will be tender, three to five minutes.

11 Some information was not transmitted due to technical issues when they are broadcasting the news.

新 [12 ~ 17] 밑줄 친 부분에 들어갈 말로 가장 적절한 것을 고르시오.

12 In the summer of 2001, he __________ Asan, Korea, to participate in a house-building project.

① visit
② visited
③ has visited
④ had visited

13 By the time he arrives at the office, his coworkers ____________ their morning tasks and meetings.

① already start
② would already start
③ will already start
④ will have already started

14 For the last fifty years, advances in chemistry ______________ many positive changes to the American lifestyle.

① have brought
② were being brought
③ had brought
④ had been brought

15 The air quality in this city has improved significantly since stricter emission regulations _______ implemented.

① were
② to be
③ will be
④ been

16 When I shopped at the market yesterday, I realized that the prices of many items ________ sharply in recent weeks.

① has risen
② have raised
③ had risen
④ had been raising

17 As soon as she __________ her housework, she will be busy preparing dinner for the guests attending the business meeting.

① finishes
② finished
③ will finish
④ will be finished

전략

11 'If'가 나오면 가정법을 떠올려라

if가 있고 주절에 should/would/could/might가 나왔으면 가정법이다. 그러나 if가 없더라도 주절에 should/would/could/might가 나온다면 가정법일 가능성도 염두에 두자. 만약 문장 형태가 가정법을 말하고 있다면, 시간 부사구 및 문맥을 통해서 현재 사실의 반대(가정법 과거)인지 과거 사실의 반대(가정법 과거완료)인지를 구별한다.

PART 2
문법

전략 노트 가정법의 형태

가정법은 그 형태를 외우는 게 핵심이다. (단, 가정법에서 if가 생략되면 주어와 동사가 도치되므로 함께 익혀 두자.)

가정법 과거	If + S + 동사의 과거형/were ~, Were + S ~,	S + should/would/could/might + RV
가정법 과거완료	If + S + had p.p. ~, Had + S + p.p. ~,	S + should/would/could/might + have p.p.
가정법 미래	If + S + should + RV ~, Should + S + RV ~,	S + should[shall]/would[will] + RV
혼합 가정법	If + S + had p.p. ~, Had + S + p.p. ~,	S + should/would/could/might + RV + (now/today)

예제

01 If I **[were / had been]** rich now, I **[could buy / could have bought]** a super luxury car.

➲ 종속절의 if와 주절의 could가 있으므로 가정법 ▶ now는 현재시제를 나타내는 signal ▶ 현재 사실의 반대를 가정하는 가정법 과거 'If + S + 동사의 과거형/were ~, S + 조동사의 과거형 + RV' ▶ were, could buy

내가 지금 부자라면, 최고급 차를 살 수 있을 텐데.

02 If I **[were / had been]** more careful then, I would not **[get / have gotten]** in trouble with him now.

➲ 종속절의 if와 주절의 would가 있으므로 가정법 ▶ 종속절의 then은 과거시제를, 주절의 now는 현재시제를 나타내는 signal ▶ 혼합 가정법 'If + S + had p.p. ~, S + 조동사의 과거형 + RV + (now/today)' ▶ had been, get

내가 그때 좀 더 조심했더라면, 나는 지금 그와 문제가 생기지 않았을 텐데.

03 I regret having paid little attention to him. In other words, I **[should pay / should have paid]** more attention to him.

➲ 앞 문장(동명사의 완료형)의 의미: '(과거에) 그에게 관심을 거의 주지 못한 것을 (현재) 후회한다' ▶ 뒤 문장의 의미('In other words(다시 말해서)'로 바꾸어 말함): 과거 사실에 대한 후회를 나타내는 '그에게 관심을 더 기울였어야 했다 (하지만 그러지 못했다)'가 적절 ▶ 과거 사실의 반대를 가정하는 가정법 과거완료 should have paid

나는 그에게 관심을 거의 주지 못한 것에 대해 후회한다. 다시 말해서, 나는 그에게 관심을 더 기울였어야 했다.

전략
12 'I wish' 또는 'V + as if'가 보이면 뒤는 가정법이다

'I wish'나 'V + as if[though]' 뒤에는 가정법 형태가 와야 한다. 이때 두 동사의 시간 전후 관계를 잘 따져서 가정법 과거인지 가정법 과거완료인지를 파악하자.

전략 노트 가정법 특수 구문

1. I wish 가정법 '~라면 좋을 텐데'

I wish 현재	+ 가정법 과거 현재 사실의 반대 + 가정법 과거완료 과거 사실의 반대	I wished 과거	+ 가정법 과거 과거 사실의 반대 + 가정법 과거완료 대과거 사실의 반대

ex I wish I were rich.
나는 (지금) 부자면 좋을 텐데.
I wish I had been rich.
나는 (과거에) 부자였으면 좋았을 텐데.

2. as if[though] 가정법 '마치 ~처럼'

V + as if[though] 현재	+ 가정법 과거 현재 사실의 반대 + 가정법 과거완료 과거 사실의 반대	Ved + as if[though] 과거	+ 가정법 과거 과거 사실의 반대 + 가정법 과거완료 대과거 사실의 반대

ex My friend **talks as if** he **were** rich.
내 친구는 마치 (지금) 부자인 것처럼 말한다.
My friend **talks as if** he **had been** rich.
내 친구는 마치 (과거에) 부자였던 것처럼 말한다.

3. It is (high/about) time 가정법 '~할 시간이다'

It is (high/about) time	+ S + should(생략 불가) + RV + S + 과거동사

ex **It is high time** you **went[should go]** home.
집에 가야 할 시간이다.

예제

01 I wish it **[is not / were not]** raining right now.

➲ I wish가 있으므로 가정법 ▶ right now는 현재시제를 나타내는 signal ▶ 현재 사실의 반대되는 일을 소망하는 I wish 가정법 과거 'I wish + S + 동사의 과거형/were' ▶ were not

나는 지금 비가 오지 않기를 바란다.

02 I wished he **[went / had gone]** there the previous day.

➲ I wished가 있으므로 가정법 ▶ 주절은 과거시제(wished), 종속절의 the previous day는 과거시제를 나타내는 signal ▶ 종속절은 주절의 바랐던 시점보다 더 이전인 대과거 ▶ 대과거 사실의 반대되는 일을 소망하는 I wish 가정법 과거완료 'I wished + S + had p.p.' ▶ had gone

나는 그 전날 그가 그곳에 갔기를 바랐다.

전략 적용 연습

정답 및 해설 p. 20

[01 ~ 11] 밑줄 친 부분 중 어법상 옳은 것은 O, 옳지 않은 것은 X로 표시하고 틀린 부분을 올바르게 고치시오.

01 The party was so much fun. I wish you have been there.

02 You failed the test. You should prepare for it more thoroughly.

03 He speaks English fluently as if he were an American.

04 I wish I'd known that Diana was sick. I would have gone to see her.

05 If I studied Mathematics harder when young, I could get into Harvard now.

06 I might have prevented the project from failing if I had maintained my original judgment.

07 If Hitler hadn't invaded other European countries, World War II might not take place.

08 If the item should not be delivered tomorrow, they would have complained about it.

09 Had I given up the project at that time, I could not have achieved such a splendid result.

10 He had to quit school because of some trouble at home. Otherwise, he would graduate last June.

11 Those victims of education should receive training to develop creative talents while they were in school.

新 [12 ~ 16] 밑줄 친 부분에 들어갈 말로 가장 적절한 것을 고르시오.

12 I wish I ________ more time to spend with my family and friends when I was not busy.

① have
② would have
③ have had
④ had had

13 If he had worked hard when he was in high school, he ________ a college student now.

① were
② would be
③ had been
④ would have been

14 Our country's economic situation is growing worse and worse: it is high time we ________ it seriously.

① discuss
② discussed
③ discuss about
④ discussed about

15 ________ your flight be delayed, the airline will notify you by email with updated departure information.

① If
② As though
③ Should
④ Will

16 A policeman said that if Clauss ________ so quickly and decisively, there would have been two drownings instead of one.

① didn't react
② couldn't react
③ hasn't reacted
④ hadn't reacted

전략

13 '조동사 + have p.p.'는 문맥을 통해 파악하라

과거의 일에 대한 추측/기대/후회/충고 등을 나타내는 'must/should/may/cannot have p.p.'가 쓰였다면, 문맥을 통해서 의미와 시제가 맞는지 확인해야 한다.

PART 2 문법

전략 노트 조동사 구문

1. 조동사 + have p.p.

must have p.p.	~했음이 틀림없다	must not have p.p.	~하지 않았음이 틀림없다
should[ought to] have p.p.	~했어야 했는데 (하지 않았다)	should not[ought not to] have p.p.	~하지 말았어야 했는데 (했다)
may[might] have p.p.	~했었을 것이다	may[might] not have p.p.	~하지 않았을 것이다
-	-	cannot[can't] have p.p.	~했었을 리가 없다
had better[would rather/may as well/might as well] have p.p.	~하는 게 나았을 텐데 (그런데 안 했다)	need not have p.p.	~할 필요는 없었는데 (했다)

2. 'used to RV' vs 'be used to RV' vs 'be used to RVing'

used to RV	~하곤 했다
be used to RV	~하는 데 사용되다
be[get] used to RVing	~하는 데 익숙하다[익숙해지다]

예제

01 She **[must / should]** have been a beautiful girl when young.

➲ 문맥상 확인: must have been '아름다운 소녀였음이 틀림없다' vs should have been '아름다운 소녀였어야 했는데 (그러지 못했다)' ▶ 과거 일에 대한 추측이 적절 ▶ must

그녀는 분명히 어렸을 때 아름다운 소녀였을 것이다.

02 I should **[form / have formed]** a habit of reading in my boyhood.

➲ in my boyhood는 과거시제를 나타내는 signal ▶ 문맥상 '(과거에) 당연히 습관을 형성했어야 했는데 (하지 않았다)'라는 의미의 과거 일에 대한 후회가 적절 ▶ have formed

나는 어린 시절에 독서하는 습관을 들였어야 했다.

03 Mark **[is used to / used to]** fear public speaking, but now he finds himself volunteering for presentations.

➲ 문맥상 확인: is used to fear '두려워하는 데 사용되다' vs used to fear '두려워하곤 했다' ▶ 등위접속사 but으로 대조를 이루는 두 문장 ▶ 뒤 문장의 의미: '현재 발표에 자원하는 자신을 발견한다' ▶ 앞 문장의 의미: '(과거에) 대중 앞에서 발표하는 것을 두려워하곤 했다'라는 의미의 과거 사실이 적절 ▶ used to

Mark는 (과거에) 대중 앞에서 말하는 것을 두려워하곤 했지만, 지금은 발표에 자원하는 자신을 발견한다.

전략

14 주·요·명·제·충·결 동사는 that절의 동사를 조심하라

주장·요구·명령·제안·충고·결정 동사가 보이면, 다음에 나오는 that절의 동사가 '(should) RV'의 형태인지 먼저 확인해 보도록 한다.

전략 노트 주·요·명·제·충·결 동사의 that절

1. 주·요·명·제·충·결 동사 + that + S + (should) RV

주장·요구·명령·제안·충고·결정 동사가 당위(~해야 한다)의 의미를 지니는 that절을 목적어로 취할 경우, that절 내의 동사는 '(should) RV'의 형태로 쓴다.

주장	insist, urge, argue	요구	ask, demand, require, request
명령	order, command	제안	suggest, propose
충고	advise, recommend	결정	decide

* suggestion처럼 명사화되어 동격의 that절을 취하는 경우도 있다.

ex They **insist** that she (should) be released from prison.
그들은 그녀가 교도소에서 석방되어야 한다고 주장한다.

2. 주·요·명·제·충·결 동사의 that절이 당위의 의미를 지니지 않는 경우

insist(주장하다)나 suggest(암시하다)의 경우, that절이 당위가 아닌 '사실'을 나타낼 수 있다. 이때 that절 내의 동사는 '(should) RV'가 아니라, 시제와 수를 일치시킨 동사의 일반적인 형태로 쓴다.

ex He **insisted** that the party had been canceled. (실제 일어난 일)
그는 파티가 취소되었다고 주장했다. (실제로 취소됨)

He **insisted** that the party (should) be canceled. (당위의 의미)
그는 파티가 (당연히) 취소되어야 한다고 주장했다. (실제로 취소된 것은 아님)

The result of the research **suggested** that the animal had used the tool. (실제 일어난 일)
그 연구의 결과는 그 동물이 그 도구를 사용했다는 사실을 시사했다. (실제로 사용함)

3. 이성적 판단의 형용사 + that + S + (should) RV

that절의 내용에 대해 판단하는 형용사가 올 경우, that절의 동사는 '(should) RV'의 형태를 취한다.

중요한, 필수적인	important, vital, necessary, essential, required
당연한, 마땅한	advisable, desirable, natural

ex It's **necessary** that the firefighter (should) wear protective gear while extinguishing a fire.
소방관이 화재 진압 시에 보호 장비를 착용하는 것은 필수적이다.

예제

01 To ensure accuracy, the editor requests that all articles **[be proofread / are proofread]** before publication.
➜ 요구 동사 requests의 목적어 역할을 하는 that절 내 동사 자리 ▶ '(should) RV' ▶ should가 생략된 be proofread
정확성을 보장하기 위해 편집자는 게시 전에 모든 기사가 교정을 거치도록 요구한다.

02 The faint tire tracks suggested that a car **[drive / had driven]** off the road.
➜ 제안 또는 암시 동사 suggested의 목적어 역할을 하는 that절 내 동사 자리 ▶ 문맥상 that절의 내용이 당위가 아닌 '사실'을 나타냄 ▶ 차가 도로를 벗어난 것은 (그 사실을) 암시하는(suggested) 것보다 더 이전의 일 ▶ 과거완료시제 had driven
희미한 타이어 자국은 차가 도로를 벗어났다는 것을 암시했다.

전략 적용 연습

정답 및 해설 p. 22

[01 ~ 09] 밑줄 친 부분 중 어법상 옳은 것은 O, 옳지 않은 것은 X로 표시하고 틀린 부분을 올바르게 고치시오.

01 Michael wasn't at work. He must be sick yesterday.

02 They used to loving books much more when they were young.

03 The celebrity rejected the suggestion that he say something more specific.

04 The doctor firmly insisted that he had operated on the patient the day before.

05 Peter Thompson mentioned your name to me and suggested I had contacted you to get admission.

06 It is necessary that the patient follows the doctor's instructions for proper medication and recovery.

07 The athlete should not ignore the coach's advice before the big game, which led to a poor performance.

08 Most of President Cleveland's upper left jaw was removed. The president ordered that the operation had been kept secret.

09 The teeth had been bothering David for some time. He knew he should have gone to the dentist's earlier. But he had put it off.

新 [10 ~ 15] 밑줄 친 부분에 들어갈 말로 가장 적절한 것을 고르시오.

10 Today, we ____________ women play sports in pants.

① used to see
② used to seeing
③ are used to see
④ are used to seeing

11 He insisted that his son ________ at home when the murder had been committed.

① is
② be
③ has been
④ had been

12 The lost city hidden deep in the jungle ________ centuries ago due to disease or natural disasters.

① may be abandoned
② should be abandoned
③ may have been abandoned
④ should have been abandoned

13 With the fiscal year ending soon, it is essential that every department ____________ its budget report promptly.

① are submitting
② submit
③ be submitted
④ will be submitted

14 The French Minister promoted a law asking that 3,000 English words widely used in France ________________ by newly created French equivalents.

① be replaced
② are replaced
③ have replaced
④ would have replaced

15 Even before Mr. Kay announced his move to another company, the manager requested that the HR team __________ advertising for a new accountant.

① begin
② began
③ has begun
④ had begun

FURTHER STUDY 혼동하기 쉬운 전치사 및 접속사

▶ **until[till]** vs **by** vs **since**

until[till]	~까지	동작·상태의 지속성(keep/stay) → '계속'을 넣어 해석
by	~까지	동작의 완료(finish) → '늦어도'를 넣어 해석
since	~ 이래로	완료시제와 함께 쓰임

▶ **for** vs **during**

for	~ 동안	+ 불특정 기간(주로 숫자를 포함)	ex for two weeks, for a long time
during	~ 동안	+ 특정 기간(주로 한정사를 포함)	ex during his vacation, during the spring

▶ **beside** vs **besides**

beside	~의 옆에(전치사)
besides	~ 외에도(전치사), 게다가(접속부사)

▶ **주의해야 하는 접속사**

now (that)	이제는 ~이니까
in order that / so (that)	~하기 위해서
providing[provided] (that)	만약 ~한다면
in case (that)	~하는 경우에 (대비해서)
in that	~라는 점에서

- Tell me **[until / by]** Friday whether you can come to the party.
  네가 파티에 갈지 안 갈지 금요일까지 말해 줘.
- The cafe down the street is open **[until / by]** midnight if you want to grab a late-night snack.
  야식을 먹고 싶다면 길 아래 카페가 자정까지 영업한다.
- **[In / Since]** 2008, blockchain technology has been developing and influencing various industries.
  2008년 이후 블록체인 기술은 다양한 산업에 발전을 이루고 영향을 미치고 있다.
- Despite my efforts to stay active, I'd gained weight **[for / during]** this winter.
  활동량을 늘리려고 노력했음에도 불구하고 이번 겨울 동안 나는 살이 쪘다.
- I can't believe we have been married **[for / during]** two years already.
  우리가 결혼한 지 벌써 2년이 되었다는 게 믿기지 않는다.
- **[Now that / In order for]** you understand the rules, don't break them during the game.
  이제 규칙을 이해했으니 게임 중에 규칙을 어기지 마라.
- I'll lend you some money, **[provide / provided]** you pay me back by the end of the month.
  이달 말까지 갚는다는 조건으로 너에게 돈을 빌려주겠다.

정답 by | until | Since | during | for | Now that | provided

FURTHER STUDY 자동사 vs 타동사

▶ '자동사 vs 타동사'를 혼동하기 쉬운 동사

현재형	과거형	과거분사형	현재분사형	의미
lie lay lie	lay laid lied	lain laid lied	lying laying lying	㉶ 눕다; 놓여 있다 ㉹ ~을 눕히다, 놓다; 낳다 ㉶ 거짓말하다
rise raise arise	rose raised arose	risen raised arisen	rising raising arising	㉶ 오르다, 뜨다 ㉹ ~을 들어 올리다; 인상하다; 기르다 ㉶ 일어나다, 발생하다
sit seat	sat seated	sat seated	sitting seating	㉶ 앉다 ㉹ ~을 앉히다
wait await	waited awaited	waited awaited	waiting awaiting	㉶ 기다리다 ㉹ ~을 기다리다

- For example, a child **[lying / laying]** on the floor, coloring, can't help but hum.
  예를 들어, 바닥에 누워 색칠을 하고 있는 아이는 콧노래를 부를 수밖에 없다.
- He was **[risen / raised]** by his grandparents, who taught him traditional values.
  그는 전통적인 가치관을 가르친 조부모님 밑에서 자랐다.
- She glanced at the man **[seating / sitting]** next to her.
  그녀는 자기 옆에 앉아 있는 남자를 힐끔 쳐다봤다.
- Hiding behind the curtain, I **[waited / awaited]** the shadow to reappear.
  나는 커튼 뒤에 숨어서 그림자가 다시 나타나기를 기다렸다.

▶ 타동사로 착각하기 쉬운 자동사

graduate from	~을 졸업하다	arrive at[in]	~에 도착하다
operate on	~을 수술하다	account for	~을 설명하다
dispose of	~을 처리하다	dispense with	~없이 지내다 (without X)
consist of	~로 구성되다	consist in/with	~에 있다/~와 일치하다
result in	~을 야기하다	result from	~에서 기인하다
interfere with/in	~을 방해하다/~에 간섭하다	deal with	~을 다루다, 처리하다

- How do you **[explain / account]** for your absence yesterday?
  너는 어제의 결석을 어떻게 설명할 거니?
- The summer festival **[composes / consists]** largely of live music and food stalls.
  여름 축제는 주로 라이브 음악과 먹거리 장터로 구성된다.
- Missing the payment deadline will **[result / cause]** in a late fee charge.
  납부 기한을 놓치면 연체료가 부과된다.
- Social media often **[disturbs / interferes]** considerably with work tasks.
  소셜 미디어는 종종 업무에 상당한 방해가 된다.
- Some of our chefs had to **[deal / handle]** with last-minute catering orders.
  일부 셰프들은 급작스러운 케이터링 주문을 처리해야 했다.

정답 lying | raised | sitting | awaited | account | consists | result | interferes | deal

▶ 자동사로 착각하기 쉬운 완전타동사(REMALIODA)

R	resemble ~~like/to~~	~와 닮다	reach ~~at~~	~에 도착하다
E	enter ~~(in)to~~ *cf.* enter into	~에 들어가다 (논의 등을) 시작하다		
M	marry ~~with/to~~ *cf.* be[get] married to	~와 결혼하다 ~와 결혼하다	mention ~~on~~	~에 대해 언급하다
A	accompany ~~with~~	~와 동행하다	affect ~~on~~	~에 영향을 미치다
	approach ~~to/on~~	~에 다가가다		
L	leave ~~from~~ *cf.* leave A for B	~을 떠나다 A를 떠나 B로 향하다		
I	influence ~~on~~	~에 영향을 미치다		
O	obey ~~to~~	~에 복종하다	oppose ~~to~~ *cf.* be opposed to object to	~에 반대하다 ~에 반대하다 ~에 반대하다
D	discuss ~~about~~	~에 대해 토론하다		
A	answer ~~to~~	~에 답하다	attend ~~at~~ *cf.* attend on attend to	~에 참석하다 ~을 시중들다 ~에 유의하다
	address ~~to~~	~에게 연설하다		
기타	consider ~~about~~	~에 대해 고려하다	contact ~~to~~	~에게 연락하다

- Something very remarkable happened to the astronauts soon after they **[arrived / reached]** the International Space Station.
  국제우주정거장에 도착한 직후 우주비행사들에게 매우 놀라운 일이 일어났다.
- Seohee agreed to **[accompany / accompany with]** her father on a trip to France.
  서희는 프랑스 여행에 그녀의 아버지와 동행하는 것에 동의했다.
- The two brothers closely **[resemble / resemble with]** each other, sharing the same features and attitudes.
  두 형제는 같은 특징과 태도를 공유하며 서로를 매우 닮았다.
- The main topic for this webinar is to **[discuss / talk]** methods for effective team collaboration.
  이 웨비나의 주요 주제는 효과적인 팀 협업을 위한 방법을 논의하는 것이다.
- In the debate, each candidate had two minutes to **[answer to / respond to]** a question from the moderator.
  토론에서 각 후보자에게는 사회자의 질문에 응답할 수 있는 2분이라는 시간이 주어졌다.

정답 reached | accompany | resemble | discuss | respond to

FURTHER STUDY 분리·박탈/인지/제공/금지·억제 동사

▶ 분리·박탈 동사 + A + of + B

동사		A				B		의미
rob deprive relieve	+	A A에게서	+	of	+	B B를	▶	강탈하다 박탈하다 덜어 주다

▶ 인지 동사 + A + of + B / A + that

동사		A			의미
convince inform remind warn assure notify	+	A A에게	+	of + B (B를) that (~라는 것을)	▶ 확신시키다 알리다 상기시키다 경고하다 확신시키다 통보하다

cf.

동사						의미
say/mention explain suggest/propose announce	+	[to A(사람)] (A에게)	+	that ~라는 것을	▶	말하다 설명하다 제안하다 발표하다

▶ 제공 동사 + A + with + B

동사		A				B		의미
provide supply present equip	+	A A에게	+	with	+	B B를	▶	제공하다 공급하다 주다 갖추게 하다

▶ 금지·억제 동사 + A + from + RVing

동사		A						의미
prevent prohibit discourage stop keep deter	+	A A가	+	from	+	RVing ~하는 것을	▶	막다, 예방하다 금지하다 막다, 단념하게 하다 막다 막다 단념하게 하다

- The pervasive use of technology can deprive people **[outdoor activities / of outdoor activities]**, leading to sedentary lifestyles.
  만연한 기술 사용은 사람들이 야외 활동을 하지 못하게 하고, 늘 앉아 있는 생활을 하게 만든다.

- The manager will **[suggest / notify]** employees of the new company policies at the staff meeting.
  관리자는 직원회의에서 새로운 회사 정책을 직원들에게 알릴 것이다.

- The teacher will **[say / explain to]** students that there will be a change in the exam schedule.
  선생님은 학생들에게 시험 일정이 변경될 것임을 설명할 것이다.

- Upon arrival, guests will be **[provided / offered]** with a complimentary breakfast to start their day off right.
  도착 즉시, 손님들은 하루를 활기차게 시작할 수 있도록 무료 조식을 제공받을 것이다.

- Passengers **[are prohibited / are prohibited from]** opening airplane doors mid-flight for security reasons.
  보안상의 이유로 승객이 비행 중 비행기 문을 여는 것이 금지되어 있다.

- Regular exercise can keep you **[with gaining / from gaining]** excess weight and help you maintain a healthy body.
  규칙적인 운동은 과체중을 방지하고 건강한 신체를 유지하는 데 도움이 된다.

정답 of outdoor activities | notify | explain to | provided | are prohibited from | from gaining

PART 2
문법

UNIT 02

준동사 핵심 전략

전략

15 준동사를 묻는다면, 먼저 본동사를 파악하라

부정사의 경우, 'to RV vs RV', 'to RV vs RVing'와 같이 둘 중 무엇이 적절한지를 묻는데, 대개 앞에 나온 본동사가 무엇이냐에 따라 결정된다. 따라서 문장에 이미 동사가 있는 상황에서 준동사의 형태를 묻는 문제라면, 앞에 나온 본동사의 성격을 파악하는 것이 먼저다.

전략 노트 부정사 vs 동명사 vs 분사

1. to 부정사와 동명사 둘 다 목적어로 취하지만 의미가 다른 동사

	to RV (미래지향적/동작이 안 일어남)	RVing (과거지향적/동작이 일어남)
remember/forget	~하기로 한 것을 기억하다/잊다	~한 것을 기억하다/잊다
stop	~하기 위해 걸음을 멈추다	~하는 것을 그만두다
regret	~하게 돼서 유감이다	~한 것을 후회하다
try	~하기 위해 노력하다	시험 삼아 ~해보다

2. 동명사를 목적어로 취하는 동사(MEGAPEPFA) * p. 103 〈동명사 관용 표현〉 참고

Mind	꺼리다	Enjoy	즐기다	Give up	포기하다
Avoid	피하다	Postpone	연기하다	Escape	피하다
Practice	연습하다	Finish	끝내다	Appreciate	감사하다

cf. to 부정사를 목적어로 취하는 동사: wish, want, expect, hope, plan, promise, choose, decide, agree, afford, fail

3. 지각동사·사역동사의 5형식 문장

목적어와 목적격 보어의 관계가 능동이냐 수동이냐에 따라 답이 달라진다. 목적어를 목적격 보어의 의미상 주어로 보고 앞에서 배운 '능·수동 구별법'을 활용하도록 한다.

지각동사	see, watch, hear, notice, feel	+ O + RV 또는 RVing (능동) / p.p. (수동)
사역동사	have, make	+ O + RV (능동) / p.p. (수동)
	let	+ O + RV (능동) / be p.p. (수동)
준사역동사	get	+ O + to RV (능동) / p.p. (수동)
	help	+ (O) + (to) RV

❶ let의 목적어와 목적격 보어의 관계가 수동일 때, 목적격 보어에 p.p.가 아니라 be p.p.를 쓴다는 점에 유의한다.

※ 지각동사·사역동사의 수동태

지각동사와 사역동사의 문장을 수동태로 전환할 때 목적격 보어로 쓰인 원형부정사를 반드시 to RV로 바꿔야 한다.

(능동태) S + 지각/사역동사 + O + RV
→ (수동태) O + be p.p. + to RV (+ by S)

4. to 부정사를 목적격 보어로 취하는 5형식 동사(COREAF/P)

Cause, Order, Require, Enable, Expect, Encourage, Ask, Allow, Advise, Force, Permit, Persuade	+ O + to RV

예제

01 I remember **[to email / emailing]** my boss yesterday.

➡ 타동사 remember의 목적어 자리 ▶ remember to RV: '~할 것을 기억하다' vs remember RVing: '~한 것을 기억하다' ▶ 과거 시점 부사 yesterday가 있음 ▶ 문맥상 '어제 이메일을 보낸 것을 기억한다'라는 의미가 자연스러움 ▶ emailing

나는 어제 사장님께 이메일을 보낸 것을 기억하고 있다.

02 I enjoy **[to eat / eating]** ice cream.

➡ 타동사 enjoy의 목적어 자리 ▶ enjoy는 동명사를 목적어로 취하는 동사 ▶ eating

나는 아이스크림 먹는 것을 즐긴다[좋아한다].

03 I could hear a dog **[barking / barked]**.

➡ 지각동사 hear의 목적격 보어 자리 ▶ O와 OC의 관계 - 능동: RV 또는 RVing vs 수동: p.p. ▶ 개가 '짖는' 것 ▶ 능동의 barking(또는 bark)

나는 개가 짖는 것을 들을 수 있었다.

04 Please let me **[know / to know]** the result as soon as possible.

➡ 사역동사 let의 목적격 보어 자리 ▶ O와 OC의 관계 - 능동: RV vs 수동: be p.p. ▶ 내가 '결과를 아는' 것 ▶ 능동의 know

가능한 한 빨리 제가 결과를 알도록 해 주세요[제게 결과를 알려 주세요].

05 I had the project **[finish / finished]**.

➡ 사역동사 have의 목적격 보어 자리 ▶ O와 OC의 관계 - 능동: RV vs 수동: p.p. ▶ 프로젝트가 '완료되는' 것 ▶ 수동의 finished

나는 그 프로젝트가 완료되게 했다[그 프로젝트를 완료했다].

06 Let the work **[finished / be finished]** by him.

➡ 사역동사 let의 목적격 보어 자리 ▶ O와 OC의 관계 - 능동: RV vs 수동: be p.p. ▶ 그 일이 '끝내지는' 것 ▶ 수동의 be finished

그 일이 그에 의해 끝나도록 해라[그가 그 일을 끝내게 해라].

07 We were made **[watch / to watch]** him perform a magic trick.

➡ 사역동사 make가 수동태로 쓰인 문장 구조 ▶ 능동태의 목적격 보어로 쓰인 원형부정사는 수동태로 전환 시 to 부정사로 바뀜 ▶ to watch

우리는 그가 마술을 하는 모습을 지켜보게 되었다.

08 He was seen **[enter / entering]** the building when the crime was committed.

➡ 지각동사 see가 수동태로 쓰인 문장 구조 ▶ 능동태의 목적격 보어로 쓰인 RVing는 수동태로 전환 시 그대로 남음(원형부정사는 to 부정사로 바뀜) ▶ entering

그 범행이 저질러졌을 때 그가 그 건물에 들어가는 것이 목격되었다.

09 My father allowed me **[to travel / travelling]** around Korea alone.

➡ 5형식 동사 allow의 목적격 보어 자리 ▶ allow는 to 부정사를 목적격 보어로 취하는 동사 ▶ to travel

우리 아버지는 내가 혼자서 한국을 여행하는 것을 허락하셨다.

10 I got him **[do / to do]** the chores.

➡ 준사역동사 get의 목적격 보어 자리 ▶ O와 OC의 관계 - 능동: to RV vs 수동: p.p. ▶ 그가 '집안일을 하는' 것 ▶ 능동의 to do

나는 그가 집안일을 하게 했다.

11 I got the chores **[to do / done]**.

➡ 준사역동사 get의 목적격 보어 자리 ▶ O와 OC의 관계 - 능동: to RV vs 수동: p.p. ▶ 집안일이 '끝마쳐지는' 것 ▶ 수동의 done

나는 집안일이 끝마쳐지게 했다[집안일을 끝마쳤다].

전략 적용 연습

정답 및 해설 p. 24

[01 ~ 11] 밑줄 친 부분 중 어법상 옳은 것은 O, 옳지 않은 것은 X로 표시하고 틀린 부분을 올바르게 고치시오.

01 As I went out for work, I saw a family moved in upstairs.

02 Please remember putting out the light before you go to bed.

03 As I forgot to post the letter yesterday, I must visit the post office again.

04 She tried to avoid to answer the difficult question, but the teacher insisted.

05 After many failed attempts, he finally gave up trying to learn how to play the guitar.

06 We regret to inform you that the delivery of your package has been delayed due to logistical issues.

07 The Chicago Dairy Farm was forced to discard 50 percent of its milk because it failed meeting quality standards.

08 I was really happy to see his kind and caring face, but there wasn't anything he could do to make the flu to go away.

09 Since the city stopped registering handguns in 1976, no one who hadn't registered by then can have a handgun at home.

10 Living in areas with high levels of air pollution and poor air quality can cause people increase their risk of developing chronic diseases.

11 To his horror, the examiner had forgotten fastening his seatbelt. He moved forward and hit his head against the windshield, then fell back.

新 [12 ~ 17] 밑줄 친 부분에 들어갈 말로 가장 적절한 것을 고르시오.

12 Let the problem ________ from all angles before making a decision.

① analyze
② to analyze
③ analyzed
④ be analyzed

13 Journalists are expected ________ their sources before releasing news stories.

① verification
② verifies
③ to verify
④ verifying

14 Even dogs yawn in response to seeing their owners, or even strangers, ________.

① yawn
② to yawn
③ yawned
④ be yawned

15 When my computer stopped working, I took it to the computer store to get it ________.

① fix
② to fix
③ fixed
④ fixing

16 As a consequence, she was made ________ for her mistake in front of the entire class.

① apologize
② to apologize
③ apologized
④ to be apologized

17 The guidebook helps tourists ________ the best attractions in the city, offering detailed maps, reviews, and tips for an enjoyable visit.

① find
② finds
③ finding
④ to finding

전략

16 준동사는 결국 능·수동을 묻는다

동사의 기능을 가진 준동사도 능동과 수동의 형태가 있다. 동사의 능·수동에서 주어가 핵심 단서인 것처럼, 준동사 역시 의미상 주어를 찾아 해석으로 능·수동을 판별해야 한다. 여기서 한 가지 더 기억해야 할 것은, 준동사의 역할과 위치에 따라 의미상 주어는 문장의 주어가 될 수도 있고, 목적어나 수식을 받는 명사 등이 될 수도 있다는 점이다.

전략 노트 준동사의 능·수동

1. 준동사의 능·수동 구별법

❶ 준동사의 의미상 주어를 찾아라.

❷ 'S와 V의 해석'을 통해서 능·수동을 따져라. (의미상 주어: S, 준동사: V)

'S가 V하다'로 해서 말이 되면 → **능동** vs ┌ 'S가 V되어지다'로 해서 말이 되면 → **수동**
└ 'S를 V하다'로 해서 말이 되면 → **수동**

❸ 준동사 뒤 목적어의 유무를 확인하라. (단, 예외가 있으니 조심할 것)

목적어가 **있으면** → **능동** vs 목적어가 **없으면** → **수동**

2. with/keep + O + OC

목적어와 목적격 보어의 관계가 능동이면 RVing를, 수동이면 p.p.를 쓴다.

with + O + OC(전명구 / 형용사 / RVing: 능동 / p.p.: 수동)	~가 ~하면서[~한 채로]
keep + O + OC(전명구 / 형용사 / RVing: 능동 / p.p.: 수동)	~을 ~한 상태로 유지하다

예제

01 I'm sorry to have kept you **[waiting / waited]**.

➲ 5형식 동사 keep의 목적격 보어 자리 ▶ O와 OC의 관계 - 능동: RVing vs 수동: p.p. ▶ 네가 '기다리는' 것 ▶ 능동의 waiting

기다리게 해서 죄송합니다.

02 I'll keep my fingers **[crossing / crossed]** for you.

➲ 5형식 동사 keep의 목적격 보어 자리 ▶ O와 OC의 관계 - 능동: RVing vs 수동: p.p. ▶ 내 손가락이 '겹쳐 놓이는' 것 ▶ 수동의 crossed

나는 너를 위해 내 손가락들이 겹쳐 놓이도록 할게[너를 위해 행운을 빌게].

03 I would like the chicken **[to cook / to be cooked]** in the oven.

➲ 5형식 동사 would like의 목적격 보어 자리 ▶ would like는 to 부정사를 목적격 보어로 취하는 동사 ▶ 닭이 '요리되는' 것 ▶ 수동의 to be cooked

나는 오븐에서 닭을 요리하고 싶다.

04 Then a robot, **[calling / called]** Robo, goes to work.

➲ 명사 a robot을 수식하는 분사 자리 ▶ 분사의 의미상 주어인 a robot이 Robo라고 '불리는' 것 ▶ 수동의 called

그러고 나서 Robo라고 불리는 로봇은 일하러 간다.

05 Birds can fly without **[teaching / being taught]** by anyone.

➲ 전치사 without의 목적어 자리 ▶ 동명사의 능동 vs 수동 ▶ 동명사의 의미상 주어인 Birds가 '가르침을 받는' 것 ▶ 수동의 being taught

새는 누구의 가르침을 받지 않아도 날 수 있다.

06 My car pulled into the garage with its tires **[replacing / replaced]** recently.

➲ 'with + O + OC' 구문의 목적격 보어 자리 ▶ O와 OC의 관계 - 능동: RVing vs 수동: p.p. ▶ 그것의 타이어가 '교체되는' 것 ▶ 수동의 replaced

내 차가 최근에 타이어를 교체한 상태로 차고에 들어왔다.

전략 적용 연습

정답 및 해설 p. 25

[01 ~ 11] 밑줄 친 부분 중 어법상 옳은 것은 O, 옳지 않은 것은 X로 표시하고 틀린 부분을 올바르게 고치시오.

01 This is the most terrifying story ever written.

02 Ignoring my English teacher's advice, I wasted my time and money.

03 Michael was sure of electing president of his school this year.

04 Sitting with the legs crossed for a long period can raise blood pressure.

05 They wanted cats to kill the rats eaten their food supplies on their ships.

06 Motivating by feelings of guilt, they are inclined to make amends for their actions.

07 New features for the mobile app are expected to introduce in the upcoming update.

08 Guests are reminded to keep their personal belongings store in the designated lockers.

09 Including in this series is "The Enchanted Horse," among other famous children's stories.

10 Situated at an elevation of 1,350m, the city of Kathmandu enjoys a warm climate year-round that makes living here pleasant.

11 In other words, birth order may define your role within a family, but as you mature into adulthood, accepted other social roles, birth order becomes insignificant.

新 [12 ~ 17] 밑줄 친 부분에 들어갈 말로 가장 적절한 것을 고르시오.

12 Princess Diana spent most of her life ________ to helping poor children.

① devoting
② being devoted
③ to devote
④ was devoted

13 Losing a beloved pet is a ________ event that leaves you feeling sad and lonely.

① depress
② depressed
③ depressing
④ depressingly

14 Locations ________ for the new movie include New York City and the Grand Canyon.

① will film
② are being filmed
③ filming
④ to be filmed

15 If you don't show your boarding pass when ______ to by the airline staff, you won't be able to board the plane.

① ask
② asked
③ asking
④ to ask

16 The beautiful necklace ________ of pearls and a diamond was an inheritance passed down through many generations.

① consisted
② consistent
③ consisting
④ consistency

17 The enhanced design, ________ a Voltaic pile, was made by stacking some discs made from these metals between discs made of cardboard soaked in sea water.

① called
② was called
③ calling
④ to call

전략
17 준동사의 시제는 signal을 준다

동사와 마찬가지로, 대부분 준동사의 시제를 알려주는 signal이 있다. 시간 부사구를 통해 명백히 시제 구분이 되는 경우가 있는 반면, 문맥상 본동사와 준동사 간의 시간상 전후 관계를 따져서 준동사의 시제를 결정해야 하는 경우도 있다.

PART 2 문법

전략 노트 **준동사의 시제와 의미상 주어**

1. 준동사의 시제를 따져야 하는 3가지 경우

본동사의 시제와 같을 때(단순시제)와 본동사의 시제보다 앞설 때(완료시제)	to RV vs to have p.p. RVing vs having p.p.
동사 seem/be p.p. 뒤에 올 때	to RV vs to have p.p.
명백한 과거시제를 나타내는 signal이 있을 때(완료시제)	to have p.p./having p.p.

* 명백한 과거시제를 나타내는 signal: when young / in her youth / yesterday / last week / 시간 + ago / in + 과거 연도

2. 준동사의 의미상 주어

부정사	동명사	분사
for + 목적격	소유격(대명사·일반명사일 때) 또는 목적격(일반명사일 때)	주격

3. It is + 사람 성격 형용사 + of + 목적격 + to RV

to 부정사의 경우, 사람의 성격을 나타내는 형용사 뒤에 쓰인 to 부정사의 의미상 주어는 'of + 목적격'의 형태로 나타낸다.

사람의 성격을 나타내는 형용사
kind, wise, clever, thoughtful, considerate, careful, generous, stupid, foolish, cruel, rude, careless

예제

01 She seems **[to lose / to have lost]** her watch yesterday.

➲ 동사 seems의 주격 보어 자리 ▶ 과거 시점 부사 yesterday가 있음 ▶ to 부정사구가 현재시제의 본동사보다 앞선 시제 ▶ 부정사의 완료형 to have lost

그녀는 어제 시계를 잃어버린 것 같다.

02 **[They arriving / Their arriving]** early was crucial for the smooth running of the event.

➲ 문장의 주어 자리(본동사 was) ▶ 동명사 arriving의 의미상 주어가 대명사일 경우 소유격으로 표시 ▶ Their arriving

그들이 일찍 도착한 것은 원활한 행사 진행에 있어서 매우 중요했다.

03 It's really kind **[for you / of you]** to help me.

➲ 사람 성격 형용사 kind 뒤 to 부정사의 의미상 주어 자리 ▶ 'of + 목적격' ▶ of you

나를 도와주다니 너는 정말 친절하다[나를 도와줘서 정말 고마워].

전략

18 뒤에 목적어가 없으면 명사, 목적어가 있으면 동명사가 답이다

동명사와 명사는 둘 다 명사라는 공통점이 있지만, 둘의 가장 큰 차이점은 목적어 유무이다. 동명사는 뒤에 목적어 역할을 하는 명사가 올 수 있지만, 명사는 바로 이어서 명사가 올 수 없다(단, 복합명사는 제외).

전략 노트 동명사 vs 명사

1. 동명사와 명사의 공통점과 차이점

	동명사	명사
공통점	문장 내 주어, 목적어, 보어 역할	
차이점	목적어 O	목적어 X
	부사로 수식	형용사로 수식
	관사 X	관사 O

(1) [**동명사** vs 명사] + 목적어/보어

ex analyzing the data 데이터를 분석하는 것

cf. 명사 + 전치사 + 명사

ex the analysis of the data 데이터의 분석

(2) 부사 + [**동명사** vs 명사]

ex carefully **choosing** your words 신중히 말을 고르는 것

(3) 형용사 + [동명사 vs **명사**]

ex intensive **training** 집중적인 훈련

(4) 관사 + 형용사 + [동명사 vs **명사**]

ex an important **decision** 중요한 결정

2. 전치사의 목적어 자리에 to 부정사는 올 수 없다.

ex for to love her (X) / for loving her (O)

예제

01 He knows very well the way of **[expressing / expression]** his feelings.

➡ 전치사 of의 목적어 자리 ▶ 뒤에 목적어 his feelings 있음 ▶ 동명사 expressing

그는 자신의 감정을 표현하는 방법을 매우 잘 알고 있다.

02 In agriculture, technology enables rapid **[producing / production]** of high-yield crops.

➡ 동사 enables의 목적어 역할을 하며 형용사 rapid의 수식을 받는 자리 ▶ 명사 production

농업 분야에서는 기술이 다수확 작물의 급속한 생산을 가능하게 한다.

03 He thanks his grandmother for always **[to treat / treating]** him kindly.

➡ 전치사 for의 목적어 자리 ▶ 뒤에 목적어 him 있음 ▶ 동명사 treating

그는 언제나 자신을 친절하게 대해 주시는 자기 할머니에게 감사해한다.

전략 적용 연습

정답 및 해설 p. 27

[01 ~ 10] 밑줄 친 부분 중 어법상 옳은 것은 O, 옳지 않은 것은 X로 표시하고 틀린 부분을 올바르게 고치시오.

01 Having drunk three cups of coffee, she can't fall asleep.

02 The disease is thought to emerge in the tropics 100 years ago.

03 Hearing the story before, she didn't want to hear it again.

04 There is also the possibility of damage your stuff, some of which is valuable.

05 The paper charged her with use the company's money for her own purposes.

06 The tools for analysis these patterns were not even available until the early 1990s.

07 My father would not accompany us to the place where the Smiths were staying but insisted on my going.

08 It's important to recognize that communication inner thoughts is crucial for your mental well-being.

09 In this blind taste test, participants are asked to rank the wines in order of preferring among red varieties.

10 The explaining for the explosive force of volcanoes lies in the pressure of the gases imprisoned within the molten rock.

新 [11 ~ 16] 밑줄 친 부분에 들어갈 말로 가장 적절한 것을 고르시오.

11 I am ashamed of __________ all the money on that stock last year.

① being spent
② having spent
③ to spent
④ to have spent

12 By __________ how to allocate the budget, expenditures on office equipment will be reduced.

① regulations
② regulate
③ regulating
④ to regulate

13 __________ to affordable housing remains a challenge in many urban centers.

① Access
② Accessing
③ Accesses
④ Accessible

14 All these things __________, it might be better to ask for the services of a moving company.

① consider
② considering
③ considered
④ to be considered

15 Goodwill Foundation has shown a strong commitment to _______ hunger by distributing food to those in need.

① fights
② fighting
③ fought
④ be fought

16 It is very thoughtful _______ to remember my birthday each year and send such a heartfelt card filled with beautiful words.

① you
② your
③ for you
④ of you

FURTHER STUDY 동명사 관용 표현

▶ '전치사 to + 동명사' 표현

look forward to RVing	~을 고대하다
be used[accustomed] to RVing	~에 익숙하다
object to RVing(= be opposed to RVing)	~에 반대하다
with a view[eye] to RVing	~할 목적으로
when it comes to RVing	~에 관해 말하자면
What do you say to RVing?	~하는 건 어때?
be devoted[dedicated/committed] to RVing	~에 몰두하다, 전념하다
contribute to RVing	~에 기여하다

▶ 동명사 관용 표현

be worth RVing	~할 가치가 있다
be busy (in) RVing	~하느라 바쁘다
have difficulty[trouble/a hard time] (in) RVing	~하는 데 어려움을 겪다
spend + 시간/돈 + (in) RVing	~하는 데 시간/돈을 쓰다
It is no use[good] RVing	~해도 소용없다
There is no RVing	~하는 것은 불가능하다
It goes without saying that	~은 말할 것도 없다
make a point of RVing(= make it a rule to RV)	꼭 ~하다, ~하는 것을 원칙으로 삼다
be on the point[edge/brink/verge] of RVing(= be about to RV)	막 ~하려고 하다
come near to RVing	거의 ~할 뻔하다
above RVing	결코 ~하지 않는
How[What] about RVing?	~하는 게 어때?

- We look forward to **[receive / receiving]** your prompt reply.
  우리는 당신의 빠른 답장을 받기를 고대한다.
- The criminal suspect objected to **[give / giving]** an answer when questioned by the police.
  그 범죄 용의자는 경찰에게 심문받았을 때 답변을 거부했다.
- Plenty of fresh air contributes to **[maintain / maintaining]** good health.
  신선한 공기를 충분히 마시는 것은 좋은 건강을 유지하는 데 도움이 된다.
- The dog is busy **[chasing / to chase]** squirrels in the backyard.
  개가 뒷마당에서 다람쥐를 쫓느라 바쁘다.
- Even a short walk in nature can be worth **[taking / to take]** to clear your head.
  자연 속에서의 짧은 산책이라도 머리를 맑게 위해서는 충분히 할 만한 가치가 있다.
- It is no use **[worrying / to worry]** about things beyond our control.
  우리가 통제할 수 없는 일에 대해 걱정하는 것은 아무 소용이 없다.
- They endure day after day, and just when they're about **[making / to make]** it, decide they can't take any more.
  그들은 매일 인내하다가 막 성공하려고 할 때, 더 이상 참고 견딜 수 없다고 결정을 내린다.

정답 receiving | giving | maintaining | chasing | taking | worrying | to make

UNIT 03

관계사/의문사/접속사 핵심 전략

전략

19 who/which/what/where는 결국 '격 → 완전/불완전'이다

who/which/that/what/when/where/why는 앞에 명사가 나오면 관계사, 앞에 동사가 나오면 의문사이다(that은 접속사). 관계사라면, ① 격이 맞는지, ② 뒤에 완전한 문장이 왔는지 불완전한 문장이 왔는지를 확인한다. 그러고도 답이 헷갈릴 때는 해석까지 해보는 것이 좋다.

전략 노트 관계사 vs 의문사 vs 접속사

1. 관계대명사 vs 관계부사

명사	+ who(m)/which/that(관계대명사: 그런데 그 명사)	+ 불완전한 문장
명사	+ when/where/why/how(관계부사: 그런데 그 명사에서)	+ 완전한 문장
명사	+ 전치사 + 관계대명사 whom/which	+ 완전한 문장

* '명사, 부정대명사 + of + 목적격 관계대명사 + V' 구조에는 whom 또는 which만 올 수 있다.

2. 의문사 vs 접속사 that

동사/전치사	+ who(m)/which/what(의문대명사: 누가/어느 것/무엇)	+ 불완전한 문장
동사/전치사	+ when/where/why/how(의문부사: 언제/어디서/왜/어떻게)	+ 완전한 문장
동사/형용사	+ that(접속사: ~것/사실)	+ 완전한 문장

* '의문사 what vs 선행사를 포함하는 관계대명사 what'은 해석을 통해서 구분한다.

3. 소유격 관계대명사 vs 의문형용사

명사	+ whose(소유격 관계대명사: 그런데 그 명사의) + 명사	+ 불완전한 문장
동사	+ whose/which/what(의문형용사: 누구의/어느/무슨) + 명사	+ 불완전한 문장

* 선행사가 동물·사물일 때 소유격 관계대명사 whose 대신 of which로도 쓸 수 있다.

4. 관계대명사 which는 명사(구)뿐만 아니라 문장 전체를 선행사로 받을 수 있다.

5. '전치사 + 관계대명사'의 경우, ① 뒤에 완전한 문장이 와야 하고, ② '전치사 + 관계대명사'를 동사나 목적어 뒤에 넣어서 해석하면 답이 보인다.

예제

01 I love Paris **[which / where]** there are lots of beautiful buildings.
➜ 앞에 명사 Paris가 나옴 ▶ which는 관계대명사이고 where는 관계부사 ▶ 뒤에 완전한 문장이 옴 ▶ 관계부사 where
나는 아름다운 건물이 많은 파리를 좋아한다.

02 In Barcelona, there is a cathedral **[which / where]** Antoni Gaudi designed in the late 19th and early 20th centuries.
➜ 앞에 명사 a cathedral이 나옴 ▶ which는 관계대명사이고 where는 관계부사 ▶ 뒤에 designed의 목적어가 없는 불완전한 문장이 옴 ▶ 관계대명사 which
바르셀로나에는 Antoni Gaudi가 19세기 말 20세기 초에 설계한 성당이 있다.

03 In Rouen, there is a cathedral **[which / where]** Joan of Arc prayed before battle.
➜ 앞에 명사 a cathedral이 나옴 ▶ which는 관계대명사이고 where는 관계부사 ▶ 뒤에 완전한 문장이 옴 ▶ 관계부사 where
루앙에는 Joan of Arc가 전투 전에 기도했던 성당이 있다.

04 She is the only person **[whom / on whom]** I can depend.
➜ 앞에 명사 the only person이 나옴 ▶ whom과 on whom 둘 다 관계대명사 ▶ 뒤에 완전한 문장이 옴 ▶ '전치사 + 관계대명사' on whom
* '~에 의존하다'라는 뜻의 depend on은 '자동사 + 전치사' 형태의 타동사구
그녀는 내가 의지할 수 있는 유일한 사람이다.

05 The host mentioned **[who / that]** the event would be rescheduled.
➜ 앞에 동사 mentioned가 나옴 ▶ who는 의문사이고 that은 접속사 ▶ 뒤에 완전한 문장이 옴 ▶ 접속사 that
그 진행자는 행사 일정이 변경될 것이라고 언급했다.

06 The host mentioned **[who / that]** would attend the event.
➜ 앞에 동사 mentioned가 나옴 ▶ who는 의문사이고 that은 접속사 ▶ 뒤에 주어가 없는 불완전한 문장이 옴 ▶ 의문사 who
그 진행자는 행사에 누가 참석할지 언급했다.

07 I don't know **[what / how]** you solve the problem.
➜ 앞에 동사 don't know가 나옴 ▶ what과 how 둘 다 의문사 ▶ 뒤에 완전한 문장이 옴 ▶ 의문부사 how
나는 네가 그 문제를 어떻게 풀었는지 모르겠다.

08 Do you know **[what / how]** the weather is like tomorrow?
➜ 앞에 동사 know가 나옴 ▶ what과 how 둘 다 의문사 ▶ 뒤에 전치사 like의 목적어가 없는 불완전한 문장이 옴 ▶ 의문대명사 what
내일 날씨가 어떤지 아세요?

09 We passed by the art gallery **[which / whose]** windows were adorned with intricate stained glass.
➜ 앞에 명사 the art gallery가 나옴 ▶ which와 whose 둘 다 관계사 ▶ 뒤에 완전한 문장이 옴 ▶ '소유격 관계대명사 whose + 명사 windows + 불완전한 문장' 형태(명사를 포함하면 뒤에 완전한 문장이 온 것으로 볼 수 있음) ▶ 소유격 관계대명사 whose
우리는 창문이 정교한 스테인드글라스로 장식된 미술관을 지나쳤다.

전략 적용 연습

정답 및 해설 p. 29

[01 ~ 18] 밑줄 친 부분 중 어법상 옳은 것은 O, 옳지 않은 것은 X로 표시하고 틀린 부분을 올바르게 고치시오.

01 I remember the day which we first met.

02 She had a teddy bear, both of whose eyes were missing.

03 Green tea is one of the things in which Boseong is famous.

04 Providing the room is clean, I don't mind which hotel we stay at.

05 This garden has the most beautiful pond where I have ever seen.

06 I met the woman whose husband is the president of the corporation.

07 At tourist sites, I usually head for buildings who are different from ours.

08 The knee is the joint which the thigh bone meets the large bone of the lower leg.

09 We drove on to the hotel, from whose balcony we could look down at the town.

10 A mutual aid group is a place where an individual brings a problem and asks for assistance.

11 The head of the department, <u>which</u> earns twice the average salary and oversees the entire team, has to take responsibility.

12 Imagine <u>how</u> your life would have been like if you had begun working in a factory at the age of six or seven.

13 If you are in Japan, you must go to RoboStore. It's the first store in the world <u>that</u> there are no humans at work.

14 To find a good starting point, one must return to the year 1800 <u>during which</u> the first modern electric battery was developed.

15 Alongside endangered species exists a group of supporters who fight for their protection, <u>to whom</u> we call environmental activists.

16 Schubert wrote music as freely as one would write a friendly letter. He just produced <u>which was</u> in him and brought us a rich treasure of music.

17 As she lived in a small house, <u>which</u> she could not practice without disturbing the rest of the family, she usually practiced her high notes outside.

18 Movies were first seen as an exceptionally potent kind of illusionist theatre, the rectangle of the screen corresponding to the proscenium of a stage, <u>on which</u> appear actors.

新 [19 ~ 30] 밑줄 친 부분에 들어갈 말로 가장 적절한 것을 고르시오.

19 I do aerobics three times a week, _______ helps me stay in shape.

① it
② who
③ which
④ where

20 The novel _________ my mother was interested was found in the garret.

① which
② whose
③ in which
④ for which

21 Who would have guessed _______ baking soda is a great cleaning agent?

① that
② where
③ who
④ about

22 The boy drew pictures of people at an airport __________ waiting for their planes.

① who was
② who were
③ which was
④ which were

23 The building was destroyed in a fire, the cause of ________ was never confirmed.

① it
② which
③ that
④ where

24 By tracking purchases, you can see __________ products customers buy most frequently.

① who
② which
③ that
④ of which

25 The NGO worked on a campaign with volunteers, most of _______ dedicated their time to the cause.

① who
② them
③ that
④ whom

26 There are those in the cities _______ want to be industrial workers and want to learn only about machines.

① who
② which
③ where
④ what

27 Everyone is curious about _______ will win the championship this year, especially with the close competition.

① that
② whose
③ who
④ when

28 His sense of responsibility urged him to undertake the dangerous task _________ he eventually sacrificed himself.

① which
② what
③ for which
④ for what

29 The National Museum of Korea, _____ collection includes ancient artifacts, is hosting a special exhibit this month.

① whose
② which
③ that
④ its

30 On January 10, 1992, a ship traveling through rough seas lost 12 cargo containers, __________ held 28,800 floating bath toys.

① it
② one of them
③ one of whom
④ one of which

전략 20 'when/where'는 뒤에 어순을 확인하고, 'that'은 앞에 전치사나 콤마를 확인한다

문장 중간에 when/where와 같은 의문사가 나온 경우, 보통 다른 문장의 주어, 목적어, 보어, 전치사의 목적어 등으로 쓰이는 간접의문문이며, 특히 의문사 뒤에 오는 '주어 + 동사'의 어순에 유의해야 한다. 뒤를 조심해야 하는 의문사와는 반대로, 관계대명사 that은 앞에 전치사나 콤마(,)가 올 수 없다는 점을 명심해야 한다.

전략 노트 주의해야 하는 의문사·관계사의 문장 구조

1. ~ when/where/why/how + S + V

문장 중간에 나온 의문사 뒤에는 반드시 '주어 + 동사'의 어순이어야 한다.

cf. 의문대명사(who, which, what)와 '의문형용사(whose, which, what) + 명사'가 간접의문문의 주어 자리에 올 경우, 뒤에 바로 동사가 온다.

2. '전치사 또는 콤마(,) + that'은 틀리다.

관계대명사 that은 전치사의 목적어로 올 수 없으며, 계속적 용법의 콤마(,) 뒤에도 올 수 없다.

cf. in that(~한다는 점에서), except that(~을 제외하고도)

예제

01 Do you know **[what am I saying / what I am saying]**?

➲ 동사 know의 목적어 자리 ▶ 의문사 what이 이끄는 간접의문문 ▶ '의문사 + 주어 + 동사'의 어순 ▶ what I am saying

너는 내가 무슨 말을 하고 있는지 알겠니?

02 The farmer, **[who / that]** was poor, was honest.

➲ 앞에 명사 The farmer가 나옴 ▶ 뒤에 주어가 없는 불완전한 문장이 옴 ▶ 콤마(,) 뒤에 올 수 있는 주격 관계대명사 ▶ who

그 농부는, 가난한데, 정직했다.

03 When we compared the universities, we had to think carefully about **[that / which]** had the better reputation.

➲ 앞에 전치사 about이 나옴 ▶ 뒤에 주어가 없는 불완전한 문장이 옴 ▶ 전치사 about의 목적어 역할을 하는 간접의문문의 주어 자리 ▶ 의문대명사 which

우리는 대학을 비교했을 때 어느 대학이 더 평판이 좋은지 신중하게 생각해야 했다.

04 Science is fascinating **[in what / in that]** it unveils mysteries of the universe, just as a telescope reveals distant galaxies.

➲ 앞에 형용사 fascinating이 나옴 ▶ 뒤에 완전한 문장이 옴 ▶ '전치사 + 의문대명사' in what vs 접속사 in that ▶ 완전한 구조의 두 문장을 연결하는 접속사 자리 ▶ in that

과학은 망원경이 먼 은하계를 보여 주듯 우주의 신비를 밝혀낸다는 점에서 매혹적이다.

전략
21 'what vs that'은 앞에 명사가 왔는지 동사/전치사가 왔는지로 구별한다

관계대명사 what(= the thing(s) which/that)은 선행사를 포함하고 있으므로 앞에 명사가 올 수 없는 반면, 관계대명사 that은 앞에 명사가 온다. 또한 관계대명사 what은 불완전한 구조의 명사절을, 접속사 that은 완전한 구조의 명사절을 이끌어 문장에서 주어, 목적어, 보어로 쓰인다.

전략 노트 what vs that

명사	+ that(관계대명사)	+ 불완전한 문장
동사/형용사	+ that(접속사)	+ 완전한 문장
동사/전치사	+ what(관계대명사)	+ 불완전한 문장

cf. 보통 선행사를 포함하는 관계대명사 what 앞에는 명사가 오지 않는다. 하지만 4형식 문장에서 what절이 직접목적어로 쓰인 경우 앞에 간접목적어(명사)가 나올 수 있다.

ex He offered his parents **what** he had saved from his allowance.
그는 자신의 용돈에서 아껴둔 것을 부모님께 드렸다.

예제

01 There are many commercials **[that / what]** give incorrect information.
➲ 앞에 명사 many commercials가 나옴 ▶ 뒤에 주어가 없는 불완전한 문장이 옴 ▶ 주격 관계대명사 that
부정확한 정보를 주는 광고들이 많다.

02 **[That / What]** we all need is patience.
➲ 문장의 본동사는 is ▶ 주어 자리에 온 명사절을 이끌어야 하는 자리 ▶ 뒤에 need의 목적어가 없는 불완전한 문장이 옴 ▶ 관계대명사 What
우리 모두에게 필요한 것은 인내다.

03 **[That / What]** the vacation days have been reduced by half is frustrating news for all employees.
➲ 문장의 본동사는 is ▶ 주어 자리에 온 명사절을 이끌어야 하는 자리 ▶ 뒤에 완전한 문장이 옴 ▶ 접속사 That
휴가 일수가 절반으로 줄었다는 것은 모든 직원에게 실망스러운 소식이다.

04 Through curiosity and exploration, you will discover in life **[that / what]** you seek and remain open to.
➲ 동사 discover의 목적어 자리 ▶ 뒤에 동사 seek의 목적어와 전치사 to의 목적어가 없는 불완전한 문장이 옴 ▶ 관계대명사 what
호기심과 탐험을 통해 인생에서 자신이 추구하고 열려 있는 것을 발견할 것이다.

전략 적용 연습

정답 및 해설 p. 33

[01 ~ 10] 밑줄 친 부분 중 어법상 옳은 것은 O, 옳지 않은 것은 X로 표시하고 틀린 부분을 올바르게 고치시오.

01 Do you remember when and where did you see the picture?

02 He wanted to know that they had agreed on behind closed doors.

03 The woman about that I was talking suddenly walked into the room.

04 Traveling alone can be challenging in that you have to rely on yourself for everything.

05 I showed my father a picture of the car what I was going to buy as soon as I saved enough money.

06 First, there is critical thinking, emphasizing the skill to analyze information and question what we are told.

07 The gift from my friend, that arrived in a small box, turned out to be a rare book from my favorite author.

08 Many social scientists have believed for some time what birth order directly affects both personality and achievement in adult life.

09 The doctor suggested that both the husband and wife sit down at the dining table and write down on paper that they were unhappy about with each other.

10 Robert was going steady with Susan and was thinking of marrying her. He wanted to know what kind of girls her sisters were, what her father was like, and how long her mother had been dead.

* go steady with: ~와 지속적으로 사귀다

新 [11 ~ 16] 밑줄 친 부분에 들어갈 말로 가장 적절한 것을 고르시오.

11 By skimming, you can understand __________ presenting the material.

① what is the writer
② what the writer is
③ how is the writer
④ how the writer is

12 Please be aware _____ customs regulations can vary significantly between countries.

① of
② to
③ what
④ that

13 _______ the adult smoking rate is gradually dropping is not good news for big tobacco companies.

① Which
② That
③ What
④ Who

14 There is an ancient bridge in the village, built by craftsmen, ________, it is said, possessed exceptional knowledge and precision.

① who
② which
③ that
④ what

15 Local libraries host book clubs at ______ patrons can discuss intriguing novels and share recommendations at their convenience.

① what
② that
③ which
④ where

16 Rocks and soil show geologists _______ the earth consisted of millions of years ago, how it has changed since then, and whether it is still changing.

① who
② that
③ what
④ whom

PART 2
문법

전략

22 복합관계대명사는 결국 '격 → 완전/불완전'을 묻는다

복합관계대명사가 나온 경우, ① 그 복합관계대명사가 그 문장 안에서 주어로 쓰였는지 목적어로 쓰였는지 격을 따져봐야 한다.(whoever vs whomever) 그런 다음, ② 뒤에 불완전한 문장이 왔는지 확인한다.(복합관계대명사는 뒤에 반드시 불완전한 문장이 와야 한다.) 그리고 명사절을 이끄는 복합관계대명사와 의문사의 구분은 해석을 통해 문맥에 따라 결정한다.

전략 노트 복합관계사

1. 복합관계대명사 + 불완전한 문장: 명사절 또는 부사절

whoever/whomever	명사절	~하는 사람이면 누구든(지)(= anyone who/whom)
	부사절	~하는 사람이면 누구든지 간에(= no matter who/whom)
whichever/whatever	명사절	~하는 것이면 무엇이든(= anything that)
	부사절	~하는 것이면 무엇이든지 간에(= no matter which/what)

* 복합관계형용사 whichever/whatever + 명사 + 불완전한 문장

2. 복합관계부사 + 완전한 문장: 부사절

whenever	부사절	~할 때면 언제든지(= no matter when)
wherever		~하는 곳이면 어디든(= no matter where)
however		아무리 ~해도(= no matter how)

* 복합관계부사 however는 바로 뒤에 형용사나 부사와 같이 쓰인다.

예제

01 **[Whoever / Whomever]** comes early before 11 a.m. will get the promotion goods.
➡ 문장의 본동사는 will get ▶ 주어 자리에 온 명사절을 이끌어야 하는 자리 ▶ 뒤에 주어가 없는 불완전한 문장이 옴 ▶ 복합관계대명사 Whoever
오전 11시 전에 일찍 오는 사람이면 누구든 그 홍보 상품을 받게 될 것이다.

02 Choose **[whatever / whenever]** you like from the menu for dinner.
➡ 문장의 본동사는 Choose ▶ 동사 Choose의 목적어 역할을 하는 명사절을 이끌어야 하는 자리 ▶ 뒤에 like의 목적어가 없는 불완전한 문장이 옴 ▶ 복합관계대명사 whatever
저녁 메뉴에서 네가 원하는 것은 무엇이든 골라라.

03 **[What / Whatever]** the topic of conversation might be, active listening shows respect for the speaker.
➡ 동사 2개(might be / shows) ▶ '_______ + S + V, S + V' 구조 ▶ 부사절을 이끌어야 하는 자리 ▶ 뒤에 be의 주격 보어가 없는 불완전한 문장이 옴 ▶ 복합관계대명사 Whatever
대화의 주제가 무엇이든 적극적으로 경청하는 것은 화자를 존중하는 태도를 보여 준다.

04 You must apply what you learn to see results **[how / however]** many books you read.
➡ 동사 3개(must apply / learn / read), 접속사/관계사/의문사 1개(what) ▶ 'S + V + _______ + 형용사 + 명사 + S + V' 구조 ▶ 뒤에 온 형용사 many를 수식하면서 부사절을 이끌어야 하는 자리 ▶ 복합관계부사 however
아무리 많은 책을 읽어도 배운 것을 적용해야 결과를 볼 수 있다.

전략

23 and/or/상관접속사는 같은 품사를 연결한다

'A and B', 'A, B, or C', 상관접속사는 주로 접속사를 중심으로 서로 같은 품사가 연결됐는지를 묻는다. 특히 단어가 짝을 이루고 있는 상관접속사는 서로의 짝을 찾는 문제로도 출제된다.

PART 2

문법

전략 노트 등위접속사와 상관접속사

1. 등위접속사

단어와 단어, 구와 구, 절과 절을 대등하게 연결하며, 반복되는 부분은 생략될 수 있다. (단, so와 for는 문장만 연결한다.)

and 그리고	or 또는	but/yet 그러나	so 그래서	for 왜냐하면

2. 상관접속사

두 단어 이상이 짝을 이루어 대등하게 연결한다.

both A and B A와 B 둘 다	neither A nor B A와 B 둘 다 아닌
either A or B A와 B 둘 중 하나	not A but B A가 아니라 B인
not only A but (also) B A뿐만 아니라 B도	B as well as A A뿐만 아니라 B도

예제

01 Almost every student hates taking tests and **[does / doing]** homework.

➲ 등위접속사 and 있음 ▶ 문장의 본동사 hates와 병렬 구조 vs 동명사 taking과 병렬 구조 ▶ 문맥상 '거의 모든 학생이 시험 보는 것과 숙제 하는 것을 싫어한다'라는 의미가 자연스러움 ▶ 동명사 doing

거의 모든 학생은 시험을 보는 것과 숙제를 하는 것을 싫어한다.

02 Companies looking for **[experience / experienced]** and competent staff may find it difficult to do so.

➲ 등위접속사 and 있음 ▶ 명사 staff를 수식하는 형용사 competent와 병렬 구조 ▶ 형용사 experienced

경험 있고 유능한 직원을 찾는 회사들은 그게 어렵다는 것을 알게 될지도 모른다.

03 With fairness in mind, the judge neither **[favor / favors]** nor discriminates against any party in the courtroom.

➲ 상관접속사 'neither A nor B' 구문 ▶ 주어 the judge에 대한 단수 동사 discriminates와 병렬 구조 ▶ 단수 동사 favors

공정성을 염두에 둔 채 판사는 법정에서 어떤 당사자도 편애하거나 차별하지 않는다.

04 What a pet needs most isn't just food and water, but **[to love / love]**, companionship, and regular exercise.

➲ 상관접속사 'not A but B' 구문 ▶ 주격 보어 역할을 하는 명사 food and water와 병렬 구조 & 뒤에 등위접속사 and로 연결된 명사 companionship, regular exercise와 병렬 구조 ▶ 명사 love

반려동물에게 가장 필요한 것은 단순히 음식과 물이 아니라 사랑, 교감, 그리고 규칙적인 운동이다.

전략 적용 연습

정답 및 해설 p. 35

[01 ~ 12] 밑줄 친 부분 중 어법상 옳은 것은 O, 옳지 않은 것은 X로 표시하고 틀린 부분을 올바르게 고치시오.

01 I'm sure the team is willing to do whatever he wants.

02 I stopped going out with friends and practiced the cello constantly.

03 Planning a wedding can be not only joyful but also occasionally stress.

04 Give this note to whomever is in charge of organizing the event promptly.

05 However weary you may be, you must keep moving forward step by step.

06 Children need a place where they can learn to swim, surf, and enjoying the water safely.

07 No matter what cold it may be outside, you should let in some fresh air from time to time.

08 In the Metro, you have to open the doors yourself by pushing a button, depressing a lever, or sliding them.

09 You should remember that however struggles you encounter, you are not alone with your friends and family by your side.

10 But a human is much more capable of operating those instruments correctly and to place them in appropriate and useful positions.

11 As an architect, you design a building based on how it integrates with the environment and evaluates its functionality and sustainability.

12 To ensure long-term success and satisfaction, you must avoid making hasty decisions and taking the time to consider all your options carefully.

新 [13 ~ 18] 밑줄 친 부분에 들어갈 말로 가장 적절한 것을 고르시오.

13 City parks offer _______ recreational facilities and scenic walking trails for residents.

① whichever
② both
③ in that
④ either

14 Her ambition is to start her own business and eventually ________ it internationally.

① expand
② expands
③ expanding
④ expansion

15 If you have any questions during the lecture, do not hesitate to ask them, _________ basic they may seem.

① how
② what
③ whoever
④ no matter how

16 As neither the cash register _______ the credit card machine is working, exact change will be required.

① but
② both
③ or
④ nor

17 The supervisor was advised to give the assignment to _________ he believed had a strong sense of responsibility.

① who
② whom
③ whoever
④ whomever

18 Please conduct a safety drill ________ the risk of fire rises due to increased temperatures or hazardous materials in the facility.

① whatever
② whenever
③ whose
④ how

UNIT 04

형용사/부사 핵심 전략

전략

24 '형용사 vs 부사'는 명사를 설명하는지 동사를 수식하는지를 따져라

형용사는 ① 명사 앞뒤에서 명사를 수식하거나 ② 주격/목적격 보어로서 명사를 설명하고, 부사는 명사를 제외한 동사, 형용사, 부사, 구, 절, 그리고 문장 전체를 수식한다. 따라서 '형용사 vs 부사' 문제는 문장에서 어떤 역할을 하는지 파악해서 형용사를 쓸지 부사를 쓸지 판단해야 한다. (단, 부사는 문장 성분에 포함되지 않는 수식어이므로 생략되어도 문법적 오류가 없다는 점에 유의한다.)

전략 노트 **형용사 vs 부사**

1. 형용사는 주격 보어나 목적격 보어 자리에 오고, 부사는 동사를 수식한다.

(1) S + V + [형용사 vs 부사]: S + V + 형용사(SC) (S를 설명) vs S + V + 부사 (V를 수식)

(2) S + V + O + [형용사 vs 부사]: S + V + O + 형용사(OC) (O를 설명) vs S + V + O + 부사 (V를 수식)

※ 동사를 수식하는 부사 자리에 형용사는 올 수 없다.

조동사 + (부사) + RV — 형용사 (X)
be/have + (부사) + p.p. — 형용사 (X)
to + (부사) + RV — 형용사 (X)

2. 형용사는 명사를 수식하고, 부사는 형용사/부사를 수식한다.

a/the + 형용사 + 명사 vs a/the + 부사 + 형용사 + 명사

3. -ly가 붙어 혼동하기 쉬운 형용사와 부사는 따로 암기하자. * p. 126 〈주의해야 하는 형용사와 부사〉 참고

예제

01 You should walk **[careful / carefully]** after it has snowed.
➡ 동사 walk를 수식하는 자리 ▶ 문맥상 '조심해서 걷다'라는 의미가 자연스러움 ▶ 부사 carefully
눈이 온 뒤에는 조심해서 걸어야 한다.

02 It rarely happens that this disease proves **[fatal / fatally]**.
➡ 2형식 동사 proves의 주격 보어 자리 ▶ 주어인 질병이 '치명적인' 것 ▶ 형용사 fatal
이 질병이 치명적인 것으로 드러나는 일은 좀처럼 없다.

03 Her painting displayed **[extraordinary / extraordinarily]** talent and creativity.
➡ 명사구 talent and creativity를 수식하는 자리 ▶ 형용사 extraordinary
그녀의 그림은 뛰어난 재능과 창의성을 보여 주었다.

04 The cafe is **[convenient / conveniently]** located next to the university campus.
➡ 수동태의 be동사(is)와 p.p.(located) 사이에서 동사를 수식하는 자리 ▶ 부사 conveniently
그 카페는 대학 캠퍼스 옆에 편리하게 위치해 있다.

전략

25 보어 자리에 형용사를 취하는 2형식 동사와 5형식 동사는 무조건 암기한다

형용사 문제는 주로 명사를 수식하거나 보어 자리를 묻는 문제로 출제된다. 그중 주격/목적격 보어 자리인지를 빠르게 판단하려면 대표적 2형식 동사와 5형식 동사를 암기해 두어야 한다.

전략 노트 대표적인 2·5형식 동사

1. 2형식 동사

be동사		+ 형용사
become형 동사(~이 되다)	become, get, turn, grow, go, come, run, fall	
remain형 동사(유지하다)	remain, keep, stay, hold	
오감/표정 동사	look, smell, taste, sound, feel, seem	+ 형용사 + like 명사
판단·입증 동사	seem, appear, prove, turn out	+ (to be) 형용사

2. 5형식 동사

make, keep, find, think	+ 명사	+ 형용사

* make/find의 가목적어-진목적어 구문: 'make/find + 가목적어(it) + 형용사 + 진목적어(to RV)'

3. 보어로만 쓰이는 서술적 용법의 형용사와 명사 앞에만 쓰이는 제한적 용법의 형용사를 구분하자. * p. 126 〈주의해야 하는 형용사와 부사〉 참고

예제

01 The answer to that question sounds **[obvious / obviously]**.

➲ 2형식 동사 sounds의 주격 보어 자리 ▶ 형용사 obvious

그 질문에 대한 답은 분명한 것처럼 들린다.

02 Sometimes the variation is as **[subtle / subtly]** as a pause.

➲ as ~ as 원급 비교 구문 ▶ be동사 is의 주격 보어 자리 ▶ 형용사 subtle

가끔 그 변화는 정지 상황만큼이나 미묘하다.

03 We must keep our room **[clean / cleanly]**.

➲ 5형식 동사 keep의 목적격 보어 자리 ▶ 형용사 clean

우리는 우리 방을 깨끗하게 유지해야 한다.

04 She found the instructions quite **[simple / simply]** to follow and understand.

➲ 5형식 동사 found의 목적격 보어 자리 & 부사 quite의 수식을 받는 자리 ▶ 형용사 simple

그녀는 지침이 따르고 이해하기에 매우 간단하다는 것을 알았다.

전략 적용 연습

정답 및 해설 p. 37

[01 ~ 11] 밑줄 친 부분 중 어법상 옳은 것은 O, 옳지 않은 것은 X로 표시하고 틀린 부분을 올바르게 고치시오.

01 She would like to be financial independent.

02 Each officer must perform his or her duties efficient.

03 Your problems and challenges suddenly seem insignificant.

04 The population of the city will increase sharply over the next quarter.

05 The lower the resolution, however, the less clearly the image will become.

06 The hotel lobby offers conveniently seating areas for guests waiting to check in.

07 With rising gas prices, many drivers will short be looking for fuel-efficient cars.

08 For maintaining good oral hygiene, brushing your teeth after meals proved essential for preventing cavities.

09 He soon found the prevailing musical idioms inadequately and began to explore new and radical forms of expression.

10 The air feels fresher, the flowers smell sweeter, the food tastes more delicious, and the stars shine more brilliant in the night sky.

11 People with the condition find it easy to interpret large images or scenes, but struggle to "spot the difference" in fine detail.

新 [12 ~ 17] 밑줄 친 부분에 들어갈 말로 가장 적절한 것을 고르시오.

12 Scientists have conducted ________ research to develop a vaccine for the recent global pandemic.

① extensive
② extensively
③ extend
④ extension

13 In order to make energy consumption highly ___________, the city council installed solar panels on all public buildings.

① sustain
② sustainable
③ sustainably
④ sustainability

14 The legal team has reviewed all documentation thoroughly, and they expect the case to be resolved ________ in court.

① success
② succeed
③ successful
④ successfully

15 Cultures as ________ as the Guatemalan Maya and the Inuit of Northwestern Canada, practice parent-infant 'co-sleeping.'

① diverse
② diversely
③ diversity
④ diversify

16 Our university is creating a mentorship program which will be especially _______ for freshmen adjusting to campus life.

① using
② use
③ useful
④ usefully

17 As researchers learn more about how children's intelligence develops, they are _______ surprised by the power of parents.

① repeating
② repeated
③ repeatedly
④ repeat

전략

26 enough/so/such/too가 나오면 어순과 해석에 주의하라

문장 중간에 enough/so/such/too가 나오면 뒤에 to RV나 that절이 나오는지를 확인하고, 어순과 해석까지 적절한지 살펴보아야 한다. 만약 부사 자리를 묻는데, 선택지에 enough/so/such/too 중 하나가 있다면 특정 구문을 완성하는 구조인지 꼭 확인하도록 하자.

전략 노트 to RV나 that절과 함께 특정 구문을 나타내는 형용사/부사

1. enough

부사로 쓰일 때 형용사 앞이 아니라 형용사 뒤에서만 수식이 가능하다.

형용사	enough + 명사 + to RV (O)	명사 + enough + to RV (O)
부사	형용사 + enough + to RV (O)	enough + 형용사 + to RV (X)

2. so vs such vs too

뒤에 ① 형용사/부사가 왔는지 명사(a + 형용사 + 명사)가 왔는지, ② to RV나 that절이 왔는지 확인한 후 해석으로 마무리한다.

so + 형/부 that / so + 형 + a(n) + 명 + that	너무 ~해서 (그 결과) ~하다
such + a(n) + 형 + 명 + that	너무 ~해서 (그 결과) ~하다
too + 형/부 + to RV	너무 ~해서 ~할 수 없다

예제

01 Tom is **[old enough / enough old]** to see the movie.

➡ 형용사 old를 수식하는 부사 자리 ▶ enough는 형용사를 뒤에서 수식 ▶ old enough

Tom은 그 영화를 볼 수 있을 만큼 나이가 들었다.

02 He is **[so / such]** an honest man that everyone trusts him.

➡ 뒤에 명사구(an honest man)와 that절이 옴 ▶ '______ + an + 형(honest) + 명(man) + that'의 어순 ▶ such

그는 정말 정직해서 모두가 그를 믿는다.

03 She is **[so / too]** young to realize that not everyone will always agree with her opinions.

➡ 뒤에 형용사(young)와 to RV(to know)가 옴 ▶ 문맥상 '너무 어려서 깨닫지 못한다'라는 의미가 자연스러움 ▶ too

그녀는 너무 어려서 모든 사람이 항상 자신의 의견에 동의하는 것은 아니라는 것을 깨닫지 못한다.

전략
27 very/much/many/little/few는 뒤를 잘 봐야 한다

very는 뒤에 원급이, much는 뒤에 비교급이나 단수 명사가 왔는지를 확인하고, many/little/few는 뒤에 단수 명사가 왔는지 복수 명사가 왔는지를 확인한다. 특히 부정·수량형용사는 단/복수 명사와 짝을 이루고 있으므로 서로를 단서 삼아서 푸는 문제가 주로 출제된다.

PART 2
문법

전략 노트 뒤와 짝꿍 관계를 이루는 형용사/부사

1. very vs much

very	much
형용사/부사 **원급** 수식	형용사/부사 **비교급** 수식
the very 최상급	much the 최상급
현재분사 수식	**과거분사** 수식
동사 수식 **불가**	동사 수식 **가능**

2. 부정·수량형용사는 뒤에 오는 명사가 단/복수인지를 구별해서 푼다.

every / each / another (a) little / much / a large amount of / a great deal of / many a	+ **단수** 명사
other / one[each/either/neither] of (a) few / many / a number of / a variety of	+ **복수** 명사

* 부정대명사 one/each/either/neither of + 복수 명사 + 단수 동사

예제

01 This is **[very / much]** expensive car.
➲ 뒤에 온 원급 형용사 expensive를 수식(강조)하는 부사 자리 ▶ very
이것은 매우 비싼 차이다.

02 This car is **[very / much]** more expensive than yours.
➲ 뒤에 온 비교급 형용사 more expensive를 수식(강조)하는 부사 자리 ▶ much
이 차는 너의 것보다 훨씬 더 비싸다.

03 My father never gave me **[many / much]** advice.
➲ 뒤에 온 불가산명사(단수 명사) advice를 수식하는 형용사 자리 ▶ much
우리 아버지는 나에게 많은 충고를 해준 적이 없다.

전략 적용 연습

정답 및 해설 p. 39

[01 ~ 10] 밑줄 친 부분 중 어법상 옳은 것은 O, 옳지 않은 것은 X로 표시하고 틀린 부분을 올바르게 고치시오.

01 The artist's much colorful paintings brighten the whole gallery.

02 He felt enough comfortable to tell me about something he wanted to do.

03 As many as twenty states have already restricted the sale of junk food.

04 Looking up new words in a dictionary is very important in learning languages.

05 The travelers didn't anticipate that prices would rise so many during the holiday season.

06 He was so distracted by a text message to know that he was going over the speed limit.

07 But it can also happen that one's memories grow much sharper even after a long passage of time.

08 His address at the luncheon meeting was too great that the entire audience appeared to support him.

09 Their beginner's dance class covered just a little basic steps such as walking, turning, and practicing simple choreography.

10 Such imprudent are we that we wander about in times that are not ours and do not think of the one that belongs to us.

新 [11 ~ 16] 밑줄 친 부분에 들어갈 말로 가장 적절한 것을 고르시오.

11 This morning it was ________ cooler than yesterday morning.

① too
② very
③ more
④ much

12 This bookstore's ambition is to stock ________ genre of literature for its customers.

① all
② every
③ a few
④ each of

13 My parents were ______ poor at that time that they couldn't afford to buy the house.

① so
② too
③ very
④ such

14 Her explanation was clear _______ to convince everyone that she was innocent.

① enough
② many
③ other
④ such

15 In the grocery store, there are ________ fresh fruits and vegetables available, perfect for creating healthy meals.

① each
② every
③ many
④ much

16 A principal was committed to making sure that ________ of the classrooms was equipped with the necessary teaching materials.

① every
② a number
③ much
④ each

FURTHER STUDY 주의해야 하는 형용사와 부사

▶ '명사 + -ly' 형태의 형용사

friendly	친근한	costly	값비싼	lively	활기찬
likely	~할 것 같은	deadly	치명적인	lonely	외로운
timely	시기적절한	leisurely	한가로운	orderly	질서정연한, 정돈된

▶ 형태가 비슷하나 다른 의미의 부사

late	형 늦은	부 늦게	lately	부 최근에 (*cf.* latest 최신의)
hard	형 힘든; 열심인	부 열심히	hardly	부 거의 ~하지 않는
near	형 가까운	부 가까이	nearly	부 거의
short	형 부족한; 짧은	부 부족하게; 짧게	shortly	부 즉시
high	형 높은	부 높이, 높게	highly	부 매우, 고귀하게

▶ 서술적 용법으로만 쓰이는 형용사

alive	살아 있는	alone	혼자인	awake	깨어 있는
asleep	잠자는	afraid	두려워하는	aware	알고 있는
alike	비슷한	ashamed	부끄러운		

▶ 제한적 용법으로만 쓰이는 형용사

live	살아 있는	lone	외로운	drunken	술 취한
golden	금으로 만든	wooden	나무로 만든	former/latter	앞의/뒤의

- Weather alerts should be issued in a **[timing / timely]** manner to warn residents of severe storms.
  주민들에게 강력한 폭풍에 대해 경고할 수 있도록 기상 경보를 적시에 발령해야 한다.

- **[Late / Lately]**, he has been working extra hours to meet the deadline.
  최근에 그는 마감 기한을 맞추기 위해 초과 근무를 해왔다.

- He discovered his passion for music **[late / lately]** in life, but it was never too late to pursue his dreams.
  그는 만년에[인생 후반에] 음악에 대한 열정을 발견했지만 꿈을 이루기에는 절대 늦지 않았다.

- Her debut novel has received **[high / highly]** praise from literary critics.
  그녀의 데뷔 소설은 문학 평론가들로부터 높은 평가를 받았다.

- She was **[high / highly]** praised for her debut novel by literary critics.
  그녀는 문학 평론가들로부터 데뷔 소설로 높은 평가를 받았다.

- The nature reserve is home to a variety of **[live / alive]** wildlife species.
  자연 보호 구역에는 다양한 종의 살아 있는 야생 동물이 서식하고 있다.

- Her storytelling skills made the bedtime story fascinating, imaginative, and **[live / alive]** with wonder.
  그녀의 스토리텔링 능력은 잠들기 전 들려주는 이야기를 매혹적이고 상상력이 풍부하며 경이로움이 살아 숨 쉬게 했다.

- The siblings looked so **[like / alike]** that distinguishing between them was difficult.
  그 남매는 너무 비슷하게 생겨서 그들을 구분하기란 어려웠다.

- The siblings argued **[like / alike]** cats and dogs, but soon they were back to laughing and playing together.
  그 남매는 고양이와 개처럼 다투었지만, 곧 다시 함께 웃고 놀았다.

정답 timely | Lately | late | high | highly | live | alive | alike | like

UNIT 05

비교/도치/대명사 핵심 전략

전략

28 문두에 '부정어'나 'Only + 부사(구/절)'를 보는 순간, 바로 도치 문제임을 눈치채자

'부정어'나 'Only + 부사(구/절)'가 문장 맨 앞에 오는 경우, 주어와 동사가 도치된다. 도치 구문은 어순이 올바르게 되어 있는지, 주어와 동사의 수가 일치하는지를 확인하는 것이 가장 중요하다.

전략 노트 도치 구문

1. '부정어' 또는 'Only + 부사(구/절)'의 도치

부정어	Not/Never ~이 아닌/결코 ~않다 Little/Rarely/Scarcely/Seldom/Hardly 거의 ~않다 Not only(~ but also S + V) ~할 뿐만 아니라 (~하다) No sooner(~ than S + V) ~하자마자 (~하다) On no account/Under no circumstances 어떠한 경우에도 ~않다	+ V + S
Only + 부사(구/절)	Only then/Only recently 그때서야/최근에서야 Only when S + V ~할 때에야 비로소 ~하다	

❶ 알맞은 동사의 형태와 주어-동사의 수일치에 유의한다. (본동사가 be동사/조동사일 때 주어와 be동사/조동사의 위치가 바뀌고, 일반동사일 때는 do/does/did를 주어 앞에 쓰고 뒤에 동사원형이 온다.)

2. '장소·방향·위치의 부사구/There/Here'의 도치

장소·방향·위치의 부사구	+ V + S(일반명사)
유도부사[There/Here]	+ S(대명사) + V

3. be동사의 보어 도치

형용사/RVing/p.p.	+ be동사 + S

예제

01 Never **[he thought / did he think]** his joke would cause such a misunderstanding.
➲ 문두에 부정어 Never가 나옴 ▶ 주어와 동사의 도치 일어남 ▶ 본동사가 일반동사인 경우 'do/does/did + 주어 + 동사원형'의 어순 ▶ did he think
그는 자신의 농담이 그런 오해를 불러일으킬 줄은 전혀 생각지 못했다.

02 Only on weekends **[John was / was John]** able to see his family.
➲ 문두에 'Only + 부사구(on weekends)'가 나옴 ▶ 주어와 동사의 도치 일어남 ▶ be동사인 경우 'be동사 + 주어'의 어순 ▶ was John
오직 주말에만 John은 자신의 가족을 볼 수 있었다.

03 Beside the old oak tree **[was / were]** children playing happily in the warm glow of the afternoon sun.
➲ 문두에 장소 부사구 Beside the old oak tree가 나옴 ▶ 주어와 동사의 도치 일어남 ▶ 주어 children에 대한 동사 자리 ▶ 복수 주어에 수일치 ▶ were
오래된 떡갈나무 옆에는 아이들이 오후의 따사로운 햇살을 받으며 즐겁게 놀고 있었다.

전략
29 'so[neither] + V + S'는 3가지를 확인하라

문장 뒤에 and so[neither]가 나오면, ① 앞 문장이 긍정인지 부정인지 ② 뒤에 'V + S'의 어순인지 ③ V 자리의 (대)동사 쓰임이 적절한지를 확인해야 한다.

전략 노트 **so/neither 도치 구문**

앞 문장의 내용을 간단히 so나 neither로 대신할 때 주어와 동사가 도치되는데, 동사는 앞 문장의 동사와 동일한 형태로 쓴다. (단, 주어와의 수일치에 유의한다.)

긍정문,	and so + be동사/조동사/대동사 + S	~도 또한 그렇다
부정문,	and neither[nor] + be동사/조동사/대동사 + S	~도 또한 그렇지 않다

* neither는 부사이므로 접속사 and가 필요하고, nor는 접속사이므로 다른 접속사 없이 절을 연결한다.

예제

01 I don't agree with you, and **[so does Steve / neither Steve does / neither does Steve]**.

➡ 앞 문장이 부정문 ▶ 부정 동의 표현 '부정문, and neither[nor] + V + S' ▶ 앞 문장의 동사가 현재시제의 일반동사 don't agree ▶ 주어(Steve)와의 수일치 ▶ neither does Steve

나는 네 의견에 동의하지 않고 Steve도 또한 그렇다[동의하지 않는다].

02 The timeless artworks are still with us, and as a result, so **[is / are / does]** their beauty.

➡ 긍정 동의 표현 '긍정문, and so + V + S' ▶ 앞 문장의 동사가 현재시제의 be동사 are ▶ 주어(their beauty)와의 수일치 ▶ is

시대를 초월한 예술 작품은 여전히 우리와 함께하며, 그 결과 그 아름다움 또한 그렇다[여전히 우리와 함께한다].

03 She wasn't impressed with the presentation, **[and neither was I / and neither did I / nor did I]**.

➡ 앞 문장이 부정문 ▶ 부정 동의 표현 '부정문, and neither[nor] + V + S' ▶ 앞 문장의 동사가 과거시제의 be동사 wasn't impressed ▶ 주어(I)와의 수일치 ▶ and neither was I

그녀는 발표가 인상 깊게 느껴지지 않았고, 나도 또한 그렇다[인상 깊게 느껴지지 않았다].

전략 적용 연습

정답 및 해설 p. 41

[01 ~ 12] 밑줄 친 부분 중 어법상 옳은 것은 O, 옳지 않은 것은 X로 표시하고 틀린 부분을 올바르게 고치시오.

01 Under no circumstances <u>you should leave</u> here.

02 Peggy did not go to see the drama, and <u>so I did</u>.

03 Right beside his desk <u>was a stack of books</u> waiting to be read.

04 No sooner <u>she met</u> her husband than she started to complain.

05 So important to the training program <u>the emphasis is</u> on hands-on experience.

06 The company prioritizes ESG principles in its investments, and <u>so do its shareholders</u>.

07 Not only <u>did they send</u> the wrong components, but they also sent them to the wrong department.

08 At certain times <u>dreams are</u> realized through perseverance and unwavering determination.

09 When he left his hometown thirty years ago, little <u>does he dream</u> that he could never see it again.

10 On the southern shore of Lake Erie <u>lies Cleveland</u>, the greatest metropolitan area in Ohio.

11 If a river is heavily polluted, then there <u>is</u> likely to be significant health impacts on local wildlife.

12 Only recently have municipalities across the globe <u>began</u> experimenting with innovative designs for urban trash cans to improve usability.

新 [13 ~ 18] 밑줄 친 부분에 들어갈 말로 가장 적절한 것을 고르시오.

13 I was born in Seoul, and so ________, deeply rooted in its culture.

① my parents did
② did my parents
③ my parents were
④ were my parents

14 ________ did he know that he was fueling his son with a passion that would last for a lifetime.

① Although
② No sooner
③ Few
④ Little

15 Only when the pandemic restrictions eased did theaters ________ to the public.

① reopen
② reopened
③ reopening
④ not reopened

16 ________ will the mechanic fix your car, but he will also perform routine maintenance checks.

① Not only
② So as to
③ In spite of
④ Just as

17 Due to a scheduling conflict, the keynote speaker cannot attend the conference, and ________ can the industry expert.

① however
② neither
③ so
④ also

18 ________ along with the formal invitation is a map that shows the venue location and parking information for your convenience.

① Attach
② Attaching
③ Attached
④ To attach

전략

30 대명사에 밑줄이 있으면 수일치나 재귀대명사를 묻는다

대명사, 특히 it/them에 밑줄이 있으면 그 대명사가 가리키는 대상을 찾아서 수일치가 제대로 되었는지 먼저 확인한다. 그리고 만약 목적어로 쓰인 대명사가 주어와 같다면(행위의 주체와 대상이 동일할 때) 목적어 자리에 재귀대명사가 와야 한다.

전략 노트 지시대명사와 부정대명사

1. 대명사의 쓰임

it/them	앞뒤에 수식어구가 붙지 않는다.
[수식어구] + one/ones	앞에 수식어구가 붙을 수 있다.
that/those + [수식어구]	뒤에 수식어구가 붙을 수 있다.

2. 부정대명사 one, another, others, the other(s)의 구분

대상이 둘일 때		대상이 셋 이상일 때		
one 처음 하나	the other 나머지 하나	one 처음 하나	another another + 단수 명사	또 다른 하나[명사]
			others other + 복수 명사	다른 것들[명사들]
			the other the other + 단수 명사	마지막 하나[명사]
			the others the other + 복수 명사	나머지 것들[명사들]

❶ 항상 '마지막 것(들)'에만 정관사 the를 붙인다는 것에 주의하자.

※ one ~ another를 이용한 관용 표현

A is one thing and B is another.	A와 B는 별개의 문제이다

ex Understanding theory is **one thing** and applying it practically is **another**.
이론을 이해하는 것과 그것을 실제로 적용하는 것은 별개의 문제이다.

예제

01 One of five students is tall, but **[the other / the others]** are short.
➲ 등위접속사 but으로 대조를 이루는 두 문장 ▶ 학생 다섯 명 중 키가 큰 '한 명(one)'과 키가 작은 '나머지 모두' ▶ 뒤 문장의 동사가 복수 동사(are) ▶ 복수의 나머지 모두(네 명)를 지칭 ▶ the others
학생 다섯 명 중 한 명은 키가 크고 나머지는 키가 작다.

02 We can't give up electricity, but we can control the ways we use **[it / them]**.
➲ 문맥상 우리가 '전기'를 사용하는 방법을 제어하는 것 ▶ 단수 명사 electricity를 대신하는 대명사 ▶ it
우리는 전기를 포기할 수 없지만, 그것을 사용하는 방법을 제어할 수는 있다.

03 The fairness of a law should be assessed from the viewpoint of the citizen, not from **[that / those]** of the legislator.
➲ 문맥상 법의 공정성은 입법자의 '관점'이 아닌 시민의 '관점'에서 평가되어야 하는 것 ▶ 단수 명사 the viewpoint를 대신하며 수식어구(of the legislator)의 수식을 받을 수 있는 대명사 ▶ that
법의 공정성은 입법자의 관점이 아닌 시민의 관점에서 평가되어야 한다.

전략

31 원급·비교급·최상급이 나오면 '혼용·중복'과 '비교 대상의 급'을 확인하라

비교 구문에서 가장 핵심은 ① 'as ~ as', '-er/more ~ than'처럼 상관어구의 올바른 사용과 ② 비교되는 대상의 품사가 일치하는지 여부이다. 비교 구문의 형태와 잘 쓰이는 어구를 공식처럼 알아두면 의외로 문제가 쉽게 풀린다.

전략 노트 비교 구문의 주의 사항

1. 비교 구문의 혼용·중복 금지

원급, 비교급, 최상급의 상관어구 및 기본적인 형태가 정해져 있다.

혼용 금지	ex more beautiful as (X) / as beautiful than (X) → than → as
중복 금지	ex as younger as (X) / more younger than (X) / the most youngest (X) → young → younger → youngest

2. 비교 대상의 급 일치

비교되는 두 대상은 품사, 격, 내용이 같아야 한다.

ex The population of New York is smaller than Tokyo. (X)
뉴욕의 인구는 도쿄의 인구보다 더 적다. → that of Tokyo

3. The 비교급 ~, the 비교급 ~ '~하면 할수록 더 ~하다'

두 비교급 앞에 the가 반드시 있어야 하며, 문장 구조에 따라 형용사/부사의 비교급이 온다.

ex **The more** you read, **the wider** your vocabulary will grow.
책을 많이 읽을수록 어휘력이 더 넓어질 것이다.

4. 비교급 강조 부사

much, still, even, (by) far, a lot은 비교급을 강조하고, very는 원급을 강조한다.

ex This year's festival was **even** more exciting than last year's.
올해 축제는 작년 축제보다 훨씬 더 흥미진진했다.

5. 라틴계 비교급

라틴계 형용사가 쓰인 비교급을 말하며, 비교 대상 앞에 than 대신 to를 쓴다. 비교급이기 때문에 much로 강조할 수 있으나 very로 강조할 수 없다.

superior to ~보다 우수한	inferior to ~보다 열등한	preferable to ~보다 더 나은

ex Walking is **much preferable to** driving for short distances.
짧은 거리는 운전하는 것보다 걷는 것이 훨씬 더 낫다.

예제

01 Fifteen thousand more computers were sold in 2005 **[as / than]** in 2004.
➔ 앞에 more가 있음 ▶ 비교 대상은 in 2005과 in 2004 ▶ 비교급 비교 ▶ 비교급의 비교 대상 앞에 오는 상관어구 ▶ than
2005년에는 2004년보다 만 오천 대의 컴퓨터가 더 팔렸다.

02 The taste of homemade cookies is **[very / much]** superior to store-bought ones without question.
➔ 라틴계 비교급인 superior to(~보다 우수한)를 강조하는 부사 자리 ▶ much
직접 만든 쿠키의 맛은 의심할 여지 없이 시중에서 파는 쿠키보다 훨씬 더 뛰어나다.

03 **[The less / The least]** you multitask, the more focused you will be on each task.
➔ 뒤에 'the 비교급 + 주어 + 동사' 형태의 the more focused you will be가 있음 ▶ 'the 비교급 + 주어 + 동사, the 비교급 + 주어 + 동사' 구문 ▶ 부사 little의 'the 비교급' ▶ The less
멀티태스킹을 덜 할수록 각 작업에 더 집중할 것이다.

전략 적용 연습

정답 및 해설 p. 43

[01 ~ 12] 밑줄 친 부분 중 어법상 옳은 것은 O, 옳지 않은 것은 X로 표시하고 틀린 부분을 올바르게 고치시오.

01 This year's fashion trends are quite different from those of last year.

02 Here are four suitcases, but I can carry only two. Please bring the other.

03 Visiting a farm is far more educational than to look at the farm in the book.

04 The more they tried to explain their mistakes, the worst their story sounded.

05 The detective in the mystery novel was as cleverer as Sherlock Holmes, solving the case with ease.

06 The flags showed which way the wind blew and helped soldiers see the direction to aim their arrows.

07 When you attempt to do something and fail, you have to ask you why you have failed to do what you intended.

08 In spite of their close location to these countries, however, Korea has remained free of the deadly disease.

09 Both major events, like the World Cup, and minor one, such as local soccer matches, bring communities together.

10 Knowing they exercised for their health gives themselves a boost of energy, regardless of how tired they felt initially.

11 The modernized opera house will now comfortably accommodate 3,000 patrons, four times as many as before, enhancing the overall experience.

12 Unlike the architecture of ancient Rome, which featured grand arches and domes, those of ancient Greece emphasized columns and symmetry.

新 [13 ~ 20] 밑줄 친 부분에 들어갈 말로 가장 적절한 것을 고르시오.

13 Jane is not ____________ she looks.

① as younger as
② as young as
③ as young than
④ very younger than

14 Organic pet foods tend to be more expensive than standard ______.

① ones
② another
③ each
④ all

15 A small town seems to be ____________ a big city for raising children.

① very preferable than
② much preferable than
③ very preferable to
④ much preferable to

16 She asked her sisters to accompany __________ on a shopping trip for new clothes.

① her
② herself
③ themselves
④ on her own

17 Even if the restaurant is busy, ______ who made reservations will have guaranteed seating.

① they
② those
③ them
④ theirs

18 Among the public parks in the city, Central Park is the ____________ to reach by public transportation.

① easily
② easiest
③ more easily
④ most easily

19 The career advancements of female executives in an oil company are _________ achieved than those of their male counterparts.

① less steadily
② more steady
③ least steady
④ steadily

20 Of the two job candidates, _________ has experience in project management, while the other specializes in customer relations.

① whom
② either
③ one
④ each

PART 3

독해

新 UNIT 01 신유형 핵심 전략 (전략 01 ~ 전략 04)

UNIT 02 독해 핵심 전략 (전략 05 ~ 전략 13)

독해 핵심 공략법

1 신유형

지문 유형	이메일	안내문	웹페이지 글
2025년 출제 기조 전환	지식 암기 위주 ⇨ 현장 직무 중심		
출제 기조 전환 예시 문항 수1)	1지문 2문항	1지문 2문항	2지문 2문항 (지문당 1문항)
출제 기조 전환 예시 문제 유형2)	[set 문제] 목적+동의어	[set 문제] 제목+불일치	[단일 문제] 일치 [단일 문제] 불일치
출제 기조 전환 예시 지문 소재	민원	행사 안내	▶ 어플리케이션을 통한 세관 신고 안내 ▶ 정부 부처 역할 소개
신유형 대비 공통 전략	최대한 빠르고 정확하게 문제 풀이를 진행하여, 기존 유형의 고난도 독해 문제 풀이를 위한 시간 확보용 문제로 접근하기		

1) 실제 시험은 이와 다르게 나올 수 있음을 염두에 두어야 한다.

2) 각 지문 유형별로 출제 가능한 문제 유형은 아래와 같다.
- ▶ 이메일: 목적/요지, 동의어, 일치/불일치
- ▶ 행사/안내문: 제목/목적/주제, 동의어, 일치/불일치
- ▶ 웹페이지 글: 일치/불일치, 동의어, 제목/목적/주제

2 기존 유형

출제 유지되는 기존 유형	주제·제목, 요지·주장, 일관성, 문장 삽입, 순서 배열, 빈칸 추론
출제 불분명한 기존 유형	연결사, 기존 일치/불일치, 심경
소재	정해진 범위는 없으나, 출제 기조 전환 예시 기준 교육, 식약품, 환경, 출산율 등 국가 및 사회적인 이슈 중점적으로 출제

UNIT 01

신유형 핵심 전략

전략

01 이메일은 형식으로 접근하라

보통 이메일은 '인사 → 목적 → 부연 설명 → 당부하는 말' 순서로 전개된다. 이 형식에 맞춰 정답을 찾아 나가는 방식으로 문제 풀이에 접근해야 한다.

전략 노트

1. 이메일 상단 내용을 통해 글의 방향성을 잡아라

To(수신), From(발신), Subject(제목)를 통해 글의 내용을 예상할 수 있다. 특히 Subject 부분에서는 글의 소재를 파악할 수 있다.

To: reserve@metropolitan.com	수신: reserve@metropolitan.com
From: BruceTaylor@westcity.com	발신: BruceTaylor@westcity.com
Date: June 22, 2024	날짜: 2024년 6월 22일
Subject: Venue facilities	제목: 행사장 시설

❶ 이메일의 목적을 묻는 문제의 경우 오답 선지들도 Subject의 소재와 관련 있게 나오는 편이다. 따라서 Subject만 읽고 답을 골라서는 안 된다.

2. 초반부에서 글의 목적이 나온다

이메일의 초반부에서 목적이 명시되는 편이며, 사용되는 표현 또한 정형화되어 있다. 이 표현들에 익숙해진다면 내용을 쉽고 빠르게 파악할 수 있다.

목적 관련 표현

- I am writing to express/request/ask ~ ~하기 위해 글을 씁니다
- I am reaching out to you because ~ ~때문에 연락 드립니다
- I would like to inquire about ~ ~에 대해 문의드리고 싶습니다
- I am pleased to inform you ~ ~을 알려 드리게 되어 기쁩니다
- I am sorry / I regret / I am afraid / Unfortunately, I have to inform you ~ ~을 알려 드리게 되어 유감입니다
- regarding = in regard to = with regard to = concerning = with respect to = in respect of = relating to = as to = as for ~와 관련해서

이메일 대표 문제 유형과 전략

❶ **목적** » 윗글의 목적으로 가장 적절한 것은?

주로 이메일 초반부에 목적이 언급된다. 이 부분에서 목적 관련 표현이 나오는 경우 표시해 두도록 하자.

❷ **일치/불일치** » OOO에 관한 윗글의 내용과 일치하지 않는 것은?

선지 순서는 지문의 흐름 순서와 동일하므로, 선지와 지문 내용을 차근차근히 대조하며 풀도록 하자. * p. 154 〈전략 03〉 참고

❸ **동의어** » 밑줄 친 "______"의 의미와 가장 가까운 것은?

밑줄 친 단어가 포함된 문장의 맥락을 보고 그 단어의 쓰임새를 파악하자. * p. 161 〈전략 04〉 참고

3. 중간 2~3번째 단락에서 배경 설명 또는 추가 요청 사항이 나온다

이메일의 중간 단락에서는 앞서 언급한 이메일의 목적에 대한 배경 설명 또는 추가 요청 사항이 언급된다. 일치/불일치 문제가 나올 경우에는 출제 포인트가 될 만한 내용에 표시해 두는 것이 좋다.

요청 사항 관련 표현

- I kindly request that ~ ~을 부탁드립니다
- Could you please ~? ~해주실 수 있으실까요?
- I would like you to ~ 당신이 ~을 해주셨으면 합니다
- We need to have ~ 저희는 ~이 필요합니다

4. 지문 마지막의 당부의 말에는 크게 주의를 기울이지 않아도 된다

당부를 통해 앞에서 언급한 내용을 강조하거나 마지막 마무리 인사가 나올 경우 지문 파악에 중점을 두지 않아도 된다.

당부하는 표현

- If you have any questions, feel free to contact me via email at any time.
  궁금한 점이 있으시다면 언제든 이메일로 연락주세요.
- If you want to talk more about it, please respond directly to this e-mail.
  더 논의하고 싶으시다면 바로 이 이메일로 회신 부탁드립니다.
- If this sounds good, give me a call at ~.
  위 사항이 괜찮으시다면 ~로 제게 전화주세요.

❶ 이메일에서 일치/불일치 문제가 나올 경우, 위 표현들에서 연락 방식을 묻는 선지가 나올 수 있음에 유의한다.

심슨쌤 꿀팁! **이메일의 인사말 및 끝맺음 표현은 스킵해서 시간을 절약하자**

이메일에는 정해진 인사말과 끝맺음 표현이 있다. 이메일의 상단과 하단 부분에 해당 표현들이 나오는데, 이 부분을 하나하나 읽는 건 시간 낭비이다. 따라서 해당 부분이 어떤 의미인지만 파악해 두고, 관련 내용이 나오면 읽지 않고 넘어 가는 것이 문제 풀이에서 시간을 줄일 수 있는 전략 중 하나이다.

❶ 인사말

- To whom it may concern ~ 귀하
- Dear [회사명/직함] ~ 귀하
- Greetings 안녕하세요
- I hope this email finds you well 이 이메일이 잘 전달되길 바랍니다

❷ 끝맺음 표현

- We look forward to ~ ~을 기대하고 있겠습니다
- Thank you for ~ ~에 감사드립니다
- Sincerely/Regards/Best wishes/Yours truly 진심을 담아/안부를 전하며

적중 100% 이메일 출제 예상 소재

▶ 공무 ▸ 항의·불평: 공사, 주차, 제설 작업 요청, 쓰레기 처리 등
▸ 제안·요청: 복지 관련(일자리 창출, 지원금, 공간 대여, 장애인 지원 등)
▸ 문의: 서류 발급 문의, 지자체 프로그램 관련 문의 등
▸ 시설 운영 관련: 도서관, 체육 시설 등
▶ 업무 ▸ 업무 관련 사항(회의 참석 요청, 일정 변경 등) ▸ 행사 및 사내 프로그램 관련
▶ 기타 ▸ 특정 문제점과 해결책 관련 ▸ 예약 일정 확인 및 취소

예제

다음 글의 목적으로 가장 적절한 것은? 2025 출제기조 전환 예시

To	Clifton District Office
From	Rachael Beasley
Date	June 7
Subject	Excessive Noise in the Neighborhood

To whom it may concern, ↝ 첫 인사말은 스킵해서 시간을 절약하자!

I hope this email finds you well. I am writing to express my concern and frustration regarding the excessive noise levels in our neighborhood, specifically coming from the new sports field.

As a resident of Clifton district, I have always appreciated the peace of our community. However, the ongoing noise disturbances have significantly impacted my family's well-being and our overall quality of life. The sources of the noise include crowds cheering, players shouting, whistles, and ball impacts.

I kindly request that you look into this matter and take appropriate steps to address the noise disturbances. Thank you for your attention to this matter, and I appreciate your prompt response to help restore the tranquility in our neighborhood.

Sincerely,
Rachael Beasley ↝ 끝 인사말은 스킵해서 시간을 절약하자!

1 이메일 상단 내용을 통해 글의 방향성을 잡아라

클리프턴 군청에 Rachael Beasley가 주변 지역의 과도한 소음에 대해 무언가를 요청하는 내용이 올 것임을 예상 가능

2 초반부에서 글의 목적이 나온다

동네 소음, 특히 새 운동장에서 발생하는 소음 때문에 메일을 작성함을 알 수 있음

③ 인근 스포츠 시설의 소음에 대한 조치를 요청하려고 → 이메일의 목적과 일치

3 중간 2~3번째 단락에서 배경 설명 또는 추가 요청 사항이 나온다

운동장 소음으로 인한 피해 호소

4 지문 마지막에 등장하는 당부의 말에는 크게 주의를 기울이지 않아도 된다

적절한 조치를 신속히 취해 달라고 앞에서 나온 요청 사항을 반복해서 강조

① 체육대회 소음에 대해 주민들의 양해를 구하려고
→ 체육대회 언급 X, 주민들의 양해 구하는 내용 X

② 새로 이사 온 이웃 주민의 소음에 대해 항의하려고
→ 새로 이사 온 이웃 주민에 관한 언급 X

③ 인근 스포츠 시설의 소음에 대한 조치를 요청하려고
→ 이메일의 목적과 일치

④ 밤시간 악기 연주와 같은 소음의 차단을 부탁하려고
→ 밤시간 악기 연주에 관한 언급 X

받는 사람: 클리프턴 군청
보낸 사람: Rachael Beasley
날짜: 6월 7일
제목: 주변 지역의 과도한 소음

관계자분께,

이 이메일이 잘 전달되기를 바랍니다. 저는 우리 동네의 과도한 소음, 특히 새 운동장에서 발생하는 소음에 대한 우려와 불만을 표하기 위해 이 글을 씁니다.

저는 클리프턴 지역의 주민으로서 항상 우리 커뮤니티의 평화에 감사해 왔습니다. 그러나 계속되는 소음 방해로 인해 제 가족의 안녕과 전반적인 삶의 질에 큰 영향을 미치고 있습니다. 소음의 원인으로는 관중의 환호, 선수들의 고함, 호루라기 소리, 공이 부딪치는 소리 등이 있습니다.

이 문제를 조사하여 소음 방해를 해결하기 위한 적절한 조치를 취해 주시기를 부탁드립니다. 이 문제에 관심을 가져 주셔서 감사드리며, 우리 동네의 평온을 되찾을 수 있도록 신속하게 대응해 주심에 (미리) 감사합니다.

진심을 담아,
Rachael Beasley 드림

어휘 district office 군청 excessive 과도한 frustration 불만 ongoing 계속되는 disturbance 방해 significantly 크게, 심하게 address 해결하다 prompt 신속한 restore 되찾다 tranquility 평온

정답 ③

전략 적용 연습

정답 및 해설 p. 46

01 다음 이메일의 목적으로 가장 적절한 것은?

To	Tiffany Holland 〈tholland@athens.gov〉
From	Artis Malone 〈a_malone@jersey.com〉
Subject	Your Schedule
Date	May 12

Dear Ms. Holland,

This is Artis Malone. Two weeks ago, we spoke on the telephone regarding the restaurant on Melville Street I intend to open soon. I would like to have an inspector visit my establishment as soon as possible.

You advised me that I needed to have the area inspected by one of your employees before I could be permitted to open my establishment. You remarked that once the restaurant is certified by your department, I will be able to provide food and beverages to members of the public.

The construction work on my restaurant is now complete, so I would appreciate it if one of your employees visited my restaurant. Please call me at (552) 555-1183 any time during regular business hours to let me know when we can schedule the inspection.

Regards,

Artis Malone

① 식당 개업 파티에 초대하려고
② 식당 검사 결과에 대해 항의하려고
③ 검사관의 식당 방문 일정을 잡으려고
④ 식당 위생 검사 기준에 대해 문의하려고

[02 ~ 03] 다음 글을 읽고 물음에 답하시오.

To	Melanie James ⟨melanie@springfielddcc.org⟩
From	Ernie Powers ⟨ep@powermail.com⟩
Subject	Fall Term Classes
Date	August 27

Dear Ms. James,

I just read the announcement on the Springfield Community Center's website regarding classes for the fall term. I noticed there is a need for a volunteer to teach a woodworking class.

I have been employed as a carpenter for approximately thirty-five years. And though I am self-employed at the moment, I worked at Mason, Inc. for eighteen years. I specialize in making handcrafted furniture, especially tables and chairs. I have also led numerous workshops during which I demonstrated the finer points of carpentry.

It would be my great pleasure to serve as an unpaid instructor at the community center. Should you wish to meet me in person to see a demonstration of my skills, I would be more than happy to comply. Feel free to respond to this email or to call me at (552) 239-9733.

Sincerely,

Ernie Powers

02 Ernie Powers가 이 글을 쓴 목적으로 가장 적절한 것은?

① To propose working as a volunteer
② To discuss a workshop he recently led
③ To request opening a carpentry class for students
④ To respond to a question about his work experience

03 Ernie Powers에 관한 윗글의 내용과 일치하지 않는 것은?

① 목수로 30년 넘게 일했다.
② 현재 Mason 회사에서 근무하고 있다.
③ 탁자와 의자를 전문으로 제작한다.
④ 목공 시연 워크숍을 진행한 적이 있다.

04 다음 이메일의 내용과 일치하지 않는 것은? 2024 지방직 9급

To	reserve@metropolitan.com
From	BruceTaylor@westcity.com
Date	June 22, 2024
Subject	Venue facilities

Dear Sir,

I am writing to ask for information about Metropolitan Conference Center.

We are looking for a venue for a three-day conference in September this year. We need to have enough room for over 200 delegates in your main conference room, and we would also like three small conference rooms for meetings. Each conference room needs wi-fi as well. We need to have coffee available mid-morning and mid-afternoon, and we would also like to book your restaurant for lunch on all three days.

In addition, could you please let me know if there are any local hotels with discount rates for Metropolitan clients or large groups? We will need accommodations for over 100 delegates each night.

I look forward to hearing from you.

Best regards,

Bruce Taylor, Event Manager

① 주 회의실은 200명 이상의 대표자를 수용할 수 있어야 한다.
② wi-fi가 있는 작은 회의실 3개가 필요하다.
③ 3일간의 저녁 식사를 위한 식당 예약이 필요하다.
④ 매일 밤 100명 이상의 대표자를 위한 숙박시설이 필요하다.

05 Midland Spring Festival에 관한 다음 글의 내용과 일치하지 않는 것은?

To	inquiries@pleasantvalley.gov
From	manuel_diaz@norman.com
Subject	Midland Spring Festival
Date	March 11

To Whom It May Concern,

I am writing this email with regard to the Midland Spring Festival scheduled to be held from April 2 to 6.

I am the owner of a food truck specializing in Mexican food. I attended the festival two years ago, and had a fantastic experience. I am eager to apply for a spot at this year's festival as well, especially since it is to be the biggest one yet.

In previous years, food vendors were permitted to set up stalls or booths at the festival. Will this be the case again this year? I searched your website but was unable to find the relevant information anywhere on it. If you could let me know how to apply and how much the registration fee is, I would be grateful.

Best regards,

Manuel Diaz

① 4월 초에 진행될 예정이다.
② 2년 전에도 개최되었다.
③ 올해 사상 최대 규모로 개최된다.
④ 음식 부스 정보는 웹사이트에 있다.

전략
02 안내문은 키워드로 접근하라

안내문의 경우 행사 일정, 장소, 비용, 주의 사항 등과 관련된 정보가 언급된다. 글의 초반부에서 안내문의 소재가 나오므로, 제목을 물을 경우에 초반부만 보고도 문제가 풀리는 경우가 많다.

전략 노트

1. 안내문 메인 키워드

다음은 안내문에서 잘 등장하는 키워드로, 일치/불일치 문제의 출제 포인트가 된다.

- Details 세부 사항
- When/Dates 일정
- Times/Opening hours (운영) 시간
- Where/Location 장소
- Highlights/Features 볼거리/특징
- Registration/How to register 등록 방법
- Registration fee/Participation fee/Price/Cost 비용
- Reminder/Note/Notice/※ 주의[참고] 사항
- Contact 연락처

❶ 주의 사항을 나타내는 키워드(Reminder/Note/Notice/※)와 연관된 문제가 잘 출제되므로, 해당 내용이 나온다면 유심히 살펴보자.

2. 세부 조건 키워드

❶ 인원
- be capped at ~이 상한이다
- limited to ~ persons ~명으로 한정된

❷ 등록 방법
- in-person 직접
- at the door 현장에서
- walk-in 예약 없는 방문
- book in advance 미리 예약하기

❸ 비용
- free of charge 무료
- per person 인당
- free admission 무료 입장

❹ 기타 조건
- first-come, first-served 선착순
- by invitation only 초대를 받은 사람만
- due/no later than 적어도 ~까지
- while supplies last 재고가 있을 때까지
- RSVP 회신 바람
- rain or shine 날씨와 상관없이
- exclusive event 소수를 위한 행사
- until further notice 추후 안내 전까지
- sold out 매진된

❺ 날짜/기간/숫자
- annual 매년의
- only for a week 일주일 동안만
- twice a month 한 달에 두 번
- every two years 2년마다
- decade 10년
- every other week 격주마다
- once a year 1년에 한 번
- one-day/two-day tickets 1일/2일 입장표

❻ 연락 방법
- visit us at www.abc.com 이 웹사이트를 방문하세요
- contact us at (111) 222-3333 여기로 전화 주세요

3. 안내문 빈출 어휘

- □ booth/stall 부스/가판대
- □ exhibit 전시
- □ attraction 명소, 즐길 거리
- □ wait(ing) list 대기자 명단
- □ upcoming 다가오는
- □ tasting 시음
- □ reminder 주의
- □ host/organize 주최하다/조직하다
- □ wrap up 마무리
- □ dress code 복장 규정
- □ break/intermission 휴식 시간
- □ venue 장소
- □ fundraiser/benefit 모금 행사/자선 행사
- □ cap 상한을 정하다
- □ capacity 정원
- □ annual/yearly 연례의
- □ refreshments 다과, 간식
- □ postpone 연기하다
- □ kick-off 개시, 시작
- □ cater 음식을 공급하다
- □ keynote speaker 기조 연설자
- □ meet and greet 만남과 대화의 행사

안내문 대표 문제 유형과 전략

❶ 제목 » (A)에 들어갈 윗글의 제목으로 가장 적절한 것은?

안내문은 글의 목적이 지문의 첫 단락에서 언급되는 편이므로 제목을 묻는 문제는 글 초반부를 집중적으로 읽어 보자. 단, 오답 선지들도 글에서 언급된 단어들로 구성되므로 개별 단어에 집중하기보다는 선지의 전체적인 뜻을 파악해야 한다.

❷ 일치/불일치 » OOO에 관한 윗글의 내용과 일치하지 않는 것은?

- 안내문의 일치/불일치 문제에서는 발제에서도 힌트를 얻을 수 있다. (단, 위처럼 발제에 안내문 관련 사항이 포함될 경우에 해당된다.)
- 선지 순서는 지문의 흐름 순서와 동일하므로, 선지와 지문 내용을 차근차근히 대조하며 풀도록 하자. * p. 154 〈전략 03〉 참고

❸ 동의어 » 밑줄 친 "______"의 의미와 가장 가까운 것은?

밑줄 친 단어가 포함된 문장의 맥락을 보고 그 단어의 쓰임새를 파악하자. * p. 161 〈전략 04〉 참고

적중 100% 안내문 출제 예상 소재

▶ **행사** ▸ 지역 축제/공연 ▸ 대회 및 콘테스트 안내 ▸ 모금/자선 행사
▶ **공지** ▸ 주민 지원 교육 프로그램 ▸ 지자체 신설 사업/시설 안내
▸ 사내 공지(인사 발령, 세미나, 교육, 정책 변화) ▸ 사내 행사 및 프로그램 관련
▶ **기타** ▸ 공사 정보 안내(신규 시설, 도로/지하철 공사 등) ▸ 채용 안내/채용 박람회 ▸ 지역 봉사활동

예제

다음 글을 읽고 물음에 답하시오. 2025 출제기조 전환 예시

(A)

글의 제목을 묻는 문제

일치/불일치 문제 정답 근거

1 We're pleased to announce the upcoming City Harbour Festival, 2-① an annual event that brings our diverse community together to celebrate our shared heritage, culture, and local talent. Mark your calendars and join us for an exciting weekend!

2 Details

- **Dates**: Friday, June 16 - Sunday, June 18
- **Times**: 10 : 00 a.m. - 8 : 00 p.m. (Friday & Saturday)
  2-② 10 : 00 a.m. - 6 : 00 p.m. (Sunday)
- **Location**: City Harbour Park, Main Street, and surrounding areas

Highlights

- **Live Performances**
  Enjoy a variety of live music, dance, and theatrical performances on multiple stages throughout the festival grounds.

- **Food Trucks**
  Have a feast with a wide selection of food trucks offering diverse and delicious cuisines, as well as 2-③ free sample tastings.

For the full schedule of events and activities, please 3 2-④ visit our website at www.cityharbourfestival.org or contact the Festival Office at (552) 234-5678.

1 안내문 목적
도시의 유산, 문화, 지역 인재들을 기념하며 지역 주민을 화합하기 위한 축제

2 안내문 메인 키워드
세부 사항: 축제 날짜, 시간, 장소

볼거리: 라이브 공연, 푸드 트럭

3 세부 조건 키워드
일정 확인을 위해 웹사이트를 방문하거나 전화로 연락

01 (A)에 들어갈 윗글의 제목으로 가장 적절한 것은?

① Make Safety Regulations for Your Community
당신의 지역사회를 위한 안전 규정을 만드세요 → 안전 규정에 관한 언급 X

② Celebrate Our Vibrant Community Events
우리의 활기찬 지역 공동체 행사를 맞이하세요 → 안내문의 목적과 일치

③ Plan Your Exciting Maritime Experience
흥미진진한 해양 체험을 계획하세요 → 해양을 체험하는 것 X

④ Recreate Our City's Heritage
우리 도시의 유산을 재창조하세요 → 지문에 있는 단어로 만든 오답 선지로, 이 지문은 유산을 '재창조'하는 것과 관련 X

PART 3 독해

02 City Harbour Festival에 관한 윗글의 내용과 일치하지 않는 것은?

① 일 년에 한 번 개최된다. → 글의 초반부에서 언급

② 일요일에는 오후 6시까지 열린다. → Details의 Times에서 언급

③ 주요 행사로 무료 요리 강습이 진행된다. → 무료 요리 강습 X 시식 O

④ 웹사이트나 전화 문의를 통해 행사 일정을 알 수 있다. → 글 후반부에서 언급

우리의 활기찬 지역 공동체 행사를 맞이하세요

우리의 공유된 유산과 문화, 지역 인재들을 기념하기 위해 다양한 지역사회를 한데 모으는 연례 행사인, 다가오는 도시 항구 축제를 알려드리게 되어 기쁩니다. 달력에 표시해 두시고 저희와 신나는 주말을 함께하세요!

세부 사항
- **날짜**: 6월 16일 금요일 – 6월 18일 일요일
- **시간**: 오전 10시 – 오후 8시 (금요일과 토요일)
  오전 10시 – 오후 6시 (일요일)
- **장소**: 도시 항구 공원, 중심가 및 주변 지역

주요 행사
- **라이브 공연**
  축제장 곳곳에 마련된 여러 무대에서 다양한 라이브 음악, 댄스, 연극 공연을 즐겨보세요.

- **푸드 트럭**
  무료 시식뿐만 아니라 다양하고 맛있는 요리를 제공하는, 다양하게 엄선된 푸드 트럭과 축제를 함께 하세요.

전체 행사 및 활동 일정을 확인하시려면, 저희 웹사이트 www.cityharbourfestival.org를 방문하시거나 (552) 234-5678로 저희 축제 사무국에 연락해 주세요.

어휘 upcoming 다가오는 harbour 항구 annual 연례의 heritage 유산 theatrical performance 연극 a selection of 엄선된 cuisine 요리 sample tasting 시식 regulation 규칙 vibrant 활기찬 maritime 바다의

정답 01 ② 02 ③

전략 적용 연습

정답 및 해설 p. 47

[01 ~ 02] 다음 글을 읽고 물음에 답하시오.

Announcement about Roseville Park

After undergoing several months of renovations, Roseville Park will once again open to the public soon. The city of Hackenberg is pleased to announce the park's grand reopening this Saturday, April 23. All local residents are welcome to attend the reopening ceremony.

The festivities commence at 9:00 A.M. with a speech by Mayor Duncan. Following that, a guided tour of the renovated facilities will take place. Visitors can check out the changes made to the welcome center, the outdoor swimming pool, and the indoor basketball court. They can also view the cycling track, the skateboarding area, and the tennis courts, which are all new.

A picnic will be held in the park from 11:00 A.M. to 2:00 P.M. Hamburgers, hotdogs, and other typical picnic food will be available for purchase.

For more information regarding the park's facilities, contact Marsha Bradley at 555-9510.

01 윗글의 목적으로 가장 적절한 것은?

① To invite residents to visit a park
② To announce the start of renovations
③ To promote a visit by a city mayor
④ To request donations for a park

02 Roseville Park에 관한 윗글의 내용과 일치하지 않는 것은?

① It was closed for a period of several months.
② The city mayor will give a speech there.
③ Its indoor swimming pool was newly built.
④ Food is not complimentary at its upcoming picnic.

[03 ~ 04] 다음 글을 읽고 물음에 답하시오.

Destin Fall Music Festival

After a two-year absence, the Destin Fall Music Festival is once again scheduled to occur. This year's festival promises to be bigger and better than ever with sixty-two singers and bands scheduled to perform during the entire week.

Date: Monday, October 2 – Sunday, October 8
Time: 11:00 A.M. to 10:00 P.M.
Location: Ramona Park, Destin

Jessica Harper, the Rainmakers, and the Eddie Matthews Band headline the attending performers. Local entertainers such as Mal Reynolds, Thaddeus Watson, and Emily Hatfield will also make appearances. For a complete list of performers, visit our website at www.destinfallmusicfestival.org.

Tickets
Tickets may be purchased online or at Ramona Park. One-day, three-day, and seven-day tickets are all available.

	Adult	**Child/Elderly**
One-Day Ticket	$10	$5
Three-Day Ticket	$25	$12
Seven-Day Ticket	$50	$25

Food and beverages will be sold at the park. Those wishing to volunteer at the festival should contact Mary Rose at (242) 555-1831.

03 윗글의 목적으로 가장 적절한 것은?
① 행사가 취소되었음을 알리려고
② 참가자에게 일정 변경을 안내하려고
③ 행사에서 공연할 사람을 모집하려고
④ 개최되는 행사에 관한 정보를 제공하려고

04 Destin Fall Music Festival에 관한 윗글의 내용과 일치하는 것은?
① It is scheduled to last for more than one week.
② Some of the performers are from the local area.
③ Tickets for the elderly are cheaper than children's.
④ It only accepts volunteers through online application.

[05 ~ 06] 다음 글을 읽고 물음에 답하시오.

(A)

The city of Madison will be hosting its first ever job fair in an effort to help secure jobs for local residents during these difficult economic times.

Date: Friday, April 11
Time: 9:00 A.M. – 5:00 P.M.
Location: Gold Room & Silver Room, Madison Conference Center, 37 Western Avenue

Attending Companies
More than eighty domestic and international businesses will send representatives. These companies are in the manufacturing, pharmaceutical, IT, education, hospitality, and shipbuilding industries.

Attendees
Attendees must register in advance by visiting www.madison.gov/springjobfair. No registration fee is required. Attendees should dress in formal business attire and bring copies of their résumés, portfolios, and other relevant personal documents. Some companies have expressed a desire to conduct onsite interviews with job candidates, so attendees should be prepared to answer questions from potential employers.

05 (A)에 들어갈 윗글의 제목으로 가장 적절한 것은?
① A Lecture on How to Manage Your Employees
② Call for Companies to Attend a Job Fair
③ Online Job Training Classes Available
④ Register for the Madison Job Fair

06 job fair에 관한 윗글의 내용과 일치하지 않는 것은?
① It will be held at a conference center.
② Companies from other countries will attend it.
③ There is no dress code for its attendees.
④ Some interviews will take place there.

[07 ~ 08] 다음 글을 읽고 물음에 답하시오.

(A)

The Salem Library proudly presents the fourth special event of the summer with a book reading by renowned author Seymour Hamilton. Mr. Hamilton will read a couple of chapters from his latest thriller, *Racing the Clock*. Be sure not to miss this once-in-a-lifetime event with one of the country's bestselling writers.

Details
Date: Sunday, July 16
Time: 3:00 P.M. – 5:00 P.M.
Location: Auditorium, Salem Library

Mr. Hamilton will autograph copies of *Racing the Clock* prior to the start of the reading. Attendees can purchase books at the library for $19.99 or bring their own copies. Following the book signing, Mr. Hamilton will read from his novel. He will then conduct a Q&A session with audience members.

There is no admission fee, but space is limited to 150 individuals. Seats are available on a first-come, first-served basis and must be reserved online at www.salemlibrary.org/summerseries.

07 (A)에 들어갈 윗글의 제목으로 가장 적절한 것은?
① Salem Library to Purchase New Books
② Register to Be a Member of the Salem Library
③ Salem Library Summer Event with a Famous Author
④ Sign Up for a Writing Course with Seymour Hamilton

08 the special event에 관한 윗글의 내용과 일치하지 않는 것은?
① It will take place on the weekend.
② It will last for around two hours.
③ It will feature a book signing.
④ It will cost money to attend.

전략

03 웹페이지 글은 선지가 핵심이다

웹페이지 글은 일치/불일치 문제 유형으로 출제될 가능성이 크다. 이는 기존의 일치/불일치 문제 유형과 푸는 방식이 동일하다. 따라서 새로운 형태의 지문이 나왔다고 당황하지 말고, 기존에 알고 있던 일치/불일치 문제 풀이 방식으로 편안하게 접근해야 한다.

전략 노트

1. 지문의 흐름 순서대로 선지가 제시된다

지문의 순서와 선지의 순서가 똑같이 제시되므로 지문과 선지를 대조하며 문제를 풀어나가는 것이 관건이다. 통계적으로 불일치 문제의 정답은 ③이나 ④인 경우가 압도적으로 많으므로 만약 문제 풀이 시간이 부족하다면 글을 뒤에서부터 읽으며 선지와 1:1 대응을 해보는 것도 방법이다. ('일치' 문제의 경우에는 해당 없음)

2. 선지의 극단적인 표현에 유의해야 한다

all/every, only, always, never 등의 극단적인 표현이 포함된 선지는 글의 내용과 일치하지 않을 확률이 크다.

3. 웹페이지 글에서 나올만한 주제는 미리 익혀 두자

각 정부 부처의 역할이나 나라에서 운영하는 앱 또는 시스템에 대한 지문이 나올 가능성이 높다. 따라서 생소한 용어가 나오더라도 당황하지 않도록 관련 어휘는 익혀 놓는 것이 좋다. 다만, 이 명칭들은 암기하기보다는 참고로만 알아두자. * p. 160 〈웹페이지 글 출제 예상 소재〉 참고

심슨쌤 꿀팁! **웹페이지 글은 발제와 제목에서 힌트를 얻어라**

문제를 풀기 전, 웹페이지 글의 발제 'OOO에 관한 다음 글의 내용과 일치하지 않는 것은?'에서 글의 소재에 대한 힌트를 얻고, 지문 상단의 제목에서 좀 더 디테일하게 글의 소재를 파악할 수 있다.

적중 100% 웹페이지 글 출제 예상 소재

- 정부 부처 업무 소개 ▸ 업무 분야에 대한 설명
- 디지털 공공 서비스 소개 ▸ 정부 앱, 온라인 상담 서비스, 전자 증명서 등
- 기타 ▸ 사내 공지 ▸ 채용 안내, 각종 보고서

예제

Enter-K 앱에 관한 다음 글의 내용과 일치하지 않는 것은?　2025 출제기조 전환 예시

발제와 제목에서 글의 소재에 대한 힌트를 얻자!

Enter-K

http://enter-k.org

Use the new Enter-K app for your customs declaration.

Use the new Enter-K app upon your arrival at the airport. One notable feature offered by Enter-K is the Advance Declaration, which allows travellers the option ①to submit their customs declaration in advance, enabling them to save time at all our international airports. As part of the ongoing Traveller Modernization initiative, ②Enter-K will continue to introduce additional border-related features in the future, further improving the overall border experience. ③Simply download the latest version of the app from the online store before your arrival. ④There is also a web version of the app for those who are not comfortable using mobile devices.

지문의 흐름 순서대로 선지가 제시된다

선지 ① 내용 일치 ◎
세관 신고서를 미리 제출할 수 있음

선지 ② 내용 일치 ◎
국경 관련 기능을 추가로 도입할 예정

선지 ③ 내용 일치 ◎
온라인 스토어에서 최신 버전 다운로드 가능

선지 ④ 내용 일치 ⊗
웹 버전도 존재함
⇨ 정답 ④

① It allows travellers to declare customs in advance.
여행자가 미리 세관을 신고할 수 있게 해준다.

② More features will be added later.
추후 더 많은 기능이 추가될 예정이다.

③ Travellers can download it from the online store.
여행자는 온라인 스토어에서 그것을 다운로드할 수 있다.

④ It ~~only~~ works on personal mobile devices.
개인 모바일 기기에서만 작동한다. → 'only' 부적절: 선지의 극단적인 표현에 유의해야 함

세관 신고 시 새로운 Enter-K 앱을 사용하세요.

공항에 도착할 때 새로운 Enter-K 앱을 사용하세요. Enter-K에서 제공하는 주목할 만한 기능 중 하나는 여행자가 세관 신고서를 미리 제출할 수 있는 사전 신고 기능으로, 모든 국제공항에서 시간을 절약할 수 있도록 합니다. 현재 진행 중인 여행자 현대화 계획의 일환으로 Enter-K는 향후 국경 관련 기능을 지속적으로 추가 도입하여 전반적인 국경 경험을 더욱 개선할 예정입니다. 도착하기 전에 온라인 스토어에서 최신 버전의 앱을 다운로드하세요. 모바일 기기 사용에 익숙하지 않은 분들을 위한 이 앱의 웹 버전도 있습니다.

어휘 customs declaration 세관 신고 notable 주목할 만한 in advance 사전에 initiative 계획 border 국경
정답 ④

전략 적용 연습

정답 및 해설 p. 49

01 Ministry of Health and Welfare의 정책에 관한 다음 글의 내용과 일치하지 않는 것은?

The Ministry of Health and Welfare

http://gov.kr/healthandwelfare/newpolicy

Enhanced Family Support with New Policies

The Ministry of Health and Welfare announced the New Birth and Childcare Support Policies to improve child welfare and support systems. Key policies include direct financial aid for families with newborns, extended parental leave, increased childcare subsidies, and comprehensive healthcare coverage. Specifically, childcare subsidy coverage is to be widened by removing parental income limits. Tax benefits for companies implementing family-friendly policies will be offered as well, such as flexible working hours and on-site childcare. These policies will be implemented on a trial basis before being expanded, and the scope of support will continue to be broadened.

① It includes financial aid for families with newborns.
② It ensures childcare subsidies regardless of parental income.
③ It allows family-friendly firms to receive tax benefits.
④ It will take effect immediately without a trial period.

02 Office of the Labor Commissioner에 관한 다음 글의 내용과 일치하는 것은?

2025 출제기조 전환 예시

Office of Labor Commissioner

http://olc.gov.org/introduction

Office of the Labor Commissioner (OLC) Responsibilities

The OLC is the principal labor regulatory agency for the state. The OLC is responsible for ensuring that minimum wage, prevailing wage, and overtime are paid to employees, and that employee break and lunch periods are provided. In addition, the OLC has authority over the employment of minors. It is the vision and mission of this office to resolve labor-related problems in an efficient, professional, and effective manner. This includes educating employers and employees regarding their rights and responsibilities under the law. The OLC takes enforcement action when necessary to ensure that workers are treated fairly and compensated for all time worked.

① It ensures that employees pay taxes properly.
② It has authority over employment of adult workers only.
③ It promotes employers' business opportunities.
④ It takes action when employees are unfairly treated.

03 City Council의 새 프로그램에 대한 다음 글의 내용과 일치하는 것은?

City Council

www.cc.org/announcement

Gathering Ideas to Improve City Administration

The City Council has announced the launch of a new program to collect ideas for better city administration. Residents can only submit their suggestions online at www.cityvoice.org, and no offline suggestions will be accepted. The ten top submissions with the most 'likes' will be thoroughly reviewed every month by a dedicated committee, and selected ideas will be implemented to enhance city services. Examples of ideas include solutions for reducing traffic congestion, improving parks and green spaces, and enhancing recycling programs. The Council will accept submissions indefinitely until further notice.

① Only government officials can participate in it.
② Suggestions that aren't made online won't be accepted.
③ Submissions to be reviewed will be selected at random.
④ The program will run until the end of the year.

04 Ministry of Employment and Labor의 프로그램에 관한 다음 글의 내용과 일치하지 않는 것은?

Ministry of Employment and Labor

www.mel.org/info

Education for Empowering Midlife Careers

The Ministry of Employment and Labor has launched a specialized education program for the middle-aged population who have recently retired or are approaching retirement. A wide range of tailored education and training courses will be offered to enhance skills for reemployment. To encourage participation, we offer cash incentives to all program graduates. Additionally, we provide various financial incentives to companies that hire these graduates. Through this initiative, individuals can secure good jobs, and companies will find valuable workers. For more information on this program and how to participate, please visit our official website or contact our support centers located in your region.

① Those near retirement can receive the education.
② Graduates of the program earn a cash reward.
③ Firms that offer education in the program get benefits.
④ Support centers are available to provide more details.

FURTHER STUDY 웹페이지 글 출제 예상 소재

❶ 대표 중앙행정기관 명칭

- Ministry of Personnel Management 인사혁신처
- Ministry of Government Legislation 법제처
- Ministry of Food and Drug Safety 식품의약품안전처
- Ministry of Economy and Finance 기획재정부
- National Tax Service 국세청
- Korea Customs Service 관세청
- Statistics Korea 통계청
- Ministry of Justice 법무부
- Ministry of Culture, Sports and Tourism 문화체육관광부
- Korea Forest Service 산림청
- Korea Intellectual Property Office 특허청
- Ministry of Health and Welfare 보건복지부
- Korea Disease Control and Prevention Agency 질병관리청
- Ministry of Environment 환경부
- Korea Meteorological Administration 기상청
- Ministry of Employment and Labor 고용노동부
- Ministry of Land, Infrastructure, and Transport 국토교통부
- Ministry of SMEs and Startups 중소벤처기업부

❷ 디지털 공공서비스

- Digital Tax Filing Systems 디지털 세금 신고 시스템
- E-Government Services 전자정부 서비스
- Public Health Apps 공중 보건 앱
- Digital Identity Verification 디지털 신원 확인
- E-Passport Systems 전자여권시스템
- Online Crime Reporting 온라인 범죄 신고
- Environmental Monitoring Apps 환경 모니터링 앱
- Digital Legislative Tracking 디지털 공공 기록 접근
- Online Social Welfare Applications 온라인 사회복지 신청
- Emergency Alert Systems 비상 경보 시스템
- Library Mobile Apps 도서관 모바일 앱

전략

04 동의어 문제는 문맥으로 파악하라

동의어를 찾는 문제는 출제 기조가 전환되며 아예 새롭게 출제된 문제 유형이다. 동의어 문제에서 지문의 밑줄 친 단어는 여러 가지 뜻을 가진 다의어로 선정될 가능성이 높다. 따라서 밑줄 친 단어의 대표적인 뜻으로 정답을 고르기보다는 앞뒤 문장을 읽고 문맥을 파악하여 접근해야 한다.

전략 노트

1. 동의어 문제 풀이 방법

밑줄 친 단어가 해당 '문맥'에서 어떤 뜻으로 사용되었는지 묻는 문제이다. 확실히 틀린 선지는 소거한 뒤에, 헷갈리는 선지는 직접 밑줄 친 단어 자리에 넣어 본 후 가장 자연스럽게 해석되는 것을 고르면 된다.

STEP별 풀이법

'동의어 문제' 이렇게 풀 수 있다

STEP 1 밑줄 친 단어 지문에서 확인
STEP 2 밑줄 친 단어의 문장과 앞뒤 문맥 파악
STEP 3 헷갈리는 선지는 직접 단어 자리에 넣어 보기
STEP 4 문맥상 가장 자연스러운 단어 선택

2. 동의어는 신유형의 모든 지문에 출제될 수도 있다

출제 기조 예시 문제에서는 이메일 지문에서 두 번째 문항으로 동의어를 찾는 문제가 출제되었으나, 다른 지문에서도 동의어를 찾는 문제가 출제될 수 있다. 출제 확률이 높은 만큼, 필수 다의어는 미리 학습해 두어야 한다. * p. 166 〈출제 예상 다의어〉 참고

예제

밑줄 친 "steps"의 의미와 가장 가까운 것은? 2025 출제기조 전환 예시 변형

As a resident of Clifton district, I have always appreciated the peace of our community. However, the ongoing noise disturbances have significantly impacted my family's well-being and our overall quality of life. The sources of the noise include crowds cheering, players shouting, whistles, and ball impacts.

I kindly request that you look into this matter and take appropriate steps to address the noise disturbances. Thank you for your attention to this matter, and I appreciate your prompt response to help restore the tranquility in our neighborhood.

① movements
움직임, (사회적) 운동 → 적절한 움직임을 취해 달라는 말은 어색

② actions
조치 → 문맥에 가장 적합

③ levels
수준, 단계 → 적절한 수준을 취해 달라는 말은 어색

④ stairs
계단 → 문맥에 맞지 않음

STEP별 풀이법

1 밑줄 친 단어 지문에서 확인
steps

2 밑줄 친 단어의 문장과 앞뒤 문맥 파악
단어 문장: 문제를 조사하여 소음 방해 해결을 위한 조치 요청
앞뒤 문맥: 소음으로 인한 피해 호소 및 신속한 대응 요청

3 헷갈리는 선지는 직접 단어 자리에 넣어 보기
take appropriate ______ to address the noise disturbances
① movements ⊗
② actions
③ levels ⊗

4 문맥상 가장 자연스러운 단어 선택
⇨ 정답 ② actions
→ 문맥상 '조치'의 뜻으로 쓰임

저는 클리프턴 지역의 주민으로서 항상 우리 커뮤니티의 평화에 감사해 왔습니다. 그러나 계속되는 소음 방해로 인해 제 가족의 안녕과 전반적인 삶의 질에 큰 영향을 미치고 있습니다. 소음의 원인으로는 관중의 환호, 선수들의 고함, 호루라기 소리, 공이 부딪치는 소리 등이 있습니다.

이 문제를 조사하여 소음 방해를 해결하기 위한 적절한 조치를 취해 주시기를 부탁드립니다. 이 문제에 관심을 가져 주셔서 감사드리며, 우리 동네의 평온을 되찾을 수 있도록 신속하게 대응해 주심에 (미리) 감사합니다.

어휘 ongoing 계속되는 disturbance 방해 significantly 크게, 심하게 address 해결하다 prompt 신속한 restore 되찾다 tranquility 평온
정답 ②

전략 적용 연습

정답 및 해설 p. 51

01 밑줄 친 "critical"의 의미와 가장 가까운 것은?

> I am writing to highlight the necessity of providing used laptops to digitally vulnerable youth who struggle to access essential information.
>
> Owning a laptop is <u>critical</u> for young people. It enables them to explore their interests and talents through online tools and resources, making it a key factor in their ability to succeed in an increasingly digital world. Unfortunately, the rising cost of laptops makes it harder for them to afford one, which limits their participation in educational and career development activities.

① severe
② crucial
③ analytical
④ dangerous

02 밑줄 친 "address"의 의미와 가장 가까운 것은?

I am writing to propose the development of a special program tailored to the needs of young students, also known as a comprehensive STEM (Science, Technology, Engineering, and Mathematics) curriculum.

I believe that this program can greatly influence the development and future success of our children. Currently, many young students struggle to reach their full potential within the standard educational framework, which often fails to incorporate real-world applications and foster creativity. I believe that Wellington District can address this issue by implementing the STEM system.

① apply
② handle
③ present
④ communicate

03 밑줄 친 "terms"의 의미와 가장 가까운 것은?

I hope to emphasize the necessity of providing financial subsidies for rent to small business owners. They are the backbone of our economy and are currently experiencing hardships that require immediate assistance.

Since the onset of COVID-19, the operational costs for businesses have significantly increased. As a small business owner in Maryland, I'm personally experiencing challenges in meeting rental obligations as the prices of rent have surged. I urge you to consider implementing a rent subsidy program so that small business owners could negotiate more favorable rental <u>terms</u> with the landlords.

① interactions
② definitions
③ conditions
④ periods

FURTHER STUDY 출제 예상 다의어

* 별표는 출제 가능성이 큰 다의어

001	abstract	ⓝ 개요 ⓐ 추상적인
002	access	ⓝ 접근, 이용 ⓥ 접근하다, 이용하다
003	accommodate	ⓥ 수용하다, 숙박시키다, (상황에) 맞추다
004	* account	ⓝ 계좌, 거래처, 설명 ⓥ 간주하다, 설명하다, 차지하다
005	acquire	ⓥ 매입하다, 습득하다
006	* address	ⓝ 주소 ⓥ 연설하다, 처리하다
007	adjust	ⓥ 적응하다, 조정하다
008	advance	ⓝ 발전, 진보 ⓥ 전진시키다, 추진하다, 나아가다 ⓐ 사전의
009	* allowance	ⓝ 허가, 수당, 허용량, 용돈
010	alter	ⓥ 수선하다, 개조하다, 달라지다, 변경되다
011	* amount	ⓝ 액수, 양 ⓥ 총계가 ~에 이르다
012	appear	ⓥ 나타나다, ~인 것 같다
013	* apply	ⓥ 적용하다, 신청하다, 바르다
014	appointment	ⓝ 약속, 임명
015	* appreciate	ⓥ 감사하다, 인정하다, 이해하다, 감상하다, 가격을 올리다
016	arrange	ⓥ 배열하다, 정리하다, 준비하다, 미리 정하다
017	assemble	ⓥ 모으다, 조립하다
018	assume	ⓥ 추정하다, 떠맡다
019	* attach	ⓥ 붙이다, 첨부하다, 연관짓다
020	* attend	ⓥ 참석하다, 주의를 기울이다, 돌보다
021	* attribute	ⓝ 속성, 특질 ⓥ ~탓으로 돌리다
022	authority	ⓝ 권한, 권위자, 당국(보통 *pl.*)
023	* balance	ⓝ 잔고, 잔액, 균형 ⓥ 균형을 잡다, 상쇄되다, 견줘 보다
024	* bill	ⓝ 청구서, 법안 ⓥ 청구서를 보내다
025	board	ⓝ 이사회, 판자 ⓥ 탑승하다
026	* book	ⓝ 책, 회계 장부 ⓥ 예약하다

027	* break	ⓝ 휴식, 단절, 틈 ⓥ 부서지다, 고장나다, (법 등을) 어기다, (관계를) 끊다, (기록을) 깨다
028	* brief	ⓥ 보고하다, 이야기하다 ⓐ 짧은, 간단한
029	* capacity	ⓝ 용량, 능력
030	carry	ⓥ 나르다, 전하다, 진행시키다, 가지고 있다, 수반하다, 지탱하다
031	* case	ⓝ 경우, 사건, 사례, 주장, 상자
032	* charge	ⓝ 요금, 청구 금액 ⓥ 청구하다, 책임을 지우다
033	* check	ⓝ 조사, 점검, 수표 ⓥ 조사하다, 점검하다
034	clear	ⓥ 치우다, 승인하다, 맑아지다 ⓐ 맑은, 명백한 ⓐⓓ ~에 닿지 않게
035	close	ⓥ 닫다, 종료하다 ⓐ 가까운, 거의 ~할 것 같은
036	command	ⓝ 명령 ⓥ 명령하다, 요구하다, 지휘하다
037	* complimentary	ⓐ 무료의, 칭찬하는
038	* concern	ⓝ 걱정, 관심 ⓥ 관련되다
039	* conduct	ⓝ 행위, 지도, 운영 ⓥ 수행하다, 지휘하다
040	consult	ⓥ 상의하다, 참고하다
041	* contract	ⓝ 계약서 ⓥ 계약하다, 수축하다, (병에) 걸리다
042	* cover	ⓝ 덮개, 표지 ⓥ 덮다, 다루다, 보호하다, 보상하다, 대신 해주다
043	credit	ⓝ 외상, 신용, 학점 ⓥ 공을 ~으로 돌리다, 입금하다
044	* critical	ⓐ 비판적인, 결정적인, 매우 중요한
045	deal	ⓝ 거래 ⓥ 처리하다, 다루다, (상품을) 취급하다
046	declare	ⓥ 선언하다, 세관에서 신고하다
047	decline	ⓝ 쇠퇴, 감소 ⓥ 감소하다, 거절하다
048	* degree	ⓝ 학위, 정도, 단계
049	* deliberate	ⓥ 숙고하다 ⓐ 고의의, 신중한
050	deliver	ⓥ 전달하다, 배달하다, 아이를 낳다, (약속을) 이행하다
051	deposit	ⓝ 보증금, 예금, 침전물 ⓥ 예금하다
052	direct	ⓥ 지시하다, 안내하다 ⓐ 직접적인, 똑바른, 솔직한
053	* division	ⓝ 부서, 분할, 분열, 나눗셈
054	duty	ⓝ 임무, 관세, 세금

055	economy	ⓝ 경제, 경기, 절약
056	establish	ⓥ 설립하다, 확립하다, 임명하다, 입증하다
057	* exercise	ⓝ 운동, 연습 ⓥ 운동하다, 행사하다
058	extension	ⓝ 연장, 구내 전화
059	* face	ⓝ 얼굴, 체면, 정면 ⓥ 향하다, 직면하다
060	* fine	ⓝ 벌금 ⓥ 벌금을 부과하다 ⓐ 멋진, 괜찮은, 미세한
061	firm	ⓝ 회사 ⓐ 확고한
062	form	ⓝ 모양, 양식, 종류 ⓥ 형성하다
063	forward	ⓥ 편지를 전달하다 ⓐⓓ 앞으로
064	foundation	ⓝ 토대, 근거, 창립, 재단
065	fuel	ⓝ 연료 ⓥ 연료를 공급하다, 부채질하다
066	* grant	ⓝ 보조금, 연구비, 장학금, 허가 ⓥ 수여하다, 허가하다
067	hold	ⓝ 잡기, 예약, 영향력, 보류 ⓥ 잡고 있다, 품다, 소유하다, 개최하다, 견디다, 유효하다
068	* host	ⓝ 주인, 주최 측, 진행자 ⓥ 주최하다
069	* initiative	ⓝ 계획, 진취성, 발의권
070	institute	ⓝ 협회 ⓥ (제도를) 마련하다
071	* interest	ⓝ 관심, 이자, 이익 ⓥ 흥미를 끌다
072	introduce	ⓥ 소개하다, 출시하다, 도입하다
073	* issue	ⓝ 쟁점, 출판물 ⓥ 발행하다
074	last	ⓥ 계속하다, 견뎌 내다 ⓐ 최후의, 최근의, 지난 ⓐⓓ 최후에, 최근에
075	* launch	ⓥ 발사하다, 출시하다, 착수하다 ⓝ 개시, 출시
076	* leave	ⓝ 휴가 ⓥ 떠나다, ~ 채로 놓아 두다, (처리를) 맡기다
077	level	ⓝ 수준, 단계, 층 ⓥ 평평하게 만들다 ⓐ 평평한, 대등한
078	* liable	ⓐ 책임이 있는, ~하기 쉬운
079	live	ⓥ 살다 ⓐ 생방송의
080	local	ⓝ 지역사람 ⓐ 지방의, 현지의
081	locate	ⓥ 위치시키다, ~의 위치를 알아내다
082	* long	ⓥ 간절히 바라다 ⓐ 긴, 거리가 먼 ⓐⓓ 오랫동안

083	major	ⓝ 전공 ⓥ 전공하다 ⓐ 주된, 심각한
084	* manage	ⓥ 관리하다, 경영하다, 해내다
085	* match	ⓝ 상대, 적수, 경기, 성냥 ⓥ 대등하다, 어울리다, 경쟁시키다
086	* matter	ⓝ 문제, 물질 ⓥ 중요하다, 문제가 되다
087	mean	ⓝ 평균, 수단(means) ⓐ 비열한 ⓥ 의미하다, 의도하다, 가치가 있다
088	* measure	ⓝ 수단, 조치, 기준 ⓥ 측정하다, 평가하다
089	* meet	ⓥ 만나다, 충족시키다
090	miss	ⓥ 놓치다, 그리워하다
091	* note	ⓝ 메모, 지폐 ⓥ 주목하다, 유념하다, 언급하다
092	* notice	ⓝ 주목, 통지 ⓥ 알아차리다, 주목하다
093	object	ⓝ 물건, 대상, 목적 ⓥ 반대하다
094	* objective	ⓝ 목적 ⓐ 객관적인
095	offer	ⓝ 제의, 제안 ⓥ 제공하다, 제안하다
096	official	ⓝ 공무원, 관리 ⓐ 공식적인
097	* opening	ⓝ 개시, 공석, 구멍
098	operate	ⓥ 작동하다, 운영하다, 수술하다, 작전을 수행하다
099	* order	ⓝ 주문, 명령, 순서, 질서 ⓥ 주문하다, 명령하다
100	organize	ⓥ 정리하다, 조직하다, 계획하다
101	own	ⓝ 자기의 것 ⓥ 소유하다, 인정하다 ⓐ 자신의, 고유의
102	paper	ⓝ 종이, 논문, 신문, 문서
103	party	ⓝ 파티, 당사자, 단체, 정당
104	* performance	ⓝ 공연, 실적, 성능
105	personnel	ⓝ 직원, 인원, 인사과
106	* place	ⓝ 장소, 지역, 부분, 입장 ⓥ 놓다, 주문하다, 정하다
107	poor	ⓐ 가난한, 불쌍한, 실력 없는, 부족한
108	* practice	ⓝ 실행, 연습, 관행 ⓥ 실행하다, 연습하다
109	premium	ⓝ 보험료, 할증료 ⓐ 고급의
110	* present	ⓝ 현재, 선물 ⓥ 건네주다, 소개하다, 공개하다 ⓐ 현재의, 참석한

111	press	ⓝ 언론, 출판사 ⓥ 누르다, 압박하다
112	principal	ⓝ 교장, 단체의 장 ⓐ 주요한
113	process	ⓝ 과정 ⓥ 처리하다
114	proceed	ⓝ 수익금 ⓥ 진행하다, 나아가다
115	produce	ⓝ 농산물 ⓥ 생산하다
116	promote	ⓥ 홍보하다, 촉진하다, 승진시키다
117	property	ⓝ 재산, 부동산, 속성
118	quality	ⓝ 품질 ⓐ 질 좋은
119	raise	ⓝ (임금, 물가) 인상 ⓥ 올리다, (자금을) 모으다, (의문을) 제기하다
120	rate	ⓝ 요금, 비율, 속도 ⓥ 평가하다
121	receipt	ⓝ 영수증, 수령
122	reception	ⓝ 수령, 환영회, 접수처, 수신 상태
123	refer	ⓥ 참조하다, 언급하다, 조회하다
124	* reference	ⓝ 추천서, 참고, 언급
125	remote	ⓐ 희박한, 원격의, 멀리 떨어진
126	rest	ⓝ 나머지, 휴식 ⓥ 쉬다, 기대다, 머물다
127	resume	ⓝ 이력서 ⓥ 다시 시작하다, 되찾다
128	* return	ⓝ 반납, 복귀, 수익 ⓥ 반환하다, 돌아오다
129	run	ⓥ 뛰다, 입후보하다, 운행하다, 진행되다, 경영하다
130	safe	ⓝ 금고 ⓐ 안전한
131	* save	ⓥ 구하다, 저축하다, 절약하다, 모으다, (수고를) 덜어 주다
132	secure	ⓥ 확보하다, 고정시키다, 잠그다 ⓐ 안전한
133	* sense	ⓝ 감각, 느낌, 정신, 의미 ⓥ 감지하다, 느끼다
134	sentence	ⓝ 문장, (형의) 선고 ⓥ (형을) 선고하다
135	short	ⓐ 부족한, 짧은
136	* sign	ⓝ 징후, 표지, 흔적, 신호 ⓥ 서명하다, 계약하다, 신호를 보내다
137	* sound	ⓝ 소리 ⓥ ~인 것 같다, (소리를) 내다, (경보를) 울리다 ⓐ 타당한, 괜찮은, 건강한
138	spot	ⓝ 장소, 점, 얼룩, 관광지 ⓥ 발견하다

139	statement	ⓝ 성명, 진술서, 입출금 내역서
140	* step	ⓝ 단계, 조치, 걸음, 계단
141	stock	ⓝ 재고품, 주식 ⓥ 물품을 들여놓다
142	store	ⓝ 가게 ⓥ 저장하다
143	strike	ⓝ 파업, 타격 ⓥ 치다, (갑자기) 발생하다, 느낌을 주다
144	* subject	ⓝ 주제, 과목, 대상, 피험자 ⓐ 영향을 받는, 종속된
145	succeed	ⓥ 성공하다, 계승하다
146	* sustain	ⓥ 살아가게 하다, 지탱하다, 인정하다, 피해를 입다
147	tear	ⓝ 눈물, 갈라진 틈 ⓥ 찢다, 분열시키다
148	* term	ⓝ 조건, 임기, 기한, 용어, 학기
149	* tip	ⓝ (뾰족한) 끝, 조언, 팁 ⓥ 기울이다, 살짝 건드리다, 팁을 건네다
150	* transfer	ⓝ 이체, 양도 ⓥ 옮기다, 이동하다, 넘겨주다, 전근시키다
151	* value	ⓝ 가치 ⓥ 평가하다, 중시하다
152	versatile	ⓐ 다재다능한, 다용도의, 잘 변하는
153	waive	ⓥ (권리 등을) 포기하다, (세금 등을) 면제하다
154	well	ⓝ 우물 ⓐ 건강한 ⓐⓓ 잘, 훨씬
155	will	ⓝ 의지, 유언 ⓥ ~할 것이다, 바라다
156	yield	ⓝ 산출량, 수익 ⓥ 이익을 가져오다, 산출하다, 권리를 양보하다

UNIT 02

독해 핵심 전략

전략 05 먼저 소재를 잡아야 한다

'하나의 단락(One Paragraph)'에는 반드시 '하나의 소재(One Topic)'가 있다. 그 소재에 대해 필자가 전하고자 하는 바를 파악하는 것이 독해의 목적이다. 대부분의 문제는 세세한 부분보다는 큰 개념을 묻기 때문에 글의 도입부에서 소재만 잘 잡는다면 쉽게 풀리는 경우가 많다. 이때, 반복적으로 같은 소재를 다른 표현으로 기술하는 패러프레이징(Paraphrasing)에 특히 유의해야 한다.

전략 노트

1. 도입부에서 글의 소재를 먼저 파악한다

다음은 2024 지방직 9급에서 출제된 주제 문제의 도입부와 그 정답 선지이다. 이와 같이 도입부에서 글의 소재를 잡는 것이 매우 중요하다.

In recent years Latin America has made huge strides in exploiting its incredible wind, solar, geothermal and biofuel energy resources. Latin America's electricity sector has already begun to gradually decrease its dependence on oil…

⇨ advancement of renewable energy in Latin America

최근 몇 년 동안 라틴 아메리카는 풍력, 태양열, 지열 및 바이오 연료 에너지 자원을 활용하는 데 큰 진전을 이루었다. 라틴 아메리카의 전력 부문은 이미 석유에 대한 의존도를 점차 낮추기 시작했다…

⇨ 라틴 아메리카의 재생 에너지 발전

2. 패러프레이징(Paraphrasing) 표현을 찾아라

The only problem with pens is that they eventually run out. And most of us have no trouble tossing the ones that fail to perform. But many people can't get rid of pens that no longer function. ... Don't accumulate pens that have uncertain functionality.

펜의 유일한 문제점은 결국 다 쓴다는 것이다. 그리고 우리 대부분은 성능이 떨어지는 펜을 버리는 데 아무런 문제가 없다. 하지만 많은 사람들은 더 이상 기능하지 않는 펜을 버리지 못한다. ... 기능이 불확실한 펜을 쌓아 두지 마라.

심슨쌤 꿀팁!

소재 vs 주제

'소재'와 '주제'의 정의는 주관적일 수도 있으나, 본 교재에서는 소재와 주제를 아래의 방식으로 정의한다. 참고로, 설명이 목적인 글에서는 소재와 주제가 동일할 수도 있다.

❶ **소재:** 글을 구성하고 내용을 전달하는 데 사용되는 주요 요소

❷ **주제:** 소재에 대한 필자의 생각이나 의견

예제

다음 빈칸에 들어갈 말로 가장 적절한 것은?

글의 소재

One of the main principles I follow when I draw outside is ________________. I try to stay away from houses or barns that have unusual angles of the roof, or objects that look incorrect in size, perspective, or design. If the subject is confusing when you look at it, it will be more confusing when you attempt to draw it. I know a beautiful barn where the corners are not at right angles. No matter how many times I have drawn it, the perspective does not look right. If I were to make an accurate drawing of this barn and put it in a show, I'm sure I would get all kinds of criticism for my poor perspective. I would not be there to tell my critics that the barn is actually constructed this way. So, I stay away from subjects that do not look right to me.

1 도입부에서 글의 소재를 먼저 파악한다
글의 소재: 밖에서 그림을 그릴 때의 원칙

2 패러프레이징 표현을 찾아라
unusual
= incorrect
= confusing
= not at right angles
= not look right

결론
그림 그릴 때 가급적이면 이상한 대상을 그리지 않는다

① not to select a subject that is too difficult or odd
너무 어렵거나 이상한 대상을 선택하지 않는 것 → 소재 및 패러프레이징 표현들과 일치

② to draw an object with imagination
상상력을 발휘하여 대상을 그리는 것 → 상상력으로 그리는 것에 대한 내용은 글에 없으므로 오답

③ to get information from abstract subjects
추상적인 주제에서 정보를 얻는 것 → '추상적인' 것과 '이상한' 것은 다르며, 후자로 보더라도 글과 반대되므로 오답

④ to convert inaccurate drawings into accurate ones
부정확한 그림을 정확한 그림으로 변환시키는 것 → 패러프레이징 표현으로 함정을 준 오답, 변환시키는 것과 관계 X

밖에서 그림을 그릴 때 내가 따르는 중요한 원칙들 중의 하나는 너무 어렵거나 이상한 대상을 선택하지 않는 것이다. 난 특이한 각도의 지붕이 있는 집이나 헛간, 혹은 크기와 원근감 또는 디자인이 정확하지 않아 보이는 대상들은 그리지 않으려고 한다. 그것을 바라볼 때 대상이 너무 헷갈린다면, 그것을 그리려고 할 때 더욱 혼란스럽다. 난 모퉁이가 직각을 이루지 못하는 멋진 헛간을 알고 있다. 그것을 아무리 여러 번 그려도 그 원근감이 적절해 보이지 않는다. 이 헛간을 정확하게 그려서 사람들에게 보여 준다면, 형편없는 원근감 때문에 난 온갖 종류의 비난을 받을 거라고 확신한다. 난 그 헛간이 실제로 이런 식으로 지어졌다고 비평가들에게 말하기 위해 그곳에 있지는 않을 것이다. 그러므로 난 내게 올바르게 보이지 않는 대상으로부터 거리를 둔다.

어휘 principle 원칙 barn 헛간 subject 대상 confusing 혼란스러운 right angle 직각 perspective 원근감 accurate 정확한 criticism 비난 construct 건설하다 abstract 추상적인 convert 바꾸다

정답 ①

PART 3 독해

전략 적용 연습

정답 및 해설 p. 51

01 다음 글의 주제로 가장 적절한 것은?

The e-book applications available on tablet computers employ touchscreen technology. Some touchscreens feature a glass panel covering two electronically-changed metallic surfaces lying face-to-face. When the screen is touched, the two metallic surfaces feel the pressure and make contact. This pressure sends an electrical signal to the computer, which translates the touch into a command. This version of the touchscreen is known as a resistive screen because the screen reacts to pressure from the finger. Other tablet computers feature a single electrified metallic layer under the glass panel. When the user touches the screen, some of the current passes through the glass into the user's finger. When the charge is transferred, the computer interprets the loss in power as a command and carries out the function the user desires. This type of screen is known as a capacitive screen.

① how users learn new technology
② how e-books work on tablet computers
③ how touchscreen technology works
④ how touchscreens have evolved

02 다음 글의 제목으로 가장 적절한 것은?

With the help of scientists, the commercial fishing industry has found out that its fishing must be done scientifically if it is to be continued. With no fishing pressure on a fish population, the number of fish will reach a predictable level of abundance and stay there. The only fluctuation would be due to natural environmental factors. But if a fishery is developed to take these fish, we must be careful not to reduce the population below the ideal point where it can replace all of the fish we take out each year. If we fish at this level, called the *maximum sustainable yield*, we can maintain the greatest possible yield, year after year. If we catch too many, the number of fish will decrease each year until we fish ourselves out of a job. Fishing just the correct amount to maintain a maximum annual yield is both a science and an art. Research is constantly being done to help us better understand the fish population and how to utilize it to the maximum without depleting the population.

① Say No to Commercial Fishing
② Sea Farming Seen As a Fishy Business
③ Overfished Animals: Cases of Illegal Fishing
④ Why Does the Fishing Industry Need Science?

03 다음 글의 제목으로 가장 적절한 것은? 2024 국가직 9급

It seems incredible that one man could be responsible for opening our eyes to an entire culture, but until British archaeologist Arthur Evans successfully excavated the ruins of the palace of Knossos on the island of Crete, the great Minoan culture of the Mediterranean was more legend than fact. Indeed its most famed resident was a creature of mythology: the half-man, half-bull Minotaur, said to have lived under the palace of mythical King Minos. But as Evans proved, this realm was no myth. In a series of excavations in the early years of the 20th century, Evans found a trove of artifacts from the Minoan age, which reached its height from 1900 to 1450 B.C.: jewelry, carvings, pottery, altars shaped like bull's horns, and wall paintings showing Minoan life.

① King Minos' successful excavations
② Appreciating artifacts from the Minoan age
③ Magnificence of the palace on the island of Crete
④ Bringing the Minoan culture to the realm of reality

04 다음 빈칸에 들어갈 말로 가장 적절한 것은?

There's a knock at your door. Standing in front of you is a young man who needs help. He's injured and is bleeding. You take him in and help him, make him feel comfortable and safe and phone for an ambulance. This is clearly the right thing to do. But if you help him just because you feel sorry for him, according to Immanuel Kant, ______________________. Your sympathy is irrelevant to the morality of your action. That's part of your character, but nothing to do with right and wrong. Morality for Kant wasn't just about *what* you do, but about *why* you do it. Those who do the right thing don't do it simply because of how they feel: the decision has to be based on reason, reason that tells you what your duty is, regardless of how you happen to feel.

① that wouldn't be a moral action at all
② your action is founded on reason
③ then you're exhibiting ethical behavior
④ you're encouraging him to be an honest person

전략

06 주제를 나타내는 표현을 찾아라

글 앞부분에서 소재를 잡은 뒤에는 필자가 전달하고자 하는 바, 즉 주제를 파악해야 문제를 정확히 풀 수 있다. 여러 지문을 접하다 보면, '글의 주제를 나타내는 표현'이 있다는 것을 알게 될 것이다.

전략 노트 글의 주제를 나타내는 표현

❶ S + V + that 구조	S가 연구 사례, 전문가, 소수의 사람 등으로 특정되는 경우 that절 이하가 글의 주제가 된다. • The researchers showed that socializing boosts happiness. 연구원은 사교 활동이 행복감을 높인다는 사실을 보여 주었다.
❷ 비교급 표현	대상 간의 우위 / 인과 관계가 글의 주제가 된다. • It is proven that walking is healthier than running. 걷기가 달리기보다 건강에 좋다는 것은 입증되었다. • The more effort you make, the more you achieve. 당신이 더 많이 노력할수록 더 많은 것을 성취한다.
❸ 역접의 연결사	글 도중에 역접의 연결사가 나오면 바로 뒷부분이 글의 주제가 된다. • Many of us think that caffeine is bad. But, it is actually good for health. 많은 사람은 카페인이 나쁘다고 생각한다. 그러나, 이것은 사실 건강에 좋다.
❹ A, B의 상관관계	공통점, 차이, 영향, 인과 등 A와 B의 관계가 글의 주제가 된다. • The difference between success and failure is perseverance. 성공과 실패의 차이는 인내심이다.
❺ One of A is B	이 표현 뒤에 B에 관한 내용이 계속된다면, 그것이 글의 주제가 된다. • One of the reasons for obesity is poor diet. 비만의 원인 중 하나는 잘못된 식습관이다.
❻ 필자의 강조 표현	▪ Instead of A, B / It is not A but B A가 아니라 B ▪ Although A, B 비록 A이지만, B / Not only A but also B A뿐만 아니라 B도 ▪ It is ~ that 강조 구문 / It is 형용사(당위) + to RV/that ▪ must, should, need to RV / 명령문 ▪ : (콜론)

심슨쌤 꿀팁! 'S + V + that'에서 S가 다수일 때 / According to

❶ 'S + V + that'에서 S가 다수의 생각(통념)일 때 이 내용은 부연일 뿐인 경우가 많다. 특히 뒤에 역접의 연결사가 나온다면 이후 내용이 진짜 주제이다.

❷ 'According to ~'가 나오면 보통 그 앞부분이 소재/주제이고, 뒤는 부연 설명이다.

예제

다음 글의 요지로 가장 적절한 것은?

1 It's long been part of folk wisdom that birth order strongly affects personality, intelligence and achievement. 2 However, most of the research claiming that firstborns are radically different from other children has been discredited, and it now seems that 3 any effects of birth order on intelligence or personality will likely be washed out by all the other influences in a person's life. In fact, the belief in the permanent impact of birth order comes from the psychological theory that your personality is fixed by the time you're six. 4 That assumption simply is incorrect. 5 The better, later and larger studies are less likely to find birth order a useful predictor of anything. When two Swiss social scientists, Cecile Ernst and Jules Angst, reviewed 1,500 studies a few years ago 6 they concluded that "birth order differences in personality are nonexistent in our sample. In particular, there is no evidence for a firstborn personality."

1 A와 B의 상관관계
출생 순서가 성격, 지능, 성취에 미치는 영향 (글의 소재)

2 역접의 연결사
출생 순서가 영향력이 있다는 믿음을 반박
= 출생 순서는 아무런 영향력 X (글의 주제)

3 A와 B의 상관관계
출생 순서가 지능이나 성격에 미치는 영향
→ 이 영향은 다른 요인들에 의해 씻겨 없어짐

4 필자의 강조 표현
성격이 어렸을 때 정해진다는 가정이 틀리다는 것을 강조

5 비교급 표현
'더 나은' 연구에서는 출생 순서의 영향력 X

6 S + V + that 구조
출생 순서로 인한 성격 차이 존재X
⇨ 정답 ④

① A firstborn child is kind to other people.
맏이는 다른 사람들에게 친절하다. → 맏이의 성격을 단정 짓는 선지는 오답

② Birth order influences a person's intelligence.
출생 순서는 사람의 지능에 영향을 미친다. → 출생 순서가 영향력이 있다는 선지는 오답

③ Personality traits are fixed early in childhood.
성격 특성은 어릴 때 정해진다. → 성격이 어릴 때 정해진다는 선지는 오답

④ Birth order has nothing to do with personality.
출생 순서는 성격과 관련이 없다. → 주제와 일치

출생 순서가 성격, 지능, 성취에 강하게 영향을 미친다는 것은 오랫동안 전통적인 지혜의 일부였다. 하지만 맏이가 다른 형제들과 근본적으로 다르다고 주장하는 연구의 대부분은 신빙성이 없어졌으며, 이제는 출생 순서가 지능이나 성격에 미치는 모든 영향은 한 사람의 인생에서의 다른 모든 영향력에 의해 씻겨 없어지는 것으로 보인다. 사실 출생 순서의 영구적 영향에 대한 믿음은 당신의 성격이 6살쯤에 정해진다는 심리학 이론에서 온 것이다. 그러한 가정은 전혀 옳지 않다. 더 나은, 더 최근의, 더 큰 규모의 연구는 출생 순서가 무언가에 대한 유용한 예측 변수임을 발견할 가능성이 더 작다. 몇 년 전 Cecile Ernst과 Jules Angst라는 두 명의 스위스 사회과학자들이 1,500개의 연구들을 검토한 결과, 그들은 "우리의 표본에서는 성격에 있어 출생 순서로 인한 차이는 존재하지 않는다. 특히 맏이의 성격이라는 것에 대해서는 그 어떠한 증거도 없다."라고 결론지었다.

어휘 folk 전통적인 firstborn 맏이(의) radically 근본적으로 discredit 신빙성을 없애다 have nothing to do with ~와 관련 없다

정답 ④

전략 적용 연습

정답 및 해설 p. 53

01 다음 글의 요지로 가장 적절한 것은?

My students often believe that if they simply meet more important people, their work will improve. But it's remarkably hard to engage with those people unless you've already put something valuable out into the world. Achievements show you have something to give, not just something to take. In life, it certainly helps to know the right people. But how hard they go to bat for you, how far they stick their necks out for you, depends on what you have to offer. Building a powerful network doesn't require you to be an expert at networking. It just requires you to be an expert at something. If you make great connections, they might advance your career. If you do great work, those connections will be easier to make. Let your insights and your outputs — not your business cards — do the talking.

① Sponsorship is necessary for a successful career.
② Building a good network starts from your accomplishments.
③ A powerful network is a prerequisite for your achievement.
④ Your insights and outputs grow as you become an expert at networking.

02 다음 글의 주제로 가장 적절한 것은?

Recently, researchers have suggested that the purpose of laughter is not just to communicate that one is in a playful state, but to actually induce this state in others as well. According to this view, the peculiar sounds of laughter have a direct effect on the listener, inducing positive emotional arousal that mirrors the emotional state of the laughter, perhaps by activating certain specialized brain circuits. In this way, laughter may serve an important biosocial function of coupling together the positive emotions of members of a group and thereby coordinating their activities. This would explain why laughter is so infectious; when we hear someone laughing, it is almost impossible not to feel cheerful and begin laughing too.

① effects of laughter on others
② benefits of activating brain circuits
③ strategies for coordinating activities
④ importance of grouping in communication

03 다음 빈칸에 들어갈 말로 가장 적절한 것은?

As more and more leaders work remotely or with teams scattered around the nation or the globe, as well as with consultants and freelancers, you'll have to give them more ________. The more trust you bestow, the more others trust you. I am convinced that there is a direct correlation between job satisfaction and how empowered people are to fully execute their job without someone shadowing them every step of the way. Giving away responsibility to those you trust can not only make your organization run more smoothly but also free up more of your time so you can focus on larger issues.

① work
② rewards
③ restrictions
④ autonomy

04 다음 글의 요지로 가장 적절한 것은?

People with plenty of money are happier than people who don't have much money, but the difference is quite small. Apparently money can buy happiness, but not very much of it. There is only one objective circumstance that has been shown to make a big difference in happiness, and that involves social connections. People who are alone in the world are much less happy than people who have strong, rich social networks. This strong link shows that inner processes, in this case happiness, are linked to interpersonal relationships, in this case forming and maintaining good connections to other people. The human emotional system is set up so that it is very hard for a person to be happy while alone in life. For all other circumstances, even including health, injury, money, and career, the differences are small.

① A happy relationship is based on shared value.
② Some people can live quite happily in solitude.
③ There are many variables that bring happiness.
④ Happiness rarely comes in the absence of social relationships.

05 다음 글의 제목으로 가장 적절한 것은?

One of the areas where efficiency can be optimized is the work force, through increasing individual productivity — defined as the amount of work (products produced, customers served) an employee handles in a given time. In addition to making sure you have invested in the right equipment, environment, and training to ensure optimal performance, you can increase productivity by encouraging staffers to put an end to a modern-day energy drain: multitasking. Studies show it takes 25 to 40 percent longer to get a job done when you're simultaneously trying to work on other projects. To be more productive, says Andrew Deutscher, vice president of business development at consulting firm The Energy Project, "do one thing, uninterrupted, for a sustained period of time."

① How to Create More Options in Life
② How to Enhance Daily Physical Performance
③ Multitasking is the Answer for Better Efficiency
④ Do One Thing at a Time for Greater Efficiency

MEMO

전략

07 선지를 정확하게 해석하고 역추론하라

본문을 이해하지 못한 경우에는 선지를 통해 본문 내용을 유추할 수도 있다. 각 선지가 답일 경우 본문에 어떤 내용이 전개될지 생각해 보는 것이다. 이때 선지를 정확하게 해석하는 것이 중요하다.

전략 노트 선지 역추론 연습 방법

1. 선지에서 핵심 어구들을 표시한다. 특히 긍정/부정 표현이 있는 경우 이를 체크한다.
2. 선지들끼리 공통된 핵심 어구가 있는지 확인한다. 만약 있다면, 그것이 글의 소재일 가능성이 크다.
3. 각 선지가 답이려면 본문에 어떤 내용이 나와야 하는지 유추해 본다.

ex 아래 선지들을 보고 각 선지가 답일 경우 본문에 어떤 내용이 올지 유추해 보자.

01

① emphasis(+) on [cooperation] in sports
스포츠에서 협력의 강조

② importance(+) of [competition] and [cooperation]
경쟁과 협력의 중요성

③ attitudes on [competition] and [cooperation]
경쟁과 협력에 대한 태도

④ interrelationship between [competition] and [cooperation]
경쟁과 협력의 연관성

핵심 어구
경쟁과 협력 (②, ③, ④), 협력 (①)

역추론
① 스포츠에서 협력이 얼마나 중요한지를 강조하는 글
② 경쟁과 협력 둘 다의 중요성에 관한 글
③ 경쟁과 협력에 관해 우리가 어떻게 생각하는지, 또는 어떻게 생각해야 하는지에 관한 글
④ 경쟁과 협력 간에 어떤 관계가 있는지를 설명하는 글

02

① reasons [scientists] are [respected(+)]
과학자들이 존경을 받는 이유

② the process of [correcting(+) scientific errors(-)]
과학적 오류를 바로잡는 과정

③ the [problem(-)] of [openness in scientific researches]
과학 연구의 개방성에 대한 문제점

④ [advantages(+)] derived from [scientific researches]
과학 연구에서 비롯되는 이점

핵심 어구
과학 연구 (③, ④), 과학자에 대한 존경 (①), 과학적 오류 (②)

역추론
① 과학자들이 존경받는 이유를 서술하는 글
② 과학적 오류를 지적하고 이를 바로잡는 과정을 설명하는 글
③ 과학 연구가 개방되어 있는 문제를 지적하는 글
④ 과학 연구가 우리에게 주는 이점을 나열하는 글

예제

다음 빈칸에 들어갈 말로 가장 적절한 것은?

In most of the world, **1** capitalism and free markets are accepted today as constituting the best system for allocating economic resources and encouraging economic output. Nations have tried other systems, such as socialism and communism, but in many cases they have either switched wholesale to or adopted aspects of free markets. **2** Despite the widespread acceptance of the free-market system, ______________________. **3** Government involvement takes many forms, ranging from the **4** enactment and enforcement of laws and regulations to direct participation in the economy through entities like the U.S.'s mortgage agencies. Perhaps **5** the most important form of government involvement, however, comes in the attempts of central banks and national treasuries to **6** control and affect the ups and downs of economic cycles.

1 글의 소재
자본주의와 자유 시장

2 화제 전환
앞에서는 자유 시장의 보편성을 서술하는 듯했으나, Despite을 통해 이와 다른 맥락의 내용이 올 것을 알 수 있음

3 ~ **6** 정부 개입 존재
법, 규정, 직접적인 경제 참여, 경기의 부침을 통제하려는 움직임 등 시장에 대한 정부 개입이 존재한다는 내용
→ 시장은 자유롭지 않음
⇨ 정답 ①

① markets are rarely left entirely free ⇨ 시장이 자유롭지 않은, 즉 외부 요인이 시장에 개입하는 상황에 관한 글
시장이 완전히 자유로운 경우는 거의 없다

② governments are reluctant to intervene ⇨ 정부가 어떤 것에 간섭하거나 통제하지 않는다는 내용의 글
정부는 개입하기를 꺼려한다

③ economic inequality continues to get worse ⇨ 경제 불평등이 심화되는 상황에 관한 글
경제적 불평등은 계속해서 악화되고 있다

④ competition does not guarantee the maximum profit ⇨ 경쟁이 최선이 아니라는 내용의 글
경쟁이 최대 이익을 보장하지 않는다

오늘날 세계 대부분에서 자본주의와 자유 시장은 경제 자원을 배분하고 경제적 생산을 장려하는 데 가장 적합한 시스템을 구성하는 것으로 받아들여지고 있다. 국가들은 사회주의나 공산주의와 같은 다른 체제를 시도해 왔지만, 많은 경우 그들은 자유 시장으로 전면 전환하거나 자유 시장의 측면들을 채택했다. 자유 시장 시스템이 널리 받아들여지고 있음에도 불구하고, 시장이 완전히 자유로운 경우는 거의 없다. 정부의 개입은 법과 규정의 제정과 집행에서부터 미국의 담보 기관과 같은 실체를 통한 직접적인 경제 참여에 이르기까지 다양한 형태로 이루어진다. 그러나 아마도 가장 중요한 형태의 정부 개입은 중앙은행과 국가 재무 기관이 경기의 부침을 통제하고 영향을 미치려는 시도로 나타날 것이다.

어휘 capitalism 자본주의 constitute 구성하다 allocate 배분하다 encourage 장려하다 output 생산 socialism 사회주의 communism 공산주의 wholesale 전면적으로, 완전히 adopt 채택하다 aspect 측면 widespread 널리 퍼져 있는 acceptance 수용 enactment 제정 enforcement 집행 regulation 규정 entity 실체 mortgage 담보 agency 기관 involvement 참여 attempt 시도하다 treasury 재무부 ups and downs 부침

정답 ①

PART 3 독해

전략 적용 연습

정답 및 해설 p. 54

01 다음 글의 요지로 가장 적절한 것은?

Aggressive behavior largely results from the scarcity of resources such as food and shelter. As a given animal population increases, the competition for available food and territory rises. Animals engage in aggressive behavior to relieve these growing tensions by eliminating competitors, either by forcing weaker members of the population to relocate, or by killing them outright. As the population density decreases, so too does the need for aggressive behavior. Animal species that seldom compete for food or shelter, either due to an abundance of resources or to a small population density, rarely exhibit aggressive tendencies.

① Aggressive behavior in animals forces others to leave the area.
② There is no rule for when animals show aggressive behavior.
③ Aggression in animals can be controlled through training.
④ Resource and space account for aggression in animals.

02 다음 빈칸에 들어갈 말로 가장 적절한 것은?

In a classic set of studies over a ten-year period, biologist Gerald Wilkinson found that, when vampire bats return to their communal nests from a successful night's foraging, they frequently vomit blood and share it with other nest-mates, including even non-relatives. The reason, it turns out, is that blood-sharing greatly improves each bat's chances of survival. A bat that fails to feed for two nights is likely to die. Wilkinson showed that the blood donors are typically sharing their surpluses and, in so doing, are saving unsuccessful foragers that are close to starvation. So the costs are relatively low and the benefits are relatively high. Since no bat can be certain of success on any given night, it is likely that the donor will itself eventually need help from some nestmate. In effect, the vampire bats have created a kind of ____________________.

① complex social hierarchy
② ecological diversity
③ mutual insurance system
④ parasitic relationship

03 다음 글의 요지로 가장 적절한 것은?

If someone makes you an offer and you're legitimately concerned about parts of it, you're usually better off proposing all your changes at once. Don't say, "The salary is a bit low. Could you do something about it?" and then, once she's worked on it, come back with "Thanks. Now here are two other things I'd like..." If you ask for only one thing initially, she may assume that getting it will make you ready to accept the offer (or at least to make a decision). If you keep saying "and one more thing...," she is unlikely to remain in a generous or understanding mood. Furthermore, if you have more than one request, don't simply mention all the things you want — A, B, C, and D; also signal the relative importance of each to you. Otherwise, she may pick the two things you value least, because they're pretty easy to give you, and feel she's met you halfway.

① Negotiate multiple issues simultaneously, not serially.
② Avoid sensitive topics for a successful negotiation.
③ Choose the right time for your negotiation.
④ Don't be too direct when negotiating salary.

전략

08 + / -를 통해 글을 단순화하라

글에서 대립 구도가 눈에 띄는 경우가 있다. 이때는 반드시 대조되는 개념을 일차원적으로 분류해야 한다. 기억해야 할 점은 단어 자체의 뉘앙스를 넘어서 '필자'가 소재에 대해 어떤 입장인지를 파악해야 한다는 것이다. 따라서 대조되는 표현을 '글의 맥락'에 알맞게 + / - 표시로 분류하는 연습을 해야 한다.

전략 노트 + / - 분류 표

❶ 긍정적 vs 부정적

긍정적		부정적	
positive	긍정적인	negative	부정적인
optimistic	낙관적인	pessimistic	비관적인
admit	인정[시인]하다	deny	부인[부정]하다
bright	밝은	dark	암울한
hopeful	희망에 찬	hopeless	희망이 없는
favorable	호의적인	unfavorable	호의적이 아닌
confident	자신감 있는	unconfident	자신감이 없는
rational	이성[합리]적인	irrational	비이성[비합리]적인
agreeable	동의할 수 있는	disagreeable	동의하기 힘든
pleasant	쾌적한	unpleasant	불쾌한
approving	찬성하는	disapproving	반대하는
true	사실[진실]의	false	거짓의
sympathize	동감[공감]하다	ignore	무시하다
support	지지[옹호]하다	counter	반박하다

❷ 공통된 vs 다른

공통된		다른	
same	같은	different	다른
common	흔한	uncommon	흔치 않은
usual	보통의	unusual	특이한
universal	보편적인	unique	유일무이한
widespread	광범위한	rare	희귀한
similar	유사한	distinctive	독특한
homogeneous	동종[동질]의	heterogeneous	이종[이질]의
public	공공의	private	사유의
integrated	통합적인	fragmented	분열된
globalized	세계화된	localized	국지[국부]적인
uniform	획일적인	disparate	서로 이질적인
standardized	표준화된	diverse	다양한
comprehensive	포괄적인	selective	선택적인
uncontroversial	논란의 여지가 없는[적은]	extraordinary	특이한

❸ 영향력 있는 vs 영향력 없는

영향력 있는		영향력 없는	
effective	효과적인	ineffective	효과[효력] 없는
influential	영향력 있는	powerless	힘없는
strong	강력한	weak	약한
superior	우월한	inferior	열등한
crucial	중대한	trivial	하찮은
major	주요한	minor	중요하지 않은
helpful	도움이 되는	unhelpful	도움이 되지 않는
dominant	지배적인	secondary	부차[부수]적인
capable	유능한	incapable	무능한
persuasive	설득력 있는	unclear	명확하지 않은
convincing	납득이 가는	inadequate	부족한
successful	성공적인	unsuccessful	성공하지 못한
useful	쓸모 있는	useless	쓸모 없는
meaningful	의미 있는	futile	헛된
certain	확실한	uncertain	불확실한
profound	엄청난[깊은]	superficial	깊이 없는
powerful	영향력 있는	limited	제한된
significant	중요한	ambiguous	애매모호한
central	중심되는	marginal	가장자리의
maximal	최대[한]의	minimal	최소의

❹ 변하는 vs 변하지 않는

변하는		변하지 않는	
changeable	변하기 쉬운	unchangeable	변하지 않는
innovative	획기적인	conventional	전통적[인습적]인
flexible	융통성[신축성] 있는	inflexible	융통성[신축성] 없는
temporary	일시적인	permanent	영구[영속]적인
variable	가변적인	invariable	불변의
irregular	불규칙적인	constant	끊임없이 계속되는
volatile	변덕스러운	steady	꾸준한
inconsistent	일관성 없는	consistent	일관된
unstable	불안정한	stable	안정된
fluctuating	동요하는	fixed	고정된
movable	움직일[이동할] 수 있는	settled	정착된
adjustable	조절[조정] 가능한	firm	견고한
adaptable	적응할 수 있는	static	정적(靜的)인
conformable	순응하는	loyal	충실한
dynamic	역동적인	stationary	움직이지 않는
mobile	유동적인	rigid	엄격한

❺ 객관적 vs 주관적

객관적		주관적	
objective	객관적인	subjective	주관적인
unbiased	선입견[편견] 없는	biased	선입견이 있는
unprejudiced	한쪽으로 치우치지 않은	prejudiced	한쪽으로 치우친
impartial	공정한	partial	불공평한
absolute	절대적인	relative	상대적인
standardized	표준화된	individualized	개별화된
neutral	중립적인	personalized	(개인) 맞춤형의
balanced	균형 잡힌	one-sided	한쪽으로 치우친
logical	논리적인	emotional	감정적인

❻ 쉬운 vs 어려운

쉬운		어려운	
easy	수월한	difficult	힘든
simple	간단한	hard	어려운
plain	평이한	complicated	복잡한
effortless	힘이 들지 않는	challenging	도전적인
light	가벼운	heavy	무거운

❼ 선천적 vs 후천적

선천적		후천적	
nature	천성	nurture	양육
genes	유전자	habits	습관
born	타고난	learned	학습된
inherent	내재하는	acquired	습득한
intrinsic	본질적인	trained	훈련된
innate	선천적인	formed	형성된
instinctive	본능적인	developed	발달된

❽ 실증적 vs 이론적

실증적		이론적	
empirical	경험[실험]에 의거한	theoretical	이론적인
factual	사실에 기반을 둔	hypothetical	가설[가정]의
measurable	측정 가능한	conceptual	개념의, 구상의
concrete	구체적인	abstract	추상적인

예제

다음 빈칸에 들어갈 말로 가장 적절한 것은?

In a famous essay on Tolstoy, the liberal philosopher Sir Isaiah Berlin distinguished between 1 two kinds of thinkers by recalling an ancient saying: "2 The fox knows many things, but 3 the hedgehog knows one big thing." Hedgehogs have one central idea and see the world exclusively through the prism of that idea. They 4 overlook complications and exceptions, or mold them to fit into their world view. There is one true answer that fits at all times and all circumstances. Foxes, 5 for whom Berlin had greater sympathy, have a variegated take on the world, which 6 prevents them from ________________. They are 7 skeptical of grand theories as they feel the world's complexity 8 prevents generalizations. Berlin thought Dante was a hedgehog while Shakespeare was a fox.

1 글의 소재
두 가지 유형의 사상가
→ 대조 관계

2 첫 번째 유형: the fox
→ 관련 표현:

3 두 번째 유형: the hedgehog
→ 관련 표현:

4 overlook = (-)
뒤에 hedgehog와 대조되는(fox와 어울리는) 표현이 와야 함
→ complications and exceptions = fox

5 Berlin은 fox에 더 공감함
Berlin에게 fox = (+)

6 prevent = (-)
뒤에 fox와 대조되는 표현이 와야 함
→ hedgehog 관련 또는 (-) 표현
⇨ 정답 ③

7 skeptical = (-)
뒤에 fox와 대조되는 표현이 와야 함
→ grand theories = hedgehog

8 prevent = (-)
뒤에 fox와 대조되는 표현이 와야 함
→ generalizations = hedgehog

① behaving rationally
이성적으로 행동하는 것 → rational = (+)이므로 fox와 어울림

② finding multiple solutions
여러 가지 해결책을 찾는 것 → fox와 어울림

③ articulating one big slogan
하나의 큰 구호를 분명하게 표현하는 것 → hedgehog와 어울림

④ grasping the complications of the world
세상의 복잡성을 파악하는 것 → fox와 어울림

Tolstoy에 관한 유명한 에세이에서, 자유주의 철학자인 Isaiah Berlin 경은 "여우는 많은 것을 알지만, 고슴도치는 큰 하나를 안다."라는 고대의 격언을 상기시킴으로써 두 종류의 사상가들을 구분하였다. 고슴도치들은 하나의 중심 생각을 가졌으며 오로지 그 생각의 프리즘을 통해서만 세계를 본다. 그들은 복잡한 문제들과 예외들을 간과하거나, 그것들을 그들의 세계관에 맞추기 위해 틀에 끼워 넣는다. 모든 시간과 모든 환경에 맞는 하나의 진정한 답만 있다. Berlin은 여우에게 더 크게 공감했는데, 여우는 그들로 하여금 하나의 큰 구호를 분명하게 표현하지 않도록 하는, 세계에 관한 다양한 의견을 가졌다. 세계의 복잡성이 일반화를 막는다고 느끼기 때문에 그들은 웅장한 이론들에 대하여 회의적이다. Berlin은 Dante는 고슴도치였던 반면 Shakespeare는 여우였다고 생각했다.

어휘 liberal 자유주의의 saying 격언 hedgehog 고슴도치 exclusively 오로지 overlook 간과하다 mold into ~에 끼워 넣다 variegated 다양한 skeptical 회의적인 rationally 합리적으로 articulate 표현하다 slogan 구호

정답 ③

전략 적용 연습

정답 및 해설 p. 55

01 다음 글의 빈칸에 들어갈 말로 가장 적절한 것은?

Social sciences study the area of human behavior. Human behavior patterns vary from place to place and group to group. However, natural sciences are somewhat different. When a chemist studies hydrogen, he can assume that one hydrogen atom is very much like another, wherever it is found, and that the conditions surrounding it can be quite accurately controlled. The same is true when a physicist measures a metal bar; he can be quite sure that it will not stretch or shrink in length as long as natural conditions are the same. Because of __________________ of their subject matter, natural sciences are often called "easy sciences."

① the predictable nature
② the irregular application
③ the unmeasurable quality
④ the changeable properties

02 다음 글의 주제로 가장 적절한 것은?

It is easy to look at the diverse things people produce and to describe their differences. Obviously a poem is not a mathematical formula, and a novel is not an experiment in genetics. Composers clearly use a different language from that of visual artists, and chemists combine very different things than do playwrights. To characterize people by the different things they make, however, is to miss the universality of how they create. For at the level of the creative process, scientists, artists, mathematicians, composers, writers, and sculptors use a common set of what we call "tools for thinking," including emotional feelings, visual images, bodily sensations, reproducible patterns, and analogies. And all imaginative thinkers learn to translate ideas generated by these subjective thinking tools into public languages to express their insights, which can then give rise to new ideas in others' minds.

① distinctive features of various professions
② the commonality of the creative process
③ the difference between art and science
④ obstacles to imaginative thinking

03 다음 글의 빈칸 (A), (B)에 들어갈 말로 가장 적절한 것은?

At certain times in history, cultures have taken it for granted that a person was not fully human unless he or she learned to master thoughts and feelings. In ancient Sparta, in Republican Rome, and among the British upper classes of the Victorian era, ___(A)___, people were held responsible for keeping control of their emotions. Anyone who lost his or her temper too easily was deprived of the right to be accepted as a member of the community. In other historical periods such as the one in which we are now living, ___(B)___, the ability to control oneself is not always highly respected. People who attempt it are often thought to be odd.

	(A)	(B)
①	for example	therefore
②	for example	however
③	in addition	moreover
④	in addition	similarly

PART 3 독해

04 다음 글의 빈칸 (A), (B)에 들어갈 말로 가장 적절한 것은?

Today the technology to create the visual component of virtual-reality (VR) experiences is well on its way to becoming widely accessible and affordable. But to work powerfully, virtual reality needs to be about more than visuals. ___(A)___ what you are *hearing* convincingly matches the visuals, the virtual experience breaks apart. Take a basketball game. If the players, the coaches, the announcers, and the crowd all sound like they're sitting midcourt, you may as well watch the game on television — you'll get just as much of a sense that you are "there." ___(B)___, today's audio equipment and our widely used recording and reproduction formats are simply inadequate to the task of re-creating convincingly the sound of a battlefield on a distant planet, a basketball game at courtside, or a symphony as heard from the first row of a great concert hall.

	(A)	(B)
①	If	By contrast
②	Unless	Consequently
③	If	Similarly
④	Unless	Unfortunately

05 주어진 문장이 들어갈 위치로 가장 적절한 곳은?

> Older workers, in contrast, more often have skills that are quite specific to the industry or firm in which they are currently employed.

Younger workers tend to have more general skills and are less certain about where their skills might be put to their best uses. Hence, they tend to move between jobs on a regular basis. (①) But when they leave their old job, they have little trouble finding a new one. (②) They already know their best employment option and are not inclined to move around between jobs. (③) When they do leave work, however, finding a position that matches well with their precise skills is often difficult and time-consuming. (④) Thus, unemployment that is a nuisance for a younger worker can be a damaging and financially draining experience for a mature worker.

* nuisance: 성가신 일

PART 3 독해

06 다음 글의 흐름상 어색한 문장은?

Consider the following implication involving the role of social bonds and affection among group members. If strong bonds make even a single disagreement less likely, the performance of groups and institutions will be impaired. ① A study of investment clubs showed that the worst-performing clubs were built on affective ties and were primarily social, while the best-performing clubs limited social connections and focused on making money. ② Disagreement was far more frequent in the high-performing clubs. ③ When a decision needed to be made, the low performers usually voted unanimously, with little open debate. ④ As illustrated in the study, the high performers placed more importance on social bonds than the low performers, resulting in their high rate of success. The central problem is that the voters in low-performing groups were trying to build social cohesion rather than to produce the highest returns.

07 다음 빈칸에 들어갈 말로 가장 적절한 것은?

One of the most frequently used propaganda techniques is to convince the public that the propagandist's views reflect those of the common person and that he or she is working in their best interests. A politician speaking to a blue-collar audience may roll up his sleeves, undo his tie, and attempt to use the specific idioms of the crowd. He may even use language incorrectly on purpose to give the impression that he is "just one of the folks." This technique usually also employs the use of glittering generalities to give the impression that the politician's views are the same as those of the crowd being addressed. Labor leaders, businesspeople, ministers, educators, and advertisers have used this technique to win our confidence by appearing to be ______________________.

*glittering generalities: 화려한 추상어(만인의 호의를 얻기 위한 미화 기법)

① beyond glittering generalities
② just plain folks like ourselves
③ something different from others
④ better educated than the crowd

전략

09 빈칸 유형에서는 선지 분석 3법칙을 이용하라

빈칸 유형의 경우 출제자는 본문에 자주 등장하거나 인상적인 단어를 사용하여 매력적인 오답 선지를 구성한다. 이 함정에 빠지지 않기 위해서는 선지 분석 3법칙을 알아야 한다. 이 법칙을 통해 선지를 '감'이 아닌 '논리'로 분석하는 연습을 한다면, 답을 정확하게 골라낼 수 있을 것이다.

전략 노트 선지 분석 3법칙

소재 소거법	글의 소재를 파악한 후, 소재와 관련 없는 선지를 제거한다.
+ / - 단순화	글에 대립 구도가 나타나는 경우, 선지도 + / -로 분류한다. * p. 191 〈전략 08〉 참고
역추론	소재 소거법과 + / - 단순화로도 안 풀리는 경우, '이 선지가 답이 되려면 본문에 어떤 내용이 나와야 할까?' 라고 물으며 역추론해 본다. * p. 186 〈전략 07〉 참고

심슨쌤 꿀팁! 빈칸의 위치가 어디에 있든, 빈칸 문장과 그 앞뒤 문장을 살피는 것이 가장 중요하다. 특히 연결사가 있는 경우에 이것이 큰 힌트가 된다.

❶ 빈칸이 글 앞부분에 오는 경우

빈칸 문장이 글의 주제문인 경우가 많다. 따라서 글 전체를 읽으며 글의 소재/주제를 잡아야 한다.

❷ 빈칸이 글 중간에 오는 경우

흔히 빈칸이나 그 앞뒤 문장에 연결사가 온다. 이 경우 글 앞부분에서 소재를 잡고 연결사를 중심으로 앞뒤 문맥만 파악해도 문제가 풀릴 때가 많다. 만약 연결사가 없더라도, 글의 핵심은 빈칸과 그 앞뒤 문장에 있으므로 이 부분에 중점을 두고 글을 읽어야 한다.

❸ 빈칸이 글 뒷부분에 오는 경우

글 앞에서 소재를 잡고 글을 읽어 내려가며 글의 주제를 파악해야 한다. 특히, 빈칸 뒤에 마지막 문장이 있는 경우에는 이 문장이 글의 핵심이므로 주의 깊게 봐야 한다.

❶ 빈칸 앞에 not, rarely, never 등의 부정어가 있을 때 주제와 정반대되는 내용이 빈칸에 올 수도 있다는 점에 유의해야 한다.

예제

다음 빈칸에 들어갈 말로 가장 적절한 것은?

So often, we get caught up in **1** the tiny details of our jobs — tedious annoyances and struggles that may be temporary roadblocks but feel more like concrete mountains. While there's plenty of research that shows that people who work with their brains create all kinds of stresses for themselves, it's the people who focus on **2** the *why* of their jobs (as opposed to the *what* and the *how*) that can manage the day-to-day problems more easily. That is, if you can **3** define the purpose of your career or feel passionate about the mission of your company, you can much more easily handle the occasional server maintenance that disrupts your in-box. The flip side is that **4** if you're working in any area (or company) that doesn't match your own value, all the little stuff ______________________.

1 일의 사소한 부분 = (-) (글의 소재)
골칫거리와 어려움(-)과 동일한 것

2 the *why* = (+)
이것에 집중하면 일상의 문제(-)를 더 잘 관리할 수 있음
↔ the what and the how = (-)

3 일에 대한 목적과 열정 = (+)
이것이 있다면 the occasional ~ inbox(-)를 잘 관리할 수 있음

4 가치관에 맞지 않는 곳에서 일하는 경우 = (-)
사소한 것(-)은 문제가 될 것이므로 빈칸에는 부정적인 표현이 와야 함
⇨ 정답 ③

① focuses on the *why*, belittling the *what* and the *how*
'왜'에 초점을 맞추어 '무엇'과 '어떻게'를 경시한다 → (+)

② liberates you from the prison of daily routines
일상의 감옥에서 해방시킨다 → (-)에서 자유롭게 해주므로 (+)

③ snowballs into a big ball of daily disasters
눈덩이처럼 커져 매일 매일의 재앙이라는 거대한 공이 된다 → (-)

④ paves your way to climb up the corporate ladder
승진할 수 있는 길을 열어 준다 → 소재와 관련성이 적으나, 넓게 보면 (+)

너무나도 자주 우리는 사소한 일에 사로잡히는데, 그것은 일시적인 장애물일 수도 있지만 그보다는 오히려 콘크리트로 된 산과 같이 느껴지는 진저리나는 골칫거리와 어려움이다. 뇌로 일하는 사람들은 스스로에게 온갖 종류의 스트레스를 유발한다는 것을 보여주는 많은 연구가 있지만, 매일 매일의 문제를 좀 더 용이하게 관리할 수 있는 사람은 바로 자신의 일을 ('무엇'과 '어떻게'가 아니라) '왜' 하는지에 초점을 두는 사람들이다. 즉, 만일 당신이 당신의 일에 대한 목적을 정의할 수 있고 당신의 회사의 과업에 대한 열정을 느낄 수 있다면, 당신의 이메일 수신함에 지장을 주는 때때로의 서버 관리를 훨씬 더 용이하게 다룰 수 있다. 그 반대로 만일 당신의 가치관과 맞지 않는 어느 분야(또는 회사)에서 일을 한다면, 모든 사소한 것들이 눈덩이처럼 커져 매일 매일의 재앙이라는 거대한 공이 된다.

어휘 be caught up in ~에 휘말리다 tedious 따분한, 지루한 annoyance 짜증, 골칫거리 struggle 힘든 일 roadblock 장애물 define 정의하다, 규정하다 mission 임무, 과제 handle 다루다, 처리하다 server maintenance 서버 관리 disrupt 방해하다, 지장을 주다 in-box (이메일) 받은 편지함 flip side 다른 면, 뒷면 value 가치관

정답 ③

전략 적용 연습

정답 및 해설 p. 57

01 다음 빈칸에 들어갈 말로 가장 적절한 것은?

Sensitivity in its literal sense is mainly a change detector; it is usually expressed in a certain feeling. Like a burglar alarm, emotional sensitivity indicates the presence of something that needs attention. The optimal nature of emotional sensitivity may be that the more sensitive the system, the more changes it will detect, and thus the better it will fulfill its task. But, although it is the task of emotional sensitivity to detect changes, it is meant to detect only significant changes, those that are meaningful to our emotional concern. Being indiscriminately sensitive may be counterproductive as it will quickly overload the system with irrelevant and even destructive noise. When it comes to emotional sensitivity, it is often the case that up to a certain point "the more the merrier," but after that, it is too much to detect more changes. So for your emotional health, it is necessary for you ______________________________.

① to express your emotions in sensible ways
② to detect every change as early as you can
③ to practice indifference to insignificant things
④ to focus on present events as well as past ones

02 다음 빈칸에 들어갈 말로 가장 적절한 것은?

Nobel Prize-winning psychologist Daniel Kahneman changed the way the world thinks about economics, upending the notion that human beings are rational decision-makers. Along the way, his discipline-crossing influence has altered the way physicians make medical decisions, and investors evaluate risk on Wall Street. In a paper, Kahneman and his colleagues outline a process for making big strategic decisions. Their suggested approach, labeled as "Mediating Assessments Protocol," or MAP, has a simple goal: To put off gut-based decision-making until a choice can be informed by a number of separate factors. "One of the essential purposes of MAP is basically to _________ intuition," Kahneman said in a recent interview with *The Post*. The structured process calls for analyzing a decision based on six to seven previously chosen attributes, discussing each of them separately and assigning them a relative percentile score, and finally, using those scores to make a holistic judgment.

① improve
② delay
③ possess
④ facilitate

03 다음 빈칸에 들어갈 말로 가장 적절한 것은?

My friend was disappointed that scientific progress has not cured the world's ills by abolishing wars and starvation; that gross human inequality is still widespread; that happiness is not universal. My friend made a common mistake — a basic misunderstanding in the nature of knowledge. Knowledge is amoral — not immoral but morality-neutral. It can be used for any purpose, but many people assume it will be used to further *their* favorite hopes for society — and this is the fundamental flaw. Knowledge of the world is one thing; its uses create a separate issue. To be disappointed that our progress in understanding has not remedied the social ills of the world is a legitimate view, but ________________________________.
To argue that knowledge is not progressing because of the African or Middle Eastern conflicts misses the point. There is nothing inherent in knowledge that dictates any specific social or moral application.

① to confuse this with the progress of knowledge is absurd
② to know the nature of knowledge is to practice its moral value
③ to remove social inequality is the inherent purpose of knowledge
④ to accumulate knowledge is to enhance its social application

04 다음 빈칸에 들어갈 말로 가장 적절한 것은?

When we behave irrationally, our behavior usually seems reasonable to us. When challenged, the mind says (to itself), "Why are these people giving me a hard time? I'm just doing what makes sense. Any reasonable person would see that!" In short, we naturally think that our thinking is fully justified. As far as we can tell, we are only doing what is right and proper and reasonable. Any fleeting thoughts suggesting that we might be at fault typically are __________ by more powerful self-justifying thoughts: "I don't mean any harm. I'm just! I'm fair! It's the others who are wrong!" It is important to recognize this nature of the human mind as its natural state. In other words, humans don't have to learn self-justifying, self-serving, self-deceptive thinking and behavior. These patterns are innate in every one of us.

① authorized
② unveiled
③ fortified
④ overcome

05 다음 빈칸에 들어갈 말로 가장 적절한 것은?

Excellence is the absolute prerequisite in fine dining because the prices charged are necessarily high. An operator may do everything possible to make the restaurant efficient, but the guests still expect careful, personal service: food prepared to order by highly skilled chefs and delivered by expert servers. Because this service is, quite literally, manual labor, only marginal improvements in productivity are possible. For example, a cook, server, or bartender can move only so much faster before she or he reaches the limits of human performance. Thus, only moderate savings are possible through improved efficiency, which makes an escalation of prices ____________. (It is an axiom of economics that as prices rise, consumers become more discriminating.) Thus, the clientele of the fine-dining restaurant expects, demands, and is willing to pay for excellence.

① absurd
② inevitable
③ ridiculous
④ inconceivable

06 다음 빈칸에 들어갈 말로 가장 적절한 것은?

Our kitchens owe much to the brilliance of science, and a cook experimenting with mixtures at the stove is often not very different from a chemist in the lab: we add vinegar to red cabbage to fix the color and use baking soda to counteract the acidity of lemon in the cake. It is wrong to suppose, however, that ______________________________. It is something more basic and older than this. Not every culture has had formal science — a form of organized knowledge about the universe that starts with Aristotle in the fourth century BC. The modern scientific method, in which experiments form part of a structured system of hypothesis, experimentation, and analysis is as recent as the seventeenth century; the problem-solving technology of cooking goes back thousands of years. Since the earliest Stone Age humans cut raw food with sharpened flints, we have always used invention to devise better ways to feed ourselves.

① science has nothing to do with philosophy
② technology is just the appliance of scientific thought
③ cooking has always been independent from formal science
④ cooking is not a direct result of structured scientific analysis

전략

10 순서/삽입 문제는 Signal이 핵심이다

문장 삽입/순서 배열 문제는 단순 독해력보다는 사고력을 요구하는 문제이므로, '논리'에 초점을 맞춰 문제를 풀어야 한다. 이 논리 구조 형성에 핵심 역할을 하는 것이 바로 'Signal'이다. 따라서, 먼저 Signal을 찾아야 한다.

전략 노트

1. 문장 삽입/순서 배열 문제 푸는 법

문장 삽입	① 본문 앞부분을 읽고 소재를 파악한다. ② Box를 읽고 Signal에 유의하며 앞뒤에 어떤 내용이 나올지 유추한다. ③ 본문을 읽으면서 보이는 Signal에 모두 표시한다. ④ Box 앞뒤에 올 것으로 추론한 내용 + Signal의 연결이 맞아 떨어지는 위치가 정답이다.
순서 배열	① 제시된 Box를 읽으면서 글의 소재를 파악한다. ② (A), (B), (C) 중 무엇을 먼저 읽을지는 선지 구성/Signal/길이로 판단한다. → 대조의 Signal이 있는 경우 소재를 기준으로 + / - 구분 ③ Signal의 논리에 맞게 순서 배열한다.

2. 강력한 Signal

❶ **대조의 Signal:** 앞 내용과 뒤 내용이 서로 반대(+/-)되며, 소재가 바뀌기도 한다.

A(+) + On the contrary + B(-)
(on the other hand, by contrast / but, yet, however)

ex I find crowded areas exciting. On the contrary, many people prefer quiet places.
나는 사람이 많은 곳이 흥미롭다고 생각한다. 반면에, 많은 사람들은 조용한 장소를 선호한다.

❷ **반대의 Signal:** 앞 내용과 뒤 내용이 서로 반대(+/-)되며, 대개 소재는 같다.

A(+) + Nevertheless + A(-)
(nonetheless, still, and yet, even so / but, yet, however)

ex The company's stock price jumped. Nevertheless, it soon fell back down.
그 회사의 주가는 급등했다. 그렇지만, 그것은 곧 다시 하락했다.

❸ **지시어 + 명사:** 앞에 해당 명사가 직접 또는 간접적으로 나온다.

This + 명사
(these, that, those, such, another)

ex The population is aging quickly. This trend is concerning.
인구는 빨리 고령화되고 있다. 이 추세는 우려된다.

❹ **예시의 Signal:** 앞에 큰(추상적) 개념이 나오고, 뒤에는 작은(구체적) 개념이 나온다.

A(큰 개념) + For example + B(작은 개념)
(for instance / specifically, particularly / one is)

ex I have many hobbies. For example, I enjoy reading books and playing the guitar.
나는 취미가 많다. 예를 들면, 나는 독서와 기타 연주를 즐긴다.

3. 준 Signal

❶ 나열의 Signal: 앞과 뒤 내용의 소재는 같지만, 서로 다른 내용을 말한다.

A + Also + B
(in addition, besides, furthermore, moreover, what is more)

ex Apples are delicious. Also, they are good for your health.
사과는 맛있다. 또한, 그것들은 건강에 좋다.

❷ 비교의 Signal: 앞과 뒤 내용의 소재는 다르지만, 서로 같은 내용을 말한다.

A + Likewise + B
(similarly, in the same way)

ex Soccer players need to train hard. Likewise, students should study hard.
축구 선수들은 열심히 훈련해야 한다. 마찬가지로, 학생들은 열심히 공부해야 한다.

❸ 원인·결과의 Signal: 앞에 원인이 나오고 뒤에 결과가 나온다.

A+ Therefore + B
(thus, so, hence, as a result)

ex Shimson is nice to everyone. Therefore, he is popular.
Shimson은 모두에게 친절하다. 그래서, 그는 인기가 있다.

심슨쌤 꿀팁! 이외의 Signal

❶ 의문문 + 그 대답

앞에 질문이 나오고 뒤에 답이 제시되는 구조이다.

ex Why is this problem so hard to solve? The answer lies in the lack of data.
왜 이 문제는 풀기가 이렇게 어려울까? 그 답은 데이터 부족에 있다.

❷ the + 명사

'the + 명사'가 나오는 경우, 앞에 해당 명사가 이미 나왔을 수도 있다. 특히 'a + 명사'와 'the + 명사' 둘 다 글에 있다면, 'a + 명사'가 순서상 앞에 있다.

ex I bought a hat yesterday. The hat cost $20.
나는 어제 모자를 샀다. 그 모자 가격은 20달러였다.

예제

주어진 문장 다음에 이어질 글의 순서로 가장 적절한 것은?

South Korea boasts of being the most wired nation on earth.

(A) 4 This addiction has become a national issue in Korea in recent years, as users started dropping dead from exhaustion after playing online games for days on end. A growing number of students have skipped school to stay online, shockingly self-destructive behavior in this intensely competitive society.

(B) In fact, perhaps 1 no other country has so fully embraced the Internet.

(C) 2 But 3 such ready access to the Web has come at a price as legions of obsessed users find that they cannot tear themselves away from their computer screens.

① (A)−(B)−(C)
② (A)−(C)−(B)
③ (B)−(A)−(C)
④ (B)−(C)−(A)

(C)로 시작하는 선지가 없으므로, (A)나 (B)부터 읽어야 한다.
그런데 (A)의 길이가 월등히 길기 때문에 (B) → (C) → (A) 순으로 읽는 것이 효율적이다.

글의 소재
한국의 인터넷 발달

4 지시어 + 명사
앞에 '중독'에 관한 내용이 왔어야 함
⇨ 순서: Box → (B) → (C) → (A)
⇨ 정답 ④

1 지시어 + 명사
다른 나라들은(no other country) 인터넷을 그만큼(so) 발달시키지 못했다는 내용이므로, 앞에는 한국의 인터넷 발달 수준이 높다는 내용이 왔어야 함
⇨ 순서: Box(주어진 문장) → (B)

2 역접의 연결사 But
뒤에 인터넷 중독에 관한 부정적인 내용이 오므로, 앞에는 긍정적인 내용이 왔어야 함

3 지시어 + 명사
한국 인터넷 발달의 높은 수준을 가리킴
⇨ 순서: Box → (B) → (C)

한국은 지구상에서 네트워크 시스템화가 가장 잘된 나라라는 것을 자랑한다. (B) 실제로, 다른 어떤 나라도 인터넷을 그렇게 완벽히 담아내지 못한다. (C) 그러나 이런 웹에 대한 빠른 접근은 많은 중독된 유저들이 컴퓨터 화면에서 자신을 떼어 낼 수 없다는 것을 알게 되면서 대가를 치르게 되었다. (A) 유저들이 여러 날 동안 온라인 게임을 하고 난 뒤 기진맥진하여 즉사하면서 이런 중독은 최근 한국에서 국가적 이슈가 되었다. 많은 학생들이 온라인 게임을 하기 위해 학교에 가지 않았는데, 이는 그러한 치열한 경쟁 사회에서 충격적일 정도로 자기 파괴적인 행동이었다.

어휘 wired 컴퓨터 시스템에 연결된 self-destructive 자멸적인 competitive 경쟁적인 embrace 받아들이다, 담아내다 ready 재빠른 come at a price 대가가 따르다 legion 부대 obsess 사로잡다 tear away from ~에서 떼어 놓다

정답 ④

전략 적용 연습

정답 및 해설 p. 59

01 주어진 문장이 들어갈 위치로 가장 적절한 곳은?

> The same thinking can be applied to any number of goals, like improving performance at work.

> The happy brain tends to focus on the short term. (①) That being the case, it's a good idea to consider what short-term goals we can accomplish that will eventually lead to accomplishing long-term goals. (②) For instance, if you want to lose thirty pounds in six months, what short-term goals can you associate with losing the smaller increments of weight that will get you there? (③) Maybe it's something as simple as rewarding yourself each week that you lose two pounds. (④) By breaking the overall goal into smaller, shorter-term parts, we can focus on incremental accomplishments instead of being overwhelmed by the enormity of the goal in our profession.

02 주어진 글 다음에 이어질 글의 순서로 가장 적절한 것은?

Year after year, we hear the same thing: If you want to be happy in life, be happy in your job. Okay, but what will make me happy in my job? Some researchers have come up with an interesting way to quantify the seemingly unquantifiable.

(A) For example, trust in management — by far the biggest component of job satisfaction — is worth as much in your overall happiness as a substantial raise. Say you get a new boss and your trust in your workplace's management goes up a bit.

(B) By analyzing life-satisfaction surveys that consider four key factors in job satisfaction, they have figured out how much each is worth when compared with salary increases.

(C) Even that small increase in trust is like getting a thirty-six percent pay raise, the researchers calculate. In other words, that will boost your level of overall satisfaction in life by about the same amount as a thirty-six percent raise would.

① (A)－(B)－(C)
② (B)－(A)－(C)
③ (C)－(A)－(B)
④ (C)－(B)－(A)

03 주어진 문장 다음에 이어질 글의 순서로 가장 적절한 것은?

Devices that monitor and track your health are becoming more popular among all age populations.

(A) For example, falls are a leading cause of death for adults 65 and older. Fall alerts are a popular gerotechnology that has been around for many years and has now improved.

(B) This is particularly true for seniors as these technologies can be lifesaving for them.

(C) This simple technology can automatically alert 911 or a close family member the moment a senior has fallen.

*gerotechnology: 노인을 위한 양로 기술

① (B)−(A)−(C)
② (B)−(C)−(A)
③ (C)−(A)−(B)
④ (C)−(B)−(A)

04 주어진 문장 다음에 이어질 글의 순서로 가장 적절한 것은?

Depression afflicts more than 19 million people in the United States at any given time, and almost one in five over the course of a lifetime.

(A) This is because there is a tendency for men to tough it out rather than ask for help. This is one of the several reasons why experts believe the often-quoted statistics are misleading.

(B) According to statistics, approximately 20 percent of all women suffer from depression and about 10 percent of men do.

(C) But some researchers question the latter number. "Men are less likely than women to seek mental-health treatment in general," says Michael Addis, an assistant professor of psychology at Clark University.

① (B)－(A)－(C)
② (B)－(C)－(A)
③ (C)－(A)－(B)
④ (C)－(B)－(A)

05 주어진 글 다음에 이어질 글의 순서로 가장 적절한 것은?

Through the ages, industrious individuals have continuously created conveniences to make life easier. From the invention of the wheel to the lightbulb, inventions have propelled society forward.

(A) In addition, interactive media can be used to question a lecturer or exchange opinions with other students via e-mail. Such computerized lectures give students access to knowledge that was previously unavailable.

(B) One recent modern invention is the computer, which has improved many aspects of people's lives. This is especially true in the field of education. One important effect of computer technology on higher education is the availability of lectures.

(C) As a result of the development of computer networks, students can obtain lectures from many universities in real time. They are now able to sit down in front of a digital screen and listen to a lecture being given at another university.

① (A)－(B)－(C)
② (B)－(C)－(A)
③ (C)－(A)－(B)
④ (C)－(B)－(A)

전략

11 강력한 Signal이 없을 땐 글의 흐름으로 풀어라

간혹 문장 삽입/순서 배열 문제에서 강력한 Signal이 없어서 답을 내기가 어려울 때가 있다. 이러한 경우 '글의 흐름'에 초점을 맞춰야 한다. 흐름 전개 방식에는 크게 ① Process, ② 문제점과 해결책, ③ 실험 구조가 있다.

먼저 Process, 즉 어떠한 '과정'을 서술하는 글에서는 이야기나 과학적 프로세스가 그 소재로 등장한다.
(② 문제점과 해결책 ③ 실험 구조는 각각 전략 12와 13에서 다루고 있다.)

전략 노트 Process

Process를
파악해야 하는
글의 구조

이야기

- 일화, 사회 현상, 역사 속 사건을 서술하는 글
- '꼬리에 꼬리를 무는' 구조로, 문장간의 '연결고리'를 찾아야 함
- then, next와 같은 선후 관계를 나타내는 표현에 유의

과학적 프로세스

- 기기 작동이나 과학 현상의 원리를 설명하는 글
- 생소한 개념은 부연 설명을 동반한다는 점을 이용
- 지시어와 같이 용어의 재언급을 암시하는 Signal을 잘 봐야 함
- 이야기와 마찬가지로 선후 관계를 나타내는 표현에 유의

예제

주어진 문장 다음에 이어질 글의 순서로 가장 적절한 것은?

> A technique that enables an individual to gain some voluntary control over autonomic, or involuntary, body functions by observing electronic measurements of those functions is known as 1 biofeedback.

(A) 4 Then, when 5 a variable moves in the desired direction (for example, blood pressure down), it triggers 6 visual or audible displays — feedback on equipment such as television sets, gauges, or lights.

(B) 2 Electronic sensors are attached to various parts of the body to measure such variables as heart rate, blood pressure, and skin temperature.

(C) Biofeedback training teaches one to produce a desired response by reproducing thought patterns or actions that triggered 3 the displays.

① (A)−(B)−(C)
② (B)−(C)−(A)
③ (B)−(A)−(C)
④ (C)−(A)−(B)

(B)로 시작하는 선지가 2개이므로 (B)부터 읽는다.
(A)와 (C) 둘 다 강력한 Signal이 보이지 않으므로, 길이가 더 짧은 (C)를 읽는 것이 낫다.
따라서 (B) → (C) → (A) 순으로 읽는 것이 효율적이다.

1 과학 개념
biofeedback: 전자적 측정을 통해 불수의적인 신체 기능에 대한 수의적인 통제가 가능하도록 해주는 기술 (글의 소재)

4 순서 관계 표현 Then
biofeedback 작동 원리에 대한 설명인데 Then이 있으므로 앞에 선행되는 과정이 와야 함
→ (A)는 (B) 다음에 와야 함

5 (B)의 such variables와 연결

6 생소한 개념
바로 뒤에서 대시(—)를 통해 부연 설명됨
→ 이 개념이 처음 등장하는 것임을 암시

2 주어진 문장의 electronic measurements와 연결
내용상 biofeedback 작동 원리에 대한 구체적인 부연 설명
⇨ 순서: Box(주어진 문장) → (B)

3 the + 명사
처음 등장하는 개념인데, 'the'가 있으므로 앞에는 displays와 관련된 내용이 왔어야 함
→ (B)와 바로 연결되지 않음
⇨ 순서: Box → (B) → (A) → (C)
⇨ 정답 ③

자율적이거나 불수의적인 신체 기능들의 전자적 측정을 관찰함으로써 그 기능들에 대하여 개인이 어느 정도 수의적인 통제를 얻을 수 있도록 해주는 기술은 생체 자기 제어라고 알려져 있다. (B) 전자 센서가 심박수, 혈압, 그리고 피부 온도와 같은 변수들을 측정하기 위하여 몸 곳곳에 부착된다. (A) 그러한 변수가 원하는 방향대로 움직일 때 (예를 들어, 혈압 저하) 그것은 시각적 혹은 청각적 디스플레이, 즉 텔레비전 세트, 측정기, 조명과 같은 장치에 반응을 발생시킨다. (C) 생체 자기 제어 훈련은 그 디스플레이를 발생시킨 생각의 패턴이나 행동을 재형성해서 원하는 반응을 만들어 내도록 가르친다.

어휘 voluntary 수의[자발]적인 autonomic 자율적인 involuntary 불수의적인 trigger 유발하다 display 표시

정답 ③

PART 3 독해

전략 적용 연습

정답 및 해설 p. 60

01 주어진 문장이 들어갈 위치로 가장 적절한 곳은?

As conditions improved, more permanent dwellings began to emerge throughout the colonies.

Did you know that many of the first European settlers in America lived in caves? It is true. These early arrivals had neither the time nor the tools to build anything better. (①) This was especially the case in New England, where winters were harsh. (②) Some type of immediate shelter was needed, and caves would serve this purpose. (③) These hardy colonists thus dug caves along the side of a cliff and made a roof of bark supported by poles — and now, at least for a time, they had a place to call their own. (④) Each section of the colonies developed its own fixed-style housing, dependent on the climate and the materials at hand.

02 주어진 문장 다음에 이어질 글의 순서로 가장 적절한 것은? 2025 출제기조 전환 예시

Before anyone could witness what had happened, I shoved the loaves of bread up under my shirt, wrapped the hunting jacket tightly about me, and walked swiftly away.

(A) When I dropped them on the table, my sister's hands reached to tear off a chunk, but I made her sit, forced my mother to join us at the table, and poured warm tea.

(B) The heat of the bread burned into my skin, but I clutched it tighter, clinging to life. By the time I reached home, the loaves had cooled somewhat, but the insides were still warm.

(C) I sliced the bread. We ate an entire loaf, slice by slice. It was good hearty bread, filled with raisins and nuts.

① (A)−(B)−(C)
② (B)−(A)−(C)
③ (B)−(C)−(A)
④ (C)−(A)−(B)

03 주어진 문장이 들어갈 위치로 가장 적절한 곳은?

> It was then he remembered his experience with the glass flask, and just as quickly, he imagined that a special coating might be applied to a glass windshield to keep it from shattering.

> In 1903 the French chemist, Edouard Benedictus, dropped a glass flask one day on a hard floor and broke it. (①) However, to the astonishment of the chemist, the flask did not shatter, but still retained most of its original shape. (②) When he examined the flask he found that it contained a film coating inside, a residue remaining from a solution of collodion that the flask had contained. (③) He made a note of this unusual phenomenon, but thought no more of it until several weeks later when he read stories in the newspapers about people in automobile accidents who were badly hurt by flying windshield glass. (④) Not long thereafter, he succeeded in producing the world's first sheet of safety glass.

전략

12 문제점이 나오면 해결책을 찾아라

글 도입 부분에서 문제점이 나오면 뒤에 해결책이 나오는지를 살펴보자. 해결책이 제시되는 경우, 그것이 글의 주제가 된다. 뒷부분에 해결책이 없으면, 문제점 자체 또는 문제점과 그 원인이 글의 주제이다. 특히 순서 배열 유형의 경우, 문제점 부분과 해결책 부분을 분리해보면 순서가 보인다.

전략 노트 **문제점-해결책 구조**

문제점 → 해결책	Climate change is a serious issue. 기후 변화는 심각한 문제이다. ↓ We need to implement strict regulations. 우리는 엄격한 규제를 시행해야 한다. 주제: 엄격한 규정을 도입할 필요성
문제점 → 원인 → 해결책	Climate change is a serious issue. 기후 변화는 심각한 문제이다. ↓ It is largely due to fossil fuels. 그것은 대체로 화석 연료 때문이다. ↓ We must limit their use. 우리는 그것의 사용을 제한해야 한다. 주제: 화석 연료 사용을 제한할 필요성
문제점 → 문제점 (+ 원인)	Climate change is a serious issue. 기후 변화는 심각한 문제이다. ↓ It has a devastating impact on wildlife, human health, and the economy. 이는 야생동물, 인간 건강, 경제에 치명적인 영향을 미친다. 주제: 기후 변화의 심각성

심슨쌤 꿀팁!

❶ 문제점-해결책이 '의문문 + 그 대답' 형식으로 나올 때

문답 형식으로 글에서 문제점-해결책이 제시되기도 한다. 종종 순서 배열 문제에서 이 연결고리로 답이 풀리는 경우가 있다.

ex How do we prevent ourselves from procrastinating?
어떻게 우리는 일을 미루지 않을 수 있을까?

→ It is by adhering to a daily schedule.
그것은 매일 일정을 고수하는 것이다.

❷ 해결책 제시 방법

- by RVing ~함으로써
- the best way[solution] to RV ~할 최선의 방법[해결책]
- to avoid[solve] the problem 그 문제를 피하기[해결하기] 위해
- need to RV ~해야 한다
- through A ~을 통해
- if 만약 ~라면

예제

주어진 글 다음에 이어질 글의 순서로 가장 적절한 것은?

There's been a shift in the Japanese work culture. Workers are less devoted to one employer, viewing their roles as short-term and more frequently considering rival job offers.

글의 소재
변화하고 있는 일본의 업무 문화
→ 경쟁사로 이직하는 경우가 많아짐 (문제점 제기)

(A) In addition, these companies are collaborating with the Japanese government to modify the legal system and establish aid measures for preventing the leak of technologies.

(B) In response, Japanese companies are taking measures to keep their trade secrets secure by limiting access to sensitive information and compartmentalizing the production process so only certain factories handle specific secret technologies.

(C) In some instances, they even leak confidential information from their former company for personal gain, causing core technologies to be leaked abroad.

해결책
In addition이 나오므로 (A) 앞에도 해결책이 왔어야 함
→ (C)와 바로 연결되지 않음
⇨ 순서: Box → (C) → (B) → (A)
⇨ 정답 ④

해결책
앞에 In response가 나오므로 (B) 앞에는 문제점이 왔어야 함
→ (B)는 (C) 뒤에 와야 함

문제점 부연 설명
(C)는 문제점을 언급한 Box 뒤에 와야 함
⇨ 순서: Box(주어진 글) → (C)

① (B)−(A)−(C)
② (B)−(C)−(A)
③ (C)−(A)−(B)
④ (C)−(B)−(A)

(A)로 시작되는 선지가 없으므로 (B) 또는 (C)를 먼저 읽어야 하는데,
(C)에 강력한 Signal도 있고 길이도 짧으므로 (C)부터 읽는다.
그다음에는 강력한 Signal이 있는 (A)를 읽는 것이 낫다.
따라서 (C) → (A) → (B) 순으로 읽는 것이 효율적이다.

일본의 업무 문화에 변화가 생겼다. 근로자들은 한 고용주에게 덜 헌신하고, 자신의 역할을 단기적인 것으로 여기며, 경쟁사의 일자리 제안을 더 자주 고려한다. (C) 어떠한 경우에는, 심지어 개인적 이익을 위해 전 직장의 기밀 정보를 흘려 핵심 기술이 해외로 유출되기도 한다. (B) 이에 대해 일본 기업들은 민감한 정보에 대한 접근을 제한하고 특정 공장에서만 특정 비밀 기술을 취급하도록 생산 공정을 구획화하여 영업 비밀을 안전하게 유지하기 위한 조치를 취하고 있다. (A) 또한 이 기업들은 일본 정부와 협력하여 법 제도를 정비하고 기술 유출 방지를 위한 지원책을 마련하고 있다.

어휘 shift 이동, 변화 be devoted to ~에 전념하다 employer 고용주 short-term 단기의 rival 경쟁자 job offer 일자리 제안 collaborate with ~와 협동하다 modify 수정하다 legal 법률과 관련된 aid 도움, 보조 leak 누설, 유출; 새다, 유출하다 secure 안심하는, 안전한 access 접근, 접속 sensitive 민감한 compartmentalize 구분하다 confidential 비밀의 former 이전의, 전자의 personal gain 개인 이득 core 핵심적인, 가장 중요한

정답 ④

전략 적용 연습

정답 및 해설 p. 61

01 주어진 문장 다음에 이어질 글의 순서로 가장 적절한 것은?

Past research has shown that experiencing frequent psychological stress can be a significant risk factor for cardiovascular disease, a condition that affects almost half of those aged 20 years and older in the United States.

(A) Does this mean, though, that people who drive on a daily basis are set to develop heart problems, or is there a simple way of easing the stress of driving?

(B) According to a new study, there is. The researchers noted that listening to music while driving helps relieve the stress that affects heart health.

(C) One source of frequent stress is driving, either due to the stressors associated with heavy traffic or the anxiety that often accompanies inexperienced drivers.

① (A)－(C)－(B)
② (B)－(A)－(C)
③ (C)－(A)－(B)
④ (C)－(B)－(A)

02 다음 빈칸에 들어갈 말로 가장 적절한 것은?

Fear of loss is a basic part of being human. To the brain, loss is a threat and we naturally take measures to avoid it. We cannot, however, avoid it indefinitely. One way to face loss is with the perspective of a stock trader. Traders accept the possibility of loss as part of the game, not the end of the game. What guides this thinking is a portfolio approach; wins and losses will both happen, but it's the overall portfolio of outcomes that matters most. When you embrace a portfolio approach, you will be ______________________________ because you know that they are small parts of a much bigger picture.

① less inclined to dwell on individual losses
② less interested in your investments
③ more vulnerable to the losses
④ more sensitive to stock price fluctuations

03 주어진 글 다음에 이어질 글의 순서로 가장 적절한 것은?

Do you worry about losing your good health? Do you fear that crime, war, or terrorist attacks will disrupt the economy and your security?

(A) It's because television focuses on news that makes the world seem like a more dangerous place than it actually is. Afraid of the world that is portrayed on TV, people stay in their homes with close family and do not build bonds with their neighbors.

(B) These are legitimate concerns that many people share. We live in difficult and uncertain times. But are these fears real? Research shows that people who watch a lot of news on television overestimate the threats to their well-being. Why?

(C) Thus they become more vulnerable. Surrounding ourselves with a wall of fear, however, is not the answer. The only way to overcome this problem is to be more connected to others, and this connection will reduce fear and isolation.

① (B)－(A)－(C)
② (B)－(C)－(A)
③ (C)－(A)－(B)
④ (C)－(B)－(A)

04 다음 글의 주제로 가장 적절한 것은? 2025 출제기조 전환 예시

The Ministry of Food and Drug Safety warned that cases of food poisoning have occurred as a result of cross-contamination, where people touch eggs and neglect to wash their hands before preparing food or using utensils. To mitigate such risks, the ministry advised refrigerating eggs and ensuring they are thoroughly cooked until both the yolk and white are firm. Over the past five years, a staggering 7,400 people experienced food poisoning caused by Salmonella bacteria. Salmonella thrives in warm temperatures, with approximately 37 degrees Celsius being the optimal growth condition. Consuming raw or undercooked eggs and failing to separate raw and cooked foods were identified as the most common causes of Salmonella infection. It is crucial to prioritize food safety measures and adhere to proper cooking practices to minimize the risk of Salmonella-related illnesses.

① benefits of consuming eggs to the immune system
② different types of treatments for Salmonella infection
③ life span of Salmonella bacteria in warm temperatures
④ safe handling of eggs for the prevention of Salmonella infection

05 다음 글의 주제로 가장 적절한 것은?

Medications are a blessing if health care providers prescribe and provide them to patients safely and appropriately. Yet, health care providers are human, and as such, fallible. Despite their expertise and commitment to quality, errors and other adverse events with medications occur and sometimes cause human suffering. Prescribing the wrong drug, strength, or dose; mistaking one look-alike or sound-alike drug name for another; misusing medical equipment; choosing the wrong patient from a list on the computer screen — despite their best efforts, these things happen every day, to every kind of person, in every health care setting. The large number of new drugs and technologies introduced each year further complicates medication use, as does a growing elderly population with conditions that require complex treatment strategies, which can lead to medical errors.

① ways of reducing medication errors
② types and causes of medication errors
③ the importance of sharing medical records
④ the need for expanding healthcare coverage

06 다음 글의 요지로 가장 적절한 것은?

Many parents have been misguided by the "self-esteem movement," which has told them that the way to build their children's self-esteem is to tell them how good they are at things. Unfortunately, trying to convince your children of their competence will likely fail because life has a way of telling them unequivocally how capable or incapable they really are through success and failure. Research has shown that how you praise your children has a powerful influence on their development. Some researchers found that children who were praised for their intelligence, as compared to their effort, became overly focused on results. Following a failure, these same children persisted less, showed less enjoyment, attributed their failure to a lack of ability, and performed poorly in future achievement efforts. Praising children for intelligence made them fear difficulty because they began to equate failure with stupidity.

① Frequent praises increase children's self-esteem.
② Praising intelligence has negative effects on children.
③ Children should overcome fear of failure through success.
④ Parents should focus on the outcome rather than the process.

전략

13 실험이 나오면 전제와 결과를 생각하라

실험을 소개하는 글에서는 ① 전제와 ② 실험 결과가 제시된다. 먼저 전제에서 실험군과 대조군이 '어떤 기준으로' 나뉘었는지 파악해야 한다. 이때 실험군과 대조군은 대립 형태를 띠므로, 대조의 연결사가 흔히 등장한다. 그다음에 그러한 차이가 어떠한 실험 결과로 이어졌는지만 파악하면 된다.

전략 노트

1. 실험을 소개하는 글에서 자주 나오는 표현

실험 전제를 소개할 때	▪ some 일부 ↔ others 나머지 ▪ one 하나 ↔ the other 나머지 다른 하나 ▪ same, identical 같은 ↔ different, unlike 다른
대조의 연결사	▪ but/yet/however 그러나, 하지만 ▪ in[by] contrast/on the contrary 이와 반대로 ▪ on the other hand 반면에 ▪ while/whereas ~인데 반해
실험 결과를 제시할 때	▪ experiment/study/research showed[proved] that 실험/연구/조사는 ~임을 보여주었다[밝혔다] ▪ surprisingly 놀랍게도, contrary to common belief 일반적인 믿음과는 반대로 ▪ apparently 분명히, in fact 실제로

2. 원인-결과 표현

원인 → 결과	A(원인) + [cause / lead to / result in / end in / bring about / give rise to / produce / contribute to] + B(결과) ▪ 주어가 원인, 목적어가 결과가 된다. ▪ 'A 해서 B가 된다'라고 해석한다.
결과 → 원인	B(결과) + [result from / arise from / follow / be caused by / be produced by / be the consequence of / be the result of] + A(원인) ▪ 주어가 결과, 목적어가 원인이 된다. ▪ 'B는 A 때문이다'라고 해석한다.

예제

주어진 문장이 들어갈 위치로 가장 적절한 곳은?

> 2 Surprisingly, 3 the half of the group that scored higher with cheat sheets 4 predicted higher results for the next test.

2 Box 내용이 실험 결과에 해당함을 암시

3 컨닝으로 더 높은 점수를 받은 집단 = 실험군
실험 전제 = 컨닝을 통해 더 높은 점수를 받았었는지의 여부

4 실험군은 다음 시험에서 더 높은 점수를 예측함

> 1 Wishful thinking is stronger than dollars. Duke University professor Dan Ariely describes a clever experiment. (①) A group of people are given an intelligence test, but 5 half of them are "accidentally" shown a response sheet, allowing them to look up correct answers before recording their own. (②) Needless to say, they score above 6 the rest. (③) Next, everybody is asked to predict their grades on 7 the next IQ test, in which there will be absolutely no cheat sheets — and those who predict correctly will get paid. (④) 8 The cheaters wanted to believe they were very smart, even though their incorrect predictions of success would cost them money.

1 글의 소재
'돈보다 강력한 기대의 힘'을 보여준 한 실험

5 half of them = 실험군
컨닝을 할 수 있는 집단

6 the rest = 대조군
컨닝을 할 수 없는 집단

7 두 번째 실험 설명
다음 IQ 테스트에서 몇 점을 받을지 예측하고, 그 예측이 맞을 경우 돈을 받음

8 실험군
실험군이 틀린 예측을 했다는 점을 전제하고, 그러한 예측을 한 원인을 설명하는 내용
→ 맥락 단절 [중간에 그들이 어떤 예측을 했는지에 관한 내용이 빠짐]
⇨ 정답 ④

부질없는 기대는 돈보다 더 강력하다. Duke대학의 교수 Dan Ariely는 기발한 실험을 묘사한다. 한 무리의 사람들이 지능 검사를 받게 되지만, 그들 중 절반이 '우연히' 응답지를 보게 되고 이것이 그들로 하여금 자신의 답을 기재하기 전에 정답을 찾을 수 있게 해 준다. 말할 필요도 없이, 그들은 나머지 사람들보다 더 높은 점수를 받는다. 그러고 나서 모든 사람이 다음번 지능 검사 때의 자기 점수를 예측하도록 요청받는데, 그 검사에서는 부정행위용 종이가 전혀 없을 것이고 정확히 예측한 사람들은 돈을 받을 것이다. 놀랍게도 부정행위용 종이를 이용해 더 높은 점수를 받은 그 무리의 절반이 다음 검사에 대한 결과를 더 높게 예측했다. 부정행위자들은 성공에 대한 부정확한 예측으로 자신이 돈을 받지 못하게 되더라도, 자신이 매우 똑똑하다고 믿고 싶어 했다.

어휘 cheat (시험에서) 부정행위하다 wishful thinking (일어날 가능성이 희박한) 희망사항 intelligence test 지능 검사 accidentally 우연히, 뜻하지 않게 response 응답, 대답 look up 찾아보다 record 기록하다 absolutely 전적으로, 틀림없이 get paid 보수를 받다 prediction 예측, 추정 cost (사람에게 금액을) 쓰게 하다

정답 ④

전략 적용 연습

정답 및 해설 p. 63

01 주어진 글 다음에 이어질 글의 순서로 가장 적절한 것은?

When trained psychologists look through collections of photos, they can at a glance separate out genuine smiles from fake ones.

(A) All the women were contacted at ages twenty-seven, forty-three, and fifty-two and asked about their marriages and their life satisfaction.

(B) Astonishingly, women with genuine smiles, on average, were more likely to be married, to stay married, and to experience more personal well-being over the next thirty years.

(C) Dacher Keltner and LeeAnne Harker from the University of California demonstrated this skill when they analyzed 141 senior-class photos from the 1960 yearbook of Mills College. According to them, all but three of the women were smiling, and half of the smilers were genuinely smiling.

① (A)−(C)−(B)
② (B)−(C)−(A)
③ (C)−(A)−(B)
④ (C)−(B)−(A)

02 다음 글의 요지로 가장 적절한 것은?

In one study, done in the early 1970s when young people tended to dress in either "hippie" or "straight" fashion, experimenters dressed in hippie or straight attire and asked college students on campus for a dime to make a phone call. When the experimenter was dressed in the same way as the student, the request was granted in more than two-thirds of the instances; when the student and requester were dissimilarly dressed, the dime was provided less than half the time. Another experiment showed how automatic our positive response to similar others can be. Marchers in an antiwar demonstration were found to be more likely to sign the petition of a similarly dressed requester and to do so without bothering to read it first.

① People are more likely to help those who dress like themselves.
② Dressing up formally increases the chance of signing the petition.
③ Making a phone call is an efficient way to socialize with other students.
④ College students in the early 1970s were admired for their unique fashion.

03 다음 빈칸에 들어갈 말로 가장 적절한 것은?

Perhaps the first experiment ever conducted in the field of social psychology suggests that humans ________________________. That study, conducted at Indiana University in the late 1890s, was the brainchild of Norman Triplett, a cycling enthusiast and a sports aficionado. In dozens of experiments he pushed cyclists to ride as fast as they could on stationary bikes, occasionally leaving them alone in the lab and free from distraction, at other times pacing them against a motor-driven cycle, and sometimes asking them to ride in the presence of other cyclists. Across his observations, Triplett noticed that the cyclists tended to ride faster when other cyclists rode nearby. One cyclist rode a mile in 2 minutes 49 seconds when alone, but managed to ride the same mile in 2 minutes 37 seconds in the company of four pacing cyclists; similarly, he rode ten miles in 33 minutes 17 seconds while riding alone, but rode the same distance two minutes faster when riding with several pacers.

*aficionado: 열광적인 애호가

① exert less effort when they notice they're being observed
② cooperate to achieve a common goal of a group
③ perform better in the company of others
④ work things out for themselves when working alone

PART 3 독해

PART 4

생활영어

[전략 01 ~ 전략 03]

생활영어 핵심 공략법

1 신경향

출제 기조 전환 예시 문제에서 생활영어는 기존 유형(빈칸)과 신유형(문자 대화) 각각 한 문제씩 출제되었다. 신유형 문제는 형식만 다를 뿐, 기존 빈칸 유형과 사실상 동일하다. 따라서 본 교재는 두 유형을 굳이 구분하지 않고, '빈칸' 유형에 공통적으로 적용되는 전략을 소개한다.

2 문제 공략법

실무 능력 중심으로 시험이 바뀌는 만큼, 생활영어 지문도 실무적인 소재와 관련될 가능성이 크다. 또한 관용 표현의 경우, 출제된다 하더라도 지엽적인 숙어보다는 실생활에서 자주 쓰이는 표현이 나올 것이다. 오히려 이러한 부분을 학생들이 공부하기 어려워하는 경우가 있는데, 다음 소개되는 세 가지 전략과 부록의 생활영어 표현들만 익혀 두어도 생활영어는 쉽게 풀릴 것이다.

전략

01 빈칸 앞뒤가 중요하다

생활영어 지문에서는 빈칸 앞뒤에 단서가 있는 경우가 많다. 먼저 글 앞부분에서 소재를 잡고, 나머지 부분을 훑은 후에 빈칸 앞뒤를 중심으로 답을 유추해야 한다. 흔히 빈칸 앞뒤에서 화제가 전환되는 경우가 있으므로, 이에 특히 유의해야 한다.

전략 노트

1. 빈칸 앞에 단서가 있는 경우

2024 지방직 9급

A: Can I get the document you referred to at the meeting yesterday?
B: Sure. What's the title of the document?
A: I can't remember its title, but it was about the community festival.
B: Oh, I know what you're talking about.
A: Great. Can you send it to me via email?
B: I don't have it with me. Mr. Park is in charge of the project, so he should have it.
A: ______________________________
B: Good luck. Hope you get the document you want.

⇨ Thank you for letting me know. I'll contact him.

빈칸 앞에서 Mr. Park가 그것을 가지고 있다고 했으므로, 그 사실을 알려줘서 고맙다며 그에게 연락해보겠다는 반응이 나오는 것이 자연스럽다.

2. 빈칸 뒤에 단서가 있는 경우

2024 지방직 9급

A: Hello, can I ask you a question about the presentation next Tuesday?
B: Do you mean the presentation about promoting the volunteer program?
A: Yes. Where is the presentation going to be?
B: Let me check. It is room 201.
A: I see. Can I use my laptop in the room?
B: Sure. We have a PC in the room, but you can use yours if you want.
A: ______________________________
B: We can meet in the room two hours before the presentation. Would that work for you?
A: Yes. Thank you very much!

⇨ When can I have a rehearsal for my presentation?

빈칸 뒤에서 발표 2시간 전에 강의실에서 만날 수 있다고 했으므로, 빈칸에서는 발표 시작 전에 만나야 할 이유가 언급되어야 한다.

1. A: 어제 회의에서 언급하신 문서를 받을 수 있나요?
B: 네. 문서 제목이 뭔가요?
A: 제목은 기억나지 않지만, 주민 축제에 관한 것이었어요.
B: 아, 뭘 말씀하시는 건지 알겠어요.
A: 좋아요. 그것을 저에게 이메일로 보내주실 수 있나요?
B: 제가 가지고 있지 않네요. Park 씨가 그 프로젝트를 담당하고 있으니까, 그분이 가지고 있을 거예요.
A: 알려주셔서 감사합니다. 그에게 연락해 볼게요.
B: 행운을 빌어요. 원하시는 문서를 받으시길 바라요.

2. A: 안녕하세요, 다음 주 화요일에 있을 발표에 대한 질문을 해도 될까요?
B: 자원봉사 프로그램 홍보에 관한 발표를 말씀하시는 건가요?
A: 네. 발표를 어디서 하나요?
B: 확인해 볼게요. 201호실이네요.
A: 그렇군요. 강의실에서 제 노트북을 사용해도 되나요?
B: 네. 강의실에 컴퓨터가 있지만, 원하시면 당신 것을 사용하셔도 돼요.
A: 발표 예행연습은 언제 할 수 있을까요?
B: 저희는 발표 2시간 전에 강의실에서 만날 수 있어요. 괜찮으실까요?
A: 네. 정말 감사합니다!

예제

다음 빈칸에 들어갈 말로 가장 적절한 것은? 2024 국가직 9급

Brian [11:21]
Hi, can I get some information on your city tour?

Ace Tour [11:22]
Thank you for contacting us. Do you have any specific questions?

Brian [11:22]
____

Ace Tour [11:23]
It'll take you to all the major points of interest in the city.

Brian [11:24]
How much is it?

Ace Tour [11:24]
It's 50 dollars per person for a four-hour tour.

Brian [11:25]
OK. Can I book four tickets for Friday afternoon?

Ace Tour [11:25]
Certainly. I will send you the payment information shortly.

글의 소재
도시 투어

빈칸 앞뒤에서 단서 찾기
① 빈칸 앞: 문의 사항에 대한 질문
② 빈칸 뒤: 도시 투어를 통해 무엇을 경험할 수 있는지에 대한 설명
→ Brian은 도시 투어 내용에 대해 문의했을 것
⇨ 정답 ②

부연
가볍게 훑기

① How long is the tour? → 빈칸 뒤에서 투어 소요 시간 언급 X
② What does the city tour include? → 빈칸 뒤에서 도시 투어 내용을 설명했으므로 정답
③ Do you have a list of tour packages? → 빈칸 뒤에서 투어 패키지 목록 언급 X
④ Can you recommend a good tour guide book? → 빈칸 뒤에서 투어 가이드북 언급 X

Brian: 안녕하세요, 도시 투어에 관한 정보 좀 얻을 수 있을까요?
Ace Tour: 연락해 주셔서 감사합니다. 구체적으로 궁금한 점이 있으신가요?
Brian: 그 도시 투어에 무엇이 포함되나요?
Ace Tour: 도시의 모든 주요 명소로 안내해 드립니다.
Brian: 얼마인가요?
Ace Tour: 4시간 투어에 1인당 50달러입니다.
Brian: 알겠습니다. 금요일 오후로 티켓 4장을 예약할 수 있나요?
Ace Tour: 물론입니다. 곧 결제 정보를 보내 드리겠습니다.

① 투어는 얼마나 걸리나요?
② 그 도시 투어에 무엇이 포함되나요?
③ 투어 패키지 목록이 있나요?
④ 괜찮은 투어 가이드북을 추천해 주시겠어요?

어휘 point of interest 관심 지점 book 예약하다 recommend 추천하다 정답 ②

전략 적용 연습

정답 및 해설 p. 65

01 다음 빈칸에 들어갈 말로 가장 적절한 것은?

A: I heard that the university cafeteria changed their menu.
B: Yeah, I just checked it out.
A: And they got a new caterer.
B: Yes. Sam's Catering.
A: ______________________________?
B: There are more dessert choices. Also, some sandwich choices were removed.

① What is your favorite dessert
② Do you know where their office is
③ Do you need my help with the menu
④ What's the difference from the last menu

02 다음 빈칸에 들어갈 말로 가장 적절한 것은? 2024 국가직 9급

A: Have you found your phone?
B: Unfortunately, no. I'm still looking for it.
A: Have you contacted the subway's lost and found office?
B: ______________________________.
A: If I were you, I would do that first.
B: Yeah, you are right. I'll check with the lost and found before buying a new phone.

① I went there to ask about the phone
② I stopped by the office this morning
③ I haven't done that yet, actually
④ I tried searching everywhere

03 다음 빈칸에 들어갈 말로 가장 적절한 것은?

> A: Oh, another one! So many junk emails!
> B: I know, I receive more than ten junk emails a day.
> A: Can we stop them from coming in?
> B: I don't think it's possible to block them completely.
> A: ______________________________?
> B: Well, you can set up a filter on the settings.
> A: A filter?
> B: Yeah. The filter can weed out some of the spam emails.

① Do you write emails often
② Isn't there anything we can do
③ How did you make this great filter
④ Can you help me set up an email account

전략

02 오답 선지에도 유형이 있다

오답 선지는 보통 대화에서 나온 단어들로 구성된다. 따라서 생각보다 생활영어 문제를 틀리는 경우가 많다. 그러나 다음 네 가지 오답 유형을 알아둔다면, 매력적인 오답을 더 쉽게 걸러낼 수 있다.

전략 노트

동문서답	선지가 빈칸 앞 내용과 관계없는 말을 하는 경우 → 대화의 전체적인 맥락을 봐야 함 (의문사에 특히 유의) ex A: What did you do for your birthday? B: My birthday is coming up soon. ⊗ A: 생일에 뭐 했어? B: 내 생일이 곧 다가 와.
대화에서 나온 fact와 모순	선지가 대화에서 언급된 fact에 어긋날 경우 → 이 fact가 빈칸과 멀리 떨어져 있을 수 있음에 유의 ex A: I didn't have lunch yet. B: Me neither. We should grab something to eat. A: I'm full from the lunch I had. ⊗ A: 나는 아직 점심을 못 먹었어. B: 나도 못 먹었어. 우리 뭐 좀 먹자. A: 난 점심 먹은 걸로 배가 불러.
Yes/No 유형	Yes/No를 반대로 대답한 경우 또는 Yes/No는 잘 대답했지만 이어지는 내용이 문맥에 맞지 않는 경우 → Yes/No가 잘못 들어가 있는 선지들을 먼저 소거한 뒤에 나머지 선지들의 문맥 따지기 ex A: Did you do the dishes? B: Yes, I'll do them later. ⊗ A: 설거지 했어? B: 응. 나중에 할거야.
화자 뒤바뀜	화자가 뒤바뀌거나 제삼자 입장에서 말하는 경우 → 빈칸에서 누가 말할 차례인지에 유의 ex A: Thank you for visiting our hotel. B: Which name did you reserve under? ⊗ A: 저희 호텔을 방문해 주셔서 감사드립니다. B: 어떤 이름으로 예약하셨나요?

심슨쌤 꿀팁! 선지에서 Yes/No를 생략하고 본론만 이야기하는 경우도 있다.

ex A: Did you do the dishes?

B: I'll do them later.

A: 설거지 했어?

B: 나중에 할거야.

예제

다음 빈칸에 들어갈 말로 가장 적절한 것은?

> A: Have you taken anything for your **1** cold?
>
> B: No, I just blow my nose a lot.
>
> A: **2** Have you tried nose spray?
>
> B: ______________________
>
> A: It works great.
>
> B: **3** No, thanks. I don't like to put anything in my nose, so **4** I've never used it.

1 글의 소재
감기 치료

2 빈칸 앞 단서
코 스프레이 사용 여부를 물음

3 fact ①
코 스프레이를 사용하고 싶지 않음

4 fact ②
코 스프레이를 사용한 적 없음

① ~~Yes~~, but it didn't help. → 코 스프레이를 사용한 적이 있음을 전제하므로 fact ②와 모순

② No, I don't like nose spray. → B의 마지막 말과 일치

③ No, the pharmacy was closed. → 코 스프레이 사용 의향을 전제하므로 fact ①과 모순

④ ~~Yeah~~, how much should I use? → 코 스프레이를 사용한 적이 있음을 전제하므로 fact ②와 모순

A: 감기약은 먹었어?
B: 아니, 나는 그냥 코를 많이 풀어.
A: 코 스프레이는 써 봤니?
B: <u>아니, 난 코 스프레이를 좋아하지 않아.</u>
A: 그거 효과가 좋아.
B: 아냐, 괜찮아. 나는 코에 뭘 넣는 걸 싫어해서 한 번도 그걸 써 본 적 없어.

① 응, 하지만 도움이 안 되더라.
② 아니, 난 코 스프레이를 좋아하지 않아.
③ 아니, 약국이 문을 닫았어.
④ 응, 내가 얼마나 써야 할까?

어휘 pharmacy 약국

정답 ②

전략 적용 연습

정답 및 해설 p. 65

01 다음 빈칸에 들어갈 말로 가장 적절한 것은?

A: Hi there. May I help you?
B: Yes, I'm looking for a sweater.
A: Well, this one is the latest style from the fall collection. What do you think?
B: It's gorgeous. How much is it?
A: Let me check the price for you. It's $120.
B: ______________________.
A: Then how about this sweater? It's from the last season, but it's on sale for $50.
B: Perfect! Let me try it on.

① I also need a pair of pants to go with it
② That jacket is the perfect gift for me
③ It's a little out of my price range
④ We are open until 7 p.m. on Saturdays

02 다음 빈칸에 들어갈 말로 가장 적절한 것은?

A: Were you here last night?
B: Yes. I worked the closing shift. Why?
A: The kitchen was a mess this morning. There was food spattered on the stove, and the ice trays were not in the freezer.
B: I guess I forgot to go over the cleaning checklist.
A: You know how important a clean kitchen is.
B: I'm sorry. ______________________

① I won't let it happen again.
② Would you like your bill now?
③ That's why I forgot it yesterday.
④ I'll make sure you get the right order.

03 다음 빈칸에 들어갈 말로 가장 적절한 것은?

A: Thank you for calling the Royal Point Hotel Reservations Department. My name is Sam. How may I help you?
B: Hello, I'd like to book a room.
A: We offer two room types: the deluxe room and the luxury suite.
B: ______________________?
A: For one, the suite is very large. In addition to a bedroom, it has a kitchen, living room, and dining room.
B: It sounds expensive.
A: Well, it's $200 more per night.
B: In that case, I'll go with the deluxe room.

① Do you need anything else
② May I have the room number
③ What's the difference between them
④ Are pets allowed in the rooms

전략

03 비즈니스 용어 암기는 필수이다

새로운 출제 기조에서 익숙하지 않은 주제가 나온다면 당황할 수 있으므로, 자주 쓰이는 비즈니스 용어는 암기해 두는 것이 좋다. 〈심슨 전략서 암기 노트〉 p. 56 참고

예제

다음 빈칸에 들어갈 말로 가장 적절한 것은? 2024 국가직 9급

A: Thank you. We appreciate your order.

B: You are welcome. Could you send the goods by air freight? We need them fast.

A: Sure. We'll send them to your department right away.

B: Okay. I hope we can get the goods early next week.

A: If everything goes as planned, you'll get them by Monday.

B: Monday sounds good.

A: Please pay within 2 weeks. Air freight costs will be added on the invoice.

B: ________________________________

A: I am afraid the free delivery service is no longer available.

글의 소재
항공 화물로 상품을 배송하는 일

화물 배송비가 송장에 추가될 것임을 언급
배송비는 B가 부담해야 한다는 내용

A는 B에게 무료 배송 서비스가 종료됨을 설명
B는 빈칸에서 배송비 부담에 관해 물어봤을 것
⇨ 정답 ④

① I see. When will we be getting the invoice from you? → 빈칸 뒤에서 대답 X
② Our department may not be able to pay within two weeks. → 빈칸 뒤와 연결 X
③ Can we send the payment to your business account on Monday? → 빈칸 뒤에서 대답 X
④ Wait a minute. I thought the delivery costs were at your expense. → 문맥에 알맞음

A: 감사합니다. 주문해 주셔서 고맙습니다.
B: 천만에요. 항공 화물로 상품을 보내 주실 수 있나요? 저희가 빨리 필요해서요.
A: 물론입니다. 바로 그쪽 부서로 보내 드리겠습니다.
B: 알겠습니다. 다음 주 초에 상품을 받을 수 있으면 좋겠네요.
A: 예정대로 진행된다면, 월요일까지는 받으실 수 있을 겁니다.
B: 월요일 좋네요.
A: 2주 이내에 결제 부탁드립니다. 항공 화물 배송비는 송장에 추가될 것입니다.
B: 잠깐만요. 배송비는 그쪽에서 부담하시는 줄 알았는데요.
A: 죄송합니다만, 무료 배송 서비스는 더 이상 제공되지 않습니다.

① 알겠습니다. 저희가 송장을 언제 받아볼 수 있을까요?
② 저희 부서에서 2주 내로 지불할 수 없을지도 모르겠네요.
③ 월요일에 거래 계좌로 대금을 보내도 될까요?
④ 잠깐만요, 배송비는 그쪽에서 부담하시는 줄 알았는데요.

어휘 air freight 항공 화물 invoice 송장 account 계좌 at one's expense ~의 비용으로

정답 ④

전략 적용 연습

정답 및 해설 p. 66

01 다음 빈칸에 들어갈 말로 가장 적절한 것은? 2025 출제기조 전환 예시

A: Hello. I'd like to book a flight from Seoul to Oakland.
B: Okay. Do you have any specific dates in mind?
A: Yes. I am planning to leave on May 2nd and return on May 14th.
B: Okay, I found one that fits your schedule. What class would you like to book?
A: Economy class is good enough for me.
B: Any preference on your seating?
A: ______________________________
B: Great. Your flight is now booked.

① Yes. I'd like to upgrade to business class.
② No. I'd like to buy a one-way ticket.
③ No. I don't have any luggage.
④ Yes. I want an aisle seat.

02 다음 빈칸에 들어갈 말로 가장 적절한 것은?

Brad [10:20]
Pete, are you coming to the seminar this weekend?

Pete [10:32]
I haven't made up my mind yet. Who's the keynote speaker?

Brad [10:34]
Gary Jenson. He's a senior executive at Seoul Investment Bank.

Pete [10:34]
I wouldn't want to miss that. But the seminar is just so expensive.

Brad [10:36]
It's probably because they're providing catered lunch for free.

Pete [10:37]
That makes sense. I suppose it's worth the cost.

Brad [10:40]
____

Pete [10:41]
Really? I'd better hurry, then. Thanks for letting me know.

① Is the seminar by invitation only?
② I'm afraid the seminar is over.
③ I'm not sure who the caterer is.
④ There aren't many spots left.

03 다음 빈칸에 들어갈 말로 가장 적절한 것은?

Kate [15:32]
Celina, are you free next Wednesday?

Celina [15:39]
That's my day off. Why do you ask?

Kate [15:42]
That's too bad. I was wondering if you could accompany me on my business trip.

Celina [15:44]
Do you need help with something?

Kate [15:49]
Yes, I was hoping you could handle some follow-up tasks. Our boss approved of it, but I'm guessing he forgot you have Wednesday off.

Celina [15:52]
____

Kate [15:55]
No, I don't want you to change your plans. I'll manage on my own. Thanks.

① I think I'm going to call in sick.
② I can reschedule my day off for you.
③ Do you want me to brief you on my plans?
④ The agenda for the meeting isn't finalized yet.

실전 모의고사

[01 ~ 03] 다음 빈칸에 들어갈 말로 가장 적절한 것을 고르시오.

01

The scientists faced several ______________ including limited funding and strict regulatory requirements, yet they managed to achieve remarkable results.

① mistakes ② constraints
③ opportunities ④ characteristics

02

The __________ VIP lounge at the airport can only be accessed by first-class passengers.

① public ② exclusive
③ forbidden ④ complimentary

新 **03**

The implementation of advanced safety protocols __________ to enhance workplace security for employees in the manufacturing plant.

① expecting ② is expected
③ has expected ④ will be expecting

[04 ~ 05] 밑줄 친 부분 중 어법상 옳지 않은 것을 고르시오.

04

Hundreds of self-help books ① are published each year. The themes range from getting ② rich to quitting smoking to saving relationships. It is a million-dollar industry ③ which the authors use their personal experience to provide a solution for ④ attaining some goal.

05

The surge in movements advocating for animal rights ① continue to emerge in many parts of the world, including Britain — a country that ② has even banned its traditional sport of fox hunting in recent years. However, this issue leaves society ③ divided, with many ④ arguing that there are aspects of human rights that require more urgent attention.

[06 ~ 07] 다음 빈칸에 들어갈 말로 가장 적절한 것을 고르시오.

新 06

Jesse
Tiffany, have you completed drafting the agenda for our next meeting?
11:25

Tiffany
Yes, I attached it to the email I sent you a moment ago.
11:32

Jesse
____
11:33

Tiffany
Oh, I must have accidentally left it out. I'm sorry, I'll send it to you again.
11:34

Jesse
It's no problem. I'll give you feedback by tomorrow.
11:36

Tiffany
Thank you.
11:36

① We don't need an agenda for our next meeting.
② Your draft for the agenda seems perfect as it is.
③ I'm looking at it now, but I don't see any attachment.
④ You made a good choice forwarding it to the entire team.

07

A: Hi, I'm calling to book a room for a week starting from April 7 to 13. Are there any vacancies?
B: Yes, we can accommodate you with a garden-view deluxe room.
A: Okay. How much will that be?
B: The total will come to $840. A $50 deposit is required to secure your reservation.
A: Okay. And just wondering, ____________________________
B: Yes, I was just about to mention that. We provide free dinner services for multi-night reservations. How about I treat you to two dinners and a bottle of wine?
A: That's wonderful. Thank you.
B: It's my pleasure. I'll send you the payment information in a moment.

① should I pay for the deposit online?
② can you tell me what view I'll be getting?
③ can you contact me if any room becomes available?
④ are there any special offers for booking a long stay?

新 [08 ~ 09] 다음 글을 읽고 물음에 답하시오.

To	Incheon Office of Education
From	Minhee Kim
Date	May 19
Subject	Improvement for multicultural families

To whom it may concern,

To build a stronger and more unified Incheon, I propose that the city consider offering free Korean language classes for students from multicultural families like mine.

Growing up, I often found it difficult to fully integrate into the local community, mainly due to the language barrier. Unfortunately, the cost of Korean language classes is high, preventing many, particularly those from low-income families, from learning Korean.

I believe that by offering free Korean language classes, the city could provide equal opportunity for students from diverse backgrounds to learn Korean, regardless of their financial status. These classes would not only improve our language skills but also greatly aid our assimilation into Korean society.

I am confident that this initiative would foster a more inclusive and vibrant Incheon community. Thank you for your time and consideration.

Sincerely,
Minhee Kim

08 윗글의 목적으로 가장 적절한 것은?

① 다문화 가정 학생들을 위한 장학금 지원을 부탁하려고
② 다문화 가정 이해 증진을 위한 강연 주최를 제안하려고
③ 저소득 다문화 가정을 위한 생계 지원금 지급을 촉구하려고
④ 다문화 가정 학생들을 위한 무료 한국어 수업 개설을 요청하려고

09 밑줄 친 "status"의 의미와 가장 가까운 것은?

① value
② rights
③ situation
④ importance

新 [10 ~ 11] 다음 글을 읽고 물음에 답하시오.

(A)

Seoul faces a complex demographic shift, with a growing elderly population and declining birth rates. The Population Policy Ideas Competition invites Seoul residents to contribute innovative ideas and fresh perspectives for effective solutions to the demographic challenges currently facing the city.

To participate, your proposal must be about one of these three key areas:

- **Aging Populations**: Proposals that address labor shortages and ensure secure retirements
- **Birth Rate Decline**: Suggestions that encourage families to have more children
- **Migration**: Ideas to attract educated and skilled immigrants and foster social integration of migrant populations

Submissions are limited to individual proposals; team entries will not be accepted. Keep your proposal within the 10-page limit. The deadline for submission is 18:00 on June 22, 2024.

Rewards:
1st Place: ₩5,000,000
2nd Place: ₩3,000,000
3rd Place: ₩1,000,000
※ All prizes are awarded tax-free.

For more information, contact:
Email: Seouloffice@seoulmysoul.com
Phone: (02) 11-0000

10 (A)에 들어갈 윗글의 제목으로 가장 적절한 것은?

① Want to Learn about Seoul Youth Support Policies?
② Offer Your Solutions for Seoul's Demographic Issues
③ Attend the Seminar on Aging Population Concerns in Seoul
④ Participate in the Seoul Population Survey and Receive a Gift

11 Population Policy Ideas Competition에 관한 윗글의 내용과 일치하지 않는 것은?

① 서울 시민을 대상으로 한다.
② 주제는 인구 고령화, 저출생, 이민에 한정된다.
③ 개인이나 팀 단위로 참가할 수 있다.
④ 모든 상금은 세금이 면제된다.

新12 Aberdeen city government에 관한 다음 글의 내용과 일치하는 것은?

https://www.aberdeen.gov/contactus

Compliments | Complaints | Report a Problem | Suggestions

We in the Aberdeen city government are here to support you, our residents. If you have a problem to report, please complete the form below. Problems that should be reported to us include issues with city streets, electricity and gas service, power lines, and traffic lights. All reports are read within one hour of being posted (on business days only). Problems will be forwarded to the proper departments to resolve the issues as swiftly as possible. Be sure to leave your name and a telephone number or email address so that we can contact you for more details. Those who prefer to remain anonymous are not required to provide any personal information. For matters involving violations of the law, please contact the local police.

problemreport.doc

① It reads reports within one hour on weekends.
② It transfers problems to the appropriate departments.
③ It requires all residents to provide personal information.
④ It directly deals with problems involving illegal acts.

新13 TaxCare Program에 관한 다음 글의 내용과 일치하지 않는 것은?

TaxCare Program

http://taxcareprogram.org

Home > Introduction > TaxCare Program

Simplify tax filing with the free TaxCare Program

The Small Business Administration (SBA) has launched a new free tax assistance program for small business owners. It is user-friendly, secure, and efficient, helping with tax preparation and compliance. The program offers an intuitive online portal with step-by-step guides, checklists, and templates. Small business owners can get personalized advice through one-on-one online consultations with tax professionals. State-of-the-art security measures protect sensitive information, allowing small business owners to prepare taxes with peace of mind. To enroll or learn more, visit the SBA website or contact your local SBA office. We are here to help you focus on what you do best – running your business.

① It is designed for small business owners.
② It helps users prepare for tax payments.
③ It does not offer customized guidance online.
④ It protects sensitive information of users.

14 다음 글의 주제로 가장 적절한 것은?

Although a documentary shows actual events and contains interviews with real people, it is up to the documentary filmmaker to decide what footage to include and how to present it to the audience. Documentary filmmakers usually film hundreds of hours of footage which are then edited down to the length of a feature film and ordered in a particular way. The footage that the filmmakers choose to show the audience strongly influences how the audience will respond to the subject matter. For instance, a documentary filmmaker may want the audience to sympathize with one of the people in the film, so they may decide not to show the footage of that person doing and saying things that present them in a bad light.

*footage: (특정한 사건을 담은) 장면

① the ability of documentary films to evoke sympathy
② the reflection of objective reality in documentary films
③ the determinants of audience demand for documentaries
④ the documentary as a reconstructed representation of reality.

15 다음 글의 요지로 가장 적절한 것은?

For centuries, caste has dictated almost every aspect of Hindu religious and social life, with each group occupying a specific place in this complex hierarchy. Often criticized for being unjust and regressive, it has remained virtually unchanged for centuries, trapping people in fixed social orders from which it is nearly impossible to escape. Historians, though, say that until the 18th Century, the formal distinctions of caste were of limited importance to Indians, social identities were much more flexible, and people could move easily from one caste to another. New research shows that hard boundaries were set by British colonial rulers who made caste India's defining social feature. In fact, they did their best to create a single society with a common law that could be easily governed.

① Caste has long ruined the lives of Indians.
② British colonial rulers were affected by caste.
③ Britain contributed to eradicating caste in India.
④ It was British colonial rulers who shaped today's caste.

16 다음 글의 흐름상 어색한 문장은?

Teamwork is practically necessary because the work needed to complete a research project is simply too much for any one person to complete on their own. ① Consider, for example, the Human Genome Project, the purpose of which was to identify and sequence the more than 3 billion chemical units in human DNA. ② This massively collaborative project took about 15 years from inception to completion and involved research teams from twenty universities in the United States, Europe, and Asia. ③ The sheer amount of work required to complete it necessitated the collaborative set-up. ④ One tempting but mistaken assumption is that scientific knowledge is the most certain form of knowledge that we have. Even if one individual had possessed all the relevant expertise and skills, it would have been impossible for them to complete all this work within a single lifetime.

17 주어진 문장이 들어갈 위치로 가장 적절한 곳은?

However, they can be quite harmful to the environment, and they may not be healthy for humans to ingest.

The industrialization of agriculture has resulted in the development of a multitude of techniques to help increase farmers' yields immensely. Chemical compounds are used to fertilize soil and protect crops from insects and other such pests. (①) These fertilizers and pesticides are inexpensive and effective. (②) Runoff from farms enters the water supply, causing fish and other marine life to fall ill and disrupting the ecosystem. (③) Humans have been known to develop serious problems from handling or eating foods that have been treated with these chemicals. (④) For example, pesticide use has been linked to birth defects in babies born to farm laborers.

18 주어진 문장 다음에 이어질 글의 순서로 가장 적절한 것은?

When used correctly, virtual reality can be a powerful tool to change our lives for the better and revolutionize the way we go about doing things in our ordinary lives.

(A) However, despite all these benefits, possible problems such as isolation and losing a sense of reality can arise if we go overboard with it.

(B) As a matter of fact, it is already being involved in many fields to provide users with a more personalized and intuitive experience and connect people from around the world.

(C) Hence, it's important that we use virtual reality in moderation and maintain a healthy balance with real-world interactions in order to ensure we reap its benefits without suffering negative consequences.

① (B)－(A)－(C)
② (B)－(C)－(A)
③ (C)－(A)－(B)
④ (C)－(B)－(A)

[19 ~ 20] 다음 빈칸에 들어갈 말로 가장 적절한 것을 고르시오.

19

Despite its rapid spread, Islam is not a religion for those who are casual about regulations; on the contrary, adhering to its rules requires ____________________. One must rise before dawn to observe the first of five prayers required daily, none of which can take place without first ritually cleansing oneself. Sleep, work, and recreational activities take second place to prayer. Fasting during the month of Ramadan, undertaking the pilgrimage to Mecca at least once in a lifetime, paying tax for relief of the Muslim poor, and accepting Islam's creed require a serious and energetic commitment. On the whole, the vast majority of Muslims worldwide do observe those tenets.

① willingness to learn
② sympathy for the poor
③ great effort and discipline
④ inner peace and forgiveness

20

Villains are not confined to horror movies. Action movies are full of bad guys. Usually, the villains are motivated by greed for either money or power. These motives tend to be presented without much elaboration. Two additional features are common: sadism and egotism. Many of the movie villains seem to enjoy hurting their victims simply for the sake of doing so, and they tend to have very exalted opinions of themselves. Indeed, their pride often proves to be a fatal flaw, because their overconfidence gives the hero a chance to escape from their clutches and defeat them. But the sadism part is the essence of the villain. In a television special on villains in movies, the nationally prominent movie critics Siskel and Ebert emphasized this general point: "Enjoying being evil is the key to any successful villain." They added that this is the "most important feature." Thus, it is not merely performing harmful acts that defines villains; truly evil villains ______________________________.

① make their own set of laws
② are fun to watch or listen to
③ derive pleasure from inflicting harm
④ ultimately lose due to their overconfidence

MEMO

MEMO

MEMO

Staff

Writer 심우철

Director 강다비다

Researcher 정규리 / 한선영 / 장은영 / 김도현

Design 강현구

Manufacture 김승훈

Marketing 윤대규 / 한은지 / 유경철

발행일: 2024년 10월 15일 (3쇄)

내용문의: http://cafe.naver.com/shimson2000

2025
신경향

심슨 전략서

구문·문법·독해·생활영어
All in One 전략서

정답/해설

커넥츠 공단기 gong.conects.com 심슨영어연구소 카페 cafe.naver.com/shimson2000

| 심우철 지음 |

2025 신경향

심슨 전략서

구문·문법·독해·생활영어
All in One 전략서

정답/해설

커넥츠 공단기 gong.conects.com 심슨영어연구소 카페 cafe.naver.com/shimson2000

심우철 지음

PART 1 구문

UNIT 01 문장 해석 핵심 전략

전략 01

본서 p. 17

01 너의 편지의 목적

02 가장 위대한 야구 선수 중 한 명

03 가장 인기 있고 오래가는 장난감 중 하나

04 그 젊은 나라의 민주주의적 이상

05 세계의 수백만 종의 동식물 절반 이상

06 개인에게 중요한 기회균등의 원칙

07 전통 사회에서 현대 사회로의 가장 중요한 변화 중 하나

08 다른 학생들과 어울리는 효과적인 방법

09 20세기 사회주의의 쇠퇴와 자본주의의 등장

10 정서적, 지적, 그리고 행동적 재능의 혼합된 특징

11 오늘날의 형태로 스포츠가 발전된 것은 17세기 후반 영국에서 시작되었다.

12 Presley 이후 미국에서 가장 특이한 공중보건 문제 중 하나는 팝뮤직 콘서트에서의 대량 실신이다.

13 철로의 빠른 확산과 해양 운송의 증가로 원거리 여행이 보편화되었다.

14 학교는 또한 정직, 좋은 예절, 팀워크 그리고 협동과 같은 삶의 중요한 가치를 가르치려고 노력한다.

15 동아시아의 경제 변화는 20세기 후반 세계의 가장 중요한 발전 중 하나이다.

16 이 두 가지 기본 관계 외에도 동물은 주변의 다른 식물과 동물로부터 셀 수 없이 다양한 방식으로 직간접적으로 영향을 받을 수 있다.

17 20세기 과학의 모든 업적 중에 가장 위대한 것은 1953년 James Watson과 Francis Crick이 DNA의 구조를 발견한 것이다.

18 고객의 필요 사항을 엄격히 고려하고 또 재고하는 것이 새로운 또는 향상된 제품과 서비스를 개발하고 출시하기 위한 어떠한 과정에서도 중요하다.

19 1986년 첫 노트북 컴퓨터 개발은 1980년 중반 무렵 CPU 또는 컴퓨터 중앙처리 장치의 발명으로 가속화되었다.

20 인류의 여러 인종은 서로에 대해서 충분한 성적인 매력을 갖고 있어서 유전적 혼합에 대한 어떠한 지리적이거나 문화적인 장애물들이 없는 경우에 수천 년 사이에 인류는 인종적으로 단일화가 이루어질 가능성이 매우 크다.

전략 02

본서 p. 23

01 내 남자친구로부터 온 편지와 많은 연필이 내 방 책상 위에 있었다.

02 자연 세계와 만나는 기쁨은 예술가들만의 전유물이 아니다.

03 동물의 세계에서 발견된 가장 놀라운 의사소통 체계 중 하나가 유럽 꿀벌의 것이다.

04 쾌적한 생활 조건에는 화학적, 물리적 청결뿐만 아니라 사생활, 공간, 조용함도 포함된다.

05 직장에서 엄격한 사이버 보안 규정을 시행하면 무단 접근과 기밀 정보의 부주의한 공개를 방지할 수 있다.

06 폭넓은 지식과 전문 기술 지식이 합쳐져 그는 인공지능 분야의 복잡한 과제를 해결하기 위한 특별한 준비를 하게 되었다.

07 성과 피드백을 할 때, 당신은 피드백의 빈도, 양, 내용을 계획하는 데 있어 받는 사람의 과거 성과와 향후 잠재력에 대한 평가를 고려해야 한다.

08 그러나 유럽이 여러 개의 독립 국가로 분할하는 것은 종교, 언어, 그리고 풍습의 보편적인 유사성으로 서로 연결되어 인류의 자유에 가장 유익한 결과를 가져왔다.

09 컴퓨터, 휴대전화, 팩스, 스테레오, 그리고 가전제품과 같은 전자장치의 끊임없는 소음이 아침에 새들이 지저귀는 소리, 나무 사이로 부는 바람 소리, 또는 거친 종이 위에 그어지는 연필의 소리를 들리지 않게 할 것이다.

10 그들은 표지판을 통해서 승객들이 버스를 깨끗하게 유지하도록 일깨워주어야 한다.

11 여성 호르몬은 또한 신체가 몇 종류의 병을 막아내는 데도 도움을 준다.

12 아이들이 아무 영화나 볼 수 있도록 허락하는 것이 그들에게 해를 끼칠 수 있다는 것은 분명하다.

13 강렬한 브랜드의 이미지와 힘을 전략적으로 사용하는 것은 회사가 사업을 확장할 수 있게 해준다.

14 많은 사장이 그들의 원칙에 대한 근거를 설명하지 않은 채, 사람들에게 무엇을 어떻게 언제 해야 하는지를 지시한다.

15 그 결과 의사들은 사람들에게 곡물, 과일, 그리고 채소류를 더 많이 먹고, 육류와 유제품류는 덜 먹을 것을 충고한다.

16 Richardson은 우리에게 그가 프로젝트 일정의 모든 단계에서 일관되고 투명한 의사소통을 우선시할 것이라고 약속했다.

17 아이들이 돋보기를 통해 그들의 손가락을 관찰하게 해보면, 그들은 어머니들이 왜 저녁 식사 전에 손을 씻기를 원하는지를 이해하게 될 것이다.

18 선생님은 학생들에게 예외 없이 금요일까지 에세이를 제출하라고 하면서, 철저한 피드백과 건설적인 수정을 위해 마감일을 지키는 것이 중요하다고 강조했다.

19 세계 기후 변화에 대한 우려가 커지면서 활동가들은 화석 연료 추출 소비에 반대하는 캠페인뿐만 아니라 재생 가능 에너지를 지지하는 캠페인도 조직하게 되었다.

전략 03 본서 p. 28

01 우리는 아이들에게 서로 사이좋게 지내는 법을 배울 수 있는 기회를 제공해야만 한다.

02 관광 가이드가 관광객들에게 지역 축제로 인한 예상치 못한 도로 폐쇄로 인해 여행 일정 변경 사항을 알렸다.

03 감독관은 직원들에게 내일 아침에 예정된 다가오는 직원회의에 대한 시간 엄수의 중요성을 상기시켰다.

04 가장 절친한 친구에 의한 예상치 못한 배신으로 Peter는 다른 사람에 대한 신뢰를 잃었고, 그로 인해 그는 관계에서 조심스럽고 신중한 사람이 되었다.

05 가정에 연기 감지기를 설치하면 화재가 조용히 확산하여 심각한 응급 상황으로 확대되기 전에 막대한 피해를 주는 것을 방지할 수 있다.

06 경제 위기는 많은 가족이 식품, 주택 그리고 의료와 같은 필수 품목을 감당할 능력을 빼앗았고, 그러면서 그들이 생계를 이어 나가는 것을 어렵게 하고 재정적인 스트레스 가중에 직면하게 했다.

UNIT 02 절 해석 핵심 전략

전략 04 본서 p. 30

01 텔레비전은 과학, 의학, 예술 등 많은 분야의 학문을 이해할 수 있도록 도움을 주는 수준 높은 프로그램들을 방영한다.

02 열악한 도로 상황으로 인해 발생할 수 있는 교통 체증은 상품과 서비스의 배송을 지연시키고 사람들이 제시간에 출근하지 못하게 만드는 경우가 많다.

03 허리케인은 도로를 물에 잠기게 하고 집을 무너뜨리며, 생존자들이 사태를 수습하는 것을 힘들게 하는 바람과 세찬 비를 동반한다.

04 여러분의 증조부모님이 여러분의 나이 때에는 세계 각처에서 오는 전자 우편을 받는 개인용 컴퓨터를 꿈에도 상상하지 못했다.

05 특정 음식이나 양념이 흔히 있는 건강상의 문제점을 효과적으로 줄일 수 있다는 연구 결과가 점점 더 많이 나오고 있다.

06 그 종교의 중요한 믿음은 신들에게 음식이나 동물 제물의 형태로 대가를 치른 사람들에게 신들이 마술적인 힘을 준다는 것이었다.

07 어떤 사람들은 관심을 끄는 상품 포장지의 특정한 색상이 사람들이 색상이 다른 같은 종류의 다른 제품을 구매하는 대신 손을 뻗어 해당 제품을 가져가게 한다는 사실을 발견했다.

08 그는 그녀가 무대 공포증을 극복하고 완벽한 공연을 했다는 것을 믿을 수 없을 정도로 자랑스러워했다.

09 생명체가 다른 행성에 존재할 가능성과 언젠가 우리가 외계 생명체와 통신할 수 있다는 가능성은 과학적 탐험을 자극한다.

10 흡연이 폐암과 관련이 있고 금연이 건강 위험을 크게 줄일 수 있다는 증거는 공중 보건 캠페인의 중요성을 강조한다.

전략 05 본서 p. 33

01 그러나 최근에는 우리의 마음이 질병과 치유에 영향을 미친다는 사실을 입증하는 연구가 많이 있다.

02 그들은 회사가 정말로 효율성을 향상하기 위해서는 하나의 특정 방법이나 기술만 사용해야 한다고 주장한다.

03 나는 사람이 법을 어기거나 공중도덕을 해치지만 않으면, 자기가 하고 싶은 일을 해도 좋다고 생각한다.

04 때때로 어린아이들은 광고에 너무 '설득되어' 가족이 한 종류의 크림만 먹거나 특정 브랜드의 비누를 사용해야 한다고 정말로 믿는다.

05 다른 사람의 생각을 들어보는 것은 자신과 자신이 속한 세상에 대해 믿는 이야기가 정확한지, 아니면 조정이 필요한지 알 수 있는 한 가지 방법이다.

06 비록 이 사람이 여러분의 감정에 응답하지 않는다는 것을 받아들이는 것이 어렵지만, 당신을 다시 사랑하는 사람을 찾았을 때 당신이 지금 느끼는 고통은 당신의 마음에서 지워질 것이라는 것을 아는 것이 당신에게 도움이 될 수 있다.

07 마우스 포테이토(컴퓨터 앞에서 시간을 많이 보내는 사람)는 텔레비전의 카우치 포테이토(소파에 오랫동안 가만히 앉아 텔레비전만 보는 사람)의 컴퓨터 대응어구로, 텔레비전 앞에서 카우치 포테이토가 하는 것과 같은 방식으로 컴퓨터 앞에서 많은 여가 시간을 보내는 경향이 있는 사람을 말한다.

전략 06 본서 p. 35

01 텔레비전을 오랫동안 시청해 왔던 많은 나이 드신 분들은, 장시간 텔레비전을 보는 것이 사람들을 어리석게 만든다고 생각한다.

02 강한 윤리의식과 도덕감으로 무장한 젊은이들은 그러한 유해 웹사이트들에 의해 영향받지 않을 것이다.

03 당신이 미래의 고용주, 동료 또는 고객에게 남기는 마지막 인상은 당신의 첫인상만큼 중요할 수 있다.

04 아동 발달에 관한 수많은 연구를 메타 분석한 결과, 어린 나이에 독서에 대한 애정을 키운 어린이는 평생 학업 성취도가 더 좋은 경향이 있다는 결론이 나왔다.

05 전 생애를 희귀병 치료법 연구에 바친 그 과학자는 마침내 수백만 명의 생명을 구할 수 있는 의학적 발전을 이루었다.

06 라디오를 들었던 어린이들은 더 창의적인 응답을 한 반면, 텔레비전을 시청했던 어린이들은 원래 이야기를 반복하는 말을 더 많이 했다.

전략 07 본서 p. 37

01 온라인에 접속하면 당신이 말하고 있는 상대방을 모르기 때문에 나쁜 언어를 사용하고 싶은 유혹이 크다.

02 그는 여정에서 장애물을 만날 때마다 그것들이 성장의 기회인지 되돌아보고 인내심을 가지고 극복하기 위해 노력했다.

03 많은 어린이가 건강과 발달에 부정적인 영향을 경험하고 있지만, 그것이 현대 과학의 관심을 끌지 못했기 때문에 그들의 부모는 과도한 화면 시청의 위험성을 인식하지 못할 수도 있다.

04 사람들은 자신들이 좋아하는 팀이 이기면 흥분하고 행복해하며, 자신들이 좋아하는 팀이 지면 슬픔과 실망감을 느낀다.

05 당신이 재미있다고 생각하는 어떤 것이 일단 떠오르면, 상대방이 대화에 참여하고 주제에 대한 이해를 심화할 수 있도록 계속 질문하세요.

06 모든 사람이 눈에 잘 띄지 않는 눈 표범을 보았다는 형제나 사촌 혹은 친구가 있다고 말하지만, Himalaya를 방문하는 사람은 자기 눈으로 그것을 보았다는 사람을 거의 만나지 못할 것이다.

전략 08 본서 p. 39

01 생물학자와 연구자들은 DNA의 구조, 조직, 기능을 이해하는 데에 핵심적인 DNA 정보가 제공될 것이다.

02 그들은 아이들이 편안하고 안전한 느낌이 들 수 있는 즐겁고 보호받는 환경을 조성하기 위해 최선을 다한다.

03 가장 어려운 순간에 내가 도움의 손길을 내밀었던 사람은 결국 나의 가장 가까운 친구이자 평생의 친구가 되었다.

04 패션의 요구 사항으로 인해 일부 기묘한 디자인이 필요했지만, 모든 것이 걷기 쉽게 만든 것은 아니었다.

05 아마도 이것이 현재 대부분 완전히 효과가 없는 것으로 여겨지는 이러한 치료법이 일반적으로 문제를 "치료"하는 것처럼 보이는 이유일 것이다.

06 코치는 열심히 일하고 헌신함으로써 팀원들로부터 존경과 칭찬을 받았다고 자신이 생각한 사람을 팀 주장으로 임명했다.

07 그녀는 누가 자신의 책상 위에 수수께끼 같은 메시지와 단서로 가득 찬 익명의 메모를 남겼을지 궁금하지 않을 수 없었다.

08 그녀는 고대 묘지 안에 깊숙이 묻혀 있는 숨겨진 보물을 누가 발견했을지 모른다는 소문에 몹시 흥미를 느꼈다.

09 팀원들은 프로젝트의 새로운 팀 리더로 누구를 임명해야 할지와 의사 결정 과정에서 어떤 기준을 우선시해야 할지를 논의하고 있었다.

10 그들은 저녁 식사 장소로 어디를 갈지 며칠 동안 의논했고, 마침내 기념일을 축하하기 위해 어떤 레스토랑을 선택할지 결정했다.

11 우리에게는 또한 젊은이들이 자신의 문제에 대해 자유롭게 소통할 수 있는 게시판 공간이 있다.

12 수 시간 동안의 수색 끝에, 그들은 마침내 숲속의 개간지에 있는 오래된 참나무 아래에 보물이 깊이 묻힌 곳을 찾았다.

13 그는 규칙적인 운동이 전반적인 뇌 건강에 가져다주는 많은 이점을 강조하면서, 신체 활동이 인지 과정에 어떻게 긍정적으로 영향을 미치는지 설명했다.

14 모든 부모는 친구들의 선택이 모든 아이들에게 얼마나 중요한지 알고 있다. 어린 시절의 우정은 부모에게 그들의 자녀가 어떤 방향으로 나아가고 있는지를 말해 준다.

전략 09 본서 p. 42

01 어떤 길을 따르기로 선택하든 그것이 당신을 성취와 행복으로 인도하는지 확인하라.

02 힘든 시기에 곁을 지켜주는 사람이 누구든, 그들의 굳건한 충실함과 보살핌에 고마움과 감사를 표현해야 한다.

03 공감과 이해의 자세로 다른 사람의 이야기를 경청하는 사람이면 누구나 더 깊은 인연과 더 강한 관계를 조성한다.

04 힘든 시기에 친구들을 지원하기 위해 취하는 모든 조치는 우정을 강화하고 단결감과 연대감을 키워준다.

05 어떠한 의심이 당신의 생각을 흐리게 할지라도, 당신은 위대함을 성취할 수 있다는 것을 기억하고, 새로운 단계에 도달할 수 있는 당신의 능력을 믿어라.

06 아무리 많은 좌절에 직면하더라도, 그 각각의 좌절은 성공을 향한 디딤돌이라는 사실을 기억하라.

07 당신의 여정이 당신을 어디에 데려가든, 모든 목적지에는 저마다의 교훈과 모험이 있다는 사실을 기억하라.

UNIT 03 준동사 해석 핵심 전략

전략 10 본서 p. 44

01 무엇을 수정하고, 무엇을 수정하지 말아야 할지를 결정하는 것은 대단히 어렵다.

02 여행 중 편안함을 느낄 수 있도록 여행 일행 중 몇몇은 "로마에 오면 로마법을 따르라"라고 조언했다.

03 전국으로 나가는 좋은 일간 신문을 읽거나 TV에서 뉴스를 보는 것은 그날의 사건 정보를 놓치지 않는 가장 빠른 방법의 하나이다.

04 정부는 실직자를 위한 교육과 취업 알선 지원을 제공하기 위해 취업 능력 향상을 위한 다양한 프로그램을 시행했다.

05 낙농장에서 일하면서 그는 병의 크기가 어떠하든지 크림은 항상 꼭대기까지 온다는 것을 알았다.

06 어떤 사람들은 극도로 충격적인 사건을 경험한 뒤에 꿈과 회상을 통해 계속해서 그것을 재경험한다.

07 훌륭한 달변가가 되려면 대화를 시작하는 방법, 대화를 계속하는 방법, 대화를 끝내는 방법을 알아야 한다.

08 그날 밤 파티에 올 수 있느냐는 질문에 그는 열렬히 초대를 수락하고 호스트에게 선물을 가져다주겠다고 약속했다.

09 하이킹 여행 동안 숲속 깊은 곳에 숨겨진 폭포를 발견하고, 우리는 그 장엄한 아름다움과 고요한 주변 환경에 매료되었다.

10 자유 무역의 자연스러운 결과인 정보의 자유로운 흐름과 함께, 부유한 중산층은 결국 정치적 변화를 요구하게 될 것이며, 이는 궁극적으로 국가의 점진적인 민주화와 인권 기록의 개선으로 이어질 것이다.

11 사이버 폭력으로부터 학생들의 보호를 보장하려면 책임감 있는 디지털 시민의식을 고취하고 가상 공간에서의 존중과 공감의 문화를 조성하는 종합적인 교육 프로그램을 시행해야 한다.

전략 11 본서 p. 48

01 감기나 미열을 치료하는 가장 좋은 방법은 환자를 가능한 한 편안하게 하는 것이다.

02 슈퍼마켓 관리자는 고객이 쇼핑에 더 많은 돈을 쓰도록 장려하기 위해 다양한 전략과 기법을 사용한다.

03 학생들에게 양질의 교육에 대한 접근을 박탈하는 것은 학생들이 삶의 다양한 측면에서 잠재력을 최대한 끌어내고 성공을 거두는 데 필수적인 지식, 기술, 기회를 습득하는 능력을 저해하는 것이다.

04 창의적인 사고를 촉진하는 유머의 힘 때문에, 많은 회사가 사람들이 긴장을 풀고 창의력이 샘솟게 하려고 농담이나 다른 형태의 유머로 회의를 시작하는 전략을 채택한다.

05 복제는 심장 이식 및 시험관 아기를 포함한 과학적 업적 중 하나가 될 것이다.

06 매년 똑같은 길을 따라 지나가는 소 떼는 그것들이 가로지르는 지역의 생활과 산업에 영향을 미쳤다.

07 실신은 뇌로 가는 산소가 부족하여 발생하는 일시적인 의식 상실로, 다양한 원인에 의해 발생할 수 있다.

08 양치질은 치아에 남아 있는 음식물을 제거하고 입을 깨끗하고 건강하게 유지하기 위해 꼭 필요하다.

09 이러한 정보의 시대에 영어 실력을 향상하면 더 넓은 세상을 경험하고 시야도 넓어질 수 있다.

10 생산 라인의 컴퓨터화와 기계화로 인해 수작업의 필요성이 줄어들어 산업 전반에 걸쳐 효율성과 생산성이 향상되었다.

11 누구도 걱정으로 어떤 일도 이룰 수 없으며, 걱정 자체가 피로, 수면 부족, 과식, 전반적인 집중력 저하 등 여러 가지 문제를 쉽게 일으킬 수 있다.

12 우리는 산업 리더들과 네트워크를 구축하고 떠오르는 트렌드에 대한 소중한 통찰력을 얻는 기회를 가졌던 권위 있는 회의에 초대되어 감사했다.

UNIT 04 기타 구문 해석 핵심 전략

전략 12 본서 p. 51

01 친구가 진짜로 당신을 무시하고 있다고 믿어버리기 전에, (그가) 멍해 있거나 시력이 좋지 않은지를 고려해 보는 것은 중요하다.

02 또한 우리 아이들이 우리 부모들이 해야만 했던 지겨운 허드렛일을 할 필요가 없다는 것도 사실이다.

03 영국에 관해 글을 쓰는 몇몇 필자들은 영국인의 소속감에 대한 열망에 관해 이야기를 했고, 선술집이나 노동자의 클럽 또는 다른 수많은 클럽이 많은 사람의 삶에서 매우 중요한 역할을 한다는 것은 틀림없는 사실이다.

04 음악인으로서의 내 견해로는, 인터넷은 내가 전통적인 방식으로는 결코 닿을 수 없었을 사람들과 내 음악을 공유하는 것을 가능하게 했다.

05 많은 학생이 특히 교사의 적절한 설명 없이는 복잡한 과학 이론과 원리를 이해하기 어렵다고 생각한다.

06 용서, 수용, 신뢰, 그리고 희망을 포함한 인간 정신의 가장 위대하고 높은 이상 모두가 바탕으로 하는 것은 바로 연민이다.

07 내가 인내와 개인적 성취의 진정한 의미를 깨달은 것은 훈련 과정 내내 모든 장애물과 의심의 순간에도 불구하고 마라톤을 완주했을 때였다.

PART 2 문법

UNIT 01 동사 핵심 전략

전략 01

전략 적용 연습 본서 p. 55

01 O
02 X, does not produce → do not produce
03 X, burns → burning
04 X, providing → provides
05 X, was → were
06 O
07 X, were → was
08 O
09 ① 10 ④ 11 ②
12 ③ 13 ② 14 ①

01 정답 O

해설 전명구(in a new, unexpected way)를 괄호 치면, 뒤에 본동사 is가 있으므로 문장의 주어 자리에 온 동명사 Answering은 적절하다. 또한 this question을 목적어로 취해 '이 질문에 답변하는 것'이라는 해석도 자연스러우므로 능동태로 적절하게 쓰였다. 참고로, 동명사 주어는 단수 취급하므로 단수 동사로 수일치하였다.

해석 이 질문에 새롭고 예상치 못한 방식으로 답변하는 것이 필수적인 창조적 행위이다.

02 정답 X, does not produce → do not produce

해설 전명구(unlike carbohydrates, fats, and proteins / in our bodies)를 괄호 치면, 문장의 주어가 복수 명사인 Vitamins이므로 동사 does를 do로 고쳐야 한다.

해석 비타민은 탄수화물, 지방 및 단백질과 달리 우리 몸에서 에너지를 생성하지 않는다.

03 정답 X, burns → burning

해설 전명구(in a dark room / at full power)를 괄호 치면, 문장의 주어는 단수 명사인 A candle이고 동사가 burns와 emits 두 개다. 문맥상 emits가 본동사로 쓰여 '촛불이 많은 빛을 방출한다'라는 의미가 되는 것이 적절하므로 burns는 뒤에 온 전명구와 함께 명사 A candle을 수식하는 구조가 되어야 한다. 따라서 수식을 받는 명사인 촛불이 '타오르는' 것이므로 능동의 현재분사 burning으로 고쳐야 한다. 참고로, 비교급에서 비교 대상의 형태가 A candle burning ~ room과 a small flashlight shining ~ power로 일치된 것을 볼 수 있다.

해석 어두운 방에서 타오르는 촛불은 작은 손전등이 최대 전력으로 비추는 것만큼 많은 빛을 방출한다.

04 정답 X, providing → provides

해설 전명구(to scholars and academic researchers)를 괄호 치면, 문장에 명사구만 남고 동사가 없다. 따라서 문장의 주어인 단수 명사 The Oxford English Dictionary에 대한 동사가 필요하므로 providing을 단수 동사인 provides로 고쳐야 한다.

해석 옥스퍼드 영어 사전은 학자 및 학술 연구자에게 포괄적인 자료를 제공한다.

05 정답 X, was → were

해설 전명구(On the stage in the theater / from the 19th century)를 괄호 치면, 문장의 주어가 복수 명사인 famous actors이므로 동사 was를 were로 고쳐야 한다. 참고로, 장소 부사구가 문두에 와서 주어와 동사가 도치된 구문이다.

해석 극장 무대 위에는 19세기 고전 소설을 바탕으로 한 연극을 공연하는 유명 배우들이 있었다.

06 정답 O

해설 전명구(by Georges Brocot, a French ~ techniques)를 괄호 치면, 문장의 주어는 The replication process이고 동사는 was overseen이다. 주어가 단수 명사이므로 단수 동사 was로 수일치 하였고, 주어인 복제 과정이 '감독하는' 것이 아니라 '감독이 되는' 것이므로 수동태로도 적절하게 쓰였다.

해석 복제 과정은 주형 기술을 전문으로 하는 프랑스 화가 Georges Brocot에 의해 감독이 되었다.

07 정답 X, were → was

해설 전명구(Among her most prized ~ sale / by a ~ brand)를 괄호 치면, 문장의 주어가 단수 명사인 a 1961 bejeweled timepiece이므로 동사 were를 was로 고쳐야 한다. 참고로, 장소 부사구가 문두에 와서 주어와 동사가 도치된 구문이다.

해석 저녁 세일에서 판매된 그녀의 가장 소중한 소장품들 중에는 유명 명품 브랜드에서 1961년에 제작한 보석으로 장식된 시계가 있었다.

08 정답 O

해설 전명구(between different cultures)를 괄호 치고, 주어 자리에 온 '명사 of 명사'의 구조를 해석해 보면 '아이디어와 지식의 교환'이라고 되어 of 이하의 전명구가 명사 The exchange를 수식하는 구조임을 알 수 있다. 따라서 문장의 주어는 단수 명사인 The exchange이고, 뒤에 목적어를 취해 교환이 '우리의 집단적 이해를 풍부하게 하는' 것이므로 능동태의 단수 동사 has enriched는 적절하게 쓰였다.

해석 서로 다른 문화 간의 아이디어와 지식 교환은 인간이라는 존재의 의미에 대한 우리의 집단적 이해를 풍부하게 해 왔다.

09 정답 ①

해설 전명구(in Korean society / as the main ~ mobility)를 괄호 치면, 빈칸은 문장의 주어 Most people과 목적어 education 사이에 들어가는 동사 자리이므로 동사인 view가 와야 한다.

해석 한국 사회에서 대부분의 사람들은 교육을 사회적 이동의 주요 추진체로 여긴다.

10 정답 ④

해설 전명구(in a cash forecast / according to the company's circumstances)를 괄호 치면, 문장의 주어인 명사구 Elements of income만 있으므로 빈칸은 동사 자리이다. 주어 자리에 온 '명사 of 명사'의 구조를 해석해 보면 '소득의 요소'라고 되어 of 이하의 전명구가 명사 Elements를 수식하는 구조임을 알 수 있다. 따라서 문장의 주어는 복수 명사인 Elements이고, '다르다'라는 뜻의 완전자동사 vary는 능동태로만 가능하므로 빈칸에는 능동태의 will vary가 와야 한다.

해석 현금 예측에서 소득 요소는 회사 사정에 따라 달라질 것이다.

11 정답 ②

해설 전명구(According to Statistics Korea's data / in Seoul)를 괄호 치면, 빈칸은 문장의 주어인 동명사 buying과 목적어 9.2 years 사이에 들어가는 동사 자리이다. 이때 동명사 주어는 단수 취급하므로 빈칸에는 단수 동사인 requires가 와야 한다.

해석 통계청 자료에 따르면, 서울에서 중위 가격의 주택을 구입하는 데 9.2년이 걸린다.

12 정답 ③

해설 전명구(Like many smartphone owners / in the class / in looking at the screen)를 괄호 치면, 빈칸은 주어인 복수 명사 the students와 목적어 too much time 사이에 들어가는 동사 자리이다. 따라서 빈칸에는 복수 주어에 수일치하며 뒤에 목적어를 취하는 능동태의 were spending이 와야 한다.

해석 많은 스마트폰 소지자들처럼, 그 반의 학생들은 화면을 쳐다보는 데 너무 많은 시간을 보내고 있었다.

13 정답 ②

해설 전명구(across from the elementary school)를 괄호 치면, 빈칸은 문장의 주어 The local community center와 목적어 its operating hours 사이에서 조동사 has와 함께 현재완료 시제를 완성하는 p.p.(과거분사형) 자리이다. 따라서 빈칸에는 과거분사형인 extended가 와야 한다. 만약 has가 일반동사로 쓰였을 시에는 동사(has)와 동사(extends 또는 extend)가 같이 올 수 없고, 또한 부사 extensively가 온다면, 문맥상 '지역 문화 센터에는 광범위하게 운영 시간이 있다'라는 어색한 의미가 되며 구조상 부사는 목적어인 its operating hours 뒤에 오는 것이 적절하다.

해석 초등학교 건너편에 있는 지역 문화 센터는 더 많은 서비스를 제공하기 위해 운영 시간을 연장했다.

14 정답 ①

해설 전명구(Despite advancements ~ tools / in predicting weather patterns / mainly due to technological limitations)를 괄호 치면, 빈칸은 유도부사 there 도치 구문에서 본동사 are 뒤에 온 주어 자리이므로 명사 restrictions가 와야 한다.

해석 과학적 지식과 도구의 발전에도 불구하고, 주로 기술적 한계로 인해 날씨 패턴을 예측하는 데는 제약이 있다.

전략 02

전략 적용 연습

본서 p. 58

01 O
02 X, them → whom
03 X, has → which[that] has 또는 having
04 O
05 X, achieving → achieve
06 O
07 X, because of → because

08 ①	09 ③	10 ③
11 ④	12 ②	13 ③

01 정답 O

해설 관계사 which가 나왔으므로, 동사는 2개여야 한다. 따라서 '전치사 + 관계대명사' 형태인 for which가 이끄는 완전한 문장이 주어인 단수 명사 The treasure를 수식하고, 본동사는 주어에 수일치하여 단수 동사 was로 쓰인 것은 적절하다.

해석 그녀가 붙잡으려고 했던 보물은 진주 한 보따리였다.

02 정답 X, them → whom

해설 한 문장 안에 동사가 2개(is / are)이면 접속사/관계사/의문사가 하나 있어야 한다. 따라서 접속사 역할과 전치사 of의 목적어 역할을 동시에 하는 목적격 관계대명사가 와야 하는데, 선행사가 사람을 나타내는 10,000이므로 them을 whom으로 고쳐야 한다. 참고로, 분사구 enrolled in the online course가 명사 students를 수식하고 있는데, 학생들이 '등록된' 것이므로 수동의 과거분사 enrolled는 적절하게 쓰였다. 동사 enroll의 과거형과 과거분사형이 동일하여 문장 구조와 문맥상 파악해야 한다는 점에 유의한다.

해석 온라인 강좌에 등록된 학생 수는 1만 명이 넘는데, 그중 많은 수가 인도 출신이다.

03 정답 X, has → which[that] has 또는 having

해설 한 문장 안에 동사가 2개(has / has)이면 접속사/관계사/의문사가 하나 있어야 한다. 문맥상 뒤에 오는 has가 문장의 본동사이므로, 앞의 has는 뒤에 오는 명사구와 함께 수식어절을 이루는 것이 적절하다. 따라서 사물 명사 Coffee를 선행사로 받으며 뒤에 주어가 없는 불완전한 문장을 이끄는 주격 관계대명사 which 또는 that을 포함한 which[that] has로 고쳐야 한다. 또한 관계사절 대신 뒤에 목적어를 취하며 명사 Coffee를 수식하는 현재분사 having으로도 쓸 수 있다. 참고로, a bitter and slightly acidic flavor에서의 등위접속사 and는 형용사 bitter와 slightly acidic을 병렬 연결하기 위해 쓰였을 뿐 문장과 문장을 연결하고 있지 않다.

해석 쓴맛과 약간의 산미가 있는 커피는 사람에게 자극적인 효과를 준다.

04 정답 O

해설 관계사 which가 나왔으므로, 동사는 2개(makes / is)여야 한다. 먼저, 전명구(for a time / in a foreign country / of the merits)를 괄호 치면, 뒤에 문장의 본동사 makes가 있으므로 문장의 주어 자리에 온 동명사 Living은 적절하다. 또한 '살다'라는 뜻의 동사 live는 자동사이므로 능동태의 동명사로, 동명사 주어는 단수 취급하므로 뒤에 단수 동사로 수일치한 것도 올바르게 쓰였다. 더불어, 뒤의 문장 구조를 살펴보면, '전치사 + 관계대명사' 형태인 in which가 이끄는 완전한 문장이 복수 명사 the merits를 수식하고 있다.

해석 외국에서 한동안 거주하는 것은 우리들로 하여금 우리나라의 부족한 장점을 깨닫게 해 준다.

05 정답 X, achieving → achieve

해설 준동사에 밑줄이 쳐진 경우, 동사 자리인지 준동사 자리인지를 먼저 확인해야 한다. 문장에 관계대명사 who와 that이 있으므로 동사는 3개여야 하는데 2개(are daring / surpass)밖에 없고, 문장의 주어인 복수 명사 Persons에 대한 본동사가 없다. 따라서 준동사 achieving을 주어에 수일치한 복수 동사 achieve로 고쳐야 한다. 참고로, 주격 관계대명사 who와 that은 각각 Persons와 results를 선행사로 받아 주어가 없는 불완전한 문장을 이끌고 있다.

해석 진실을 위해 진심 어린 입장을 취하는 것에 대담한 사람들은 종종 그들의 기대를 능가하는 결과를 성취한다.

06 정답 O

해설 뒤에 '주어 + 동사'가 아닌 명사구 these similarities가 나왔으므로, 전치사 Despite가 쓰인 것은 적절하다.

해석 그러나 다른 생물들과의 이러한 유사성에도 불구하고, 인류의 진화는 다른 종의 진화와는 다르다.

07 정답 X, because of → because

해설 접속사 because 뒤에는 주어와 동사가 포함된 문장이 오고, 전치사 because of 뒤에는 명사(구)가 온다. 여기서는 뒤에 주어 every individual과 동사 has를 포함한 문장이 왔으므로 because of를 because로 고쳐야 한다.

해석 더욱이 'beach'라는 단어의 글자 그대로의 의미는 그 단어에 대한 개인적 의미를 담아내지 못한다, 왜냐하면 개인마다 그 단어에 대한 연관성이 다르기 때문이다.

08 정답 ①

해설 문장에 이미 관계사가 1개(who), 동사가 2개(had vandalized / was sentenced) 있으므로 접속사/관계사/의문사 없이 동사가 또 올 수 없다. 따라서 주어진 선택지 중 동사를 제외하면 준동사(분사, to 부정사)가 남으므로 빈칸은 주어 An American teenager를 수식할 수 있는 준동사 자리이다. 하지만 '살다'라는 뜻의 동사 live는 자동사이며, 문맥상 한 미국 십 대 청소년이 싱가포르에 '거주하는' 것이므로 빈칸에는 능동의 현재분사 living in이 와야 한다. 참고로, 뒤의 관계대명사 who는 An American teenager를 선행사로 받아 주어가 없는 불완전한 문장을 이끌고 있다.

해석 싱가포르에 거주하는 한 미국 십 대 청소년이 기물을 파손하여 싱가포르의 전통적인 형벌인 태형을 선고받았다.

09 정답 ③

해설 문장에 접속사 that이 있으므로 동사는 2개여야 하는데 1개(have to study)밖에 없고, 문장의 주어인 단수 명사 The belief에 대한 본동사가 없으므로 빈칸은 동사 자리이다. 따라서 목적어와 함께 to 부정사를 목적격 보어로 취할 수 있는 5형식 동사이며, '우리에게 동기 부여가 지속될 수 있게 해 주는' 것이므로 빈칸에는 능동태의 단수 동사 causes가 와야 한다. 참고로, 접속사 that은 완전한 문장을 이끌며 The belief를 수식하는 동격의 접속사이다.

해석 우리의 미래를 위해서 영어 공부를 열심히 해야 한다는 생각은 우리에게 동기 부여가 지속될 수 있게 해 준다.

10 정답 ③

해설 한 문장 안에 동사가 2개(went / are connected)이면 접속사/관계사/의문사가 하나 있어야 한다. 문맥상 빈칸 뒤에 오는 문장이 사람 명사 Diana's friends를 수식하는 관계사절이고, '부정대명사 + of + 목적격 관계대명사' 형태로 쓸 때 관계대명사 whom 또는 which를 쓰므로 빈칸에는 most of whom이 와야 한다.

해석 저녁에 우리는 Diana의 친구 중 한 명의 집에서 열린 파티에 갔는데, 그들 대부분이 영화 산업과 관련이 있는 사람들이었다.

11 정답 ④

해설 문장에 접속사 that, 관계대명사 that, 의문사 why가 나왔으므로 동사는 4개여야 한다. The idea를 수식하는 동격의 that 절에서 주어는 justice, 동사는 has이고, the good를 선행사로 받아 목적어가 없는 불완전한 문장을 이끄는 that 관계대명사절에서 주어는 universities, 동사는 pursue이다. 그리고 의문사 why가 이끄는 절에서 주어는 selling admission이고 동사는 is이다. 따라서 문장의 진짜 주어인 단수 명사 The idea에 대한 본동사가 없으므로 빈칸에는 주어에 수일치한 단수 동사 explains가 와야 한다.

해석 대학 입학 기회 배분의 정의가 대학이 올바르게 추구하는 공익과 관련이 있다는 생각은 입학권 판매가 왜 부당한지를 설명한다.

12 정답 ②

해설 전명구(with those ~ countries / on scientific principles / especially in their ~ wind)를 괄호 치면, 문장의 주어는 Korean kites이고, 본동사는 are based이다. 주어진 선택지를 보면, 동사 compare가 있는데 접속사/관계사/의문사 없이는 동사가 또 올 수 없다. 따라서 선택지 중 동사를 제외하면 준동사(분사, to 부정사)가 남으므로 빈칸은 주어 Korean kites를 수식할 수 있는 준동사 자리이다. 하지만 뒤에 목적어가 없으며 문맥상 한국의 연이 다른 나라의 연들과 '비교되는' 것이므로 빈칸에는 수동의 과거분사 compared가 와야 한다. 참고로, 뒤의 관계대명사 which는 their shapes를 선행사로 받아 주어가 없는 불완전한 문장을 이끌고 있다.

해석 한국의 연은 다른 나라의 연들과 비교하면 과학적 원리에 기초하고 있는데, 특히 바람을 잘 활용하는 그 모양에서 그렇다.

13 정답 ③

해설 한 문장 안에 동사가 3개(wrote / was being excavated / was found)이면 접속사/관계사/의문사가 2개 있어야 한다. 빈칸은 타동사 wrote의 목적어 자리로서 뒤에 온 문장을 이끌어야 하므로 명사절 접속사가 필요하고, 또한 명사절 안에서도 완전한 문장 2개를 연결해야 하므로 부사절 접속사가 필요하다. 따라서 빈칸에는 명사절 접속사와 부사절 접속사가 순서대로 있는 that when이 와야 한다. 참고로, 접속부사 therefore는 접속사와 달리 문장과 문장을 연결하지 못한다.

해석 Clovis Chappel은 폼페이라는 로마 도시가 발굴될 때, 베수비오산의 화산재에 의해 미라로 변한 한 여자의 시신이 발견되었다고 기록했다.

전략 03-04

전략 적용 연습

본서 p. 61

01 X, to be → are
02 X, to give → giving 또는 they give
03 O
04 X, like → likely
05 X, entrance → entering 또는 they enter
06 X, Because → Because of
07 O

08 ②	09 ①	10 ③
11 ③	12 ④	13 ③
14 ②	15 ③	

01 정답 **X, to be → are**

해설 명사 뒤에 불완전한 문장의 'S + V'가 나온 경우, 목적격 관계대명사가 생략되어 명사를 수식하는 구조임을 파악해야 한다. 즉, 목적어가 없어 불완전한 문장인 we now throw away가 주어인 복수 명사 Many things를 수식하는 구조로, 주어에 대한 본동사가 없다. 따라서 to be를 복수 동사 are로 고쳐야 한다.

해석 우리가 지금은 버리는 많은 것들이 가치 있는 자원이다.

02 정답 **X, to give → giving 또는 they give**

해설 접속사(When) 뒤에는 'S + V' 또는 분사구문(RVing/p.p./형용사)이 나올 수 있고, to 부정사는 나올 수가 없다. 따라서 to give를 giving이나 they give로 고쳐야 한다. 참고로, when은 접속사, 관계부사, 의문사로 쓰이는데, 의문사일 경우 '의문사 + to 부정사' 형태로 명사구 역할을 할 수 있다.

해석 수혈을 할 때, 의사들은 각별히 조심해야 한다.

03 정답 **O**

해설 주어는 One more thing이고 본동사는 is이며 주격 보어는 to join인 문장 구조이다. 과거형과 과거분사형 모두 Ved 형태인 타동사 devote 뒤에 목적어가 없는 것으로 보아, 여기서 과거분사이며 분사구 devoted to mathematics가 명사 a club을 수식하고 있다. 또한 동아리가 '전념시키는' 것이 아니라 '전념하는' 것이므로 수동의 과거분사 devoted가 쓰인 것은 적절하다. 참고로, do의 목적어가 없는 것으로 보아, One more thing과 you 사이에는 목적격 관계대명사가 생략되어 있으며 관계사절이 바로 앞의 명사를 수식하고 있는 구조이다.

해석 한 가지 더 해야 할 일은 수학에 전념하는 동아리에 가입하는 것이다.

04 정답 **X, like → likely**

해설 전명구(in temperature)를 괄호 치면, 주어는 The sudden drop이고 본동사는 is이며 주격 보어는 형용사구 due to ~ front인 완전한 문장 구조이다. 따라서 동사(또는 전치사/명사)인 like는 올 수 없으며, 문장 성분 중 하나를 수식하는 수식어(구)가 오는 것이 적절하다. 따라서 문맥상 '한랭 전선이 도착했기 때문일 가능성이 높다'라는 의미가 자연스러우므로 동사 like를 형용사 due를 수식하는 부사 likely로 고쳐야 한다.

해석 갑자기 기온이 떨어진 것은 한랭 전선이 도착했기 때문일 가능성이 높다.

05 정답 **X, entrance → entering 또는 they enter**

해설 접속사(before) 뒤에는 'S + V' 또는 분사구문(RVing/p.p./형용사)이 나오는데, 여기서는 명사 entrance와 명사구 restricted archaeological sites가 연달아 나와 잘못된 문장 구조가 되었다. 따라서 문맥상 '여행자들이 제한된 고고학 유적지에 들어가기 전에'라는 의미가 자연스러우므로 entrance를 능동의 현재분사 entering 또는 문장을 이루는 they enter로 고쳐야 한다. 만약 restricted를 동사의 과거형으로 보고 완전한 구조의 문장이라고 생각할 수 있으나, 문맥상 '입장이 고고학 유적지를 제한하기 전에'라는 어색한 의미가 되므로 적절치 않다.

해석 고대 유적지 탐험에 관심이 있는 여행자들은 제한된 고고학 유적지에 들어가기 전에 반드시 적절한 허가를 받아야 한다.

06 정답 X, Because → Because of

해설 명사 뒤에 불완전한 문장의 'S + V'가 나온 경우, 목적격 관계대명사가 생략되어 명사를 수식하는 구조임을 파악해야 한다. 즉, 목적어가 없어 불완전한 문장인 scientists do in Greenland가 명사 the work를 수식하는 구조로, 명사 앞에는 접속사가 아닌 전치사가 와야 한다. 따라서 접속사 Because를 전치사 Because of로 고쳐야 한다.

해석 과학자들이 그린란드에서 하는 연구 때문에, 전 세계 사람들이 날씨와 환경에 대해 더 많은 것을 배우고 있다.

07 정답 O

해설 부정대명사 everything 뒤에 touched의 목적어가 없는 불완전한 문장이 뒤따르고 있고, 바로 동사 turned가 나오고 있다. 즉, 문장의 주어는 everything이고, 본동사는 turned이며, everything과 she 사이에 목적격 관계대명사 that이 생략된 관계사절이 바로 앞의 명사를 수식하는 구조이다. 따라서 문맥상 앞에 온 과거시제의 문장과 같은 시기의 일이며, 모든 것이 '변하는' 것이므로 과거시제의 능동태 turned는 적절하게 쓰였다.

해석 바깥에서 그녀는 작은 화원을 돌보곤 했는데, 그것은 이웃들의 부러움을 샀다. 엄마와 함께하면, 그녀가 만지는 모든 것이 금으로 변했다.

08 정답 ②

해설 빈칸은 접속사 또는 전치사인 than 뒤에 오며 부사 originally의 수식을 받는 자리로, 선택지 중 빈칸에 올 수 있는 것은 분사인 expecting 또는 expected이다. 문맥상 분사의 의미상 주어인 The budget이 '예상하는' 것이 아니라 '예상되는' 것이므로 빈칸에는 수동의 과거분사 expected가 와야 한다. 참고로, 명사 expectations는 부사의 수식을 직접 받을 수 없고, 문맥상 '예산이 예상되는' 것이지 '우리가 예상되는' 것이 아니므로 we are expected도 적절치 않다.

해석 예산이 원래 예상했던 것보다 약 25% 더 높다.

09 정답 ①

해설 빈칸은 전치사 for의 목적어 자리이므로, 명사 형태(명사, 명사구, 명사절, 동명사구) 중 하나인 명사 success가 와야 한다. 참고로, to 부정사는 명사처럼 쓰일 때 문장의 주어, 목적어, 보어 자리에 올 수 있지만, 전치사의 목적어 자리에는 올 수 없다.

해석 끈기와 회복력은 어려움을 성공적으로 극복하는 데 필요한 핵심 자질이다.

10 정답 ③

해설 명사 뒤에 불완전한 문장의 'S + V'가 나온 경우, 목적격 관계대명사가 생략되어 명사를 수식하는 구조임을 파악해야 한다. 즉, faced의 목적어가 없어 불완전한 문장인 we faced ~ society가 명사 the major problems를 수식하는 구조로, 빈칸은 문장의 주어인 One of the major problems와 전치사구 through our patient efforts 사이의 본동사 자리이다. 진짜 주어가 단수 명사인 One이고 주요 문제 중 하나가 '해결되는' 것이므로 빈칸에는 단수 동사이며 수동태인 was solved가 와야 한다.

해석 우리가 개인으로서 그리고 한 사회로서 직면한 주요 문제 중 하나가 우리의 인내심 있는 노력으로 해결되었다.

11 정답 ③

해설 빈칸은 소유격 teacher's의 한정을 받으며 문장의 주어 역할을 하는 자리이므로 명사인 explanation이 와야 한다.

해석 과학적 개념에 대한 선생님의 설명은 명확하고 간결해서 학생들이 이해하기 쉬웠다.

12 정답 ④

해설 빈칸은 수동태의 be동사(is)와 p.p.(shown) 사이에서 동사를 수식하는 부사 자리이다. 문맥상으로도 '흥미롭게 드러난다'라는 자연스러운 의미가 되므로 빈칸에는 부사 interestingly가 와야 한다.

해석 극 중 인물들의 다양한 욕구와 동기를 통해 인간 본성의 복잡성이 흥미롭게 드러난다.

13 정답 ③

해설 전명구(for personal growth / for long-term fulfillment / in every aspect ~ development)를 괄호 치면, 본동사 is와 주격 보어 critical이 남는다. 따라서 빈칸은 형용사 Continuous의 수식을 받으며 문장의 주어 역할을 하는 자리이므로 명사인 improvement가 와야 한다.

해석 개인 성장을 위한 지속적인 개선은 삶의 모든 측면과 경력 개발에서 장기적인 성취를 이루는 데 매우 중요하다.

14 정답 ②

해설 Although가 이끄는 부사절에 주어 the camping gear와 본동사 is가 있으므로 빈칸을 포함한 selected는 주어를 수식하는 수식어(구/절)이다. 빈칸 뒤에 동사 selected만 있고 목적어가 없는 것으로 보아, 문맥상 '당신이 선택한'이라는 의미의 목적격 관계대명사절이 명사를 수식하는 구조인 the camping gear (that) you selected가 되는 것이 적절하다. 따라서 that이 생략된 목적격 관계대명사절의 주어 자리인 빈칸에는 대명사 you가 와야 한다.

해석 선택하신 캠핑 장비가 배낭여행용으로는 무겁지만, 무게가 가볍고 장거리 하이킹에 적합한 대안 제품도 가지고 있습니다.

15 정답 ③

해설 빈칸 뒤에 동사 means와 means의 목적어 refusing, persisting, maintaining이 and로 병렬 연결되어 있는 것으로 보아, 빈칸을 포함한 showing 부분이 문장의 주어이다. 따라서 주어 자리에 온 동명사 showing은 타동사의 성질을 가지고 있어 명사 형태의 목적어를 취할 수 있으므로 빈칸에는 명사인 perseverance가 와야 한다. 참고로, 동명사 주어는 단수 취급하므로 단수 동사 means가 쓰였다.

해석 난관에 부딪혔을 때, 인내심을 발휘한다는 것은 포기하지 않고 노력을 지속하며 좌절에도 불구하고 긍정적인 태도를 유지하는 것을 의미한다.

전략 05

전략 적용 연습

본서 p. 64

01 X, were → was
02 X, prevents → prevent
03 O
04 X, is → are
05 O
06 O
07 X, often work → often works
08 X, relies → rely
09 X, make → makes

10 ②	11 ①	12 ④
13 ②	14 ④	15 ④

01 정답 X, were → was

해설 관계사절(I had to do)을 괄호 치면, 문장의 주어는 The amount of work이다. '~의 양'이라는 뜻의 the amount of 뒤에는 '단수 명사 + 단수 동사'가 쓰이므로 동사 were를 was로 고쳐야 한다. 참고로, do의 목적어가 없는 것으로 보아, work와 I 사이에는 목적격 관계대명사가 생략되어 있으며 관계사절이 바로 앞의 명사를 수식하고 있는 구조이다.

해석 내가 해야 하는 일의 양은 나에겐 너무 많았다.

02 정답 X, prevents → prevent

해설 전명구(on pesticide use)를 괄호 치면, 문장의 주어는 복수 명사 Government controls이다. 따라서 동사는 이에 수일치한 복수 동사가 되어야 하므로 prevents를 prevent로 고쳐야 한다.

해석 살충제 사용에 대한 정부의 규제는 이러한 자연재해를 막아 준다.

03 정답 O

해설 전명구(on the sheer ~ mountain)를 괄호 치면, 문장의 주어는 복수 명사 The climbers이다. 따라서 이에 수일치한 복수 동사 need는 적절하게 쓰였다.

해석 산의 깎아지른 듯한 지형에 있는 등산객들은 구조되어야 한다.

04 정답 X, is → are

해설 At the next stage in the food chain이라는 장소 부사구가 문두에 와서 주어와 동사가 도치된 구문으로, 문장의 주어는 복수 명사 the animals이다. 따라서 동사는 이에 수일치한 복수 동사가 되어야 하므로 is를 are로 고쳐야 한다.

해석 먹이사슬의 다음 단계에는 초식동물을 잡아먹는 동물들이 있다.

05 정답 O

해설 to 부정사구(to conserve energy)를 괄호 치면, 문장의 주어는 복수 명사 Our efforts이다. 따라서 이에 수일치한 복수 동사 lead는 적절하게 쓰였다. 참고로, 여기서 lead는 'lead + O + to RV' 형태의 5형식 동사로 쓰였다.

해석 에너지를 절약하려는 우리의 노력이 회사가 새로운 지속 가능한 상품을 만들게 한다.

06 정답 O

해설 문장의 주어는 The number of children이고, 이를 현재분사구 attending school이 수식하고 있다. 따라서 '~의 수'라는 뜻의 the number of 뒤에는 '복수 명사 + 단수 동사'가 쓰이므로 단수 동사 has는 적절하게 쓰였다.

해석 지난 반세기 동안 학교에 다니는 아동의 수가 두 배 이상 증가했다.

07 정답 X, often work → often works

해설 동격의 that절(that someone ~ villagers)을 괄호 치면, 문장의 주어는 The fact이다. 따라서 동사는 단수 주어에 수일치하여 단수 동사가 되어야 하므로 often work를 often works로 고쳐야 한다.

해석 누군가가 가난한 마을 주민들에게 도움을 줄 만큼 충분한 관심을 보인다는 사실은 종종 기적을 일으킨다.

08 정답 X, relies → rely

해설 형용사구(Similar to beetles, ~ protection)와 전명구(despite their ~ shape)를 괄호 치면, 문장의 주어는 복수 명사 cuckoo bees이다. 따라서 동사는 이에 수일치한 복수 동사가 되어야 하므로 relies를 rely로 고쳐야 한다.

해석 딱딱한 날개 표피로 몸을 보호하는 딱정벌레와 마찬가지로, 왜알락꽃벌은 작은 몸집에도 불구하고 속임수에 의존해 번식한다.

09 정답 X, make → makes

해설 주절의 주어 자리에 '명사 of 명사' 형태인 the process of cleaning your house가 왔는데, 이를 해석해 보면 '집을 청소하는 과정'이 되고 여기서 진짜 주어는 단수 명사인 the process라는 것을 알 수 있다. 따라서 동사는 이에 수일치하여 단수 동사가 되어야 하므로 make를 makes로 고쳐야 한다.

해석 집 청소의 목적은 집을 더 깨끗하게 만드는 것이지만, 실제로 청소 과정 자체가 상태를 더 악화시키기도 한다.

10 정답 ②

해설 과거분사구(conducted by experienced experts)를 괄호 치면, 문장의 주어 The project와 to 부정사구 to progress smoothly만 있으므로 빈칸은 동사 자리이다. 따라서 빈칸에는 단수 주어에 수일치한 단수 동사 continues가 와야 한다.

해석 숙련된 전문가들이 진행하는 프로젝트가 계속해서 순조롭게 진행되어 고객 만족을 보장한다.

11 정답 ①

해설 뒤에 동사 study가 있는 것으로 보아, 빈칸을 포함한 doctors가 문장의 주어이다. 빈칸 뒤에 '복수 명사 + 복수 동사'의 구조가 왔고, 문맥상 '많은 의사들이 공부하는' 것이므로 빈칸에는 '많은'이라는 뜻의 A number of가 와야 한다.

해석 많은 의사들이 의학계에서의 모든 최신 발전에 뒤처지지 않기 위해서 열심히 공부한다.

12 정답 ④

해설 관계사절(who live ~ world)을 괄호 치면, 빈칸은 문장의 주어 Many people과 주격 보어 likely 사이의 동사 자리이다. 따라서 빈칸에는 복수 주어에 수일치한 복수 동사 are가 와야 한다.

해석 이쪽 지역에 살고 있는 많은 사람들은 추운 날씨가 시작되면서 다시 걱정하고 있을 것이다.

13 정답 ②

해설 문두에 Only를 포함한 부사구 Only recently가 나와 주어와 동사가 도치된 문장 구조이다. 주어 electric vehicles 뒤에 동사 become이 있는 것으로 보아, 빈칸은 조동사 자리이다. 도치 구문에서 주어와의 수일치는 조동사/be동사에 적용하는데, 선택지 중 복수 주어에 수일치한 조동사는 have밖에 없다. 따라서 빈칸에는 과거분사(p.p.) become과 함께 현재완료시제를 완성하는 have가 와야 한다. 참고로, become은 현재형과 과거분사형이 동일한 동사이며, 부사 recently는 과거시제 혹은 현재완료시제와 주로 함께 쓰인다.

해석 최근에서야 부분적이지만 정부의 장려책 덕분에 전기 자동차가 휘발유 자동차에 대한 실용적인 대안이 되었다.

14 정답 ④

해설 전명구(in the United States / from the map)와 부사(just), 부사절(as far as ~ concerned)을 괄호 치면, 문장의 주어인 명사구 as many as two hundred towns만 있으므로 빈칸은 동사 자리이다. 따라서 빈칸에는 복수 주어에 수일치한 복수 동사 disappear가 와야 한다.

해석 우정사업본부에 따르면, 매년 미국에서는 200개에 달하는 마을이 지도에서 사라지고 있다.

15 정답 ④

해설 빈칸은 a 'technology shelf'를 선행사로 받아 '전치사 + 관계대명사' 형태인 on which가 이끄는 관계사절 내 동사 자리이다. 명사 possible technical solutions가 관계사절(that other teams ~ future)의 수식을 받아 주어가 길어져서 주어와 동사가 도치된 구문으로, 주어인 가능한 기술적 해결책들이 '놓여 있는' 것이므로 수동태가 적절하다. 따라서 빈칸에는 복수 주어에 수일치하고 수동태인 were placed가 와야 한다.

해석 한 회사는 '기술 선반'이라는 것을 개발했는데, 그 위에는 다른 팀이 향후 사용할지도 모르는 가능한 기술적 해결책들이 놓여 있었다.

전략 06

전략 적용 연습

본서 p. 67

01 X, was → were
02 O
03 X, are → is
04 X, worsen → worsens
05 X, was → were
06 X, are → is
07 O
08 X, are → is
09 ② 10 ② 11 ④
12 ④ 13 ③ 14 ④

01 정답 X, was → were

해설 '부분명사(all) + of + 전체명사'가 주어로 오는 경우 of 뒤의 명사에 동사의 수를 일치시키는데, 복수 명사인 the questions가 나왔으므로 이에 수일치하여 단수 동사 was를 복수 동사 were로 고쳐야 한다.

해석 나는 그 시험의 모든 문제가 맞았다고 확신했다.

02 정답 O

해설 문장의 주어가 동명사구 Watching fireflies이므로 이에 단수로 수일치한 단수 동사 is는 적절하다.

해석 반딧불을 보는 것은 여름밤의 가장 멋진 일 중 하나이다.

03 정답 X, are → is

해설 '~ 중 하나'라는 뜻의 'one of 명사'가 주어로 오는 경우, one of 뒤에는 '복수 명사 + 단수 동사'가 온다. 따라서 문장의 본동사 자리에 온 복수 동사 are를 단수 동사 is로 고쳐야 한다. 참고로, the reasons와 some birds 사이에는 관계부사 why가 생략되었는데, '주어 + 자동사'의 완전한 구조를 갖춘 관계부사절이 the reasons를 수식하고 있다.

해석 일부 새들이 이동하는 이유 중 하나는 따뜻한 기후에서 먹이를 찾기 위해서이다.

04 정답 X, worsen → worsens

해설 문장의 주어가 동명사구 Regretting all your petty mistakes이다. 동명사구 주어는 단수 취급하므로 복수 동사 worsen을 단수 동사 worsens로 고쳐야 한다.

해석 당신의 모든 사소한 실수를 후회하는 것은 당신이 현재 직면한 상황을 악화시킬 뿐이다.

05 정답 X, was → were

해설 '부분명사(portion) + of + 전체명사'가 주어로 오는 경우 of 뒤의 명사에 동사의 수를 일치시키는데, 복수 명사인 their patients가 나왔으므로 이에 수일치하여 단수 동사 was를 복수 동사 were로 고쳐야 한다.

해석 병원에 입원한 그들의 환자 대부분은 기질성 질환이 없는 사람들이었다.

06 정답 X, are → is

해설 '부분명사(three-fourths) + of + 전체명사'가 주어로 오는 경우 of 뒤의 명사에 동사의 수를 일치시키는데, 불가산명사인 knowledge가 나왔으므로 이에 수일치하여 복수 동사 are를 단수 동사 is로 고쳐야 한다.

해석 학교에서 습득한 지식의 4분의 3 이상은 실제 상황에 적용할 수 있다.

07 정답 O

해설 '~가 있다'라는 뜻의 유도부사 'There + be동사' 구문에서 동사 다음에 나오는 명사, 즉 주어에 동사의 수를 일치시키는데, 복수 명사인 discussions가 나왔으므로 이에 수일치한 복수 동사 have는 적절하게 쓰였다.

해석 메이저리그(MLB)의 대변인 Pat Courtney는 이 문제에 대한 논의들이 있어 왔지만 아무런 진척이 없었다고 말했다.

08 정답 X, are → is

해설 문장의 주어가 what이 이끄는 명사절이다. 명사절 주어는 단수 취급하므로 복수 동사 are를 단수 동사 is로 고쳐야 한다.

해석 연구 결과에서 놀라운 점은 이전에는 알려지지 않았던 유전학과 행동 사이의 연관성을 제시한다는 것이다.

09 정답 ②

해설 빈칸은 주어와 목적어 사이의 동사 자리이다. 'A뿐만 아니라 B도'라는 뜻의 상관접속사 'B as well as A'가 주어로 오는 경우, 동사의 수는 B에 일치시킨다. 따라서 빈칸에는 B에 해당하는 복수 명사 Extensive search capabilities에 수일치한 복수 동사 distinguish가 와야 한다.

해석 사용자 친화적인 인터페이스뿐만 아니라 광범위한 검색 기능도 검색 엔진을 차별화한다.

10 정답 ②

해설 빈칸은 주어 That 명사절과 목적어 several customers 사이의 동사 자리이다. 명사절 주어는 단수 취급하며, 문맥상 '숨겨진 요금이 있다는 것이 여러 고객에게 속았다는 느낌을 주는 것'이므로 빈칸에는 능동태의 단수 동사 has left가 와야 한다. 참고로, 여기서 has left는 'leave + O + RVing' 형태의 5형식 동사로 쓰였다.

해석 월별 전화 요금 청구서에 숨겨진 요금이 있다는 것은 여러 고객이 속았다는 느낌이 들게 만들었다.

11 정답 ④

해설 빈칸은 주어에 대해 보충 설명하는 주격 보어 자리로, 문맥상 뒤에 온 복수 명사 the greatest composers와 함께 'Piccolo Paganini는 19세기의 위대한 작곡가들 중 한 명'이라는 의미가 자연스러우므로 빈칸에는 '~ 중 하나'라는 뜻의 one of가 와야 한다. 참고로, an amount of 뒤에는 단수 명사가 온다.

해석 이탈리아의 제노바에서 태어난 Piccolo Paganini는 19세기의 위대한 작곡가들 중 한 명이었다.

12 정답 ④

해설 빈칸은 since 부사절 내 주어 자리이다. 빈칸 뒤가 'of + 복수 명사(peace offers) + 단수 동사(was)'의 구조이므로 either 또는 neither가 올 수 있는데, 빈칸을 수식하는 of 전치사구의 내용과 주절과 부사절의 관계를 고려할 때 문맥상 '외교관들의 평화 제안 중 어느 것도 상대방이 받아들이지 않아 협상이 결렬되었다'라는 의미가 되어야 자연스러우므로 빈칸에는 neither가 와야 한다. 참고로, 부분명사 most는 of 뒤에 오는 전체명사에 동사의 수를 일치시키는데, 여기서 빈칸 뒤에 오는 복수 명사 peace offers와 단수 동사 was의 수일치가 맞지 않고, both는 'both of + 복수 명사 + 복수 동사'의 구조로 쓰이므로 적절치 않다.

해석 외교관들의 평화 제안 중 어느 것도 상대방이 받아들이지 않아 협상이 결렬되었다.

13 정답 ③

해설 빈칸은 that 명사절 내 동사 자리이다. that절의 주어가 동명사구 listening to ~ surgery이므로 빈칸에는 단수로 수일치한 helps가 와야 한다. 참고로, 여기서 helps는 'help + O + RV' 형태의 5형식 동사로 쓰였다.

해석 최근 한 연구에 따르면 수술 전후로 음악을 듣는 것은 환자가 관련된 스트레스에 대처하는 데 도움이 된다고 한다.

14 정답 ④

해설 빈칸은 '~가 있다'라는 뜻의 유도부사 'There + be동사' 구문의 주어 자리이다. 동사가 복수 are인 것으로 보아, 주어 자리에 온 '부분명사(30 percent) + of + 전체명사'의 전체명사는 복수가 되어야 한다. 따라서 빈칸에는 복수 동사에 수일치한 복수 명사 tasks가 와야 한다.

해석 많은 공장에서 자동화를 빠르게 도입하고 있지만 여전히 30%의 작업은 수작업으로 이루어지고 있다.

전략 07

전략 적용 연습

본서 p. 70

01 X, was suddenly occurred → suddenly occurred
02 X, excited → exciting
03 X, encouraged → was encouraged
04 X, should solve → should be solved
05 O
06 O
07 X, pleased → were pleased
08 X, was used → was using 또는 used
09 X, were carried → carried
10 ② 11 ③ 12 ②
13 ③ 14 ② 15 ②

01 정답 **X, was suddenly occurred → suddenly occurred**

해설 occur는 완전자동사이므로 수동태로 쓸 수 없다. 따라서 수동태 was suddenly occurred를 능동태 suddenly occurred로 고쳐야 한다.

해석 내가 제주도에 온 후에 그 멋진 생각이 갑자기 떠올랐다.

02 정답 **X, excited → exciting**

해설 excite는 '흥미를 일으키다[흥분시키다]'라는 뜻의 감정타동사로, 주어인 소설(The novel)이 '흥미를 느끼는' 것이 아니라 '흥미를 일으키는' 것이므로 수동의 과거분사 excited를 능동의 현재분사 exciting으로 고쳐야 한다. 참고로, '너무 ~해서 ~하다'라는 뜻의 'so + 형/부 + that' 구문이 쓰였다.

해석 그 소설이 너무 재밌어서 나는 시간 가는 줄 몰랐고 버스를 놓쳤다.

03 정답 **X, encouraged → was encouraged**

해설 완전타동사 encourage 뒤에 목적어가 없고 to 부정사가 바로 온 것으로 보아, to 부정사를 목적격 보어로 취하는 5형식 문장의 수동태인 것을 알 수 있다. 문맥상 주어인 모두(Everyone)가 자신의 채소를 기르도록 '장려된' 것이므로 능동태 encouraged를 수동태 was encouraged로 고쳐야 한다.

해석 그 당시에는 모두가 자신의 채소를 키우도록 장려되었다.

04 정답 **X, should solve → should be solved**

해설 완전타동사 solve 뒤에 목적어가 없고, 문맥상 주어인 교육 문제(Educational problems)가 '해결하는' 것이 아니라 '해결되는' 것이므로 능동태 should solve를 수동태 should be solved로 고쳐야 한다.

해석 교육 문제는 사회 구성원들의 합의에 바탕을 두고 해결되어야 한다.

05 정답 **O**

해설 the way를 수식하는 종속절의 주어는 amnesia이고 기억상실증이 '묘사되는' 것이므로 수동태 is usually portrayed로 쓰인 것은 적절하다. 참고로, 방법 명사 the way는 관계부사 how와 함께 쓸 수 없어 둘 중 하나를 생략하는데, 여기서는 관계부사가 생략된 완전한 문장이 와서 the way를 수식하고 있다.

해석 이러한 믿음은 기억상실증이 영화, 텔레비전 및 문학에서 일반적으로 묘사되는 방식을 반영하는 것일 수도 있다.

06 정답 **O**

해설 문장의 주어는 Advertising dollars이고, 뒤에 목적어인 the migration trail이 있다. 문맥상 주어인 광고비가 이동하는 경로를 '따라가는' 것이므로 능동태 have been following으로 쓰인 것은 적절하다.

해석 광고비는 이러한 새로운 기술로 이동하는 경로를 단순히 따라가고 있다.

07 정답 **X, pleased → were pleased**

해설 please는 '기쁘게 하다'라는 뜻의 감정타동사로, 문맥상 주어인 학생들(The students)이 무언가를 보고 '기쁘게 하는' 것이 아니라 '기쁜' 것이므로 능동태 pleased를 수동태 were pleased로 고쳐야 한다.

해석 학생들은 신비한 검은색 물질이 종이 위에 문질러졌을 때 어둡고 건조한 선 하나가 나타나는 것을 보고 기뻐했다.

08 정답 **X, was used → was using 또는 used**

해설 a driver를 선행사로 받는 주격 관계대명사 who가 이끄는 관계사절 내 동사인데, 뒤에 목적어 his phone이 있고 문맥상 운전자가 전화기를 '사용되는' 것이 아니라 '사용하는' 것이므로 수동태 was used를 능동태 was using 또는 used로 고쳐야 한다. 참고로, 사건이 일어났을 때 진행되고 있던 일(운전자의 전화기 사용)을 묘사하고 있으므로 과거진행시제가 조금 더 자연스럽다.

해석 최근, 나는 전화기를 사용하던 한 운전자가 주의가 산만해져서 중앙선을 침범했을 때 정면충돌을 간신히 피했었다.

09 정답 **X, were carried → carried**

해설 시간 명사 that day in May를 선행사로 받는 관계부사 when이 이끄는 관계사절 내 동사인데, 주어는 my little feet이고 뒤에 목적어 me가 있다. 문맥상 내 작은 발이 나를 '데려가진' 것이 아니라 '데려가는' 것이므로 수동태 were carried를 능동태 carried로 고쳐야 한다.

해석 나는 나의 작은 발로 계단을 올라가 자동차 경주 경기장의 관중석으로 들어갔던 5월의 어느 날 가졌던 아주 멋진 느낌을 아직도 기억한다.

10 정답 ②

해설 빈칸은 문장의 동사 자리로, 뒤에 전치사 as가 바로 온 것으로 보아 '~으로 알려지다'라는 뜻의 'be known as'가 쓰인 것을 알 수 있다. 따라서 주어인 그녀(She)가 정치 만화가로 '알려진' 것이므로 빈칸에는 수동태인 has been known이 와야 한다.

해석 그녀는 경력 내내 주로 정치 만화가로 알려져 왔다.

11 정답 ③

해설 빈칸은 주어 The Aswan High Dam과 목적어 Egypt 사이의 동사 자리로, 문맥상 Aswan High 댐이 이집트를 '보호하는' 것이므로 능동태인 has protected가 와야 한다.

해석 Aswan High 댐은 이집트를 주변 국가의 기근으로부터 보호해 왔다.

12 정답 ②

해설 빈칸은 that 명사절 내 동사 자리로, 뒤에 형용사 complete가 온 문장 구조이다. 5형식 동사 consider는 수동태가 되어도 뒤에 명사 또는 형용사를 동반할 수 있으며, 주어인 법적 거래가 '간주하는' 것이 아니라 '간주되는' 것이므로 빈칸에는 수동태인 could not be considered가 와야 한다.

해석 그 변호사는 고객에게 계약서에 서명하지 않으면 법적 거래는 완료된 것으로 간주될 수 없다고 설명했다.

13 정답 ③

해설 빈칸은 recommendations를 선행사로 받는 주격 관계대명사 that이 이끄는 관계사절의 동사 자리이다. 뒤에 목적어 없이 바로 전치사구 by environmentalists가 이어지고 있고 권고사항이 환경운동가들에 의해 '제시하는' 것이 아니라 '제시되는' 것이므로 빈칸에는 수동태인 were suggested가 와야 한다.

해석 다음은 환경운동가들이 일일 탄소발자국을 줄이기 위해 제시한 권고사항 목록이다.

14 정답 ②

해설 빈칸은 주어 crime rates와 보어 stable 사이의 동사 자리로, 복수 주어에 수일치해야 하며 '~한 상태로 남아 있다'라는 뜻의 2형식 불완전자동사 remain은 수동태로 쓸 수 없으므로 빈칸에는 능동태인 have remained가 와야 한다.

해석 철저한 데이터 분석을 기반으로 한 보고서에 따르면, 지난 10년 간 도시 지역의 범죄율은 안정적으로 유지되고 있다.

15 정답 ②

해설 과거분사구(overwhelmed by ~ success), 부사(commonly), 전명구(by the constant ~ ideals)를 괄호 치면, 빈칸은 2형식 동사 are의 보어 자리 또는 are와 함께 동사를 완성하는 자리이다. 문맥상 문장의 주어인 십 대들(Teenagers)이 끊임없는 압력에 의해 '우울하게 하는' 것이 아니라 '우울한' 것이므로 빈칸에는 수동의 과거분사 depressed가 와야 한다.

해석 비현실적인 성공 기준에 압도된 십 대들은 흔히 달성할 수 없는 이상에 순응하라는 끊임없는 압력에 우울해한다.

전략 08

전략 적용 연습

본서 p. 73

01 X, were turned → turned
02 X, be dealt → be dealt with
03 X, was reminded → was reminded of
04 O
05 O
06 X, was offering → was offered
07 X, was required → were required
08 O
09 X, review and approve → are reviewed and approved
10 O
11 ② 12 ④ 13 ①
14 ④ 15 ③ 16 ①

01 정답 X, were turned → turned

해설 문장의 주어는 The traffic lights이고 동사 뒤에 형용사 green이 와 있다. 수일치를 따지면 복수 주어에 수일치한 were는 적절한 것처럼 보이나, turn은 '(~한 상태로) 변하다'라는 뜻일 때 형용사 또는 명사를 주격 보어로 취하는 2형식 불완전자동사이므로 수동태로 쓸 수 없다. 또한 교통 신호등이 '변해지는' 것이 아니라 '변하는' 것이므로 수동태 were turned를 능동태 turned로 고쳐야 한다.

해석 교통 신호등이 파란색으로 바뀌어 나는 출발했다.

02 정답 X, be dealt → be dealt with

해설 조동사 must 뒤 동사원형 자리이므로 수일치는 안 따져도 된다. 능·수동의 경우, 문장의 주어는 The issue of climate change이고 동사 뒤에 목적어 없이 전치사구로 이어지고 있어 수동태가 적절한 것으로 보이는데, 문맥상 주어인 기후 변화 문제가 '다뤄진다'라는 의미가 되도록 '~을 다루다'라는 뜻의 'deal with'가 수동태로 쓰이는 것이 자연스럽다. 따라서 '자동사 + 전치사' 타동사구의 수동태에서는 전치사를 생략해서는 안 되므로 be dealt를 be dealt with로 고쳐야 한다.

해석 기후 변화 문제는 즉각적인 조치와 세계적 협력을 통해 다뤄져야 한다.

03 정답 X, was reminded → was reminded of

해설 문장의 주어는 I이고 동사 뒤에 명사구 precious memories ~ time이 와 있다. 수일치를 따지면 1인칭 단수 주어에 수일치한 was는 적절한 것으로 보이고, 문맥상 주어인 나에게 '떠올려진' 것이므로 수동태도 적절하다. 하지만 수동태 뒤에 명사구가 있는 것으로 보아, 인지 동사 remind가 두 개의 명사 목적어를 취하는 'remind A of B' 구문의 수동태인 'A be reminded of B' 구조여야 하므로 was reminded를 was reminded of로 고쳐야 한다. 참고로, 동사 remind는 'remind + O + to RV'와 'remind + O + that절' 구문으로도 쓰일 수 있는데, 이때의 수동태는 'be reminded to RV/that절'의 구조를 취한다.

해석 나는 옛 사진을 보며 소중한 추억과 시간의 흐름이 떠올랐다.

04 정답 O

해설 조동사 should 뒤 동사원형 자리이므로 수일치는 안 따져도 된다. 능·수동의 경우, 문장의 주어인 문제들(Problems)이 '검토하는' 것이 아니라 '검토되는' 것이므로 '자동사 + 전치사' 타동사구 look at의 수동태인 be looked at으로 쓰인 것은 적절하다.

해석 사회 문제는 효과적인 해결책을 찾기 위해 다양한 관점에서 검토되어야 한다.

05 정답 O

해설 전명구(in the neighborhood)를 괄호 치면, 문장의 주어는 The renovated park이고 동사 뒤에 명사구 "Green Haven Park"가 와 있다. 수일치를 따지면 단수 주어에 수일치한 is는 적절한 것으로 보이고, 문맥상 주어인 새롭게 단장한 공원이 "Green Haven 공원"으로 '명명된' 것이므로 수동태도 적절하다. 참고로, name은 5형식 동사로, 수동태가 되어도 뒤에 명사가 올 수 있음에 유의한다.

해석 새롭게 단장한 근처 공원은 자연의 아름다움을 기념하기 위해 "Green Haven 공원"으로 명명되었다.

06 정답 X, was offering → was offered

해설 문장의 주어는 The talented musician이고 동사 뒤에 명사구 a recording contract가 와 있다. 수일치를 따지면 단수 주어에 수일치한 was는 적절한 것처럼 보이나, 문맥상 주어인 그 재능 있는 음악가가 음반 계약을 '제안하는' 것이 아니라 '제안받는' 것이므로 수동태가 적절하다. 따라서 능동태 was offering을 수동태 was offered로 고쳐야 한다. 참고로, offer는 4형식 동사로, 수동태가 되어도 뒤에 명사가 올 수 있음에 유의한다.

해석 그 재능 있는 음악가는 대회에서 심사위원들에게 깊은 인상을 남긴 후 음반 계약을 제안받았다.

07 정답 X, was required → were required

해설 관계사절(who missed the deadline)을 괄호 치면, 문장의 주어는 The students이고 동사 뒤에 명사(구)가 아닌 to부정사가 와 있다. 수일치를 따지면 복수 주어에 수일치한 복수 동사여야 하며, 문맥상 주어인 학생들이 과제를 제출하도록 '요구되는' 것이므로 수동태가 적절하다. 따라서 단수의 was required를 복수의 were required로 고쳐야 한다. 참고로, require는 to부정사를 목적격 보어로 취하는 5형식 동사로, 수동태가 되면 뒤에 to부정사가 남는 구조가 된다.

해석 마감 기한을 놓친 학생들은 이번 주말까지 과제를 제출하도록 요구되었다.

08 정답 O

해설 전명구(from experts)를 괄호 치면, 문장의 주어는 child-rearing advice이고 동사 뒤에 목적어인 명사구 the nighttime ~ parent가 있다. 수일치를 따지면 단수 주어에 수일치한 has는 적절한 것으로 보이고, 문맥상 주어인 육아 조언이 밤 시간에 아이와 부모의 분리를 '권장한' 것이므로 능동태로도 적절하게 쓰였다.

해석 수십 년 동안, 전문가들의 육아 조언은 밤 시간에 아이를 부모로부터 분리하는 것을 권장해 왔다.

09 정답 X, review and approve → are reviewed and approved

해설 복수 명사 innovative blueprints를 선행사로 받는 주격 관계대명사 that이 이끄는 관계사절 내 동사 자리인데, 수일치를 따지면 복수인 선행사에 수일치한 review and approve는 적절한 것처럼 보이지만 타동사인 review and approve의 목적어가 뒤에 없고 문맥상 혁신적인 청사진이 '검토하고 승인하는' 것이 아니라 '검토되고 승인되는' 것이므로 수동태가 적절하다. 따라서 능동태 review and approve를 수동태 are reviewed and approved로 고쳐야 한다.

해석 현대식 건물을 설계하는 건축가들은 공사 시작 전에 검토되고 승인되는 혁신적인 청사진을 만든다.

10 정답 O

해설 전명구(with its ~ materials)를 괄호 치면, 문장의 주어는 The website이고 동사 뒤에 목적어인 명사구 valuable resources가 있다. 수일치를 따지면 단수 주어에 수일치한 provides는 적절한 것으로 보이고, 문맥상 주어인 그 웹사이트가 귀중한 자원을 '제공하는' 것이므로 능동태로도 적절하게 쓰였다.

해석 광범위한 교육 자료를 갖추고 있는 그 웹사이트는 학생들이 가정에서 학습 경험을 향상시킬 수 있는 귀중한 자원을 제공한다.

11 정답 ②

해설 빈칸은 단수 명사 a virus를 선행사로 받는 주격 관계대명사 that이 이끄는 관계사절 내 동사 자리인데, 뒤에 목적어가 없고 문맥상 바이러스가 '확인되는' 것이므로 빈칸에는 선행사에 단수로 수일치하며 수동태인 was identified가 와야 한다.

해석 중증급성호흡기증후군(SARS)은 2003년에 확인된 바이러스에 의해 발생한다.

12 정답 ④

해설 빈칸은 after가 이끄는 부사절 내 동사 자리인데, 뒤에 목적어가 없고 전치사구 by ~ motorist로 이어지고 있다. 문맥상 '~을 치다'라는 뜻의 'run over'가 수동태로 바뀐 'be run over' 구문으로, 의미상 주어인 Shimson이 주의가 산만한 운전자에게 '치였다'라는 의미가 자연스러우므로 빈칸에는 수동태인 was run over가 와야 한다.

해석 Shimson은 주의가 산만한 운전자에게 치여 불행히도 큰 부상을 입었다.

13 정답 ①

해설 빈칸은 단수 명사 too much work를 선행사로 받는 주격 관계대명사 that이 이끄는 관계사절 내 동사 자리인데, 뒤에 목

PART 2 문법

적어 my time and energy가 있고 문맥상 많은 업무가 나의 시간과 에너지를 '요구하는' 것이므로 빈칸에는 능동태인 demanded가 와야 한다.

해석 나는 나의 시간과 에너지를 지속적으로 요구하는 업무가 많다는 것을 깨닫게 되었다.

14 정답 ④

해설 빈칸은 조동사 can 뒤 동사원형 자리이며, 문장의 주어는 The *Iliad* and ~ Testaments이고 빈칸 뒤에 명사 myths가 있는 구조이다. 문맥상 'A를 B라고 부르다'라는 뜻의 'refer to A as B'가 수동태로 바뀐 'A be referred to as B' 구문으로, 주어인 〈Iliad〉, 〈Odyssey〉, 코란, 구약과 신약은 '신화라고 불릴 수 있다'라는 의미가 자연스러우므로 빈칸에는 be referred to as가 와야 한다.

해석 〈Iliad〉, 〈Odyssey〉, 코란, 구약과 신약은 모두 신화라고 불릴 수 있다.

15 정답 ③

해설 관계사절(that keeps us alive and active)을 괄호 치면, 빈칸은 문장의 주어인 명사구 The combustion of oxygen에 대한 동사 자리이다. 빈칸 뒤에 온 부사 out과 함께 타동사구(send out)를 이루며 명사 by-products를 목적어로 취하는 구조인데, 문맥상 '산소의 연소는 부산물을 내보낸다'라는 의미가 자연스러우므로 능동태가 적절하다. 따라서 빈칸에는 단수 주어에 수일치하며 능동태인 sends가 와야 한다.

해석 우리를 살아있게 하고 활동적이게 유지하는 산소의 연소는 활성 산소라고 불리는 부산물을 내보낸다.

16 정답 ①

해설 현재분사구(living in poverty)와 전명구(especially ~ countries)를 괄호 치면, 빈칸은 문장의 주어 Many children에 대한 동사 자리이다. 주어진 선택지로 보아, 분리·박탈의 동사 deprive가 오는 것을 알 수 있는데, 문맥상 빈칸 뒤에 온 명사구 proper ~ education과 연결하면 수많은 아이들이 적절한 영양, 의료, 교육을 '박탈하는' 것이 아니라 '박탈당하는' 것이므로 수동태가 적절하다. 또한 분리·박탈의 동사 deprive는 'deprive A of B' 구문으로 쓰이고, 수동태로 전환 시 'A be deprived of B'의 구조가 되므로 빈칸에는 복수 주어에 수일치하며 수동태인 are deprived of가 와야 한다.

해석 특히 개발도상국의 수많은 빈곤층 아이들은 적절한 영양, 의료, 교육을 받지 못하고 있다.

전략 09-10

전략 적용 연습

본서 p. 77

01 O
02 O
03 X, hasn't shown up → didn't show up
04 O
05 X, will be lying → am lying 또는 lie
06 X, Until → Since
07 X, is → will have been
08 X, will start → starts
09 X, has worked → had worked
10 X, will be → is
11 X, are broadcasting → were broadcasting

12 ②	13 ④	14 ①
15 ①	16 ③	17 ①

01 정답 O

해설 동사 wonder의 목적어 자리에 온 if는 명사절 접속사이며, 명사절이 미래 시점 부사구 by tonight와 함께 내용상 미래시제를 나타내므로 will finish의 쓰임은 적절하다. 참고로, if가 명사절 접속사일 땐, 시간·조건 부사절 내 현재시제가 미래시제를 대신하는 문법이 적용되지 않으며 내용상 시제를 따져야 한다.

해석 나는 그녀가 오늘 밤까지 그 일을 끝낼 수 있을지 궁금하다.

02 정답 O

해설 등위접속사 but 뒤 문장에서 since가 이끄는 절에 과거시제 started가 쓰여 '내가 일을 시작한 이후로'라는 의미를 나타내므로 주절에 현재완료시제인 have lived의 쓰임은 적절하다.

해석 나는 대만에서 태어났지만, 일을 시작한 이후로 한국에서 살고 있다.

03 정답 **X, hasn't shown up → didn't show up**

해설 명백한 과거시제를 나타내는 부사 yesterday가 있으므로, 과거시제를 써야 한다. 따라서 현재완료시제인 hasn't shown up을 과거시제인 didn't show up으로 고쳐야 한다.

해석 그가 어제 수업에 나타나지 않은 것은 매우 드문 일이었다.

04 정답 O

해설 내가 사무실을 청소하려고 했던 과거 시점(was)보다 누군가가 청소를 한 것이 더 이전이므로 과거완료시제 had already done의 쓰임은 적절하다.

해석 내가 사무실을 청소하려던 참이었는데, 누군가가 이미 청소해 놨다.

05 정답 X, will be lying → am lying 또는 lie

해설 주절의 시제가 미래시제(will think of)이고 종속절에 미래시제를 나타내는 부사구 on my next vacation이 있으므로 미래시제를 써야 하지만, when이 이끄는 시간 부사절에서는 현재시제가 미래시제를 대신한다. 따라서 will be lying을 현재시제의 am lying 또는 lie로 고쳐야 한다.

해석 나는 다음 휴가에 해변에 누워있을 때 당신을 생각할 것이다.

06 정답 X, Until → Since

해설 문장의 동사가 현재완료시제(have become)이므로 과거 시점 1920년과 함께 '1920년 이후로 현재까지 계속되어 온 일'을 나타낼 수 있는 전치사 since가 와야 한다. 따라서 '~까지'라는 뜻의 Until을 '~ 이래로'라는 뜻의 Since로 고쳐야 한다. 만약 until을 쓸 경우, '1920년까지 ~했다'라는 의미가 되므로 과거시제의 became이나 과거완료시제의 had become이 왔어야 했다.

해석 1920년 이래로, 여성들의 시합이 매우 중요해졌고, 인기가 있게 되었다.

07 정답 X, is → will have been

해설 미래 시점 부사구 by the end of next month가 있으며, 문맥상 과거의 어느 시점부터 미래 시점인 다음 달 말까지 몇 달 동안 베스트셀러 목록에 올라와 있게 되는 것이므로 과거부터 미래의 특정 시점까지 계속/완료될 때 쓰는 미래완료시제가 와야 한다. 따라서 현재시제 is를 미래완료시제 will have been으로 고쳐야 한다.

해석 이 책은 다음 달 말이면 몇 달 동안 베스트셀러 목록에 오르는 것이다.

08 정답 X, will start → starts

해설 주절의 시제가 미래시제(will be)이고 종속절에 미래시제를 나타내는 부사 tomorrow가 있으므로 미래시제를 써야 하지만, when이 이끄는 시간 부사절에서는 현재시제가 미래시제를 대신하므로 will start를 starts로 고쳐야 한다.

해석 내일 콘서트 투어가 시작될 때, 그 그룹의 팬들은 흥분할 것이다.

09 정답 X, has worked → had worked

해설 시간 부사절 'by the time + S + V(과거시제)'가 나오면 주절의 동사는 과거완료시제여야 하며, 문맥상 CEO가 된 과거 시점보다 더 이전부터 일을 시작해서 24년 넘게 일해 온 것이므로 현재완료시제인 has worked를 과거완료시제인 had worked로 고쳐야 한다.

해석 Clark 씨는 CEO가 됐을 때쯤에 24년 넘게 기술 업계에서 일했었다.

10 정답 X, will be → is

해설 until이 이끄는 시간 부사절에서는 현재시제가 미래시제를 대신하므로 will be를 is로 고쳐야 한다.

해석 브로콜리가 부드러워질 때까지 3~5분간 물에 넣고 끓이기만 하면 된다.

11 정답 X, are broadcasting → were broadcasting

해설 주절의 시제가 과거시제(was not transmitted)이므로, when이 이끄는 시간 부사절에서도 같은 시점을 나타내야 한다. 따라서 현재진행시제의 are broadcasting을 과거진행시제의 were broadcasting으로 고쳐야 한다.

해석 그들이 뉴스를 방송할 때 기술적인 문제로 인해 일부 정보가 전송되지 않았다.

12 정답 ②

해설 빈칸은 주어 he와 목적어 Asan 사이의 동사 자리로, 과거의 한 시점을 나타내는 시간 부사구 In the summer of 2001이 있으므로 빈칸에는 과거시제의 능동태인 visited가 와야 한다.

해석 2001년 여름에, 그는 주택 건축 프로젝트에 참가하기 위하여 한국에 있는 아산을 방문했다.

13 정답 ④

해설 빈칸은 주절의 주어 his coworkers와 목적어 their morning tasks and meetings 사이의 동사 자리로, 시간 부사절 'by the time + S + V(현재시제)'가 나오면 주절의 동사는 미래완료시제여야 하므로 빈칸에는 미래완료시제의 능동태인 will have already started가 와야 한다.

해석 그가 사무실에 도착할 때쯤이면, 동료들은 이미 그들의 아침 업무와 회의를 시작했을 것이다.

14 정답 ①

해설 빈칸은 주어 advances와 목적어 many positive changes 사이의 동사 자리로, 현재완료시제와 함께 쓰이는 시간 부사구 'for the last + 기간' 형태의 For the last fifty years가 있으므로, 빈칸에는 현재완료시제의 능동태인 have brought가 와야 한다.

해석 지난 50년 동안, 화학의 발전은 미국인의 생활 방식에 많은 긍정적인 변화를 가져왔다.

15 정답 ①

해설 빈칸은 '~ 이래로[~ 이후로]'라는 뜻의 시간 접속사 since가 이끄는 절 내에서 주어 stricter emission regulations에 대한 동사 자리이다. 주절이 현재완료시제 has improved이므로 과거시제의 동사가 와야 하며, 문맥상 '더 강력한 배기가스 규제가 시행된 이후'라는 수동의 의미가 자연스럽다. 따라서 빈칸에는 과거시제이면서 동시에 뒤에 온 과거분사 implemented와 함께 수동태 be p.p.를 완성하는 were가 와야 한다.

해석 이 도시의 대기질이 더 강력한 배기가스 규제가 시행된 이후 크게 개선되었다.

16 정답 ③

해설 빈칸은 that절의 주어 the prices of many items에 대한 동사 자리로, 뒤에 목적어 없이 부사와 전치사구 sharply in recent weeks로 이어지는 문장 구조이다. 문맥상 깨달은 과거 시점(realized)보다 가격이 오른 것이 더 이전이므로 빈칸에는 자동사 rise의 과거완료시제인 had risen이 와야 한다. 참고로, 진짜 주어가 복수 명사 the prices이므로 has는 수일치가 맞지 않고, raise는 완전타동사이므로 뒤에 목적어가 필요하다.

해석 어제 시장에서 쇼핑할 때 나는 최근 몇 주 동안 많은 품목들의 가격이 급격히 올랐다는 것을 깨달았다.

17 정답 ①

해설 빈칸은 '~하자마자'라는 뜻의 시간 접속사 as soon as가 이끄는 절 내에서 주어 she와 목적어 her housework 사이의 동사 자리이다. 주절이 미래시제 will be인 것으로 보아 부사절도 미래시제가 되어야 하지만, 시간 부사절에서는 현재시제가 미래시제를 대신하므로 빈칸에는 현재시제의 능동태인 finishes가 와야 한다. 참고로, 과거 동사 finished가 답이 되려면 주절의 동사가 미래시제인 will be가 아니라 과거시제 was가 돼야 한다.

해석 그녀는 집안일을 마치자마자 비즈니스 미팅에 참석하는 손님들을 위한 저녁 준비로 바쁠 것이다.

전략 11-12

전략 적용 연습

본서 p. 81

01 X, have been → had been
02 X, should prepare → should have prepared
03 O
04 O
05 X, studied → had studied
06 O
07 X, might not take place → might not have taken place
08 X, would have complained → would[will] complain
09 O
10 X, would graduate → would have graduated
11 X, should receive → should have received
12 ④ 13 ② 14 ②
15 ③ 16 ④

01 정답 X, have been → had been

해설 앞 문장은 과거의 일을 이야기하는 과거시제이고 뒤 문장이 그 과거 일과 연관된 바람을 나타내는 I wish 가정법 문장이므로 have been을 가정법 과거완료인 had been으로 고쳐야 한다.

해석 그 파티는 정말 재미있었어. 너도 거기 있었으면 좋았을 텐데.

02 정답 X, should prepare → should have prepared

해설 문맥상 과거의 일을 이야기하는 앞 문장에서 '너는 시험에 떨어졌다'라고 하였으므로, 뒤 문장에서 그 과거 사실에 대한 충고를 나타내는 내용이 나오는 것이 적절하다. 따라서 '너는 그것을 더 철저하게 준비했어야 했다 (하지만 그러지 못했다)'라는 의미로 과거 사실의 반대를 가정하는 가정법 과거완료 should have prepared로 고쳐야 한다.

해석 너는 시험에서 떨어졌다. 너는 시험 준비를 더 철저하게 했어야 했다.

03 정답 O

해설 'V + as if'를 통해 가정법 문장임을 알 수 있는데, 주절이 현재시제(speaks)이며 문맥상 '그가 (미국인이 아닌데) 마치 미국 사람인 것처럼 유창하게 영어로 말한다'라는 의미가 자연스러우므로 종속절에 현재 사실의 반대를 가정하는 가정법 과거 were가 쓰인 것은 적절하다.

해석 그는 마치 자신이 미국 사람인 것처럼 유창하게 영어로 말한다.

04 정답 O

해설 I wish를 통해 가정법 문장임을 알 수 있는데, had known의 목적어 자리에 온 that절이 과거의 일을 이야기하는 과거시제(was)이고 문맥상 'Diana가 아픈 것을 (그때) 알았더라면 좋았을 텐데'라는 의미가 자연스러우므로 과거 사실과 반대되는 일을 소망하는 가정법 과거완료 I'd known은 적절하게 쓰였다. 참고로, 뒤 문장의 would have p.p. 형태를 통해 과거 사실의 반대를 가정하는 가정법 과거완료임을 다시 한번 확인할 수 있다.

해석 Diana가 아팠다는 것을 알았더라면 좋았을 텐데. 나는 그녀를 보러 갔을 텐데.

05 정답 X, studied → had studied

해설 종속절의 if와 주절의 could를 통해 가정법 문장임을 알 수 있는데, 종속절 내 과거 시점을 나타내는 부사절 when young이 있고 주절에는 현재 시점을 나타내는 부사 now가 있으므로 가정법 과거완료와 가정법 과거가 혼합된 혼합 가정법이다. 이는 'If + S + had p.p. ~, S + 조동사의 과거형 + RV + (now/today)'의 구조를 취하므로, studied를 had studied로 고쳐야 한다.

해석 내가 어렸을 때 수학을 더 열심히 공부했더라면, 나는 지금 하버드에 들어갈 수 있을 텐데.

06 정답 O

해설 종속절의 if와 주절의 might have prevented를 통해 가정법 과거완료 문장임을 알 수 있다. 과거 사실의 반대를 가정하는 가정법 과거완료는 'If + S + had p.p. ~, S + 조동사의 과거형 + have p.p.'의 구조를 취하므로, 종속절의 had maintained는 적절하게 쓰였다.

해석 내가 원래의 판단을 유지했더라면 나는 프로젝트의 실패를 막을 수 있었을지도 모른다.

07 정답 X, might not take place → might not have taken place

해설 종속절의 'if + S + had p.p.'와 주절의 might를 통해 가정법 문장임을 알 수 있다. 문맥상 과거 역사적 사실의 반대를 가정하는 가정법 과거완료이므로 'If + S + had p.p. ~, S + 조동사의 과거형 + have p.p.'의 구조를 취해야 한다. 따라서 might not take place를 might not have taken place로 고쳐야 한다.

해석 Hitler가 다른 유럽 국가를 침략하지 않았더라면 제2차 세계대전은 일어나지 않았을지도 모른다.

08 정답 X, would have complained → would[will] complain

해설 종속절의 'if + S + should + RV'와 tomorrow, 주절의 would를 통해 가정법 미래 문장임을 알 수 있다. 가정법 미래는 'If + S + should + RV ~, S + 조동사의 현재형/과거형 + RV'의 구조를 취하므로 would have complained를 would[will] complain으로 고쳐야 한다.

해석 그 물건이 내일 배송되지 않으면 그들은 그것에 대해 불평할 것이다.

09 정답 O

해설 'Had + S + p.p.'는 가정법 과거완료에서 if가 생략된 도치 구문이다. 따라서 주절은 'S + 조동사의 과거형 + have p.p.'의 구조를 취하며, 문맥상 '그때 그 프로젝트를 포기했더라면 (그때) 그렇게 훌륭한 성과를 얻지 못했을 것이다'라는 의미도 자연스러우므로 가정법 과거완료인 could not have achieved의 쓰임은 적절하다.

해석 내가 그때 그 프로젝트를 포기했더라면 그렇게 훌륭한 성과를 얻지 못했을 것이다.

10 정답 X, would graduate → would have graduated

해설 문맥상 과거의 일을 이야기하는 앞 문장에서 '그는 학교를 그만둬야 했다'라고 하였으므로, otherwise로 대조를 이루는 뒤 문장에서는 그 과거 사실과 반대되는 내용이 올 것임을 알 수 있다. 따라서 뒤에 과거 시점을 나타내는 부사구 last June과 함께 '(그가 학교를 그만두지 않았다면) 그는 지난 6월에 졸업했을 것이다 (하지만 그러지 못했다)'라는 의미로 과거 사실의 반대를 가정하는 가정법 과거완료가 적절하므로 would have graduated로 고쳐야 한다.

해석 그는 집안 문제 때문에 학교를 그만둬야 했다. 그렇지 않았다면 그는 지난 6월에 졸업했을 것이다.

11 정답 X, should receive → should have received

해설 과거 시점을 나타내는 부사절 while they were in school이 있고 문맥상 '그러한 교육의 희생자들은 훈련을 받았어야 했다 (하지만 그러지 못했다)'라는 의미의 과거 사실에 대한 충고를 나타내는 내용이 나오는 것이 적절하므로 과거 사실의 반대를 가정하는 가정법 과거완료 should have received로 고쳐야 한다.

해석 그러한 교육의 희생자들은 학교에 다니는 동안 창의적인 재능을 발달시키는 훈련을 받았어야 했다.

12 정답 ④

해설 I wish를 통해 가정법 문장임을 알 수 있는데, 종속절 내 과거 시점을 나타내는 부사절 when I was not busy가 있는 것으로 보아 빈칸은 가정법 과거완료 동사 자리이다. 문맥상으로도 '내가 바쁘지 않을 때 가족이나 친구들과 더 많은 시간을 보냈으면 좋았을 텐데'라는 의미가 자연스러우므로 빈칸에는 가정법 과거완료인 had had가 와야 한다.

해석 내가 바쁘지 않을 때 가족이나 친구들과 더 많은 시간을 보냈으면 좋았을 텐데.

13 정답 ②

해설 빈칸은 주절의 주어 he에 대한 동사 자리로, 종속절의 if와 부사구 in high school, 주절의 a college student now를 통해서 가정법 과거완료와 가정법 과거가 혼합된 혼합가정법 문장임을 알 수 있다. 따라서 혼합가정법은 'If + S + had p.p. ~, S + 조동사의 과거형 + RV + (now/today)'의 구조를 취하므로, 빈칸에는 would be가 와야 한다.

해석 그가 고등학교 다닐 때 더 열심히 공부했더라면 그는 지금 대학생일 텐데.

14 정답 ②

해설 it is high time을 통해 가정법 문장임을 알 수 있는데, 문장의 주어 we와 목적어 it이 있으므로 빈칸은 동사 자리이다. '~할 시간이다'라는 뜻의 It is high time 가정법 동사는 'should + RV'나 과거동사로 쓰고 완전타동사 discuss는 뒤에 전치사 about을 쓰지 않으므로 빈칸에는 능동태의 과거동사 discussed가 와야 한다.

해석 우리나라의 경제 상황은 점점 더 악화되고 있다. 우리가 그것을 진지하게 논의할 때이다.

15 정답 ③

해설 빈칸 뒤에 주어와 동사로 이루어진 문장이 나와 있으므로 빈칸에 접속사가 들어가야 할 것처럼 보이지만 주어(your flight)와 동사(be delayed)의 수일치가 맞지 않는다. 따라서 이 문장은 주절의 동사 형태(will notify)를 단서 삼아, 가정법 미래 'If + S + should + RV ~, S + 조동사의 현재형/과거형 + RV'의 구조가 if가 생략되면서 주어와 should가 도치된 가정법 도치 구문으로 보는 것이 적절하므로 빈칸에는 조동사인 Should가 와야 한다. 참고로, 조동사 Will이 주어 앞으로 오는 가정법 도치 구문은 없다.

해석 항공편이 지연되면 항공사에서 업데이트된 출발 정보를 이메일로 네게 알려줄 것이다.

16 정답 ④

해설 빈칸은 if가 이끄는 절의 주어 Clauss에 대한 동사 자리로, 문장의 본동사 said의 목적어 자리에 온 that절은 종속절의 if와 주절의 would를 통해 가정법 문장임을 알 수 있다. 따라서 문장의 본동사가 과거시제이면 종속절의 동사 역시 과거시제(또는 과거완료시제)를 쓴다는 시제 일치 원칙에 따라, that절의 가정법 문장은 과거 사실의 반대를 가정하는 가정법 과거완료로 나타내는 것이 적절하므로 빈칸에는 hadn't reacted가 와야 한다.

해석 한 경찰관은 Clauss가 그렇게 신속하고 단호하게 반응하지 않았더라면 한 명이 아니라 두 명의 익사자가 발생했을 거라고 말했다.

전략 13-14

전략 적용 연습

본서 p. 85

01 X, be → have been

02 X, used to loving → used to love

03 O

04 O

05 X, had contacted → (should) contact

06 X, follows → (should) follow

07 X, should not ignore → should not have ignored

08 X, had been kept → (should) be kept

09 O

10 ④ 11 ④ 12 ③

13 ② 14 ① 15 ①

01 정답 **X, be → have been**

해설 문맥상 앞 문장에서 'Michael이 출근하지 않았다'라고 과거의 일을 이야기하였으므로 뒤 문장에는 과거 시점을 나타내는 부사 yesterday와 함께 과거의 일에 대한 내용이 나오는 것이 적절하다. 따라서 '(현재) 아픈 것임이 틀림없다'(must be sick)가 아니라 '(어제) 아팠음에 틀림없다'(must have been sick)라는 의미가 자연스러우므로 be를 have been으로 고쳐야 한다.

해석 Michael이 출근하지 않았다. 그는 어제 아팠음에 틀림없다.

02 정답 **X, used to loving → used to love**

해설 과거 시점을 나타내는 부사절 when they were young이 있는 것으로 과거시제의 문장임을 알 수 있고, '~하곤 했다'라는 뜻의 구조동사 used to 뒤에는 동사원형이 와야 하므로 used to loving을 used to love로 고쳐야 한다.

해석 그들은 어렸을 때 책을 훨씬 더 좋아하곤 했다.

03 정답 **O**

해설 '제안' 또는 '암시'라는 뜻의 명사 suggestion과 동격을 이루는 that절의 동사 자리인데, 문맥에 따라 that절이 '당위' 또는 '사실'을 나타낼 수 있다. 해석해 보면 '좀 더 구체적인 것을 말해 달라는 제안'이라는 '당위'의 의미가 자연스러우므로 should가 생략되어 동사원형만 남은 say는 적절하게 쓰였다.

해석 그 유명 인사는 좀 더 구체적인 것을 말해 달라는 제안을 거부했다.

04 정답 **O**

해설 동사 insist가 뒤에 that절을 목적어로 취하면, 문맥에 따라 that절이 '당위' 또는 '사실'을 나타낼 수 있다. 따라서 해석을 통해서 파악하는데, 문맥상 that절의 내용이 당위가 아닌 '사실'을 서술하고 있으므로 that절의 동사는 '(should) RV'가 아닌 내용상의 시제로 써 주어야 한다. 의사가 그 전날에 환자를 수술한 것이 (그 사실을) 주장하는 것보다 더 이전의 일이므로, 과거완료시제인 had operated의 쓰임은 적절하다.

해석 그 의사는 그 전날 환자를 수술했다고 단호히 주장했다.

05 정답 **X, had contacted → (should) contact**

해설 동사 suggest는 '제안하다'와 '암시하다'라는 2가지 뜻을 가지고 있으며, 문맥에 따라 목적어 자리에 온 that절이 '당위' 또는 '사실'을 나타낼 수 있다. 문맥상 '내가 당신에게 연락했다는 것을 암시했다'가 아니라 '내가 당신에게 연락해 보라고 제안했다'라는 '당위'의 의미를 나타내는 것이 적절하므로 that절의 동사는 '(should) RV'로 써야 한다. 따라서 had contacted를 (should) contact로 고쳐야 한다.

해석 Peter Thompson이 당신의 이름을 제게 언급하며 입학을 위해 당신에게 연락해 볼 것을 제안했습니다.

06 정답 **X, follows → (should) follow**

해설 necessary와 같은 이성적 판단을 나타내는 형용사가 주절에 올 때, that절의 동사는 '(should) RV'의 형태로 쓴다. 따라서 follows를 (should) follow로 고쳐야 한다.

해석 그 환자는 적절한 약물 치료와 회복을 위해 의사의 지시를 따르는 것이 필요하다.

07 정답 **X, should not ignore → should not have ignored**

해설 문맥상 which 이하 문장의 동사가 led to인 것으로 보아 앞뒤 문장이 과거의 인과관계를 나타내는 것을 알 수 있다. 따라서 과거의 결과인 '경기력 저하로 이어졌다'가 되려면 앞 문장은 '(현재) 감독의 조언을 무시해선 안 된다'가 아니라 '(과거에) 감독의 조언을 무시해선 안 되었다'라는 의미가 자연스러우므로 should not ignore를 should not have ignored로 고쳐야 한다.

해석 그 선수는 큰 경기 전에 감독의 조언을 무시해서는 안 되었으며, 이는 경기력 저하로 이어졌다.

08 정답 **X, had been kept → (should) be kept**

해설 order는 요구 동사로 당위의 의미를 지니는 that절을 목적어로 취할 경우, that절 내의 동사는 '(should) RV'의 형태로 쓴다. 따라서 had been kept를 (should) be kept로 고쳐야 한다.

해석 Cleveland 대통령의 왼쪽 위턱 대부분이 제거되었다. 대통령은 그 수술이 비밀에 부쳐져야 한다고 명령했다.

09 정답 0

해설 문맥상 첫 문장에서 '치아가 David를 괴롭혀 왔다'라고 했고, 마지막 문장에서 '그는 그것(치과에 가는 것)을 미루어 왔었다'라고 했으므로 David가 치과에 가지 않았다는 사실을 알 수 있다. 따라서 '그는 좀 더 일찍 치과에 갔어야 했다 (하지만 그러지 않았다)'라는 의미로 과거 일에 대한 후회를 나타내는 should have gone의 쓰임은 적절하다.

해석 그 치아는 David를 때때로 괴롭혀 왔다. 그는 좀 더 일찍 치과에 갔어야 했다는 것을 알았다. 하지만 그는 그것을 미루어 왔었다.

10 정답 ④

해설 빈칸은 주어 we에 대한 동사 자리로, 뒤에 완전한 문장이 목적어로 오고 있으며, 문장에 현재 시점을 나타내는 부사 Today가 있는 것으로 보아 현재시제의 동사가 적절하다. 따라서 과거의 습관을 나타낼 때 쓰는 구동사 used to는 답이 될 수 없으며, 문맥상 '우리는 보는 데에 사용된다'가 아니라 '우리는 보는 데에 익숙하다'라는 뜻이 자연스러우므로 빈칸에는 are used to seeing이 와야 한다.

해석 오늘날, 우리는 여자들이 바지를 입고 스포츠를 하는 것을 보는 데 익숙하다.

11 정답 ④

해설 빈칸은 동사 insisted의 목적어 자리에 온 that절 내 동사 자리로, 문맥에 따라 that절이 '당위' 또는 '사실'을 나타낼 수 있다. that절에 when the murder had been committed라고 과거에 이미 일어난 일을 명시하고 있기 때문에, 문맥상 '살인 사건이 일어났을 때 그의 아들은 집에 있었다'라는 '사실'을 나타내는 것이 적절하다. 따라서 종속절이 사실을 나타내는 경우 내용상 시제를 따져야 하는데, 그의 아들이 집에 있었던 것은 (그 사실을) 주장하는 것보다 더 이전의 일이므로 빈칸에는 과거완료시제인 had been이 와야 한다.

해석 그는 그 살인 사건이 일어났을 때, 그의 아들이 집에 있었다고 주장했다.

12 정답 ③

해설 문장의 주어는 The lost city, 주어를 수식하는 과거분사구 hidden deep in the jungle, 뒤에는 전치사구가 온 문장 구조로, 빈칸은 문장의 동사 자리이다. 과거 시점을 나타내는 centuries ago가 있으므로 과거의 일을 이야기하는 것이 적절하며, 문맥상 그 잃어버린 도시가 수 세기 전에 '버려져야 했었는데'라는 후회/유감의 의미보다는 '버려졌던 것일지도 모른다'라는 추측의 의미가 자연스러우므로 빈칸에는 may have been abandoned가 와야 한다.

해석 정글 깊숙이 숨겨진 그 잃어버린 도시는 수 세기 전에 질병이나 자연재해로 인해 버려졌던 것일지도 모른다.

13 정답 ②

해설 빈칸은 that절 내 주어 every department와 목적어 its budget report 사이의 동사 자리이다. 이성적 판단을 나타내는 형용사 essential이 주절에 왔으므로 that절의 동사는 '(should) RV'의 형태로 쓰며 문맥상 모든 부서가 예산 보고서를 '제출하는' 것이므로 능동태가 적절하다. 따라서 빈칸에는 should가 생략되어 능동태의 동사원형만 남은 형태인 submit가 와야 한다.

해석 회계연도가 곧 종료되므로 모든 부서는 예산 보고서를 신속하게 제출하는 것이 필수적이다.

14 정답 ①

해설 요구 동사 ask의 현재분사형인 asking이 뒤에 that절을 목적어로 취하는 구조이다. 과거분사구(widely used in France)와 전명구(by newly created French equivalents)를 괄호 치면, that절 내에 주어인 3,000 English words만 있으므로 빈칸은 동사 자리이다. 뒤에 목적어가 없고 문맥상 '3,000개의 영어 단어가 프랑스어 단어로 교체돼야 한다'라는 '당위'의 의미를 나타내므로 that 내의 동사는 '(should) RV'의 형태이며 수동태여야 한다. 따라서 빈칸에는 should가 생략되어 수동태의 동사원형만 남은 형태인 be replaced가 와야 한다.

해석 프랑스 장관은 프랑스에서 널리 사용되는 3,000개의 영어 단어를 새로 만들어진 프랑스어 단어로 교체할 것을 요구하는 법을 추진했다.

15 정답 ①

해설 빈칸은 요구 동사 requested의 목적어 자리에 온 that절 내 동사 자리로, 문맥상 that절이 '인사팀에서 광고를 시작해야 한다'라는 '당위'의 의미를 나타내므로 동사는 '(should) RV'의 형태로 써야 한다. 따라서 빈칸에는 should가 생략되어 동사원형만 남은 형태인 begin이 와야 한다.

해석 Kay 씨가 다른 회사로의 이직을 발표하기도 전에 매니저는 인사팀에서 새로운 회계사를 구하기 위한 광고를 시작해야 한다고 요청했다.

UNIT 02 준동사 핵심 전략

전략 15

전략 적용 연습

본서 p. 94

01 X, moved → move 또는 moving
02 X, putting → to put
03 O
04 X, to answer → answering
05 O
06 O
07 X, meeting → to meet
08 X, to go → go
09 O
10 X, increase → to increase
11 X, fastening → to fasten
12 ④ 13 ③ 14 ①
15 ③ 16 ② 17 ①

01 정답 **X, moved → move 또는 moving**

해설 지각동사 see는 목적어와 목적격 보어의 관계가 능동이면 RV나 RVing를, 수동이면 p.p.를 목적격 보어로 취하는데, 여기서는 한 가족이 '이사되는' 것이 아니라 '이사하는' 것이므로 과거분사 moved를 원형부정사 move 또는 현재분사 moving으로 고쳐야 한다. 참고로, 지각동사의 목적격 보어에 원형부정사 move가 올 경우 내가 출근할 때 이사 오는 '전 과정을 보았다'는 의미가 되고, 현재분사 moving이 올 경우 이사 오는 '순간을 봤다'는 의미가 된다. 여기서는 문맥상 출근할 때 잠깐 봤다는 의미로 현재분사 moving이 더 자연스럽다.

해석 내가 출근할 때 한 가족이 위층에 이사 오는 것을 보았다.

02 정답 **X, putting → to put**

해설 'remember to RV'는 '~할 것을 기억하다'라는 의미이고, 'remember RVing'는 '~한 것을 기억하다'라는 의미이다. 문맥상 잠자러 가기 전에 '불을 끈 것을 기억해라'가 아니라 '불을 끄는 것을 기억해라[잊지 말아라]'라는 의미가 자연스러우므로 putting을 to put으로 고쳐야 한다.

해석 잠자러 가기 전에 불을 끄는 것을 기억해라[잊지 말아라].

03 정답 **O**

해설 'forget to RV'는 '~하기로 한 것을 잊다'라는 의미이고, 'forget RVing'는 '~한 것을 잊다'라는 의미이다. 문맥상 주절에서 우체국에 다시 방문해야 한다고 한 것으로 보아 그 원인을 나타내는 종속절에서는 '나는 어제 편지 부치는 것을 잊었다'라는 의미가 나오는 것이 적절하므로 to post의 쓰임은 알맞다.

해석 나는 어제 편지 부치는 것을 잊어버려서 다시 우체국을 방문해야 한다.

04 정답 **X, to answer → answering**

해설 avoid는 동명사를 목적어로 취하는 동사이므로 to answer를 answering으로 고쳐야 한다.

해석 그녀는 어려운 질문에 대답하지 않으려고 했지만, 선생님은 고집을 부리셨다.

05 정답 **O**

해설 give up은 동명사를 목적어로 취하는 동사이므로 trying의 쓰임은 적절하며, 문맥상 '배우려고 노력한 것을 포기하다'라는 의미가 자연스러우므로 'try to RV' 형태인 trying to learn도 적절하게 쓰였다.

해석 많은 시도가 실패로 돌아간 끝에, 그는 마침내 기타 연주를 배우려는 노력을 포기했다.

06 정답 **O**

해설 'regret to RV'는 '~하게 돼서 유감이다'라는 의미이고, 'regret RVing'는 '~한 것을 후회하다'라는 의미이다. 문맥상 '소포 배송이 지연되었음을 알리게 돼서 유감이다'라는 의미가 자연스러우므로 to inform은 적절하게 쓰였다.

해석 물류 문제로 인해 귀하의 소포 배송이 지연되었음을 알려드리게 되어 유감입니다.

07 정답 **X, meeting → to meet**

해설 fail은 to 부정사를 목적어로 취하는 동사이므로 meeting을 to meet로 고쳐야 한다.

해석 The Chicago Dairy Farm은 품질 기준을 충족하지 못해 우유의 50%를 폐기해야 했다.

08 정답 **X, to go → go**

해설 문맥상 make는 의미상 주어인 그가 '달아나기 위해 독감을 만들다'라는 의미의 3형식 동사가 아니라 그가 '독감이 달아나게 하다'라는 의미의 사역동사로 쓰였으며, 목적어와 목적격 보어의 관계가 능동일 때는 RV 형태를 쓰므로 to go를 go로 고쳐야 한다.

해석 그의 친절하고 다정한 얼굴을 보자 나는 정말 기뻤지만, 독감이 달아나게 하기 위해 그가 할 수 있는 일은 없었다.

09 정답 **O**

해설 'stop to RV'는 '~하기 위해 멈추다'라는 의미이고, 'stop RVing'는 '~하는 것을 그만두다'라는 의미이다. 문맥상 주절에서 1976년까지 등록하지 않으면 누구도 집에 권총을 보유하고 있을 수 없다고 한 것으로 보아 종속절에서는 '1976년에 권총을 등록하는 것을 그만두다[중단하다]'라는 의미가 나오는 것이 적절하므로 registering의 쓰임은 알맞다.

해석 1976년 그 시가 권총 등록을 중단했기 때문에, 그때까지 등록하지 않은 사람은 누구도 집에 권총을 보유하고 있을 수 없다.

10 정답 X, increase → to increase

해설 5형식 동사로 쓰인 cause는 to 부정사를 목적격 보어로 취하므로 increase를 to increase로 고쳐야 한다.

해석 대기 오염이 심하고 대기질이 좋지 않은 지역에 거주하는 것은 사람들이 만성 질환에 걸릴 위험을 증가시킬 수 있다.

11 정답 X, fastening → to fasten

해설 'forget to RV'는 '~하기로 한 것을 잊다'라는 의미이고, 'forget RVing'는 '~한 것을 잊다'라는 의미이다. 뒤 문장에서 그 시험관이 앞으로 나가 차 앞 유리창에 머리를 부딪치고 뒤로 넘어진 것으로 보아, 안전벨트를 매지 않았다는 것을 알 수 있다. 따라서 문맥상 앞 문장에서는 '안전벨트를 맨 것을 잊었다'가 아니라 '안전벨트를 매는 것을 잊었다'라는 의미가 자연스러우므로 fastening을 to fasten으로 고쳐야 한다.

해석 무섭게도, 그 시험관은 안전벨트를 매는 것을 잊어버렸다. 그는 앞으로 나아갔고 차 앞 유리창에 그의 머리를 부딪치고 뒤로 넘어졌다.

12 정답 ④

해설 빈칸은 사역동사 let의 목적격 보어 자리로, 목적어와 목적격 보어의 관계가 능동이면 RV를, 수동이면 be p.p.를 쓰는데, 여기서는 문제가 '분석되는' 것이므로 빈칸에는 수동을 나타내는 be analyzed가 와야 한다.

해석 결정을 내리기 전에 문제를 모든 각도에서 분석해 봐라.

13 정답 ③

해설 주어가 Journalists이고 5형식 동사 expect가 수동태로 쓰인 문장으로, 빈칸은 보어 자리이다. expect가 5형식 동사로 쓰일 때 to 부정사를 목적격 보어로 취하는데, 수동태로 전환 시 동사 뒤에 to 부정사가 그대로 남는 구조가 된다. 따라서 빈칸에는 to 부정사인 to verify가 와야 한다.

해석 기자는 뉴스 기사를 내보내기 전에 출처를 확인해야 한다.

14 정답 ①

해설 빈칸은 동명사 seeing의 목적격 보어 자리이다. 지각동사 see는 목적어와 목적격 보어의 관계가 능동이면 RV나 RVing를, 수동이면 p.p.를 목적격 보어로 취하는데, 여기서는 주인이나 심지어 낯선 사람이 '하품하는' 것이므로 빈칸에는 능동을 나타내는 yawn이 와야 한다.

해석 개들도 주인이나 심지어 낯선 사람이 하품하는 것을 보고 반응하여 하품을 한다.

15 정답 ③

해설 빈칸은 준사역동사 get의 목적격 보어 자리로, 목적어와 목적격 보어의 관계가 능동이면 to RV를, 수동이면 p.p.를 쓰는데, 여기서는 그것(컴퓨터)이 '수리되는' 것이므로 빈칸에는 수동을 나타내는 fixed가 와야 한다.

해석 내 컴퓨터가 작동을 멈췄을 때, 나는 그것을 수리하기 위해 컴퓨터 가게로 가져갔다.

16 정답 ②

해설 주어가 she이고 사역동사 make가 수동태로 쓰인 문장으로, 빈칸은 보어 자리이다. 사역동사가 능동태에서 수동태로 전환 시 목적격 보어 자리에 온 능동의 RV는 to RV로 바뀌고, 수동의 p.p.는 p.p. 그대로 남으므로 보어 자리에는 to RV 또는 p.p. 형태가 와야 한다. 여기서는 주어인 그녀가 '사과하는' 것이라는 능동의 의미가 적절하므로 빈칸에는 to apologize가 와야 한다.

해석 그 결과로, 그녀는 자신의 실수에 대해 반 전체 학생들 앞에서 사과해야 했다.

17 정답 ①

해설 빈칸은 준사역동사 help의 목적격 보어 자리이다. help의 5형식 문장은 'help + O + OC(RV / to RV)'의 구조로 쓰이므로 빈칸에는 find가 와야 한다.

해석 가이드북은 관광객들이 도시 최고의 명소를 찾을 수 있도록 도와주며, 자세한 지도와 후기, 즐거운 방문을 위한 팁을 제공한다.

전략 16

전략 적용 연습

본서 p. 97

01 O
02 O
03 X, electing → being elected
04 O
05 X, eaten → eating
06 X, Motivating → Motivated
07 X, to introduce → to be introduced
08 X, store → stored
09 X, Including → Included
10 O
11 X, accepted → accepting
12 ② 13 ③ 14 ④
15 ② 16 ③ 17 ①

01 정답 O

해설 명사 story를 수식하는 자리에 온 분사로, 분사의 의미상 주어는 분사의 수식을 받는 명사인 story이고 이야기가 '무서움을 느끼는' 것이 아니라 '무섭게 하는' 것이므로 능동의 현재분사인 terrifying은 적절하게 쓰였다.

해석 이것은 지금까지 쓰였던 이야기 중 가장 무서운 이야기이다.

02 정답 O

해설 문장에 이미 동사 wasted가 존재하므로, 콤마로 구분되어 문장 맨 앞에 온 분사구문 자리이다. 여기서는 분사 뒤에 목적어가 있는 문장 구조이며, 분사구문의 의미상 주어는 주절의 주어인 I

이고 내가 영어 선생님의 조언을 '무시하는' 것이므로 능동의 현재분사인 Ignoring은 적절하게 쓰였다.

해석 나는 영어 선생님의 조언을 무시해서 시간과 돈을 낭비했다.

03 정답 **X, electing → being elected**

해설 전치사 of의 목적어 자리에 온 동명사로, 동명사의 의미상 주어는 주어인 Michael이고 Michael이 회장으로 '선출하는' 것이 아니라 '선출되는' 것이므로 능동의 electing을 수동의 being elected로 고쳐야 한다. 참고로, 5형식 동사 elect는 명사를 목적격 보어로 취하는데, 수동태로 전환 시 동사 뒤에 명사가 남는 문장 구조가 된다.

해석 Michael은 올해 자신의 학교 회장으로 선출될 것을 확신했다.

04 정답 **O**

해설 '~가 ~한 채로'라는 뜻의 부대 상황을 나타내는 'with + O + OC' 분사구문으로, 목적어인 다리(the legs)가 '겹치게 놓은' 것이 아니라 '겹치게 놓인' 것이므로 목적격 보어 자리에 쓰인 수동의 과거분사 crossed는 적절하다.

해석 다리를 꼰 채로 오랫동안 앉아 있는 것은 혈압을 상승시킬 수 있다.

05 정답 **X, eaten → eating**

해설 wanted가 5형식 동사로 쓰인 문장에서 문맥상 명사 the rats를 수식하는 자리이므로 분사가 올 수 있는데, 분사의 의미상 주어는 분사의 수식을 받는 명사인 the rats이고 쥐들이 그들의 배급 식량을 '먹힌' 것이 아니라 '먹은' 것이므로 수동의 과거분사인 eaten을 능동의 현재분사 eating으로 고쳐야 한다.

해석 그들은 자신들의 배에서 배급 식량을 먹는 쥐를 죽일 고양이를 원했다.

06 정답 **X, Motivating → Motivated**

해설 문장에 이미 동사 are inclined가 존재하므로, 콤마로 구분되어 문장 맨 앞에 온 분사구문 자리이며 여기서는 분사 뒤에 목적어가 없는 문장 구조이다. 분사구문의 의미상 주어는 주절의 주어인 they이고 문맥상 그들이 죄책감에 의해 '동기를 부여하는' 것이 아니라 '동기 부여를 받는' 것이므로 능동의 현재분사인 Motivating을 수동의 과거분사 Motivated로 고쳐야 한다.

해석 죄책감에 의해 동기 부여를 받은 그들은 자신들의 행동에 대해 보상하려는 경향이 있다.

07 정답 **X, to introduce → to be introduced**

해설 5형식 동사 expect가 수동태로 전환되면서 to 부정사가 그대로 남게 된 문장 구조이다. to 부정사의 의미상 주어는 주어인 New features인데, 동사 뒤에 목적어가 없고 문맥상 새로운 기능이 '소개하는' 것이 아니라 '소개되는' 것이므로 수동의 의미가 적절하다. 따라서 능동의 to introduce를 수동의 to be introduced로 고쳐야 한다.

해석 모바일 앱의 새로운 기능은 다음 업데이트에서 소개될 예정이다.

08 정답 **X, store → stored**

해설 5형식 동사 keep의 목적격 보어 자리에 원형부정사를 쓰지 않는다. keep은 목적어와 목적격 보어의 관계가 능동이면 RVing를, 수동이면 p.p.를 목적격 보어로 취하는데, 개인 소지품이 '보관하는' 것이 아니라 '보관되는' 것이므로 수동을 나타내는 stored로 고쳐야 한다.

해석 손님들은 개인 소지품을 지정된 사물함에 보관해 줄 것을 당부받는다.

09 정답 **X, Including → Included**

해설 전명구(in this series / among ~ stories)를 괄호 치면, 문장의 주어는 "The Enchanted Horse"이고 동사는 is이며 주격 보어가 Including인 문장인데, 보어가 문두에 와 도치된 구조이다. 분사 뒤에 목적어가 없고 문맥상 주어인 "The Enchanted Horse"가 '포함하는' 것이 아니라 '포함되는' 것이므로 능동의 현재분사인 Including을 수동의 과거분사 Included로 고쳐야 한다.

해석 다른 유명한 동화들 중에서, "The Enchanted Horse(마법에 걸린 말)"가 이 시리즈에 포함된다.

10 정답 **O**

해설 문장에 이미 동사 enjoys가 존재하므로, 콤마로 구분되어 문장 맨 앞에 온 분사구문 자리이며 여기서는 분사 뒤에 목적어가 없는 문장 구조이다. 분사구문의 의미상 주어는 주절의 주어인 the city of Kathmandu이고 문맥상 카트만두시가 '위치시킨' 것이 아니라 '위치된[위치한]' 것이므로 수동의 과거분사인 Situated는 적절하게 쓰였다.

해석 해발 1,350미터에 위치한 카트만두시에서는 생활을 즐겁게 해주는 온화한 기후를 일 년 내내 즐길 수 있다.

11 정답 **X, accepted → accepting**

해설 등위접속사 but 다음에 접속사 1개(as), 동사 2개(mature / becomes)이므로 두 콤마 사이는 수식어구/부사구 역할을 할 수 있는 분사구문 자리이다. 문맥상 as가 이끄는 부사절을 수식하는 분사구문으로, 분사구문의 주어는 you이고 당신이 다른 사회적 역할을 '받아들여지는' 것이 아니라 '받아들이는' 것이므로 수동의 과거분사인 accepted를 능동의 현재분사 accepting으로 고쳐야 한다. 참고로, 분사구문 대신 등위접속사 and로 주어 you에 대한 동사의 병렬 관계(mature / accept)를 이루는 형태로도 쓸 수 있다.

해석 다시 말해, 출생 순서가 가족 내에서 역할을 규정지을 수는 있지만, 성인이 되어 다른 사회적 역할을 받아들이면서 출생 순서는 중요하지 않게 된다.

12 정답 **②**

해설 '~하는 데 시간/돈을 쓰다'라는 뜻의 동명사 관용 표현 'spend + 시간/돈 + (in) RVing'가 쓰인 문장으로, 빈칸은 동명사 자리이다. 뒤에 전치사구 to helping이 오고 있고 목적어인 그녀의 일생 대부분이 '바치는' 것이 아니라 '바쳐진' 것이므로 빈칸에는 동명사의 수동형 being devoted가 와야 한다.

해석 Diana 왕세자비는 자신의 생애 대부분을 가난한 아이들을 돕는 데 헌신하며 보냈다.

13 정답 ③

해설 빈칸은 명사 event를 앞에서 수식하는 형용사 자리이다. depress는 '우울하게 하다'라는 뜻의 감정타동사로, 수식을 받는 명사(의미상 주어)인 event가 '우울한' 것이 아니라 '우울하게 하는' 것이므로 빈칸에는 능동의 현재분사 depressing이 와야 한다.

해석 사랑하는 애완동물을 잃는다는 것은 당신이 슬프고 외로운 느낌을 들게 하는 우울한 사건이다.

14 정답 ④

해설 문장에 이미 동사 include가 존재하므로 접속사 없이 동사가 또 올 수 없고, 빈칸은 명사 Locations를 뒤에서 수식할 수 있는 수식어구 자리이다. 선택지 중 명사를 수식할 수 있는 것으로는 분사와 to 부정사가 해당되는데, 수식을 받는 명사(의미상 주어)인 장소가 '촬영되는' 것이므로 수동태가 적절하다. 따라서 빈칸에는 형용사적 용법으로 쓰인 to 부정사의 수동태 to be filmed가 와야 한다.

해석 새 영화의 촬영 장소로는 뉴욕시와 그랜드 캐니언이 있다.

15 정답 ②

해설 접속사 when 뒤에는 'S + V' 또는 분사구문(RVing/p.p./형용사)이 나오는데, 주어진 선택지 중 올 수 있는 것을 따졌을 때 빈칸은 분사구문 자리이다. 빈칸 뒤에 목적어 없이 바로 전치사구 to by the airline staff로 이어지는 문장 구조이며, 분사구문의 의미상 주어는 주절의 주어인 you이고 문맥상 당신이 승무원에 의해 '요청받는' 것이므로 빈칸에는 수동의 과거분사 asked가 와야 한다. 참고로, 빈칸 뒤 to는 5형식 동사 ask의 수동태 뒤에 남은 to 부정사의 to인데, to do so(= to show your boarding pass)에서 반복을 피하기 위해 생략된 구조이다.

해석 승무원이 요청할 때 탑승권을 제시하지 않으면 비행기에 탑승할 수 없을 것이다.

16 정답 ③

해설 문장의 주어가 The beautiful necklace이고 동사는 was인 문장 구조로, 빈칸은 문장의 주어를 뒤에서 수식할 수 있는 수식어구 자리이다. 선택지 중 명사를 수식할 수 있는 것으로는 형용사와 분사가 해당되는데, 자동사(구) consist of는 수동태로 쓸 수 없으므로 과거분사 consisted of는 적절하지 못하며, consistent는 '일관성 있는'이라는 뜻으로 문맥상 어색하다. 따라서 빈칸에는 능동의 현재분사 consisting of가 와야 한다. 참고로, 명사 consistency가 The beautiful necklace와 함께 복합명사를 이룬다고 해도 '그 아름다운 목걸이 일관성'이라는 어색한 의미가 되므로 답이 될 수 없다.

해석 진주와 다이아몬드로 이루어진 그 아름다운 목걸이는 여러 세대에 걸쳐 물려받은 유산이었다.

17 정답 ①

해설 전명구(by stacking ~ metals / between discs ~ sea water)를 괄호 치면, 문장의 주어가 The enhanced design이고 동사는 was made인 완전한 문장 구조이다. 콤마로 구분되어 주어와 동사 사이에 수식어구가 왔는데, 접속사가 없으므로 동사가 또 올 수 없고, 명사 a Voltaic pile과 함께 문장 중간에 콤마로 구분되어 올 수 있는 것은 분사구이므로 빈칸은 분사 자리이다. 문맥상 빈칸은 주어를 수식하고 있으므로 분사의 의미상 주어는 The enhanced design이고 그 향상된 디자인이 Voltaic 파일이라고 '부르는' 것이 아니라 '불리는' 것이므로 빈칸에는 수동의 과거분사 called가 와야 한다.

해석 Voltaic 파일이라고 불리는 그 향상된 디자인은 바닷물에 적신 판지로 만든 디스크 사이에 이러한 금속으로 만든 몇몇 디스크를 쌓아서 만들어졌다.

전략 17-18

전략 적용 연습

본서 p. 101

01 O
02 X, to emerge → to have emerged
03 X, Hearing → Having heard
04 X, damage → damaging
05 X, use → using
06 X, analysis → analyzing
07 O
08 X, communication → communicating
09 X, preferring → preference
10 X, explaining → explanation

11 ②	12 ③	13 ①
14 ③	15 ②	16 ④

01 정답 O

해설 문장에 이미 동사 can't fall이 존재하므로, 콤마로 구분되어 문장 맨 앞에 온 분사구문 자리이며 여기서는 분사 뒤에 목적어가 있는 문장 구조이다. 분사구문의 의미상 주어는 주절의 주어인 she이고 그녀가 세 잔의 커피를 '마신' 것으로 능동의 의미이며, 문맥상 '마신' 것은 주절의 잠을 잘 수 없는 현재 시점(can't fall)보다 더 이전이므로 완료시제가 와야 한다. 따라서 능동의 현재분사 완료형인 Having drunk는 적절하게 쓰였다.

해석 커피를 석 잔이나 마셔서 그녀는 잠을 잘 수가 없다.

02 정답 X, to emerge → to have emerged

해설 문장의 본동사인 수동태 is thought 뒤 보어 자리에 온 to 부정사로, 과거 시점을 나타내는 100 years ago가 있는 것으로 보아 문맥상 '발생한' 시점은 '생각되는' 것보다 더 이전이므로 완료시제가 와야 한다. 따라서 단순시제의 to emerge를 완료시제의 to have emerged로 고쳐야 한다.

해석 그 질병은 100년 전 열대 지방에서 발생한 것으로 생각된다[여겨진다].

03 정답 X, Hearing → Having heard

해설 문장에 이미 동사 didn't want가 존재하므로, 콤마로 구분되어 문장 맨 앞에 온 분사구문 자리이며 여기서는 분사 뒤에 목적어가 있는 문장 구조이다. 분사구문의 의미상 주어는 주절의 주어인 she이고 그녀가 전에 그 이야기를 '들은' 것으로 능동의 의미이며, 문맥상 '들은' 것은 주절의 다시 듣고 싶지 않은 과거 시점(didn't want)보다 더 이전이므로 완료시제가 와야 한다. 따라서 단순시제의 Hearing을 완료시제의 Having heard로 고쳐야 한다.

해석 그 이야기를 전에 들어서, 그녀는 그것을 다시 듣고 싶지 않았다.

04 정답 X, damage → damaging

해설 damage는 명사이자 동사이다. 동사라면 문장에 이미 본동사 is가 존재하므로 접속사/관계사/의문사 없이 동사가 또 올 수 없으며, 명사라면 바로 이어서 명사를 취할 수 없다. 따라서 전치사 of의 목적어 자리에 오면서 뒤에 명사 your stuff를 목적어로 취할 수 있는 동명사가 와야 하므로 명사 또는 동사인 damage를 동명사 damaging으로 고쳐야 한다.

해석 또한 물건을 훼손할 가능성도 있는데, 물건들 중에는 귀중한 것도 일부 있다.

05 정답 X, use → using

해설 use는 명사이자 동사이다. 동사라면 문장에 이미 본동사 charged가 존재하므로 접속사/관계사/의문사 없이 동사가 또 올 수 없으며, 명사라면 바로 이어서 명사를 취할 수 없다. 따라서 전치사 with의 목적어 자리에 오면서 뒤에 명사 the company's money를 목적어로 취할 수 있는 동명사가 와야 하므로 명사 또는 동사인 use를 동명사 using으로 고쳐야 한다.

해석 그 신문은 그녀가 회사의 돈을 사적인 용도로 사용했다고 비난했다.

06 정답 X, analysis → analyzing

해설 전치사 for의 목적어 자리에 오면서 뒤에 명사 these patterns를 목적어로 취할 수 있는 것은 동명사이므로 명사 analysis를 동명사 analyzing으로 고쳐야 한다.

해석 이러한 패턴들을 분석하기 위한 도구들은 심지어 1990년대 초까지만 해도 이용할 수 없었다.

07 정답 O

해설 동명사의 의미상 주어는 소유격으로 쓰는 것이 원칙이나 일반명사의 경우 목적격도 허용한다. 따라서 동명사 going 앞에 온 인칭대명사의 소유격 my는 적절하게 쓰였다.

해석 우리 아버지는 Smith 씨 가족이 머무는 곳으로 우리와 동행하지는 않으려 하셨지만, 나는 가야 한다고 고집하셨다.

08 정답 X, communication → communicating

해설 that절 내 주어가 communication inner thoughts이고 본동사는 is이며 보어가 crucial인 문장 구조이다. 하지만 명사 communication과 명사 inner thoughts가 바로 이어서 나올 수 없고 만약 복합명사라고 해도 '의사소통 내면의 생각'이라는 어색한 의미가 되며 단수 동사와 수일치가 맞지 않는다. 따라서 inner thoughts를 목적어로 취해 '내면의 생각을 전달하는 것'이라는 의미가 되며 동사와의 수일치가 맞도록 명사 communication을 동명사 communicating으로 고쳐야 한다. 참고로, 동명사 주어는 단수 취급하므로, 단수 동사로 수일치된다.

해석 여러분의 내면 생각을 전달하는 것이 정신적 안녕에 필수적이라는 점을 인식하는 것이 중요하다.

09 정답 X, preferring → preference

해설 전치사 of 뒤에 명사 혹은 동명사가 오는데, 뒤에 타동사 prefer의 목적어가 없으므로 동명사의 쓰임은 적절치 않다. 따라서 '레드 와인 품종 중 선호도 순으로'라는 자연스러운 의미가 되며 목적어 없이 전치사 뒤에 올 수 있는 명사 preference로 고쳐야 한다.

해석 이 블라인드 맛 테스트에서 참가자들은 레드 와인 품종 중 선호도 순으로 순위를 매길 것을 요청받는다.

10 정답 X, explaining → explanation

해설 전명구(for the explosive ~ volcanoes / in the pressure ~ molten rock)를 괄호 치면, 동사 lies만 남으므로 주어 자리이다. explaining은 동명사 또는 현재분사인데, 둘 다 관사 The 뒤에 단독으로 올 수 없다. 따라서 관사의 한정을 받을 수 있는 명사 explanation으로 고쳐야 한다.

해석 화산의 폭발력에 대한 설명은 녹아내린 암석 안에 갇혀 있는 가스의 압력에 있다.

11 정답 ②

해설 빈칸은 전치사 of의 목적어 자리로, 명사(구/절)나 동명사(구)가 와야 한다. 하지만 뒤에 온 명사 all the money를 목적어로 취해야 하므로 능동태의 동명사가 적절하며 과거 시점을 나타내는 부사구 last year가 있는 것으로 보아 문맥상 돈을 쓴 시점이 그것을 부끄러워하는 것보다 더 이전이므로 완료시제로 나타내야 한다. 따라서 빈칸에는 동명사의 완료형인 having spent가 와야 한다.

해석 나는 작년에 그 주식에 모든 돈을 다 써버린 것이 부끄럽다.

12 정답 ③

해설 빈칸은 전치사 By의 목적어 자리로, 명사(구/절)나 동명사(구)가 와야 한다. 하지만 뒤에 온 명사구 how to allocate the budget을 목적어로 취해야 하므로 빈칸에는 동명사인 regulating이 와야 한다. 참고로, 전치사의 목적어 자리에 to 부정사는 올 수 없고, 명사 뒤에 바로 이어서 명사구가 올 수 없다.

해석 예산을 어떻게 배분할지 규정하면, 사무실 장비에 대한 지출이 줄어들 것이다.

13 정답 ①

해설 전명구(to affordable housing / in many urban centers)를 괄호 치면, 빈칸은 동사 remains, 보어 a challenge인 문장 구조의 주어 역할을 할 수 있는 명사 자리이다. 동사가 단수이므로 단수 형태의 명사 Access와 동명사 Accessing이 올 수 있지만, 빈칸 뒤에 타동사 access의 목적어가 없으므로 빈칸에는 단수 명사 Access가 와야 한다.

해석 많은 도심에서 저렴한 주택에 대한 접근성은 여전히 어려운 과제다.

14 정답 ③

해설 주어가 it, 동사가 might be인 완전한 문장 앞에 콤마로 구분되어 온 수식어구인데, 접속사가 없으므로 동사가 또 올 수 없고, 명사 All these things와 함께 문장 맨 앞에 위치할 수 있는 것은 분사구문이므로 빈칸은 분사 자리이다. 주절의 주어(it)와 달라 분사구문의 의미상 주어로 온 명사 All these things가 '고려하는' 것이 아니라 '고려되는' 것이므로 빈칸에는 수동의 과거분사 considered가 와야 한다. 참고로, 완전한 문장 앞에 콤마로 구분되어 온 수식어구 자리에 to 부정사도 올 수 있으나, 그 때는 명사 뒤에 온 형용사적 용법이 아니라 부사적 용법의 to 부정사가 이끄는 구조여야 한다.

해석 이러한 모든 것들을 고려해 본다면, 이삿짐 회사에 부탁하는 것이 더 좋을지도 모른다.

15 정답 ②

해설 빈칸 앞에 온 to는 to 부정사의 to일 수도 있고 전치사 to일 수도 있다. to 부정사라면 뒤에 명사 hunger를 목적어로 취하는 능동형 동사가 와야 하며, 전치사 to라면 전치사의 목적어 역할을 하며 뒤에 명사를 취할 수 있는 능동의 동명사가 와야 한다. 따라서 선택지 중 이 조건을 충족하는 것을 고르면 빈칸에는 능동의 동명사 fighting이 와야 한다. 참고로, 명사 commitment는 전치사 to와 함께 '~에 대한 의지[집념]'라는 뜻을 나타낸다.

해석 Goodwill Foundation은 도움이 필요한 사람들에게 식량을 배포함으로써 기아 퇴치에 대한 강한 의지를 보여 왔다.

16 정답 ④

해설 빈칸 앞에 사람의 성격을 나타내는 형용사 thoughtful이 있고 뒤에는 to 부정사가 있는 것으로 보아, 문맥상 빈칸은 주절의 주어와 달라 to 부정사 앞에 의미상 주어를 나타내는 자리이므로 'of + 목적격' 형태인 of you가 와야 한다.

해석 매년 내 생일을 기억해 주고 아름다운 글귀가 가득 담긴 감동적인 카드를 보내 주다니 너는 정말 생각이 깊다.

UNIT 03 관계사/의문사/접속사 핵심 전략

전략 19

전략 적용 연습

본서 p. 106

01 X, which → when 또는 on which
02 O
03 X, in which → for which
04 O
05 X, where → that
06 O
07 X, who → which 또는 that
08 X, which → where 또는 in which
09 O
10 O
11 X, which → who
12 X, how → what
13 X, that → where 또는 in which
14 O
15 X, to whom → whom
16 X, which was → what was
17 X, which → where 또는 in which
18 O

19 ③	20 ③	21 ①
22 ②	23 ②	24 ②
25 ④	26 ①	27 ③
28 ③	29 ①	30 ④

01 정답 X, which → when 또는 on which

해설 앞에 명사 the day가 나왔으므로 which는 관계대명사이다. 하지만 뒤에 주어나 목적어가 없는 불완전한 문장이 아닌 완전한 문장이 왔으므로 시간 명사 the day를 선행사로 받는 관계부사 when 또는 '전치사 + 관계대명사' 형태의 on which로 고쳐야 한다. 만약 which가 목적격 관계대명사이고 뒤에 동사 met의 목적어가 없는 불완전한 문장이 왔다고 생각된다면, 선행사를 뒤 문장에 넣어 해석해 본다. '그런데 우리는 그날을 만났다'라는 어색한 의미가 되므로 틀린 문장이라는 것을 알 수 있다. 참고로, meet는 자동사이자 타동사로 쓰인다.

해석 나는 우리가 처음 만났던 날을 기억한다.

02 정답 O

해설 앞에 명사 a teddy bear가 나왔으므로 whose는 관계대명사이다. whose의 수식을 받는 명사 eyes를 제외하면 'both of + 소유격 관계대명사 whose + 명사 eyes + 불완전한 문장' 형태로 뒤에 불완전한 문장이 온 것으로 볼 수 있으므로 소유격 관계대명사 whose는 적절하게 쓰였다. 해석도 '그런데 그 인형의 두 눈이 다 떨어져 나가고 없었다'라는 자연스러운 의미가 되어 적절하다.

해석 그녀는 곰 인형을 하나 가지고 있었는데, 인형 눈이 양쪽 다 떨어져 나가고 없었다.

03 정답 **X, in which → for which**

해설 앞에 명사 the things가 나왔으므로 in which는 '전치사 + 관계대명사'이고 뒤에 완전한 문장이 왔으므로 문법적으로는 맞다. 하지만 선행사를 뒤 문장에 넣어 해석해 보면 '그런데 보성은 그것들 중 하나에 유명하다'라는 어색한 의미가 된다. 따라서 '~으로 유명하다'라는 뜻의 'be famous for'를 써서 '그런데 보성은 그것들 중 하나로 유명하다'라는 자연스러운 의미가 되도록 전치사 in을 for로 고쳐야 한다.

해석 녹차는 보성이 유명한 것들 중 하나이다.

04 정답 **O**

해설 앞에 동사 don't mind가 나왔으므로 which는 의문사이다. which는 뒤에 오는 명사 hotel을 수식하며 전치사 at의 목적어가 없는 불완전한 문장을 이끄는 의문형용사로, 해석해 보면 '우리가 어느 호텔에 머무를지'라는 자연스러운 의미가 되므로 적절하게 쓰였다.

해석 방이 깨끗하다면, 나는 우리가 어떤 호텔에 머물든 상관없다.

05 정답 **X, where → that**

해설 앞에 명사 the most beautiful pond가 나왔으므로 where는 관계부사이다. 하지만 뒤에 완전한 문장이 아닌 타동사 have seen의 목적어가 없는 불완전한 문장이 왔으므로 앞에 온 명사를 선행사로 받아 불완전한 문장을 이끄는 관계대명사 that으로 고쳐야 한다. 참고로, 선행사에 형용사의 최상급이 있는 경우 관계대명사는 that만 쓸 수 있다.

해석 이 정원에는 내가 본 것 중 가장 아름다운 연못이 있다.

06 정답 **O**

해설 앞에 명사 the woman이 나왔으므로 whose는 관계대명사이다. whose의 수식을 받는 명사 husband를 제외하면 '소유격 관계대명사 whose + 명사 husband + 불완전한 문장' 형태로 뒤에 불완전한 문장이 온 것으로 볼 수 있으므로 소유격 관계대명사 whose는 적절하게 쓰였다. 해석도 '그런데 그 여자의 남편은 회사의 대표이다'라는 자연스러운 의미가 되어 적절하다.

해석 나는 남편이 회사 대표인 여자를 만났다.

07 정답 **X, who → which 또는 that**

해설 앞에 명사 buildings가 나왔으므로 who는 관계대명사인데, 뒤에 주어가 없는 불완전한 문장이 왔으므로 주격 관계대명사이다. 하지만 선행사(buildings)가 사물이므로 주격 관계대명사 who를 which 또는 that으로 고쳐야 한다.

해석 관광지에서, 나는 보통 우리 건물과는 다른 건물로 향하곤 한다.

08 정답 **X, which → where 또는 in which**

해설 앞에 명사 the joint가 나왔으므로 which는 관계대명사이다. 하지만 뒤에 주어나 목적어가 없는 불완전한 문장이 아닌 완전한 문장이 왔으므로 장소 명사 the joint를 선행사로 받는 관계부사 where 또는 '전치사 + 관계대명사' 형태의 in which로 고쳐야 한다.

해석 무릎은 대퇴골과 다리 아래쪽의 큰 뼈가 만나는 관절이다.

09 정답 **O**

해설 앞에 명사 the hotel이 나왔고 '전치사 + 관계대명사' 뒤에 완전한 문장이 온 구조인데, 바로 뒤의 명사 balcony를 수식하며 관계사절을 이끌어야 하므로 소유격 관계대명사 whose의 쓰임은 적절하다. 해석도 '그 호텔의 발코니에서 우리는 마을을 내려다볼 수 있었다'라는 자연스러운 의미가 되어 적절하다.

해석 우리는 호텔로 계속 운전해 갔는데, 그 호텔의 발코니에서 우리는 마을을 내려다볼 수 있었다.

10 정답 **O**

해설 앞에 명사 a place가 나왔으므로 where는 관계부사이다. where는 뒤에 완전한 문장을 이끌고 있으며, 해석해 보면 '그런데 그곳에 개인이 문제를 가지고 와서 도움을 요청한다'라는 자연스러운 의미가 되므로 적절하게 쓰였다.

해석 부조 집단은 개인이 문제를 가지고 와서 도움을 요청하는 곳이다.

11 정답 **X, which → who**

해설 앞에 명사구 The head of the department가 나왔으므로 which는 관계대명사인데, 뒤에 주어가 없는 불완전한 문장이 왔으므로 주격 관계대명사이다. 하지만 선행사가 '명사 of 명사' 형태라서 진짜 선행사를 찾아야 하는데, 문맥상 평균 연봉의 두 배를 받으며 팀 전체를 감독하는 '부서'가 아니라 '장(長)'이어야 하므로 사람 선행사 The head를 받는 주격 관계대명사 who로 고쳐야 한다.

해석 평균 연봉의 두 배를 받으며 팀 전체를 감독하는 그 부서장이 책임을 져야 한다.

12 정답 **X, how → what**

해설 앞에 동사 Imagine이 나왔으므로 how는 의문부사이다. 하지만 의문부사 뒤에는 완전한 문장이 와야 하는데 여기서는 전치사 like의 목적어가 없는 불완전한 문장이 왔다. 따라서 불완전한 문장을 이끌며 '~은 어떤지'라는 뜻의 'what + S + be동사 + like' 구조를 완성하는 의문대명사 what으로 고쳐야 한다. 참고로, imagine의 목적어 자리에 과거 사실의 반대를 가정하는 가정법 과거완료 문장이 쓰였다.

해석 만약 당신이 6~7살 때 공장에서 일을 시작했었더라면 당신의 인생이 어땠을지 상상해 봐라.

13 정답 **X, that → where 또는 in which**

해설 앞에 명사 the first store가 나왔으므로 that은 관계대명사이다. 하지만 뒤에 주어나 목적어가 없는 불완전한 문장이 아닌 완전한 문장이 왔으므로 장소 명사 the first store를 선행사로 받는 관계부사 where 또는 '전치사 + 관계대명사' 형태의 in which로 고쳐야 한다.

해석 만약 네가 일본에 있다면 RoboStore에 가 봐라. 그곳은 사람이 일하지 않는 세계 최초의 가게이다.

14 정답 **O**

해설 앞에 명사 the year 1800이 나왔으므로 전치사 during 뒤에 온 which는 관계대명사이다. '전치사 + 관계대명사' 뒤에 완전한 문장이 왔으며 해석도 '그런데 1800년에 최초의 현대식 전기 배터리가 개발되었다'라는 자연스러운 의미가 되므로 during which는 적절하게 쓰였다.

해석 좋은 출발점을 찾기 위해서는 최초의 현대식 전기 배터리가 개발된 1800년으로 돌아가야 한다.

15 정답 **X, to whom → whom**

해설 명사 a group of supporters가 관계사절(who ~ protection / to whom ~ activists)의 수식을 받아 주어가 길어져서 주어와 동사가 도치된 구문으로, 앞에 명사가 있으므로 전치사 to 뒤에 온 whom은 관계대명사이다. '전치사 + 관계대명사' 뒤에 3형식 동사 call이 쓰인 완전한 문장이 온 것처럼 보이지만 선행사를 뒤 문장에 넣어 해석해 보면 '그런데 지지자 그룹에게 우리는 환경운동가를 부른다'라는 어색한 의미가 된다. 따라서 뒤에 목적어가 없는 5형식의 불완전한 문장(environmental activists가 목적격 보어)을 이끌어 '그런데 우리는 지지자 그룹을 환경운동가라고 부른다'라는 자연스러운 의미가 되도록 목적격 관계대명사 whom으로 고쳐야 한다. 참고로, call이 5형식 동사로 쓰일 때 명사를 목적격 보어로 취할 수 있다.

해석 멸종 위기종 옆에는 그들의 보호를 위해 싸우는 지지자 그룹이 존재하는데, 우리는 이들을 환경운동가라고 부른다.

16 정답 **X, which was → what was**

해설 앞에 동사 produced가 나왔으므로 which는 의문사이며, 뒤에 불완전한 문장이 왔으므로 문법적으로는 맞다. 하지만 '어느 (것)'이라는 뜻의 의문사 which를 넣어 문장 전체를 해석해 보면 '그는 어느 것이 자신의 내면에 있는지를 만들었다'라는 어색한 의미가 된다. 따라서 '그는 자신의 내면에 있는 것을 만들었다'라는 자연스러운 의미가 되도록 선행사를 포함하며 불완전한 문장을 이끄는 관계대명사 what으로 고쳐야 한다.

해석 Schubert는 우리가 다정한 편지를 쓰듯 자유롭게 작곡했다. 그는 자신의 내면에 있는 것을 만들어 우리에게 풍성한 보물인 음악으로 가져다주었다.

17 정답 **X, which → where 또는 in which**

해설 앞에 명사 a small house가 나왔으므로 which는 관계대명사이며, 뒤에 practice의 목적어가 없는 불완전한 문장이 온 것으로 생각할 때 문법적으로는 맞다고 볼 수 있다. 하지만 선행사를 뒤 문장에 넣어 해석해 보면 '그런데 그녀는 나머지 가족들을 방해하지 않고는 작은 집을 연습할 수 없었다'라는 어색한 의미가 되므로 틀린 문장이라는 것을 알 수 있다. 따라서 장소 명사 a small house를 선행사로 받고 뒤에 온 완전한 문장을 이끌며 '그런데 그녀는 나머지 가족들을 방해하지 않고는 작은 집에서 연습할 수 없었다'라는 자연스러운 의미가 되도록 which를 관계부사 where 또는 '전치사 + 관계대명사' 형태의 in which로 고쳐야 한다. 참고로, practice는 자동사이자 타동사로 쓰인다.

해석 그녀는 나머지 가족들을 방해하지 않고는 연습할 수 없는 작은 집에 살았기 때문에, 보통 밖에서 고음 연습을 했다.

18 정답 **O**

해설 앞에 명사구 the proscenium of a stage가 나왔으므로 전치사 on 뒤에 온 which는 관계대명사이다. '전치사 + 관계대명사' 뒤에 appear actors라는 '자동사 + 주어' 형태의 도치된 완전한 문장이 왔으며 해석도 '그런데 배우들이 앞 무대 위에 등장한다'라는 자연스러운 의미가 되므로 on which는 적절하게 쓰였다. 참고로, 장소의 부사구(on which = on the proscenium of a stage)가 문장 앞에 와서 도치가 일어났다.

해석 직사각형의 화면이 배우가 등장하는 앞 무대와 유사하게 보이면서, 초기에 영화는 매우 강력한 일종의 마술 공연장으로 여겨졌다.

19 정답 ③

해설 한 문장 안에 동사가 2개(do / helps)이면 접속사/관계사/의문사가 하나 있어야 한다. 빈칸 뒤에 오는 문장이 주어가 없는 불완전한 문장이므로 관계부사 또는 의문부사인 where는 답이 될 수 없고 빈칸 앞에 선행사로 받을 수 있는 사람 명사가 오지 않았으므로 관계대명사 who도 답이 될 수 없다. 따라서 빈칸에는 문맥상 앞의 문장 전체를 선행사로 받을 수 있는 관계대명사 which가 와야 한다.

해석 나는 에어로빅을 일주일에 세 번 하는데, 그것이 내 몸매를 유지하게 돕는다.

20 정답 ③

해설 한 문장 안에 동사가 2개(was interested / was found)이면 접속사/관계사/의문사가 하나 있어야 한다. 빈칸은 The novel을 선행사로 받으면서 뒤에 온 완전한 문장을 이끌어야 하는데, 문맥상 be interested in 구문을 이루어 '그런데 그 소설에 엄마가 관심이 있다'라는 의미가 되는 것이 적절하므로 빈칸에는 '전치사 + 관계대명사' 형태인 in which가 와야 한다.

해석 다락방에서 엄마가 좋아하시는 소설이 발견되었다.

21 정답 ①

해설 빈칸 앞에 동사 guessed가 있고 뒤에 동사가 있는 문장이 오는 것으로 보아, 선택지에서 전치사 about을 제외하면 that(접속사), where(의문사), who(의문사)는 모두 명사절을 이끄는 접속사에 해당하므로 빈칸은 명사절 접속사 자리이다. 하지만 뒤에 완전한 문장이 온 것으로 보아, who는 올 수 없고, 문맥상 '베이킹소다가 훌륭한 세정제라는 사실을 짐작하다'라는 의미가 자연스러우므로 빈칸에는 접속사 that이 와야 한다.

해석 베이킹소다가 훌륭한 세정제라는 사실을 누가 짐작할 수 있었을까?

22 정답 ②

해설 빈칸 앞에 명사가 있고 뒤에 현재분사가 있는 구조에, 선택지가 모두 '관계대명사 + be동사' 형태인 것으로 보아 빈칸을 포함한 이하는 관계대명사절이라는 것을 알 수 있다. 문맥상 관계대명사절의 수식을 받는 것이 그들의 비행기를 기다리는 '공항'이 아니라 '사람들'이므로 빈칸에는 사람 명사 people을 선행사로 받으며 그에 동사의 수를 일치시킨 who were가 와야 한다.

해석 그 소년은 공항에서 비행기를 기다리는 사람들의 그림을 그렸다.

23 정답 ②

해설 한 문장 안에 동사가 2개(was destroyed / was confirmed)이면 접속사/관계사/의문사가 하나 있어야 한다. 그리고 문맥상 앞에 온 명사 a fire를 선행사로 받으면서 전치사 of 뒤에 올 수 있어야 하므로 빈칸에는 관계대명사 which가 와야 한다. '화재의 원인'이라는 뜻의 소유격을 나타내는 관계대명사절 '명사(선행사), 명사 + of which + V' 구조이다. 참고로, 전치사 뒤에 관계대명사 that은 올 수 없고, '명사 of 명사' 형태를 이루는 곳에 관계부사도 올 수 없다.

해석 그 건물은 화재로 소실되었는데, 그 화재의 원인은 전혀 확인되지 않았다.

24 정답 ②

해설 빈칸 앞에 동사 can see가 있고 뒤에 동사(buy)가 있는 문장이 오는 것으로 보아, 선택지 중 앞에 명사가 와야 하는 of which를 제외하고 who(의문사), which(의문사), that(접속사)은 모두 명사절을 이끄는 접속사에 해당하므로 빈칸은 명사절 접속사 자리이다. 하지만 뒤에 명사 products와 명사 customers가 연달아 나오는 구조이며 buy의 목적어가 없는 불완전한 문장이므로, 완전한 문장을 이끄는 that은 올 수 없고, 명사 products를 수식할 수 없는 who도 적절치 않다. 따라서 빈칸에는 '어느(것)'이라는 뜻으로 명사를 수식하며 불완전한 문장을 이끄는 의문형용사 which가 와야 한다. 문맥상 '고객이 어떤 제품을 가장 자주 구매하는지'라는 의미도 자연스럽다.

해석 구매 내역을 추적함으로써 고객이 어떤 제품을 가장 자주 구매하는지 확인할 수 있다.

25 정답 ④

해설 한 문장 안에 동사가 2개(worked / dedicated)이면 접속사/관계사/의문사가 하나 있어야 한다. 문맥상 빈칸 뒤에 오는 문장이 '그런데 자원봉사자들 대부분이 자신들의 시간을 할애했다'라는 의미로 사람 명사 volunteers를 수식하는 관계사절이고, '명사, 부정대명사(most) + of + 목적격 관계대명사 + V(dedicated)' 구조인 것으로 보아, 빈칸에는 사람 명사를 선행사로 받는 목적격 관계대명사 whom이 와야 한다.

해석 그 NGO는 자원봉사자들과 함께 캠페인을 진행했는데, 그들 대부분은 대의를 위해 자신의 시간을 할애했다.

26 정답 ①

해설 한 문장 안에 동사가 3개(are / want / want)이면 접속사/관계사/의문사가 2개 있어야 하는데 1개(and)밖에 없다. 빈칸 앞에 명사가 있고 뒤에 주어가 없는 불완전한 문장이 왔으므로 빈칸은 주격 관계대명사 자리인데, 문맥상 관계대명사절의 수식을 받는 것이 산업 근로자가 되고 싶은 '도시들'이 아니라 '사람들'이므로 빈칸에는 사람 명사 those를 선행사로 받는 관계대명사 who가 와야 한다. 참고로, those who는 '~하는 사람들'이란 표현으로 잘 쓰인다.

해석 도시에는 산업 근로자가 되고 싶고 기계에 대해서만 배우고 싶어 하는 사람들이 있다.

27 정답 ③

해설 빈칸 앞에 전치사 about이 있고 뒤에 동사(will win)가 있는 문장이 오는 것으로 보아, 빈칸은 전치사의 목적어 역할을 하는 명사절을 이끄는 접속사 자리이다. 하지만 빈칸 뒤가 주어가 없는 불완전한 구조이며 문맥상 '올해는 누가 우승을 차지할지'라는 의미가 자연스러우므로 빈칸에는 의문대명사 who가 와야 한다. 참고로, 접속사 that은 전치사 뒤에 올 수 없고, 의문형용사 whose는 뒤에 명사가 와야 하며, 의문부사 when은 뒤에 완전한 문장이 온다.

해석 특히 박빙의 승부가 펼쳐지는 가운데 올해는 누가 우승을 차지할지 모두가 궁금해하고 있다.

28 정답 ③

해설 한 문장 안에 동사가 2개(urged / sacrificed)이면 접속사/관계사/의문사가 하나 있어야 한다. 빈칸 앞에 명사 the dangerous task가 있고 뒤에 완전한 문장이 왔으므로 빈칸은 관계부사 또는 '전치사 + 관계대명사' 자리이다. 따라서 빈칸에는 둘 중 하나에 해당하는 for which가 와야 한다. 참고로, sacrifice는 'B를 위해 A를 희생하다'라는 뜻을 나타낼 때 'sacrifice A for B'의 구조로 쓰인다.

해석 책임감이 그로 하여금 결국 자신을 희생하게 한 위험한 일을 맡도록 재촉하였다.

29 정답 ①

해설 한 문장 안에 동사가 2개(includes / is hosting)이면 접속사/관계사/의문사가 하나 있어야 한다. 빈칸 앞에 명사 The National Museum of Korea가 있고 뒤에 완전한 문장이 왔으므로 빈칸은 관계부사 또는 '전치사 + 관계대명사' 자리이다. 하지만 선택지 중 이에 해당하는 것이 없는데, 사실 소유격 관계대명사도 뒤에 오는 명사를 포함해서 완전한 문장을 이끄는 구조로 볼 수 있으므로 빈칸에 올 수 있다. 또한 문맥상 '그런데 한국 국립 박물관의 소장품은 고대 유물을 포함한다'라는 자연스러운 의미가 되므로 빈칸에는 whose가 와야 한다.

해석 소장품에 고대 유물을 포함하고 있는 한국 국립 박물관에서 이번 달에 특별 전시회를 개최한다.

30 정답 ④

해설 한 문장 안에 동사가 2개(lost / held)이면 접속사/관계사/의문사가 하나 있어야 한다. 문맥상 빈칸 뒤에 오는 문장이 사물 명사 cargo containers를 수식하는 관계사절이고, '부정대명사 + of + 목적격 관계대명사' 형태로 쓸 때 관계대명사 whom 또는 which를 쓰므로 빈칸에는 one of which가 와야 한다.

해석 1992년 1월 10일, 거친 바다를 항해하던 배 한 척이 12개의 화물 컨테이너를 잃었는데, 그중 하나는 28,800개의 물에 뜨는 욕실 장난감을 담고 있었다.

전략 20-21

전략 적용 연습

본서 p. 112

01 X, did you see → you saw
02 X, that → what
03 X, that → whom
04 O
05 X, what → that 또는 which
06 O
07 X, that → which
08 X, what → that
09 X, that → what
10 O
11 ④ 12 ④ 13 ②
14 ① 15 ③ 16 ③

01 정답 X, did you see → you saw

해설 동사 remember의 목적어 자리에 온 의문사 when and where가 이끄는 간접의문문으로, 의문사 뒤에는 '주어 + 동사'의 어순으로 써야 하므로 did you see를 you saw로 고쳐야 한다.

해석 그 그림을 언제 그리고 어디서 보았는지 기억하니?

02 정답 X, that → what

해설 동사 know의 목적어 자리에 온 that은 접속사인데, 뒤에 완전한 문장이 아닌 '자동사 + 전치사' had agreed on의 목적어가 없는 불완전한 문장이 왔으므로 that은 적절치 않다. 따라서 문맥상 '무엇을 합의했는지'라는 의미가 되어 불완전한 문장을 이끄는 의문사 what으로 고쳐야 한다.

해석 그는 그들이 비공개로 무엇을 합의했는지 알고 싶어 했다.

03 정답 X, that → whom

해설 전치사 뒤에 that은 올 수 없다. 따라서 문맥상 사람 명사 The woman을 선행사로 받아 전치사 about 뒤에 온 완전한 문장을 이끄는 목적격 관계대명사 자리이므로 that을 whom으로 고쳐야 한다.

해석 내가 이야기하고 있던 여자가 갑자기 방으로 걸어 들어왔다.

04 정답 O

해설 전치사 in 뒤에 that이 온 구조로, 원래 전치사 뒤에는 that이 나올 수 없지만 예외의 경우로 '~한다는 점에서'라는 뜻의 접속사 in that으로 쓰일 수 있다. 여기서 문맥상 '모든 것을 자기 자신에게 의존해야 한다는 점에서'라는 의미가 자연스러우므로 in that은 적절하게 쓰였다.

해석 혼자 여행하는 것은 모든 것을 자기 자신에게 의존해야 한다는 점에서 어려울 수 있다.

05 정답 X, what → that 또는 which

해설 what 앞에는 명사가 올 수 없다. 따라서 문맥상 사물 명사 the car를 선행사로 받아 뒤에 buy의 목적어가 없는 불완전한 문장을 이끄는 목적격 관계대명사 자리이므로 what을 that 또는 which로 고쳐야 한다.

해석 나는 돈을 충분히 저축하자마자 아버지에게 내가 살 예정인 차의 사진을 보여드렸다.

06 정답 O

해설 앞에 동사 question이 나왔으므로 what은 관계대명사 또는 의문사이다. 뒤에 are told의 목적어가 없는 불완전한 문장이 왔으며, 해석도 '우리가 들은 것'이라는 자연스러운 의미가 되므로 관계대명사 what은 적절하게 쓰였다.

해석 첫째, 비판적 사고가 있는데, 그것은 정보를 분석하고 우리가 들은 것에 의문을 제기하는 기술을 강조한다.

07 정답 X, that → which

해설 관계대명사 that 앞에는 콤마(,)가 나올 수 없다. 따라서 문맥상 사물 명사 The gift를 선행사로 받아 뒤에 주어가 없는 불완전한 문장을 이끄는 주격 관계대명사 which로 고쳐야 한다.

해석 내 친구로부터 온 선물은 작은 상자 안에 담겨 도착했는데, 내가 가장 좋아하는 작가의 희귀본이었다.

08 정답 X, what → that

해설 전명구(for some time)를 괄호 치면 앞에 동사 have believed가 나온 것을 알 수 있으므로 what은 관계대명사 또는 의문사이다. 하지만 뒤에 불완전한 문장이 아닌 완전한 문장이 왔으므로 동사의 목적어 자리에 오며 완전한 문장을 이끄는 명사절 접속사 that으로 고쳐야 한다.

해석 많은 사회 과학자들은 한동안 출생 순서가 성인기의 성격과 성취 둘 다에 직접적으로 영향을 미친다고 믿어 왔다.

09 정답 X, that → what

해설 동사 suggested의 목적어 자리에 온 that절 내에 등위접속사 and를 중심으로 동사 sit down과 write down이 병렬 구조를 이루고 있다. 부사구(on paper)를 괄호 치면, 동사 write down의 목적어 자리에 온 that은 접속사인데, 뒤에 완전한 문장이 아닌 전치사 about의 목적어가 없는 불완전한 문장이 왔으므로 that은 적절치 않다. 따라서 동사의 목적어 역할을 하며 불완전한 문장을 이끄는 관계대명사 what으로 고쳐야 한다. 참고로, 만약 that을 앞에 온 명사 paper를 선행사로 받아 불완전한 문장을 이끄는 목적격 관계대명사로 보는 경우, 문맥상 '그런데 그들은 서로에게 종이에 대해 불만족스러워했다'라는 어색한 의미가 된다.

해석 의사는 부부 모두 식탁에 앉아 서로에게 불만이 있는 것을 종이에 적으라고 제안했다.

10 정답 O

해설 동사 know의 목적어 자리에 온 'A, B, and C' 병렬 구조에서 A, B, C 모두 간접의문문이다. 간접의문문은 '의문사 + 주어 + 동사'의 어순을 취하며, 문맥상 간접의문문의 '그녀의 어머니가 돌아가신' 것은 주절의 알고 싶은 과거 시점(wanted)보다 더 이전이므로 과거완료시제가 오는 것이 적절하다. 따라서 과거완료시제의 간접의문문 형태인 how long her mother had been dead는 적절하게 쓰였다.

해석 Robert는 Susan과 잘 사귀고 있었고 그녀와 결혼할 생각을 하고 있었다. 그는 그녀의 자매들이 어떤 사람인지, 그녀의 아버지는 어떤지, 그녀의 어머니가 돌아가신 지 얼마나 됐는지를 알고 싶었다.

11 정답 ④

해설 빈칸은 동사 understand의 목적어 자리로, 주어진 선택지로 보아 의문사가 이끄는 간접의문문이 온 구조이다. 하지만 의문대명사 what은 불완전한 문장을 이끌고 의문부사 how는 완전한 문장을 이끄는데, 빈칸 뒤에 동사와 목적어까지 온 완전한 구조의 문장을 이루고 있으므로 의문부사가 오는 것이 적절하다. 또한 간접의문문은 '의문사 + 주어 + 동사'의 어순을 취하므로 빈칸에는 how the writer is가 와야 한다.

해석 대강 훑어보면, 당신은 작가가 그 소재를 어떻게 묘사하고 있는지 알 수 있다.

12 정답 ④

해설 빈칸 앞에 형용사 aware가 있고 뒤에 완전한 문장이 온 것으로 보아, 빈칸에는 'be aware that + 완전한 문장' 구조로 aware의 보어 역할을 할 수 있는 명사절 접속사 that이 와야 한다. 참고로, '~을 알고 있는'이라는 뜻의 aware 뒤에는 'of + 명사(구/절)' 또는 that절이 온다.

해석 세관 규정은 국가마다 크게 다를 수 있다는 점에 유의하세요.

13 정답 ②

해설 한 문장 안에 동사가 2개(is dropping / is)이면 접속사/관계사/의문사가 하나 있어야 한다. 빈칸은 문장의 본동사 is의 주어 역할을 하며 완전한 문장을 이끄는 명사절 접속사 자리이므로 접속사 That이 와야 한다. 참고로, 의문대명사 who, which, what 뒤에는 불완전한 문장이 오며, 여기서 동사 drop은 '감소하다'라는 뜻의 자동사로 쓰였다.

해석 성인 흡연율이 점차 감소하고 있다는 것은 거대 담배 회사들에게 좋은 소식은 아니다.

14 정답 ①

해설 전명구(in the village), 과거분사구(built by craftsmen), 삽입절(it is said)을 괄호 치면, 동사가 2개(is / possessed)이므로 접속사/관계사/의문사가 하나 있어야 한다. 빈칸 앞에 명사(an ancient bridge / the village / craftsmen)가 있고 뒤에 주어가 없는 불완전한 문장이 왔으므로 빈칸은 주격 관계대명사 자리이다. 문맥상 선행사를 넣어 해석했을 때 '그런데 장인들은 뛰어난 지식과 정밀성을 지니고 있었다'라는 의미가 자연스러우므로 관계대명사절의 선행사는 craftsmen이다. 사람 선행사이므로 which는 올 수 없고, 콤마(,) 뒤 자리이므로 that도 올 수 없으며, 선행사를 포함하는 what은 앞에 명사가 있으므로 적절치 않다. 따라서 빈칸에는 사람 선행사를 받아 콤마 뒤에 계속적 용법으로 쓸 수 있는 주격 관계대명사 who가 와야 한다.

해석 그 마을에는 장인들이 만든 고대 다리가 있는데, 그들은 뛰어난 지식과 정밀성을 지니고 있었다고 한다.

15 정답 ③

해설 한 문장 안에 동사가 3개(host / can discuss / share)이면 접속사/관계사/의문사가 2개 있어야 하는데 1개(and)밖에 없다. 빈칸 앞에 전치사 at이 있고 뒤에 완전한 문장이 왔으므로 빈칸은 명사 book clubs를 선행사로 받아 전치사의 목적어 역할을 하며 뒤에 온 완전한 문장을 이끄는 목적격 관계대명사 자리이다. 따라서 빈칸에는 전치사 at과 함께 '전치사 + 관계대명사' 형태를 완성하는 which가 와야 한다. 참고로, 관계대명사 what은 불완전한 문장을 이끌고, that은 전치사 뒤에 올 수 없으며, 관계부사 where는 '전치사 + 관계대명사'를 대신하므로 전치사가 또 올 수 없다.

해석 지역 도서관은 고객이 편리한 시간에 흥미로운 소설에 대해 토론하고 추천 도서를 공유할 수 있는 북클럽을 주최한다.

16 정답 ③

해설 4형식 동사 show의 직접목적어 자리에 등위접속사 and를 중심으로 명사절 3개(______ / how / whether)가 병렬 구조를 이루고 있다. 빈칸은 직접목적어 역할을 하며 '자동사 + 전치사' consisted of의 목적어가 없는 불완전한 문장을 이끄는 명사절 접속사 자리이다. 의문사 who와 whom은 지구를 구성하는 게 사람이 아니므로 올 수 없고, 접속사 that 뒤에는 완전한 문장이 와야 하므로 적절치 않다. 따라서 빈칸에는 '지구가 무엇으로 구성되어 있었는지'라는 의미의 명사절을 이끄는 의문사 what이 와야 한다.

해석 암석과 토양은 지질학자들에게 수백만 년 전 지구가 무엇으로 구성되어 있었는지, 그 이후로 어떻게 변화했는지, 그리고 여전히 변화하고 있는지를 보여 준다.

전략 22-23

전략 적용 연습

본서 p. 116

01 O
02 O
03 X, stress → stressful
04 X, whomever → whoever
05 O
06 X, enjoying → enjoy
07 X, No matter what → No matter how 또는 However
08 O
09 X, however → whatever
10 X, to place → placing
11 X, evaluates → evaluate
12 X, taking → take
13 ② 14 ① 15 ④
16 ④ 17 ③ 18 ②

01 정답 O

해설 동사 do의 목적어 역할을 하는 명사절을 이끌어야 하는 자리로, 뒤에 wants의 목적어가 없는 불완전한 문장이 왔으므로 복합관계대명사 whatever의 쓰임은 적절하다. 해석상으로도 '그가 원하는 것이면 무엇이든'이라는 자연스러운 의미가 된다.

해석 나는 그 팀이 그가 원하는 것은 무엇이든 기꺼이 할 것이라고 확신한다.

02 정답 O

해설 등위접속사 and를 중심으로 문장의 본동사 stopped 또는 동명사 going out과 병렬된 구조인지 해석으로 확인한다. 문맥상 '친구들과 함께 놀러 나가는 것을 그만두고 첼로를 연습했다'라는 의미의 본동사가 병렬되는 것이 자연스러우므로 과거시제의 동사 practiced의 쓰임은 적절하다.

해석 나는 친구들과 함께 놀러 나가는 것을 그만두고 끊임없이 첼로를 연습했다.

03 정답 X, stress → stressful

해설 'A뿐만 아니라 B도'라는 뜻의 'not only A but also B' 구문으로, not only 뒤에 온 문장의 형용사 보어 joyful과 같은 형태가 but also 뒤에도 와야 하므로 명사 또는 동사 stress를 형용사 stressful로 고쳐야 한다.

해석 결혼식을 계획하는 것은 즐거운 일이지만 때때로 스트레스가 될 수도 있다.

04 정답 X, whomever → whoever

해설 전치사 to의 목적어 역할을 하는 명사절을 이끌어야 하는 자리로, 뒤에 주어가 없는 불완전한 문장이 왔다. 복합관계대명사의 격은 복합관계사절 내에서 결정되는데, 여기서는 복합관계사절 내에 주어가 없으므로 목적격인 whomever를 주격인 whoever로 고쳐야 한다.

해석 이 쪽지를 행사 조직을 책임지는 사람에게 신속히 전달해라.

05 정답 O

해설 복합관계부사 However가 뒤에 온 형용사 weary를 수식해 'however + 형/부 + S + V' 구조의 부사절을 이끌고 있으며, 해석상으로도 '아무리 네가 지치더라도'라고 자연스러운 의미가 되므로 However는 적절하게 쓰였다.

해석 아무리 네가 지치더라도, 한 걸음 한 걸음 앞으로 나아가야 한다.

06 정답 X, enjoying → enjoy

해설 등위접속사 and를 중심으로 동사 learn의 목적어 자리에 온 to 부정사의 동사 swim, surf, enjoying이 병렬 구조를 이루는 문장이므로 enjoying을 enjoy로 고쳐야 한다. 뒤에 오는 to 부정사에서 공통부분인 to를 생략한 구조이다.

해석 아이들은 수영, 서핑 및 안전한 물놀이를 배울 수 있는 곳이 필요하다.

07 정답 X, No matter what → No matter how 또는 However

해설 No matter what은 '추위가 무엇이든지 간에'라고 해석되어 문맥상 어색한 의미를 전달하므로 '아무리 추워도'라는 의미를 나타내는 No matter how 또는 However로 고쳐야 한다. 참고로, cold는 형용사이자 명사이므로 how와 함께일 때는 형용사, what과 함께일 때는 명사로 쓰인 구조이다.

해석 아무리 밖이 추워도 가끔 환기를 시켜 주어야 한다.

08 정답 O

해설 등위접속사 or를 중심으로 전치사 by의 목적어 자리에 온 동명사 pushing, depressing, sliding이 병렬 구조를 이루는 문장이므로 동명사 형태의 sliding은 적절하게 쓰였다. 또한 대명사 them은 앞에 나온 복수 명사 the doors를 가리키는 복수형으로 적절하게 쓰였다.

해석 지하철에서는 버튼을 누르거나 레버를 아래로 당기거나 옆으로 밀어서 직접 문을 열어야 한다.

09 정답 X, however → whatever

해설 부사절을 이끄는 복합관계부사 however 뒤에는 반드시 형용사나 부사가 와야 하며 완전한 문장 구조를 취한다. 여기서는 뒤에 명사 struggles를 수식하며 주어와 타동사로만 이루어진 불완전한 구조의 부사절을 이끌어야 하므로 복합관계형용사가 오는 것이 적절하다. 문맥상으로도 '어떤 어려움에 직면하더라도'라는 자연스러운 의미가 되므로 however를 whatever로 고쳐야 한다.

해석 네가 어떤 어려움에 직면하더라도 친구와 가족이 곁에 있으니, 혼자가 아니라는 사실을 기억해야 한다.

10 정답 X, to place → placing

해설 등위접속사 and를 중심으로 전치사 of의 목적어 자리에 온 동명사 operating과 함께 병렬 구조를 이루는 문장이므로 to 부정사 to place를 동명사 placing으로 고쳐야 한다. 문맥상으로도 '그러한 도구들을 올바르게 조작하고 그것들을 설치하는 데에 훨씬 더 능숙할 수 있다'라는 자연스러운 의미가 되므로 동명사가 적절하다.

해석 하지만 인간은 그러한 도구들을 올바르게 조작하고 그것들을 적절하고 유용한 위치에 설치하는 데에 훨씬 더 능숙할 수 있다.

11 정답 X, evaluates → evaluate

해설 등위접속사 and를 중심으로 how가 이끄는 명사절의 동사 integrates와 evaluates가 병렬 구조를 이루는 문장인데, 해석해 보면 '건물이 환경과 어떻게 통합되고 (건물이) 기능성과 지속 가능성을 평가하는지에 기초하여 건물을 설계한다'라는 어색한 의미가 된다. 따라서 and에 의해 문장의 본동사 design과 병렬 구조를 이루어 '당신은 건물이 환경과 어떻게 통합되는지에 기초하여 건물을 설계하고 (당신은) 기능성과 지속 가능성을 평가한다'라는 의미가 되도록 evaluates를 evaluate로 고쳐야 한다.

해석 건축가로서, 건물이 환경과 어떻게 통합되는지에 기초하여 건물을 설계하고 기능성과 지속 가능성을 평가한다.

12 정답 X, taking → take

해설 등위접속사 and를 중심으로 동사 avoid의 목적어 자리에 온 동명사 making과 taking이 병렬 구조를 이루는 문장인데, 해석해 보면 '성급한 결정을 내리는 것과 모든 선택지를 고려할 시간을 피해야 한다'라는 어색한 의미가 된다. 따라서 and에 의해 조동사 뒤 동사원형 avoid와 병렬 구조를 이루어 '성급한 결정을 내리는 것을 피하고 모든 선택지를 고려할 시간을 가져야 한다'라는 의미가 되도록 taking을 동사원형 take로 고쳐야 한다.

해석 장기적인 성공과 만족을 보장하려면 성급한 결정을 피하고 모든 선택지를 신중하게 고려하는 시간을 가져야 한다.

13 정답 ②

해설 등위접속사 and를 중심으로 동사 offer의 목적어 자리에 온 명사구 recreational facilities와 scenic walking trails가 병렬 구조를 이루는 문장이므로 빈칸은 and와 짝을 이루는 상관접속사 자리이다. 따라서 빈칸에는 'A와 B 둘 다'라는 뜻의 상관접속사 'both A and B'를 완성하는 both가 와야 한다.

해석 도시공원은 주민들을 위한 레크리에이션 시설과 경치가 좋은 산책로를 모두 제공한다.

14 정답 ①

해설 빈칸 앞에 등위접속사 and가 있으므로 앞의 문장 요소와 병렬 구조를 이루는데, 빈칸 뒤에 오는 it을 목적어로 취해야 하므로 동사 자리이다. 하지만 문맥상 문장의 보어 자리에 온 to 부정사 to start와 병렬 구조로 보는 것이 적절하므로 to expand가 오는데, to 부정사의 to가 반복될 때는 생략하므로 빈칸에는 동사원형 expand가 와야 한다.

해석 그녀의 야망은 자신의 사업을 시작하여 궁극적으로는 그것을 국제적으로 확장하는 것이다.

15 정답 ④

해설 한 문장 안에 동사가 3개(have / do not hesitate / may seem)이면 접속사/관계사/의문사가 2개 있어야 하는데 하나(If)만 있으므로 빈칸은 문장을 연결하는 접속사/관계사/의문사 자리이다. 빈칸 앞에 온 완전한 문장(명령문)이 콤마(,)로 분리되어 있고 빈칸 바로 뒤에 형용사 basic을 포함하여 완전한 문장이 이어지고 있으므로 빈칸에는 양보의 부사절을 이끌어 '아무리 그것(질문)들이 기본적인 것 같더라도'라는 의미가 되는 no matter how가 와야 한다. 참고로, 의문사 how와 what은 명사절을 이끄는데 명사절이 역할을 할 수 있는 자리가 없고, 복합관계대명사 whoever는 부사절을 이끌 수 있으나 뒤에 주어나 목적어가 없는 불완전한 문장이 와야 한다.

해석 강의 중에 질문이 있으면 아무리 그 질문이 기본적인 것 같더라도 주저하지 말고 물어봐라.

16 정답 ④

해설 빈칸은 As 부사절의 주어 자리에 온 명사구 the cash register와 the credit card machine을 연결하는 접속사 자리이다. 빈칸 앞에 neither가 있으므로 빈칸에는 'A와 B 둘 다 아닌'이라는 뜻의 상관접속사 'neither A nor B' 구문을 완성하는 nor가 와야 한다.

해석 금전 등록기와 신용 카드 기계가 모두 작동하지 않으므로 정확한 잔돈이 필요할 것이다.

17 정답 ③

해설 한 문장 안에 동사가 2개(was advised / had)이면 접속사/관계사/의문사가 하나 있어야 한다. 삽입절 he believed를 괄호치면, 빈칸은 전치사 to의 목적어 역할을 하며 뒤에 주어가 없는 불완전한 문장을 이끌어야 하는 자리이다. 관계대명사 who는 전치사 뒤에 올 수 없고, whom은 전치사 뒤에 올 수 있으나 앞에 사람 선행사가 없고 뒤에 주어가 없는 불완전한 문장이 왔기 때문에 적절치 않다. 따라서 빈칸은 명사절을 이끄는 복합관계대명사 자리인데, 복합관계사절 내에 주어가 없으므로 주격인 whoever가 와야 한다.

해석 관리자는 그가 책임감이 강하다고 생각하는 누구에게든 임무를 맡기라는 권고를 받았다.

18 정답 ②

해설 한 문장 안에 동사가 2개(conduct / rises)이면 접속사/관계사/의문사가 하나 있어야 한다. 빈칸 앞에는 완전한 문장이 왔으며 빈칸은 자동사 rises가 있는 완전한 문장을 이끌어야 하는 자리이다. 불완전한 문장을 이끄는 복합관계대명사 whatever는 올 수 없고, 이미 완전한 문장 구조이기 때문에 의문사 how가 이끄는 명사절이 역할을 할 수 있는 자리가 없다. 또한 앞에 명사가 오고 뒤에 명사를 포함한 완전한 문장을 이끌 수 있는 관계대명사 whose는 소유격이므로 뒤에 관사 the와 겹쳐서 쓸 수 없고 문맥상 '그런데 안전 훈련의 화재 위험이 커진다'라는 어색한 의미를 전달하므로 적절치 않다. 따라서 문맥상 '화재 위험이 높아질 때면 언제든'이라는 의미를 나타내도록 빈칸에는 복합관계부사 whenever가 와야 한다.

해석 시설 내 온도 상승이나 위험 물질로 인해 화재 위험이 커질 때면 언제든 안전 훈련을 실시하세요.

UNIT 04 형용사/부사 핵심 전략

전략 24-25

전략 적용 연습

본서 p. 120

01 X, financial → financially
02 X, efficient → efficiently
03 O
04 O
05 X, the less clearly → the less clear
06 X, conveniently → convenient
07 X, short → shortly
08 O
09 X, inadequately → inadequate
10 X, brilliant → brilliantly
11 O

12 ①	13 ②	14 ④
15 ①	16 ③	17 ③

01 정답 X, financial → financially

해설 be동사의 보어로 쓰인 형용사 independent 앞에서 수식하는 자리이므로 부사가 와야 한다. 문맥상으로도 '경제적으로 독립된'이라는 자연스러운 의미가 되도록 형용사 financial을 부사 financially로 고쳐야 한다.

해석 그녀는 경제적으로 독립하고 싶어 한다.

02 정답 X, efficient → efficiently

해설 형용사는 명사를 수식하므로 officer나 duties가 그 대상인데, 문맥상 적절치 않다. 따라서 동사 perform과 목적어 their duties 뒤에 와서 동사를 수식하는 구조로, '(임무를) 효율적으로 수행하다'라는 의미가 되는 것이 자연스러우므로 형용사 efficient를 부사 efficiently로 고쳐야 한다.

해석 각 경찰관은 자신의 임무를 효율적으로 수행해야 한다.

03 정답 O

해설 '~인 것 같다, ~처럼 보이다'라는 뜻의 seem은 대표적 2형식 동사로 뒤에 명사, 형용사, to 부정사를 주격 보어로 취하는데, 이 문장에서는 형용사가 와서 '대수롭지 않은 것처럼 보인다'라는 자연스러운 의미가 되므로 insignificant는 적절하게 쓰였다.

해석 당신의 고민과 난제들이 갑자기 대수롭지 않은 것처럼 보인다.

04 정답 O

해설 increase가 완전자동사로 쓰인 1형식의 완전한 문장 구조에서 동사에 의미를 더하는 수식어 역할로 부사 sharply가 왔는데, 문맥상으로도 '급격히 증가하다'라는 자연스러운 의미가 되므로 적절하게 쓰였다.

해석 그 도시의 인구는 다음 분기에 급격히 증가할 것이다.

05 정답 X, the less clearly → the less clear

해설 'the 비교급, the 비교급' 구문인데, 주절에서 'the 비교급'은 2형식 동사 become의 주격 보어 역할을 해야 한다. 따라서 문장 성분에 포함되지 않는 부사 대신 주격 보어로 쓰일 수 있는 형용사의 비교급이 와야 하므로 the less clearly를 the less clear로 고쳐야 한다.

해석 그러나 화질이 낮을수록, 이미지가 덜 선명해질 것이다.

06 정답 X, conveniently → convenient

해설 부사 conveniently가 동사 offers를 수식하여 '편리하게 제공하다'라는 의미를 나타내거나, seating을 형용사로 착각하여 부사가 형용사를 수식하는 구조로 볼 수 있으나, 둘 다 구조상으로도 문맥상으로도 적절치 않다. 따라서 형용사가 명사구 seating areas를 앞에서 수식하는 구조로, '편리한 좌석 공간'이라는 의미가 되는 것이 자연스러우므로 부사 conveniently를 형용사 convenient로 고쳐야 한다.

해석 호텔 로비에는 체크인을 기다리는 투숙객을 위한 편리한 좌석 공간이 마련되어 있다.

07 정답 X, short → shortly

해설 조동사 will과 동사 be looking 사이에서 동사를 수식하는 자리이므로 부사가 와야 한다. short는 형용사일 때 '부족한, 짧은'이라는 뜻이고 부사일 때 '부족하게, 짧게'라는 뜻인데, 문맥상 '(연비가 좋은 자동차를) 부족하게 찾게 될 것이다'라는 어색한 의미가 되므로 적절치 않다. 따라서 '곧'이라는 뜻의 부사 shortly를 써서 '곧 찾게 될 것이다'라는 자연스러운 의미가 되도록 short를 shortly로 고쳐야 한다.

해석 유가가 상승함에 따라 많은 운전자들이 곧 연비가 좋은 자동차를 찾게 될 것이다.

08 정답 O

해설 2형식 동사 proved의 주격 보어 자리에는 주어를 설명하는 형용사가 올 수 있으며, '식후 양치질이 필수적인 것으로 판명되다'라는 자연스러운 의미가 되므로 형용사 essential의 쓰임은 적절하다.

해석 구강 위생을 잘 유지하기 위해서는 식후 양치질이 충치 예방에 필수적인 것으로 판명되었다.

09 정답 X, inadequately → inadequate

해설 동사가 타동사일 때 'S + V + O + [형용사 vs 부사]'의 구조인 경우, 형용사는 목적어를 설명하며 부사는 동사를 설명(수식)한다. 문맥상 '부적당한(inadequate)' 것은 '널리 퍼져 있던 뮤지컬 언어(the prevailing musical idioms)'인 명사이지 '알아내는(found)' 동작이 아니다. 따라서 동사 find가 쓰인 5형식 문장 구조로 보고, 명사(목적어)를 설명하는 목적격 보어 자리에 온 부사 inadequately를 형용사 inadequate로 고쳐야 한다.

해석 그는 이내 널리 퍼져 있던 뮤지컬 언어가 부적당하다는 것을 깨닫고 새롭고 혁신적인 표현 방식을 탐구하기 시작했다.

10 정답 X, brilliant → brilliantly

해설 등위접속사 and를 중심으로 4개의 절이 병렬 구조를 이루고 있다. 앞에 쓰인 feel, smell, taste는 2형식 오감 동사로, 주어를 설명하는 주격 보어 자리에 형용사 fresher, sweeter, more delicious를 쓰는 것이 적절하지만, shine은 1형식 동사이다. 따라서 부사가 동사를 수식하여 '찬란하게 반짝이다'라는 의미가 되도록 형용사 brilliant를 부사 brilliantly로 고쳐야 한다.

해석 공기의 느낌이 더 신선해지고, 꽃 냄새가 더 향긋해지고, 음식 맛이 더 좋아지며, 밤하늘의 별이 더 찬란하게 반짝인다.

11 정답 O

해설 find가 5형식 동사로 쓰인 'find + 가목적어(it) + 형용사 + 진목적어(to RV)'의 문장 구조이다. 따라서 가목적어 it 뒤 목적격 보어 자리에 온 형용사 easy는 '그것(큰 이미지나 장면을 해석하는 것)이 쉽다고 여기다'라는 자연스러운 의미로 목적어를 설명하고 있으므로 적절하게 쓰였다.

해석 그런 증상이 있는 사람들은 큰 이미지나 장면을 해석하는 것이 쉽다고 여기지만, 세부 사항의 "차이점을 찾아내는" 데 어려움을 겪는다.

12 정답 ①

해설 빈칸은 명사 research를 수식하는 형용사 자리이다. 따라서 빈칸에는 '광범위한 연구'라는 자연스러운 의미가 되도록 형용사 extensive가 와야 한다. 참고로, 명사를 앞에서 수식하는 자리에 부사(extensively)와 동사(extend)는 올 수 없고, 명사(extension)와 명사(research)가 합쳐져 복합 명사가 될 수 있지만 '확대 연구'라는 어색한 의미가 되므로 적절치 않다.

해석 과학자들은 최근 전 세계적으로 유행하고 있는 전염병에 대한 백신을 개발하기 위해 광범위한 연구를 진행했다.

13 정답 ②

해설 동사가 타동사일 때 'S + V + O + [형용사 vs 부사]'를 주로 묻는데, 형용사는 목적어를 설명하며 부사는 동사를 설명(수식)한다. in order to 부정사구 구조를 보면, '지속 가능한(sustainable)' 것은 '에너지 소비(energy consumption)'인 명사이지 '만드는(make)' 동작이 아니므로 make가 5형식 동사로 쓰인 문장 구조로 보는 것이 적절하다. 따라서 빈칸에는 명사(목적어)를 설명하는 목적격 보어 역할을 하며 부사 highly의 수식을 받아 '에너지 소비를 더욱 지속 가능하게 만들다'라는 의미가 되도록 형용사 sustainable이 와야 한다. 참고로, 사역동사 make는 목적격 보어 자리에 명사, 형용사, 원형부정사를 취할 수 있는데, 완전타동사 sustain은 목적어가 필요하고 명사 sustainability는 부사의 수식을 받을 수 없으므로 적절치 않다.

해석 시의회는 에너지 소비를 더욱 지속 가능하게 만들기 위해 모든 공공건물에 태양광 패널을 설치했다.

14 정답 ④

해설 빈칸이 없어도 완전한 문장을 갖추고 있으므로 빈칸은 to 부정사의 수동태 to be resolved와 전명구 in court 사이에서 다른 문장 성분에 의미를 더하는 수식어 자리이다. 따라서 문맥상 앞에 온 동사 be solved를 수식하여 '성공적으로 해결되다'라는 자연스러운 의미가 되도록 빈칸에는 부사 successfully가 와야 한다. 참고로, 명사 success는 과거분사 resolved와 함께 명사구를 이룬다고 해도 '해결된 성공'이라는 어색한 의미가 되고, succeed는 앞의 동사와 함께 연달아 나올 수 없으며, 형용사 successful은 동사를 수식할 수 없다.

해석 법무팀은 모든 서류를 면밀히 검토했으며, 법정에서 성공적으로 사건이 해결될 것으로 예상하고 있다.

15 정답 ①

해설 문장의 동사는 practice이고 그 앞이 모두 주어인데, 주어 자리에 온 명사구 안에 as ~ as 원급 비교 구문이 쓰인 구조이다. 빈칸은 원급 비교 구문을 완성하며 앞에 나온 명사 Cultures를 수식하는 형용사 자리이다. 문맥상으로도 '다양한 문화권'이라는 자연스러운 의미가 되므로 빈칸에는 diverse가 와야 한다. 참고로, 명사를 뒤에서 수식하는 자리에 부사(diversely), 명사(diversity), 동사(diversify)는 올 수 없다.

해석 과테말라의 마야인들, 그리고 캐나다 북서부의 이누이트족처럼 다양한 문화권에서는 부모와 유아가 함께 자는 것을 행한다.

16 정답 ③

해설 빈칸은 which가 이끄는 주격 관계대명사절에서 동사 will be 뒤에 오는 주격 보어 자리이다. 따라서 빈칸 앞에 온 부사 especially의 수식을 받아 '특히 유용한'이라는 자연스러운 의미가 되도록 형용사 useful이 와야 한다. 참고로, be동사 뒤에는 현재분사 using이 올 수 있지만 뒤에 목적어가 없고 문맥상 선행사인 멘토링 프로그램이 '사용하는' 것이 아니라 '사용되는' 것이므로 수동의 과거분사 used가 오는 것이 적절하다. 또한 be동사 뒤 주격 보어 자리에 주어와 동격을 이루는 명사 use가 올 수 있지만 부사의 수식을 직접 받을 수 없고, 부사 usefully가 앞에 온 부사의 수식을 받는다고 해도 문맥상 멘토링 프로그램이 '특히 유용하게 있을 것이다'라는 어색한 의미가 되어 적절치 않다.

해석 우리 대학은 캠퍼스 생활에 적응하는 신입생들에게 특히 유용한 멘토링 프로그램을 만들고 있다.

17 정답 ③

해설 빈칸은 수동태의 be동사(are)와 p.p.(surprised) 사이에서 동사를 수식하는 부사 자리이다. 문맥상으로도 '거듭 놀라다'라는 자연스러운 의미가 되므로 빈칸에는 부사 repeatedly가 와야 한다.

해석 연구자들은 아이들의 지능이 어떻게 개발되는지에 대해 더 많이 알게 되면서, 부모들의 힘에 거듭 놀라움을 금치 못한다.

전략 26-27

전략 적용 연습

본서 p. 124

01 X, much → many 또는 very
02 X, enough comfortable → comfortable enough
03 O
04 O
05 X, many → much
06 X, so → too
07 O
08 X, too → so
09 X, a little → a few
10 X, Such → So
11 ④ 12 ② 13 ①
14 ① 15 ③ 16 ④

01 정답 X, much → many 또는 very

해설 뒤에 오는 복수 명사 paintings를 수식하는 형용사 자리이므로 불가산명사(단수 명사)를 수식하는 much는 올 수 없다. 따라서 복수의 가산 명사를 수식할 수 있는 many로 고쳐야 한다. 또한 만약 (원급) 형용사 colorful을 수식하여 '매우 다채로운 그림'이라는 의미를 나타낸다면 much를 very로 고쳐야 한다.

해석 작가의 여러/매우 다채로운 그림이 미술관 전체를 환하게 밝힌다.

02 정답 X, enough comfortable → comfortable enough

해설 2형식 오감 동사 felt의 주격 보어 자리에 온 형용사 comfortable을 수식하는 부사 자리인데, enough가 부사로 쓰일 때는 형용사 뒤에서만 수식이 가능하므로 enough comfortable을 comfortable enough로 고쳐야 한다.

해석 그는 자신이 하고 싶은 일에 대해 나에게 말할 수 있을 만큼 편안함을 느꼈다.

03 정답 O

해설 원급 비교 구문 as ~ as 사이에 온 형용사 many가 뒤에 온 복수의 가산명사 twenty states를 수식하고 있으므로 many의 쓰임은 적절하다.

해석 이미 20개 주에서 정크 푸드 판매를 금지하고 있다.

04 정답 O

해설 very는 형용사의 원급을 수식(강조)할 수 있다. 따라서 be동사 is의 주격 보어 역할로 온 원급 형용사 important를 very가 수식하고 있는 것은 적절하다.

해석 사전에서 새로운 단어를 찾아보는 것은 언어를 배우는 데에 매우 중요하다.

05 정답 X, many → much

해설 that절을 살펴보면, 완전자동사 rise가 쓰인 1형식의 완전한 구조 뒤에 온 so many가 문맥상 동사를 수식하고 있다. 하지만 many는 형용사 또는 대명사로만 쓰이므로 동사를 수식할 수 없다. 따라서 부사 so와 함께 동사를 수식하여 '그렇게 많이 오르다'라는 자연스러운 의미가 되도록 many를 much로 고쳐야 한다. 참고로, much는 형용사, 대명사 및 부사로 쓰인다.

해석 여행객들은 휴가철에 물가가 그렇게 많이 오를 것이라고는 예상하지 못했다.

06 정답 X, so → too

해설 뒤에 형용사(distracted)와 to RV(to know)가 왔으므로 '너무 ~해서 ~할 수 없다'라는 뜻의 'too ~ to' 구문으로 쓰는 것이 적절하다. 문맥상으로도 '너무 정신이 팔려서 알지 못했다'라는 자연스러운 의미가 되므로 so를 too로 고쳐야 한다. 참고로, 여기서 that은 'so ~ that' 구문의 that이 아니라 to know의 목적어 자리에 온 명사절을 이끄는 that으로 쓰였다.

해석 그는 문자 메시지에 너무 정신이 팔려서 제한 속도를 초과해서 달리고 있다는 것을 몰랐다.

07 정답 O

해설 much는 형용사의 비교급을 수식(강조)할 수 있다. 따라서 2형식 동사 grow의 주격 보어 역할로 온 비교급 형용사 sharper를 much가 수식하고 있는 것은 적절하다.

해석 그러나 사람의 기억력은 긴 시간이 지난 후에도 훨씬 더 선명해지는 일이 또한 일어날 수도 있다.

08 정답 X, too → so

해설 뒤에 형용사(great)와 that절이 왔으므로 '너무 ~해서 (그 결과) ~하다'라는 뜻의 'so ~ that' 구문으로 쓰는 것이 적절하다. 문맥상으로도 '너무 훌륭해서 청중 전체가 그를 지지하는 것처럼 보였다'라는 자연스러운 의미가 되므로 too를 so로 고쳐야 한다.

해석 오찬 회의에서의 그의 연설은 너무 훌륭해서 청중 전체가 그를 지지하는 것처럼 보였다.

09 정답 X, a little → a few

해설 수량형용사 a little은 단수 명사(불가산명사)를 수식하는데, 수식을 받는 명사가 복수인 steps이므로 a little을 a few로 고쳐야 한다. 참고로, 수량형용사 a little과 형용사 basic 모두 명사 steps를 수식하고 있는데, 이처럼 형용사가 나열되는 경우 '지시형용사 → 수량형용사 → 상태/성질형용사' 순으로 온다.

해석 그들의 초급 댄스 수업에서는 걷기, 돌기, 간단한 안무 연습과 같은 몇 가지 기본 단계만 다루었다.

10 정답 X, Such → So

해설 문장의 보어인 형용사(imprudent)가 강조를 위해 문장 맨 앞으로 와서 주어와 동사가 도치된 구문이다. 원래의 어순으로 바꾸면 We are such imprudent that ~인데, such 뒤에는 형용사가 바로 올 수 없으므로 Such를 So로 고쳐야 한다. 참고로, '너무 ~해서 (그 결과) ~하다'라는 같은 뜻을 나타내는 'so/such ~ that' 구문이라도, such(형용사)는 명사를 수식하고, so(부사)는 형용사/부사를 수식한다.

해석 우리는 너무나 경솔해서 우리의 것이 아닌 시간 속에서 방황하고 우리에게 속한 것에 대해 생각하지 않는다.

11 정답 ④

해설 빈칸은 be동사 was와 주격 보어인 형용사 cooler 사이의 부사 자리이다. 빈칸 뒤에 비교급 형용사 cooler가 나왔으므로 비교급을 수식(강조)하는 부사 much가 와야 한다. 참고로, too와 very 둘 다 원급을 수식(강조)하는 부사이고, more는 cooler가 이미 비교급 형태이므로 혼용해서 쓸 수 없다.

해석 오늘 아침은 어제 아침보다 훨씬 더 시원했다.

12 정답 ②

해설 빈칸은 동사 stock의 목적어 자리에 온 명사구 genre of literature를 수식하는 형용사 자리이다. 빈칸 뒤에 가산명사이지만 단수 형태인 genre가 왔으므로 선택지 중 이를 수식할 수 있는 형용사는 every밖에 없다. all 뒤에는 복수 가산명사 또는 불가산명사(단수 명사)가 오고, a few와 each of 뒤에는 복수 명사가 와야 한다. 따라서 빈칸에는 뒤에 수식하는 명사와 함께 '모든 장르의 문학'이라는 의미를 나타내는 every가 와야 한다.

해석 이 서점의 포부는 고객을 위해 모든 장르의 문학을 구비하는 것이다.

13 정답 ①

해설 빈칸 뒤에 형용사(poor)와 that절이 나왔으므로 '너무 ~해서 ~하다'라는 뜻의 'so ~ that' 구문이 오는 것이 적절하다. too는 형용사를 수식할 수 있지만 to 부정사와 함께 'too ~ to' 구문으로 쓰이고, very는 형용사를 수식할 수 있지만 that절과 함께 쓰일 수 없고, such는 'such ~ that' 구문으로 쓰일 때 명사를 수식하므로 형용사 뒤에 명사가 필요하다.

해석 우리 부모님은 그 당시에 너무 가난해서 집을 살 수가 없었다.

14 정답 ①

해설 빈칸이 없어도 완전한 문장을 갖추고 있으므로 빈칸은 주격 보어인 형용사(clear)와 to 부정사(to convince) 사이에서 다른 문장 성분에 의미를 더하는 수식어 자리이다. 따라서 문맥상으로도 구조상으로도 '모든 사람에게 납득시킬 수 있을 만큼 명확하다'라는 의미가 자연스러우므로 빈칸에는 '형용사 + enough + to RV' 구문을 완성하는 부사 enough가 와야 한다. 참고로, 나머지 선택지인 many, other, such는 형용사 또는 명사이므로 이 문장에서 역할을 할 수 있는 자리가 없다.

해석 그녀의 설명은 모든 사람에게 그녀의 결백을 납득시킬 수 있을 만큼 명확했다.

15 정답 ③

해설 빈칸은 문장의 주어인 복수 명사 fresh fruits and vegetables를 수식하는 형용사 자리이다. 선택지 중 복수 명사를 수식할 수 있는 형용사는 many밖에 없고, 나머지 선택지인 each, every, much 뒤에는 단수 명사가 와야 한다. 따라서 빈칸에는 뒤에 수식하는 명사와 함께 '많은 신선한 과일과 채소'라는 의미를 나타내는 many가 와야 한다.

해석 식료품점에는 건강한 식단을 만들기에 완벽한 신선한 과일과 채소가 많이 있다.

16 정답 ④

해설 빈칸은 that절의 주어 자리로, 빈칸 뒤의 of the classrooms와 함께 명사구를 완성할 수 있는 명사가 오는 것이 적절하다. every는 형용사이므로 주어 자리에 올 수 없고, a number는 뒤에 복수 명사와 함께 쓰이나 복수 동사로 수일치하여야 하며, much는 of the 뒤에 불가산명사(단수 명사)가 나와야 한다. 따라서 빈칸에는 명사구를 완성하여 '각 교실'이라는 의미를 나타내는 each가 와야 한다.

해석 교장은 각 교실에 필요한 교재가 반드시 비치될 수 있도록 하는 데 최선을 다했다.

UNIT 05 비교/도치/대명사 핵심 전략

전략 28-29

전략 적용 연습 본서 p. 130

01 X, you should leave → should you leave
02 X, so I did → neither did I
03 O
04 X, she met → had she met
05 X, the emphasis is → is the emphasis
06 O
07 O
08 O
09 X, does he dream → did he dream
10 O
11 X, is → are
12 X, began → begun
13 ④ 14 ④ 15 ①
16 ① 17 ② 18 ③

01 정답 **X, you should leave → should you leave**

해설 부정의 부사구 Under no circumstances가 문두에 나온 경우, 주어와 동사가 도치된다. 따라서 원래의 '주어 + (조)동사'의 어순이 아닌 '(조)동사 + 주어'의 어순으로 써야 하므로 you should leave를 should you leave로 고쳐야 한다.

해석 어떤 상황에서도 너는 이곳을 떠나면 안 된다.

02 정답 **X, so I did → neither did I**

해설 부정문에 이어지는 동의 표현이므로 접속사 and 뒤에 so가 아닌 neither가 와야 하며, 주어와 동사도 도치되어야 한다. 따라서 앞 문장의 동사가 과거시제의 일반동사 did not go이므로 대동사 did를 쓰고 주어와 동사는 도치되어 'neither + V + S'의 어순이 되도록 so I did를 neither did I로 고쳐야 한다.

해석 Peggy는 그 드라마를 보러 가지 않았고, 나도 또한 그렇다[가지 않았다]

03 정답 **O**

해설 장소·방향·위치의 부사구 Right beside his desk가 문두에 나왔는데, 주어가 일반명사로 이루어진 명사구 a stack of books이고 동사가 자동사인 was이므로 주어와 동사가 도치될 수 있다. 따라서 was a stack of books로 주어와 동사가 도치된 것은 적절하며 진짜 주어인 단수 명사 a stack에 수일치한 단수 동사 was의 쓰임 또한 적절하다.

해석 그의 책상 바로 옆에는 읽기를 기다리고 있는 책이 한 무더기 있었다.

04 정답 **X, she met → had she met**

해설 부정의 부사구 No sooner가 문두에 나온 경우, 주어와 동사가 도치된다. 이때, No sooner 뒤에 이어지는 문장의 내용이 than 뒤에 나오는 문장의 내용보다 시제가 앞서기 때문에 과거시제(met)가 아닌 과거완료시제(had met)로 쓰는 것이 적절하다. 따라서 과거완료시제와 '(조)동사 + 주어'의 어순에 맞춰 she met을 had she met으로 고쳐야 한다.

해석 그녀는 남편을 만나자마자 불평하기 시작했다.

05 정답 **X, the emphasis is → is the emphasis**

해설 전명구(to the training program / on hands-on experience)를 괄호 치면, 주어는 the emphasis이고 be동사(is)의 보어로 쓰인 형용사(important)가 문두에 나온 구조이다. 형용사 보어가 문두에 나오면 주어와 동사가 도치되어 'be동사 + 주어'의 어순을 취하므로 the emphasis is를 is the emphasis로 고쳐야 한다.

해석 교육 프로그램에서 매우 중요한 것은 실습 경험에 중점을 둔다는 점이다.

06 정답 **O**

해설 긍정문에 이어지는 동의 표현으로, 접속사 and 뒤에 부사 so를 쓰고 주어와 동사는 도치된 'so + V(do) + S(its shareholders)'의 어순은 적절하다. 또한 앞 문장의 동사가 현재시제의 일반동사 prioritizes이고 뒤 문장의 주어가 복수 명사 its shareholders이므로 대동사 do가 쓰인 것도 적절하다.

해석 회사는 투자에 있어 ESG 원칙을 우선시하며 주주들도 그렇다[우선시한다].

07 정답 **O**

해설 부정의 부사구 Not only가 문두에 나온 경우, 주어와 동사가 도치된다. 원래의 '주어 + (조)동사'의 어순이 아닌 '(조)동사 + 주어'의 어순으로 쓰며, 여기서 뒤 문장의 시제가 과거시제(sent)이므로 문맥상 같은 시점에 벌어진 일을 나타내도록 과거시제를 쓰는 것이 적절하다. 따라서 조동사 did를 이용하여 도치한 did they send의 쓰임은 적절하다.

해석 그들은 다른 부품을 보냈을 뿐만 아니라, 엉뚱한 부서로 보냈다.

08 정답 **O**

해설 부사구 At certain times가 문두에 나오긴 했지만 '장소·방향·위치'를 나타내는 부사구가 아니라 '시간'을 나타내는 부사구이다. 따라서 도치 없이 '주어(dreams) + 동사(are)' 어순 그대로 쓴 것은 적절하며, 주어인 꿈(dreams)이 '실현하는' 것이 아니라 '실현되는' 것이므로 수동태로 쓰인 것도 적절하다.

해석 특정한 때에 꿈은 인내와 확고한 결의를 통해 실현된다.

09 정답 **X, does he dream → did he dream**

해설 주절을 보면, 부정부사 little이 문두에 나와 '(조)동사 + 주어'의 어순으로 주어와 동사가 도치되었는데, when이 이끄는 시간 부사절의 시제가 과거시제(left)이고 주절의 시제가 현재시제

(does)이다. 하지만 문맥상 '떠났을 때 꿈에도 생각지 못했다'라는 의미로 주절과 종속절 모두 과거의 같은 시점에 일어난 일을 나타내는 것이 적절하므로 과거시제의 조동사 did를 이용하여 does he dream을 did he dream으로 고쳐야 한다. 참고로, 주절에 부정어 little과 never가 있는데, 주절과 dream의 목적어 역할인 that절이 다른 절이므로 이중부정이라고 착각하면 안 된다.

해석 30년 전 고향을 떠날 때, 그는 다시는 고향을 못 볼 거라고 꿈에도 생각지 못했다.

10 정답 **O**

해설 장소·방향·위치의 부사구 On the southern shore of Lake Erie가 문두에 나왔는데, 주어가 일반명사 Cleveland이고 동사가 자동사인 lies이므로 주어와 동사가 도치될 수 있다. 따라서 lies Cleveland로 주어와 동사가 도치된 것은 적절하며 주어인 단수 명사 Cleveland에 수일치한 단수 동사 lies의 쓰임 또한 적절하다.

해석 Erie 호의 남쪽 연안에는 오하이오에서 가장 큰 대도시인 클리블랜드가 있다.

11 정답 **X, is → are**

해설 주절을 보면, 유도부사 there가 문두에 나와 주어와 동사가 도치되었는데, 도치 구문에서는 동사 다음에 나오는 명사, 즉 주어에 동사의 수를 일치시킨다. 따라서 동사구 is likely to be 뒤에 나온 복수 명사 significant health impacts가 주어이므로 이에 수일치하여 단수 동사 is를 복수 동사 are로 고쳐야 한다.

해석 강이 심하게 오염되면 지역 야생 동물의 건강에 심각한 영향을 미칠 가능성이 높다.

12 정답 **X, began → begun**

해설 Only를 포함한 부사구 Only recently가 문두에 나와 '(조)동사 + 주어'의 어순으로 주어와 동사가 도치되었는데, 주어는 municipalities이고 동사는 현재완료시제인 have begun인 구조에서 조동사 have가 앞으로 간 것이므로 뒤에는 p.p. 형태가 와야 한다. 따라서 과거동사 began을 과거분사형(p.p.)인 begun으로 고쳐야 한다.

해석 전 세계 지자체들은 최근에서야 사용성을 개선하기 위해 도시 쓰레기통의 혁신적인 디자인을 실험하기 시작했다.

13 정답 ④

해설 주어진 선택지로 보아, 긍정문 뒤에 접속사 and로 이어지는 동의 표현 'so + V + S'를 묻는 문제이므로 빈칸은 도치된 주어와 동사 자리이다. 앞 문장의 동사가 과거시제의 be동사 was이고 뒤 문장의 주어가 복수 명사 my parents이므로 빈칸에는 대동사 were를 이용하여 도치한 were my parents가 와야 한다.

해석 나는 서울에서 태어났고, 우리 부모님들도 그렇기[서울에서 태어나셨기] 때문에 서울 문화에 깊이 뿌리를 두고 계신다.

14 정답 ④

해설 문두에 빈칸이 있고 뒤에 주어와 동사가 도치된 구조(did he know)로 보아 도치 구문인데, 빈칸을 제외하고는 완전한 문장 구조를 갖추고 있으므로 빈칸은 부사 자리이다. 선택지에서 도치를 일으키는 부사는 부정어 Little밖에 없고, '그는 ~라는 사실을 거의 알지 못했다'라는 자연스러운 의미가 되므로 빈칸에는 동사를 수식하는 부정부사 Little이 와야 한다. 참고로, 접속사 Although는 빈칸 뒤에 주어와 동사가 연결되어 있다 하더라도 주절이 있어야 하고, No sooner는 접속사 than이 이끄는 절이 있어야 하며, Few는 형용사이자 명사이므로 동사를 수식할 수 없다.

해석 그는 자신이 아들에게 평생 동안 지속될 열정을 불어넣고 있다는 사실을 거의 알지 못했다.

15 정답 ①

해설 Only를 포함한 when 부사절(when ~ eased)이 문두에 나와 있는 것으로 보아, 도치 구문이다. 도치 구문에서 주어와 동사는 '(조)동사 + 주어'의 어순으로 쓰는데, 주절의 주어 theaters 앞에 조동사 did가 있으므로 빈칸은 본동사의 동사원형 자리이다. 따라서 빈칸에는 도치 구문을 완성하는 동사원형 reopen이 와야 한다.

해석 팬데믹 제한이 완화되고 나서야 극장은 일반인에게 다시 문을 열었다.

16 정답 ①

해설 앞 문장이 '조동사(will) + 주어(the mechanic)'의 어순으로 도치되었고, 뒤 문장에 but also가 있는 것으로 보아, 빈칸은 도치를 일으키며 but also와 짝꿍을 이루는 표현이 오는 자리이다. 'Not only ~ but also' 구문에서 부정어 Not only를 앞으로 보내 주어와 동사가 도치되므로 빈칸에는 도치 구문을 완성하는 Not only가 와야 한다. 참고로, So as to는 뒤에 동사원형이 와서 '~하기 위해서'라는 뜻의 목적을 나타내는 표현이고, In spite of는 '~에도 불구하고'라는 뜻의 구전치사이므로 뒤에 명사가 와야 하며, Just as는 '~처럼'이라는 뜻의 양태부사절 접속사인데 접속사가 이끄는 절에 주어와 동사가 도치되진 않는다.

해석 그 정비공이 차를 고쳐 줄 뿐만 아니라 일상적인 정비 점검도 해 줄 것이다.

17 정답 ②

해설 접속사 and로 이어진 뒤 문장을 보면, 빈칸 뒤에 '조동사(can) + 주어(the industry expert)'의 어순으로 주어와 동사가 도치된 구조이다. 동사는 조동사 can이 대동사로 쓰였으며 앞 문장이 부정문(cannot attend)인 것으로 보아, 부정 동의 표현이 뒤 문장에 쓰인 것으로 유추할 수 있다. 따라서 빈칸은 부정 동의 표현을 완성하는 부사 자리로, '업계 전문가들도 그렇다[참석할 수 없다]'라는 부정의 뜻을 나타내는 neither가 와야 한다. 참고로, 부사 so는 앞 문장이 긍정문일 때 쓰며, 접속부사 however와 부사 also는 문두에 왔다고 해서 주어와 동사가 도치되지 않는다.

해석 일정 충돌로 인해 기조 연설자는 콘퍼런스에 참석할 수 없으며 업계 전문가도 그렇다[참석할 수 없다].

18 정답 ③

해설 전명구(along with ~ invitation / for your convenience)와 관계사절(that shows ~ information)을 괄호 치면, 주어는 a map이고 동사는 is인데 주어와 동사가 도치되었다. 주어진 선택지가 모두 동사의 변화형인 것으로 보아, be동사의 형용사 보어가 문두에 와서 도치가 일어난 것을 유추할 수 있으므로 빈칸은 주어 a map과 문맥상으로 어울리는 형용사 보어 자리이다. 따라서 문장의 주어인 지도(a map)가 '첨부하는' 것이 아니라 '첨부되는' 것이므로 빈칸에는 수동의 과거분사인 Attached가 와야 한다. 참고로, 이 문장은 형용사가 강조를 위해 문두에 와 주어와 동사의 도치가 일어난 것으로 볼 수 있고, 주어가 수식어로 인해 문장이 길어져서 도치가 일어난 것으로 볼 수도 있다.

해석 여러분의 편의를 위해 공식 초대장과 함께 행사장 위치 및 주차 정보가 표시된 지도가 첨부되어 있습니다.

전략 30-31

전략 적용 연습

본서 p. 134

01 O
02 X, the other → the others
03 X, to look → looking
04 X, the worst → the worse
05 X, as cleverer → as clever
06 O
07 X, you → yourself
08 X, their close location → its close location
09 X, one → ones
10 X, themselves → them
11 O
12 X, those → that

13 ②	14 ①	15 ④
16 ①	17 ②	18 ②
19 ①	20 ③	

01 정답 O

해설 문맥상 올해의 '패션 경향'과 작년의 '패션 경향'이 비교 대상이므로 대명사 those가 가리키는 것은 복수 명사 fashion trends이다. 따라서 복수로 수일치한 those는 적절하게 쓰였고, 뒤에 This year와 대비되는 수식어구(of last year)가 붙은 것 또한 적절하다. 참고로, 원급/비교급/최상급 외에 의미상으로 비교급을 표현하는 표현들이 있는데 그중 'A는 B와 다르다'라는 뜻의 'A is different from B'가 쓰였다.

해석 올해의 패션 경향은 작년의 패션 경향과는 사뭇 다르다.

02 정답 X, the other → the others

해설 the other는 마지막 남은 것이 하나일 때 쓴다. 여기서는 4개의 suitcases 중에서 2개를 뺀 '나머지 것들'이 2개이므로, the other를 the others로 고쳐야 한다.

해석 여기 여행 가방이 네 개 있는데, 저는 두 개만 들고 갈 수 있어요. 나머지를 가져와 주세요.

03 정답 X, to look → looking

해설 more educational than이 있는 것으로 보아 비교급 문장이다. 비교되는 두 대상은 품사, 격, 내용이 같아야 하는데, 동명사 Visiting과 달리 뒤에 to 부정사 to look으로 쓰였으므로 to look을 동명사 looking으로 고쳐야 한다.

해석 농장을 방문하는 것이 책에서 농장을 보는 것보다 훨씬 더 교육적이다.

04 정답 X, the worst → the worse

해설 '~하면 할수록 더 ~하다'라는 뜻의 'the 비교급 + 주어 + 동사, the 비교급 + 주어 + 동사' 구문이다. 따라서 최상급 the worst를 앞에 나오는 The more와 병렬되며 2형식 오감 동사 sounded의 주격 보어 역할을 하는 형용사 bad의 비교급 the worse로 고쳐야 한다.

해석 그들이 자신들의 실수에 관해 설명하려 더 노력하면 할수록 그들의 이야기는 더 나쁘게 들렸다.

05 정답 X, as cleverer → as clever

해설 뒤에 as가 있는 것으로 보아 as ~ as 원급 비교 구문이다. be동사 was의 주격 보어인 형용사가 비교 구문으로 쓰였는데, as ~ as 사이에는 원급이 들어가야 하고 비교급 형태와 혼용해서 쓸 수 없으므로 as cleverer를 as clever로 고쳐야 한다.

해석 추리 소설 속 탐정은 Sherlock Holmes만큼 영리하여 사건을 쉽게 해결했다.

06 정답 O

해설 명사 arrows를 수식하는 소유격 대명사 their가 가리키는 대상을 찾아야 한다. 문맥상 '무엇/누구의' 화살이냐를 따졌을 때 their가 복수 명사 soldiers를 받아 '깃발은 병사들이 '자신들의[그들의]' 화살을 겨냥하는 방향을 알 수 있게 도와주었다'라는 의미가 되는 것이 자연스러우므로 복수형 소유격 대명사 their의 쓰임은 적절하다.

해석 깃발은 바람이 어느 쪽으로 부는지를 보여 주었고, 병사들이 자신들의 화살을 겨냥할 방향을 알 수 있게 도와주었다.

07 정답 X, you → yourself

해설 주절의 동사 ask의 목적어 you는 주어 you와 같은 대상을 가리킨다. 주어와 목적어가 같을 때 목적어 자리에는 '~ 자신[스스로]'이라는 뜻의 재귀대명사를 써야 하고, 문맥상으로도 '여러분은 자신에게 물어봐야 한다'라는 의미가 자연스러우므로 대명사 you를 재귀대명사 yourself로 고쳐야 한다. 참고로, 이 문장이 다수의 상대방에게 전달하는 말일 경우에는 2인칭의 복수형인 yourselves로도 쓸 수 있다.

해석 여러분이 어떤 일을 시도해 보고 실패하면, 여러분은 왜 의도했던 일에 실패했을까 하고 자신에게 물어야 한다.

08 정답 X, their close location → its close location

해설 명사구 their close location과 전명구 to these countries의 의미 관계를 따지면, 이러한 국가들과 지리적으로 인접해 있는 것은 'Korea'이다. 따라서 대명사가 가리키는 것이 단수 취급하는 고유명사 Korea이므로 복수형 their를 단수형 its로 고쳐야 한다. 참고로, 명사를 수식하는 한정사가 '소유격 대명사(its) + 형용사(close) + 명사(location)'의 순서로 쓰인 것은 적절하다.

해석 그러나 한국은 이러한 국가들과 지리적으로 인접해 있으면서도 그 치명적인 질병으로부터 면역된 상태를 유지해 오고 있다.

09 정답 X, one → ones

해설 앞에 언급된 명사의 반복을 피하고 정해지지 않은 막연한 것을 가리킬 때 부정대명사 one을 쓰는데, 앞에 수식어구가 올 수 있다. 이 문장에서 형용사 minor의 수식을 받는 부정대명사 one이 대신하고 있는 것은 상관접속사 'both A and B'로 연결된 복수 명사 events이므로 이에 수일치하여 단수형 one을 복수형 ones로 고쳐야 한다. 문맥상으로도 '큰 이벤트들과 작은 이벤트들 모두 지역사회를 결속시킨다'라는 자연스러운 의미가 된다.

해석 월드컵과 같은 큰 이벤트와 지역 축구 경기와 같은 작은 이벤트 모두 지역사회를 결속시킨다.

10 정답 X, themselves → them

해설 주어가 동명사구 Knowing they ~ health이고, 동사는 gives이며, 간접목적어로 재귀대명사 themselves, 그리고 직접목적어로 명사구 a boost of energy가 쓰인 4형식 문장이다. 목적어 자리에 재귀대명사가 쓰이려면 '주어 = 목적어' 관계가 성립되어야 하는데, 여기서 '아는 것'과 '그들'은 동일한 대상을 가리키는 것이 아니므로 재귀대명사가 올 수 없다. 따라서 목적어가 가리키는 것인 'they'을 대신하기 위해서는 재귀대명사 themselves를 인칭대명사 them으로 고쳐야 한다.

해석 건강을 위해 운동했다는 사실을 알면 그들은 처음에 얼마나 피곤했는지에 상관없이 활력을 얻는다.

11 정답 O

해설 문장 구조를 살펴보면, 3,000 patrons와 four times 사이에 '주격 관계대명사 + be동사'(which is)가 생략된 구조로, 명사 3,000 patrons를 주격 관계대명사절(형용사절)이 수식하고 있다. 주격 관계대명사절의 생략된 be동사의 주격 보어 자리에 형용사 many의 원급 비교가 쓰였는데, 배수사를 포함한 원급 비교 구문은 '배수사 + as + 형용사/부사의 원급 + as' 형태로 나타내므로 four times as many as는 적절하게 쓰였다. 참고로, 명사 뒤에 '주격 관계대명사 + be동사'가 생략되어 바로 형용사가 올 경우, 형용사가 뒤에서 명사를 수식하는 것으로도 볼 수 있다.

해석 현대화된 오페라 하우스는 이제 이전보다 4배 많은 3,000명의 관객을 편안하게 수용하여 전반적인 경험을 향상시킬 것이다.

12 정답 X, those → that

해설 문맥상 고대 로마의 '건축 양식'과 고대 그리스의 '건축 양식'이 비교 대상이므로 대명사 those가 가리키는 것은 단수 명사 the architecture이다. 따라서 대명사는 가리키는 대상과 수를 일치시켜야 하므로 those를 that으로 고쳐야 한다. 참고로, that 뒤에는 수식어구(of ancient Greece)가 붙을 수 있으므로 지시대명사 that의 쓰임은 적절하다.

해석 웅장한 아치와 돔이 특징인 고대 로마의 건축 양식과 달리, 고대 그리스의 건축 양식은 기둥과 대칭을 강조했다.

13 정답 ②

해설 주어진 선택지로 보아, 빈칸은 비교 구문이 들어가는 자리이다. 원급 비교는 'as + 형용사/부사의 원급 + as' 형태로 쓰고, 비교급 비교는 '형용사/부사의 비교급 + than' 형태로 쓰는데, very는 원급을 수식(강조)하는 부사이므로 비교급을 수식(강조)할 수 없다. 따라서 빈칸에는 선택지 중 올바른 비교 구문 형태로 쓰인 원급 as young as가 와야 한다. 참고로, 부정어와 함께 쓰인 원급 비교 구문 'A not as + 형용사/부사의 원급 + as B'는 'A는 B만큼 ~하지 않다'라는 뜻이다.

해석 Jane은 보이는 것만큼 젊지 않다.

14 정답 ①

해설 빈칸은 형용사 standard의 수식을 받는 명사 자리이다. 선택지 중 another, each, all은 형용사의 수식을 받지 못하므로 빈칸에는 ones밖에 올 수 없다. 또한 비교급 문장(more expensive than)에서 비교되는 두 대상은 품사, 격, 내용이 같아야 한다. Organic pet foods와 standard pet foods가 그 비교 대상인데, 앞에 언급된 명사 pet foods의 반복적인 쓰임 대신 대명사로 대신할 수 있으므로 복수 명사에 수일치하며 형용사의 수식을 받을 수 있는 ones를 쓰는 것이 적절하다.

해석 유기농 반려동물 사료는 일반 반려동물 사료보다 더 비싼 경향이 있다.

15 정답 ④

해설 주어진 선택지로 보아, 빈칸은 라틴계 형용사 preferable의 비교급 구문이 들어가는 자리이다. 'preferable to'는 '~보다 더 나은'이라는 뜻으로, than이 아닌 to와 함께 쓰이고 또한 비교급 강조 부사로는 very가 아닌 much가 쓰이므로 빈칸에는 much preferable to가 와야 한다. 참고로, very는 원급을 수식(강조)하는 부사이므로 비교급을 수식(강조)할 수 없다.

해석 아이들을 키우는 데 있어서 작은 마을이 대도시보다 훨씬 더 나아 보인다.

16 정답 ①

해설 빈칸은 to 부정사의 동사 accompany의 목적어 자리이다. 동사 asked의 5형식 문장에서 목적격 보어 to accompany의 의미상 주어는 목적어 her sisters인데, 문맥상 그녀의 자매들이 '그녀 자신' 또는 '그녀들 자신'이 아니라 '그녀'와 함께 가는 것이므로 빈칸에는 주어 She를 가리키는 목적격 대명사 her가 와야 한다. 참고로, 재귀대명사는 (의미상) 주어와 목적어가 같을 때 목적어 자리에 쓴다.

해석 그녀는 자매들에게 새 옷을 사러 그녀와 함께 쇼핑하러 가자고 부탁했다.

17 정답 ②

해설 빈칸은 관계사절(who made reservations)의 수식을 받으며 주어 역할을 하는 명사 자리로, 선택지 중 뒤에 수식어구가 올 수 있는 것은 those밖에 없다. 대명사 those는 주로 'those who/RVing/p.p./with ~'의 구조로 관계사절, 분사, 전명구의 수식을 받으며 '~하는 사람들'이라는 뜻을 나타낸다. 여기서 문맥상으로도 '예약한 사람들이 보장된 좌석을 차지할 것이다'라는 자연스러운 의미가 되므로 빈칸에는 those가 와야 한다.

해석 레스토랑이 붐비더라도 예약을 한 사람들에게는 좌석이 보장될 것이다.

18 정답 ②

해설 주어진 선택지로 보아, 비교 범위를 나타내는 부사구 Among ~ city가 강조를 위해 문두로 나온 문장에 들어갈 적절한 비교급 형태를 묻고 있다. 빈칸은 be동사 is의 주격 보어 자리로, 부사(easily)가 아닌 형용사(easy)가 오는데 정관사 the의 한정을 받으며 '가장 ~한'이라는 뜻을 나타내야 하므로 형용사의 최상급이 오는 것이 적절하다. 따라서 문맥상으로도 'Central Park가 대중교통으로 가기에 가장 쉽다'라는 자연스러운 의미가 되도록 빈칸에는 형용사 easy의 최상급 형태인 easiest가 와야 한다.

해석 시내의 공원 중 대중교통으로 가장 쉽게 갈 수 있는 곳은 Central Park다.

19 정답 ①

해설 빈칸은 수동태의 be동사(are)와 p.p.(achieved) 사이에서 동사를 수식하는 부사 자리인데, 뒤에 than이 나오므로 부사의 비교급이 오는 것이 적절하다. 따라서 빈칸에는 '부사 little + 부사 steadily'의 비교급 형태인 less steadily가 와야 한다.

해석 한 석유 회사에서 여성 임원들의 승진은 남성 임원들의 승진보다 덜 꾸준히 이루어지고 있다.

20 정답 ③

해설 빈칸은 부사절 접속사 while로 대조를 이루는 두 문장 중 주절의 주어 자리이다. 대상이 둘(Of the two job candidates)이라고 명시되어 있는 가운데, 종속절의 주어로 the other(나머지 한 명)가 왔으므로 주절의 주어에는 '처음 하나'를 뜻하는 부정대명사가 오는 것이 적절하다. 따라서 빈칸에는 대상이 둘일 때 쓰는 'one ~, the other ~' 구문을 완성하는 부정대명사 one이 와야 한다. 참고로, 동사가 2개(has / specializes)이고 접속사가 이미 1개(while) 있으므로 관계대명사 whom이 올 수 없다.

해석 두 명의 입사 지원자 중에서 한 명은 프로젝트 관리 경험이 있는 반면, 나머지 한 명은 고객 관리에 전문성을 가지고 있다.

PART 2 문법

PART 3 독해

UNIT 01 신유형 핵심 전략

전략 01

전략 적용 연습

본서 p. 142

01 ③ 02 ① 03 ②
04 ③ 05 ④

01 정답 ③

해설 개업 허가를 받기 위해 필요한 검사 절차 일정을 문의하고자 보내는 이메일이다. 따라서 이메일의 목적으로 가장 적절한 것은 ③ '검사관의 식당 방문 일정을 잡으려고'이다.

해석 수신: Tiffany Holland 〈tholland@athens.gov〉
발신: Artis Malone 〈a_malone@jersey.com〉
제목: 귀사의 일정
날짜: 5월 12일

친애하는 Holland 씨께,

Artis Malone입니다. 저희는 2주 전에 멜빌 거리에 조만간 개업하고자 하는 식당과 관련하여 전화 통화를 했습니다. 가능한 한 빨리 검사관이 제 식당을 방문해 주셨으면 합니다.

귀하는 제가 식당의 개업 허가를 받을 수 있기 전에 귀사의 직원 중 한 명이 그 구역을 검사해야 한다고 조언해 주셨습니다. 귀하는 식당이 귀하 부서의 인증을 받으면 일반인에게 음식과 음료를 제공할 수 있을 것이라고 말씀하셨습니다.

이제 제 식당의 공사가 완료되었으므로 귀사의 직원 중 한 명이 제 식당을 방문해 주시면 감사하겠습니다. 업무 시간 중에 언제든지 (552) 555-1183으로 전화하시어 검사 일정을 언제로 잡을 수 있는지 저에게 알려 주세요.

안부를 전하며,

Artis Malone 드림

어휘 intend 의도하다 inspector 검사관 establishment 상점, 영업소 permit 허가하다 remark 언급하다 certify 인증하다 department 부서 beverage 음료 construction 공사 appreciate 고마워하다 business hour 업무 시간

02 정답 ①

해설 목공 수업을 가르칠 자원봉사자가 필요하다는 공고를 읽은 Ernie Powers가 이메일을 통해 자기 경력을 소개하며 봉사 의사를 전하고 있다. 따라서 글의 목적으로 가장 적절한 것은 ① '자원봉사자로 일할 것을 제안하기 위해'이다.
② 최근에 자신이 진행한 워크숍에 대해 논의하기 위해
③ 학생들을 위한 목공 수업 개설을 요청하기 위해
④ 자신의 업무 경험에 대한 질문에 답변하기 위해

03 정답 ②

해설 2번째 단락 2번째 문장에서 현재는 자영업을 하고 있다고 언급되므로, 글의 내용과 일치하지 않는 것은 ② '현재 Mason 회사에서 근무하고 있다.'이다.
① 목수로 30년 넘게 일했다. → 2번째 단락 첫 문장에서 언급된 내용이다.
③ 탁자와 의자를 전문으로 제작한다. → 2번째 단락 3번째 문장에서 언급된 내용이다.
④ 목공 시연 워크숍을 진행한 적이 있다. → 2번째 단락 마지막 문장에서 언급된 내용이다.

02-03 해석 수신: Melanie James 〈melanie@springfieldcc.org〉
발신: Ernie Powers 〈ep@powermail.com〉
제목: 가을 학기 수업
날짜: 8월 27일

친애하는 James 씨께,

저는 방금 스프링필드 커뮤니티 센터 웹사이트에서 가을 학기 수업에 관한 공고를 읽었습니다. 저는 목공 수업을 가르칠 자원봉사자가 필요하다는 것을 알게 되었습니다.

저는 약 35년 동안 목수로 일해 왔습니다. 현재는 자영업을 하고 있지만 저는 18년 동안 Mason 회사에서 근무했습니다. 저는 수공예 가구, 특히 탁자와 의자를 전문으로 제작합니다. 또한 목공의 더 정교한 부분을 시연하는 수많은 워크숍을 진행했습니다.

커뮤니티 센터에서 무급 강사로 봉사할 수 있게 된다면 매우 기쁠 것 같습니다. 직접 만나서 제 기술 시연을 보고 싶으시다면 기꺼이 응하겠습니다. 이 이메일에 답장하시거나 (552) 239-9733으로 전화 주셔도 좋습니다.

진심을 다해,

Ernie Powers 드림

어휘 announcement 공고 employ 고용하다, 일하다 carpenter 목수 approximately 대략 self-employed 자영업을 하는 specialize 전문으로 하다 handcrafted 수공예품인 pleasure 기쁨 instructor 강사 demonstration 시연 comply 응하다

04 정답 ③

해설 2번째 단락 마지막 문장에서 3일간 점심 식사를 할 식당을 예약하고 싶다고 언급하였다. 따라서 글의 내용과 일치하지 않는 것은 ③ '3일간의 저녁 식사를 할 식당 예약이 필요하다.'이다.
① 주 회의실은 200명 이상의 대표자를 수용할 수 있어야 한다.
② wi-fi가 있는 작은 회의실 3개가 필요하다.
④ 매일 밤 100명 이상의 대표자를 위한 숙박시설이 필요하다.

해석 수신: reserve@metropolitan.com
발신: BruceTaylor@westcity.com
날짜: 2024년 6월 22일
제목: 행사장 시설

안녕하세요,

Metropolitan Conference Center에 대한 정보를 요청하기 위해 글을 씁니다.

저희는 올해 9월에 3일간의 콘퍼런스를 개최할 장소를 찾고 있습니다. 귀사의 주 회의실에 200명 이상의 대표자를 수용할 수 있는 충분한 공간이 필요하며, 회의를 위한 소회의실 3곳도 필요합니다. 각 회의실에는 wi-fi도 필요합니다. 오전과 오후 중간에 마실 수 있는 커피가 필요하며, 3일 동안 귀사의 식당에 점심 식사 예약을 하고 싶습니다.

더불어, Metropolitan 고객이나 대규모 단체를 위한 할인 요금이 적용되는 현지 호텔이 있는지 알려 주시겠어요? 매일 밤 100명 이상의 대표자가 묵을 수 있는 숙소가 필요합니다.

귀사의 답장을 기다리겠습니다.

진심을 담아,

행사 매니저 Bruce Taylor 드림

어휘 venue 장소 delegate 대표자 book 예약하다 local 현지의 discount 할인 accommodation 숙소

05 정답 ④

해설 마지막 단락 3번째 문장에서 웹사이트에서는 음식 노점이나 부스에 대한 정보를 찾을 수 없었다고 말했으므로, 글의 내용과 일치하지 않는 것은 ④ '음식 부스 정보는 웹사이트에 있다.'이다.
① 4월 초에 진행될 예정이다. → 첫 단락에서 언급된 내용이다.
② 2년 전에도 개최되었다. → 2번째 단락 2번째 문장에서 언급된 내용이다.
③ 올해 사상 최대 규모로 개최된다. → 2번째 단락 마지막 문장에서 언급된 내용이다.

해석 수신: inquiries@pleasantvalley.gov
발신: manuel_diaz@norman.com
제목: 미드랜드 봄 축제
날짜: 3월 11일

관련자분께,

4월 2일부터 6일까지 열릴 예정인 미드랜드 봄 축제와 관련하여 이 이메일을 씁니다.

저는 멕시코 음식을 전문으로 하는 푸드트럭의 주인입니다. 저는 2년 전에 이 축제에 참석하여 환상적인 경험을 했습니다. 특히 올해 축제는 역대 최대 규모일 예정이라 꼭 자리를 신청하고 싶습니다.

예년에는 음식 노점상이 축제에서 노점이나 부스를 설치하는 것이 허용되었습니다. 올해도 마찬가지일까요? 귀사의 웹사이트를 찾아봤지만, 관련 정보를 어디에서도 찾을 수 없었습니다. 신청 방법과 등록비가 얼마인지 알려 주시면 감사하겠습니다.

안부를 전하며,

Manuel Diaz 드림

어휘 specialize 전문으로 하다 eager 간절히 바라는 vendor 노점상 stall 노점 case 경우 relevant 관련된 registration fee 등록비 grateful 고마워하는

전략 02

전략 적용 연습

본서 p. 150

01 ①	02 ③	03 ④
04 ②	05 ④	06 ③
07 ③	08 ④	

01 정답 ①

해설 이 글은 보수 공사를 통해 새롭게 변한 공원을 둘러보며 피크닉을 즐길 수 있는 행사에 주민을 초대하는 글이다. 따라서 글의 목적으로 가장 적절한 것은 ① '주민들을 공원 방문에 초대하기 위해'이다.
② 보수 시작을 알리기 위해
③ 시장의 방문을 홍보하기 위해
④ 공원을 위한 기부금을 요청하기 위해

02 정답 ③

해설 글 중반부에서 '실내'가 아닌 '실외' 수영장이며, 새로 지은 것이 아니라 기존에 있던 수영장을 보수한 것을 알 수 있으므로, 글의 내용과 일치하지 않는 것은 ③ '실내 수영장이 새로 지어졌다.'이다.
① 로즈빌 공원은 몇 달 동안 폐쇄되었다. → 글 초반부에서 언급된 내용이다.
② 시장이 그곳에서 연설할 예정이다. → 글 중반부에서 언급된 내용이다.
④ 다가오는 피크닉에서 음식은 무료가 아니다. → 글 후반부에서 언급된 내용이다.

01-02 해석 로즈빌 공원 관련 공지

몇 달간의 보수 공사를 마친 로즈빌 공원이 곧 다시 일반 시민들에게 공개됩니다. 하켄버그시는 이번 주 토요일 4월 23일에 공원이 재개장한다는 소식을 알려 드리게 되어 기쁩니다. 모든 지역 주민은 재개장식에 참석할 수 있습니다.

오전 9시에 Duncan 시장의 연설로 축제가 시작됩니다. 이어서 보수된 시설에 대한 가이드 투어가 진행됩니다. 방문객들은 웰컴 센터, 야외 수영장, 실내 농구장의 변화된 모습을 확인할 수 있습니다. 또한 사이클링 트랙, 스케이트보드 구역, 테니스 코트도 모두 새롭게 조성된 모습을 볼 수 있습니다.

오전 11시부터 오후 2시까지 공원 내에서 피크닉이 열리며 햄버거, 핫도그 등 일반적인 피크닉 음식을 구매할 수 있습니다.

공원 시설에 관한 자세한 정보는 555-9510으로 Marsha Bradley에게 문의하세요.

어휘 undergo 겪다 local 지역[현지]의 resident 주민 commence 시작하다 speech 연설 mayor 시장 renovate 보수하다 facility 시설 outdoor 실외의 indoor 실내의 purchase 구매하다 promote 홍보하다 complimentary 무료의

03 정답 ④

해설 가을 음악 축제 개최를 안내하고 축제의 일정과 출연진을 소개하고 있으므로, 글의 목적으로 가장 적절한 것은 ④ '개최되는 행사에 관한 정보를 제공하려고'이다.

04 정답 ②

해설 글 중반부에서 이 지역 출신의 유명 연예인도 출연한다고 했으므로, 글의 내용과 일치하는 것은 ② '출연자 중 일부는 이 지역 출신이다.'이다.
① 일주일보다 더 길게 진행할 예정이다. → 글 초반부에서 7일 동안만 진행되는 것을 알 수 있으므로 옳지 않다.
③ 노인 티켓은 어린이 티켓보다 저렴하다. → 글 후반부에서 노인 티켓과 어린이 티켓은 동일한 가격임을 알 수 있으므로 옳지 않다.
④ 온라인 신청을 통해서만 자원봉사자를 모집한다. → 글 후반부에서 자원봉사를 희망하는 사람들은 전화로 연락하라고 언급되므로 옳지 않다.

03-04 해석 데스틴 가을 음악 축제

2년 동안의 중단 끝에, 데스틴 가을 음악 축제가 다시 개최될 예정입니다. 올해 축제는 62팀의 가수와 밴드가 일주일 내내 공연을 펼칠 예정으로 그 어느 때보다 더 크고 멋진 축제가 될 것을 약속합니다.

날짜: 10월 2일 월요일 - 10월 8일 일요일
시간: 오전 11:00부터 오후 10:00까지
위치: 라모나 공원, 데스틴

Jessica Harper, the Rainmakers, Eddie Matthews 밴드가 공연진의 헤드라인을 장식합니다. Mal Reynolds, Thaddeus Watson, Emily Hatfield 등, 이 지역 출신의 연예인들도 출연할 예정입니다. 전체 출연자 목록은 저희 웹사이트 www.destinfallmusicfestival.org에서 확인하세요.

티켓
티켓은 온라인 또는 라모나 공원에서 구매할 수 있습니다. 1일권, 3일권, 7일권 티켓 모두 구매 가능합니다.

	성인	어린이/노인
1일권	10달러	5달러
3일권	25달러	12달러
7일권	50달러	25달러

음식과 음료는 공원에서 판매될 예정입니다. 축제에서 자원봉사를 희망하시는 분은 (242) 555-1831로 Mary Rose에게 연락하세요.

어휘 absence 부재 entire 전체의 attend 참석하다 local 지역[현지]의 appearance 출연 purchase 구매하다 available 구매[이용] 가능한 beverage 음료

05 정답 ④

해설 회사와 구직자 모두 참여할 수 있는 취업 박람회 등록을 장려하는 글이므로, 글의 제목으로 가장 적절한 것은 ④ '매디슨 취업 박람회에 등록하세요'이다.
① 직원 관리 방법에 대한 강의
② 채용 박람회에 참석할 기업을 모집합니다
③ 온라인 직무 교육 강의를 들으실 수 있습니다

06 정답 ③

해설 글 후반부에서 참석자는 정장을 착용해야 한다고 언급되므로, 글의 내용과 일치하지 않는 것은 ③ '참석자의 복장 규정은 없다.'이다.
① 콘퍼런스 센터에서 개최된다. → 글 초반부에서 언급된 내용이다.
② 외국 회사들이 참여한다. → 글 중반부에서 언급된 내용이다.
④ 그곳에서 일부 면접이 진행된다. → 글 후반부에서 언급된 내용이다.

05-06 해석 매디슨 취업 박람회에 등록하세요

매디슨시는 이러한 어려운 경제 상황 속에서 지역 주민의 일자리 확보를 지원하기 위해 사상 처음으로 채용 박람회를 개최합니다.

날짜: 4월 11일 금요일
시간: 오전 9:00 - 오후 5:00
위치: 골드 룸 및 실버 룸, 매디슨 콘퍼런스 센터, 37 웨스턴 거리

참여 기업
80개 이상의 국내외 기업이 대표자를 파견할 예정입니다. 이 기업들은 제조, 제약, IT, 교육, 서비스, 조선 산업에 종사하고 있습니다.

참석자
참석자는 www.madison.gov/springjobfair에 방문하여 사전 등록해야 합니다. 등록비는 필요하지 않습니다. 참석자는 정장을 착용하고 이력서, 포트폴리오 및 기타 관련 개인 서류 사본을 지참해야 합니다. 일부 기업에서는 입사 지원자들과 현장 면접을 진행하고자 하는 의사를 밝혔으므로, 참석자는 잠재적 고용주의 질문에 답변할 준비를 해야 합니다.

어휘 host 개최하다 fair 박람회 secure 확보하다 resident 주민 domestic 국내의 representative 대표 manufacturing 제조업 pharmaceutical 제약의 hospitality 서비스업 shipbuilding 조선업 attendee 참석자 register 등록하다 in advance 사전에 registration fee 등록비 attire 복장 relevant 관련 있는 desire 희망, 바람 conduct 진행하다 onsite 현장의 job candidate 입사 지원자 potential 잠재적인

07 정답 ③

해설 베스트셀러 작가의 낭독회 및 사인회가 기획된 세일럼 도서관의 네 번째 여름 행사를 안내하는 글이다. 따라서 글의 제목으로 가장 적절한 것은 ③ '유명 작가와 함께하는 세일럼 도서관 여름 행사'이다.
① 세일럼 도서관이 새 책을 구입하다
② 세일럼 도서관의 회원이 되기 위해 등록하세요
④ Seymour Hamilton과 함께하는 작문 강좌에 등록하세요

08 정답 ④

해설 글 후반부에서 입장료가 없다고 언급되므로, 글의 내용과 일치하지 않는 것은 ④ '참석하려면 비용이 든다.'이다.
① 주말에 열린다. → 글 초반부에서 언급된 내용이다.
② 약 2시간 동안 진행된다. → 글 초반부에서 언급된 내용이다.
③ 책 사인회가 있을 예정이다. → 글 중반부에서 언급된 내용이다.

07-08 해석 유명 작가와 함께하는 세일럼 도서관 여름 행사

세일럼 도서관은 이번 여름의 네 번째 특별 행사로 유명 작가 Seymour Hamilton의 책 낭독회를 선보입니다. Hamilton 씨는 그의 최신 스릴러인 'Racing the Clock'의 몇 챕터를 낭독할 예정입니다. 국내 베스트셀러 작가와 함께하는 일생에 단 한 번뿐인 이 행사를 놓치지 마세요.

세부 정보
날짜: 7월 16일 일요일
시간: 오후 3시 - 오후 5시
위치: 세일럼 도서관 강당

Hamilton 씨는 낭독회 시작에 앞서 'Racing the Clock' 책 사인회를 할 예정입니다. 참석자들은 도서관에서 19.99달러에 책을 구입하거나 소장본을 가져올 수 있습니다. 책 사인회에 이어서 Hamilton 씨는 자신의 소설을 낭독할 예정입니다. 그런 다음 청중들과 Q&A 세션을 진행할 것입니다.

입장료는 없지만 자리는 150명으로 제한됩니다. 좌석은 선착순으로 제공되며 www.salemlibrary.org/summerseries에서 온라인으로 예약해야 합니다.

어휘 proudly 자랑스럽게 present 선보이다 renowned 유명한 once-in-a-lifetime 평생 단 한 번뿐인 autograph 사인하다 prior to ~에 앞서 attendee 참석자 purchase 구매하다 conduct 진행하다 audience 청중 admission fee 입장료 available 이용 가능한 first-come, first-served 선착순 reserve 예약하다 register 등록하다 sign up 등록하다 last 지속되다 feature 특별히 포함하다

전략 03

전략 적용 연습

본서 p. 156

01 ④ 02 ④ 03 ②
04 ③

01 정답 ④

해설 5번째 문장에서 시범 시행 후 확대될 것이라고 언급했다. 따라서 글의 내용과 일치하지 않는 것은 ④ '시범 기간 없이 즉시 시행된다.'이다.
① 신생아가 있는 가정에 대한 재정적 지원을 포함한다. → 2번째 문장에서 언급된 내용이다.
② 부모의 소득에 관계없이 양육비를 보장한다. → 3번째 문장에서 언급된 내용이다.
③ 가족친화기업이 세제 혜택을 받을 수 있도록 한다. → 4번째 문장에서 언급된 내용이다.

해석 새로운 정책으로 강화된 가족 지원
보건복지부는 아동 복지 및 지원 시스템 개선을 위한 출산 및 보육 지원 정책을 발표했다. 주요 정책으로는 신생아가 있는 가정

에 대한 직접적인 재정 지원, 육아휴직 확대, 보육료 지원금 인상, 포괄적인 의료 보상 범위 등이 있다. 특히, 보육 지원금 보장 범위는 부모 소득 제한을 없앰으로써 확대될 것이다. 유연 근무제, 직장 내 보육과 같은 가족 친화적인 정책을 시행하는 기업에 대한 세제 혜택도 제공될 예정이다. 이러한 정책은 시범적인 시행 후 확대될 예정이며, 지원 범위도 지속적으로 확대될 것이다.

어휘 childcare 보육, 육아 direct 직접적인 financial 재정의 aid 지원 newborn 신생아 extended 확대된 parental leave 육아휴직 subsidy 보조금 comprehensive 종합적인 healthcare 보건진료 coverage (보상[보장]) 범위 parental 부모의 income 소득 implement 시행하다 family-friendly 가족 친화적인 policy 정책 flexible 유연한 trial 시험, 시범 scope 범주 broaden 확대하다

02 정답 ④

해설 마지막 문장에서 노동청은 근로자가 공정한 대우를 받도록 필요한 경우 집행 조치를 취한다고 언급했다. 따라서 글의 내용과 일치하는 것은 ④ '고용인이 부당한 대우를 받을 때 조치를 취한다.'이다.

① 직원들이 세금을 제대로 납부하는지 확인한다. → 2번째 문장에서 직원들의 세금 납부가 아닌 직원들이 임금을 제대로 받는지 확인한다고 언급되므로 옳지 않다.

② 성인 근로자의 고용에 대한 권한만 있다. → 3번째 문장에서 미성년자 고용에 대한 권한도 있다고 언급되므로 옳지 않다.

③ 고용주의 사업 기회를 촉진한다. → 5번째 문장에서 법률상의 권리와 책임에 대해 고용주를 교육한다고만 언급되므로 옳지 않다.

해석 노동청(OLC) 책무

노동청은 국가의 주요 노동 규제 기관입니다. 노동청은 최저 임금, 통상 임금 및 초과 근무 수당이 직원에게 지급되는 것과 직원 휴식 및 점심시간이 제공되는 것을 보장하는 데 책임이 있습니다. 추가적으로 노동청은 미성년자 고용에 대한 권한이 있습니다. 노동청의 비전과 사명은 노동 관련 문제를 효율적이고 전문적이며 효과적인 방식으로 해결하는 것입니다. 여기에는 법률상의 권리와 책임에 대해 고용주와 고용인을 교육하는 것이 포함됩니다. 노동청은 근로자가 근로를 제공한 모든 시간에 대해 공정한 대우와 보상을 받도록 보장하기 위해 필요한 경우 집행 조치를 취합니다.

어휘 labor 노동 commissioner 청장 regulatory 규제의 agency 기관 responsible 책임이 있는 ensure 확실히 하다 wage 임금 prevailing 일반적인 overtime 초과근무 authority 권한 employment 고용 minor 미성년자 resolve 해결하다 enforcement 집행 compensate 보상하다

03 정답 ②

해설 2번째 문장에서 온라인에서만 의견을 제출할 수 있고 다른 오프라인 제안은 받지 않는다고 말하고 있다. 따라서 글의 내용과 일치하는 것은 ② '온라인으로 제출하지 않은 제안은 접수되지 않을 것이다.'이다.

① 정부 관계자만 참여할 수 있다. → 2번째 문장에서 주민들이 제안 사항을 제출할 수 있다고 했으므로 옳지 않다.

③ 검토될 제출물은 무작위로 선정될 것이다. → 3번째 문장에서 가장 많은 '좋아요'를 받은 상위 제안이 검토될 것이라고 언급되므로 옳지 않다.

④ 프로그램은 연말까지 운영될 것이다. → 마지막 문장에서 무기한으로 제출을 받겠다고 언급되므로 옳지 않다.

해석 시 행정 개선을 위한 의견 수렴

시 의회는 더 나은 시정 운영을 위한 의견을 모으는 신규 프로그램 개시를 발표했습니다. 주민들은 www.cityvoice.org를 통해서만 제안 사항을 제출할 수 있고, 다른 오프라인 제안은 받지 않습니다. 가장 많은 '좋아요'를 받은 상위 제안 10개를 매월 전담 위원회에서 면밀히 검토할 것이며, 선정된 아이디어는 도시 서비스를 강화하기 위해 실행될 것입니다. 아이디어 예시로는 교통 혼잡 완화, 공원 및 녹지 개선, 재활용 프로그램 강화에 대한 해결책이 포함됩니다. 시의회는 추후 공지가 있을 때까지 무기한으로 제출을 받겠습니다.

어휘 launch 출시, 개시 collect 모으다 administration 행정 resident 거주민 submit 제출하다 thoroughly 면밀히, 철저히 dedicated committee 전담 위원회 submission 제출물 implement 실행하다, 실시하다 enhance 확대하다 traffic congestion 교통 혼잡 indefinitely 무기한으로 at random 무작위로

04 정답 ③

해설 4번째 문장에서 교육 프로그램 수료자들을 고용한 기업들에게 재정적 인센티브를 제공한다고만 했다. 따라서 글의 내용과 일치하지 않는 것은 ③ '프로그램에서 교육을 제공하는 기업들은 혜택을 받는다.'이다.

① 은퇴를 앞둔 사람들도 교육을 받을 수 있다. → 첫 문장에서 언급된 내용이다.

② 프로그램 수료자들은 현금 보상을 받는다. → 3번째 문장에서 언급된 내용이다.

④ 더 자세한 사항은 지원센터에서 확인할 수 있다. → 마지막 문장에서 언급된 내용이다.

해석 중년 경력 역량 강화 교육

고용노동부는 최근에 은퇴했거나 은퇴를 앞둔 중장년층을 위한 특화된 교육 프로그램을 개시했습니다. 재취업 역량 강화를 위한 다양한 맞춤형 교육 및 훈련 과정이 제공될 것입니다. 참여를 독려하기 위해 모든 프로그램 수료자에게 현금 인센티브를 제공합니다. 게다가 해당 수료자들을 고용한 기업에는 다양한 재정적 인센티브를 제공합니다. 이 조치를 통해, 개인은 좋은 일자리를 확보할 수 있고 기업들은 가치 있는 직원을 발견할 수 있습니다. 이 프로그램에 대한 더 많은 정보와 참여 방법은 저희 공식 웹사이트를 방문하거나 여러분의 지역에 위치한 지원센터로 연락해 주시기를 바랍니다.

어휘 launch 시작하다 specialized 전문적인 middle-aged 중년의 population 인구 recently 최근 retired 은퇴한 approach 접근하다 retirement 은퇴 tailored 맞춤의 reemployment 재취업, 재고용 encourage 독려하다, 장려하다 graduate 졸업생, 수료자 initiative 조치 individual 개인 secure 확보하다

전략 04

전략 적용 연습 본서 p. 163

01 ② 02 ② 03 ③

01 정답 ②

해설 청소년에게 노트북은 필수적임을 강조하는 글이다. 맥락상 critical은 '중요한'이라는 뜻으로 쓰였으므로, 이와 의미가 가장 가까운 것은 ② 'crucial(중요한)'이다.
① 심각한 ③ 분석적인 ④ 위험한

해석 저는 필수 정보에 접근하기 어려운 디지털 취약 청소년에게 중고 노트북을 제공해야 할 필요성을 강조하기 위해 이 글을 씁니다.

노트북을 소유하는 것은 청소년들에게 중요합니다. 이것은 온라인 도구와 자료를 통해 관심사와 재능을 탐색할 수 있게 함으로써 점점 더 디지털화되는 세상에서 성공하기 위한 핵심 요소로 작용합니다. 안타깝게도 노트북 가격의 상승으로 청소년들의 노트북 구입이 더 어려워져서, 교육 및 경력 개발 활동이 제한되고 있습니다.

어휘 highlight 강조하다 necessity 필요성 used 중고의 laptop 노트북 vulnerable 취약한 struggle to RV ~에 어려움을 겪다 access 접근하다 essential 필수적인 enable 가능하게 하다 factor 요소 afford ~할 형편이 되다 participation 참여

02 정답 ②

해설 STEM 교육과정을 도입하여 현재 교육의 여러 문제점을 다뤄야 한다는 글이다. 맥락상 address는 '대처하다'라는 뜻으로 쓰였으므로, 이와 의미가 가장 가까운 것은 ② 'handle(처리하다)'이다.
① 적용하다 ③ 제시하다 ④ 소통하다

해석 저는 종합적인 STEM(과학, 기술, 공학, 수학) 교육과정이라고도 하는 어린 학생들의 필요에 맞춘 특별 프로그램의 개발을 제안하기 위해 이 글을 씁니다.

저는 이 프로그램이 우리 아이들의 발달과 미래의 성공에 큰 영향을 미칠 수 있다고 믿습니다. 현재 많은 어린 학생들이 실제 세상에 적용되지 못하고 창의력을 기르지 못하는 표준적인 교육 틀 안에서 자신의 잠재력을 최대한 발휘하는 데 어려움을 겪고 있습니다. 저는 웰링턴 지역이 STEM 시스템을 시행함으로써 이 문제에 대처할 수 있다고 믿습니다.

어휘 propose 제안하다 tailor 맞추다 comprehensive 종합적인 engineering 공학 curriculum 교육과정 struggle to RV ~에 어려움을 겪다 framework 틀 incorporate 포함하다 application 적용 foster 조성하다, 발전시키다 implement 시행하다

03 정답 ③

해설 임대료를 내는 데 어려움을 겪는 소상공인을 위해 임대료 보조금을 제공하여 유리한 임대 조건을 협상할 수 있도록 요청하는 글이다. 맥락상 terms는 '조건'이라는 뜻으로 쓰였으므로, 이와 의미가 가장 가까운 것은 ③ 'conditions(조건)'이다.
① 상호작용 ② 정의 ④ 시기

해석 저는 임대료에 있어 소상공인에게 재정적인 보조를 제공하는 것의 필요성을 강조하고자 합니다. 소상공인은 우리 경제의 근간이며 현재 즉각적인 지원이 필요한 어려움을 겪고 있습니다.

코로나19가 발병한 이후 사업체의 운영 비용이 크게 증가했습니다. 메릴랜드의 소상공인인 저는 개인적으로 임대료가 급등하면서 임대 의무를 이행하는 데 어려움을 겪고 있습니다. 소상공인들이 임대인과 보다 유리한 임대 조건을 협상할 수 있도록 임대료 보조금 프로그램 시행을 고려해 주실 것을 촉구합니다.

어휘 emphasize 강조하다 necessity 필요성 subsidy 지원[보조]금 small business owner 소상공인 backbone 근간 hardship 어려움 require 요구하다 immediate 즉각적인 assistance 도움 onset 시작 operational 운영적인 significantly 크게 obligation 의무 urge 촉구하다 implement 시행하다 negotiate 협상하다 favorable 유리한 landlord 임대인

UNIT 02 독해 핵심 전략

전략 05

전략 적용 연습 본서 p. 174

01 ③ 02 ④ 03 ④
04 ①

01 정답 ③

해설 이 글은 첫 문장에서 바로 '태블릿 컴퓨터에서 사용되는 터치스크린 기술'이라는 글의 소재가 나온다. 전자책 애플리케이션은 터치스크린 기술을 응용하는 매체의 한 예시에 불과하며, 이후에는 터치스크린이 작동하는 방식에 대한 설명이 이어지고 있기 때문에 이것을 글의 소재로 보아서는 안 된다. 구체적으로는, 두 금속 표현을 덮는 유리 패널을 가진 저항성 스크린의 작동 방식에 대한 설명과 하나의 전기가 통하는 금속층을 덮는 유리 패널을 가진 정전용량식 스크린의 작동 방식에 대한 설명이 나오고 있다. 따라서 이 글의 주제로 가장 적절한 것은 ③ '터치스크린 기술이 작동하는 방식'이다.
① 사용자가 새로운 기술을 배우는 방식
② 전자책이 태블릿 컴퓨터에서 작동하는 방식
④ 터치스크린이 어떻게 발전해 왔는가

해석 태블릿 컴퓨터에서 사용할 수 있는 전자책 애플리케이션은 터치스크린 기술을 이용한다. 일부 터치스크린은 전자적으로 변화된 마주 보고 놓여 있는 두 개의 금속 표면을 덮는 유리 패널을 특징으로 한다. 화면을 터치하면 두 금속 표면이 압력을 느끼고 접촉한다. 이러한 압력은 컴퓨터로 전기 신호를 보내서 그 터치를 명령으로 변환시킨다. 이 터치스크린 버전은 화면이 손가락의 압력에 반응하기 때문에 저항성 스크린으로 알려져 있다. 다른 태블릿 컴퓨터들은 유리 패널 아래에 하나의 전기가 통하는 금속층을 특징으로 한다. 사용자가 화면을 터치하면 일부 전류가 유리를 통과해 사용자의 손가락으로 들어간다. 전하가 전달되면 컴퓨터는 전력 손실을 명령어로 해석하고 사용자가 원하는 기능을 수행한다. 이러한 유형의 화면을 정전용량식 스크린이라고 한다.

어휘 employ 이용하다 feature 특징으로 하다 electronically 전자적으로 metallic 금속의 face-to-face 마주 보는 pressure 압력 resistive 저항성의 electrify 전기를 통하게 하다 layer 층 current 전류 interpret 해석하다 capacitive 정전용량식 evolve 발전하다

02 정답 ④

해설 글의 서두에서 상업적 어업을 지속하기 위해서 과학의 도움이 필요하다고 말했으므로, 이 글의 소재는 '상업적 어업과 과학'임을 알 수 있다. 이후에는 어업이 어떠한 방식으로 과학의 도움을 받을 수 있는지에 관한 내용이 이어지는데, 특히 '지속 가능한 최대 수확량'이라는 개념을 소개하며 상업적 어업에 쓰이는 과학 개념을 설명하고 있다. 따라서 글의 제목으로 가장 적절한 것은 ④ '왜 어업은 과학을 필요로 하는가?'이다.

① 상업적인 어업에 반대하라
② 어업으로 간주되는 바다 양식업
③ 남획된 동물들 : 불법 어업의 사례들

해석 과학자들 덕분에, 상업적 어업은 그것이 지속되려면 조업을 과학적으로 해야 한다는 것을 알게 되었다. 어류 개체군에 대한 어획 압력이 없다면 어류의 수는 예측 가능한 수준의 양에 도달하고 그 상태를 유지할 것이다. 유일한 변동은 자연환경 요인으로 인한 것일 것이다. 그러나 이 물고기들을 잡기 위해 어장이 개발된다면, 우리는 매년 우리가 잡는 물고기를 모두 대체할 수 있는 이상적인 지점 이하로 개체수가 감소하지 않도록 주의해야 한다. 우리가 '지속 가능한 최대 수확량'이라고 하는 이 수준에서 물고기를 잡으면 해마다 가능한 최대 수확량을 유지할 수 있다. 너무 많이 잡으면 매년 물고기의 수가 줄어들어 결국 우리는 일자리를 잃게 될 것이다. 연간 최대 수확량을 유지하기 위해 정확한 양을 잡는 것은 과학이자 기술이다. 어류 개체수를 더 잘 이해하고 개체수를 고갈시키지 않으면서 그것을 최대한 활용할 수 있는 방법을 찾기 위한 연구가 끊임없이 이루어지고 있다.

어휘 commercial 상업적인 abundance 양 fluctuation 변동 sustainable 지속 가능한 yield 수확량 deplete 고갈시키다 overfish 남획하다

03 정답 ④

해설 첫 문장에서 고고학자 Evans를 소개하면서 그가 미노스 문명의 크노소스 궁전 유적을 성공적으로 발굴함으로써 신화로만 여겨졌던 미노스 문명이 사실로 드러났음을 기술하고 있다. 따라서 이 글의 소재는 '미노스 문명의 유적 발굴'임을 알 수 있다. 이후에는 Evans의 유적 발굴 사례가 계속해서 언급된다. 따라서 글의 주제로 적절한 것은 ④ '미노스 문명을 현실의 영역으로 가져오기'이다.

① Minos 왕의 성공적인 발굴
② 미노스 문명 시대의 유물 감상하기
③ 크레타섬 궁전의 장엄함

해석 한 사람이 어떤 문화 전체에 우리의 눈을 뜨게 해줄 수 있다는 것은 믿기 힘들지만, 영국의 고고학자 Arthur Evans가 크레타섬의 크노소스 궁전의 유적을 성공적으로 발굴하기 전까지 지중해의 위대한 미노스 문명은 사실보다는 전설에 가까웠다. 실제로 그 문명에서 가장 유명한 거주자는 신화 속에 나오는 Minos 왕의 궁전 아래에 살았다고 전해지는 반인반수의 미노타우로스라는 신화 속 생물이었다. 하지만 Evans가 증명했듯이 이 왕국은 신화가 아니었다. 20세기 초 일련의 발굴 작업을 통해 Evans는 보석, 조각품, 도자기, 황소 뿔 모양의 제단, 미노스 문명의 삶을 보여 주는 벽화 등 기원전 1900년부터 1450년까지 전성기를 누렸던 미노스 시대의 귀중한 유물들을 발견했다.

어휘 archaeologist 고고학자 excavate 발굴하다 ruins 유적 Mediterranean 지중해의 resident 거주자 mythology 신화 bull 황소 realm 왕국 trove 귀중한 발견물 artifact 유물 pottery 도자기 altar 제단 appreciate 감상하다 magnificence 장엄함

04 정답 ①

해설 글 서두에서 한 상황을 가정한 뒤에, 빈칸 앞에서 다친 사람을 돕는 일은 '분명 올바른 일'이라고 하였다. 따라서 이 글의 소재는 도덕적인 행동과 관련됨을 알 수 있다. 그런데 뒤에서 역접의 접속사 But이 나오므로, 이 행위가 '올바르지 않은' 경우에 대한 내용이 나와야 한다. 이때 빈칸 뒤에서 동정심은 도덕성과 무관하다고 하였기 때문에 그것이 동정심에서 한 행동이라면 도덕적인 행동이라고 할 수 없다는 맥락으로 연결된다. 따라서 빈칸에 들어갈 말로 가장 적절한 것은 ① '그것은 전혀 도덕적인 행동이 아닐 것이다'이다.

② 당신의 행동은 이성에 기초한다
③ 그렇다면 당신은 윤리적 행위를 드러내고 있는 것이다
④ 당신은 그가 정직한 사람이 되도록 격려하고 있는 것이다

해석 당신의 문에 누군가 노크를 한다. 당신 앞에는 도움이 필요한 한 젊은이가 서 있다. 그는 부상을 당했고 피를 흘리고 있다. 당신은 그를 데리고 들어와 도와주며, 그가 편안하고 안전하게 느끼도록 한 뒤, 전화를 걸어 구급차를 부른다. 이것은 분명 올바른 일이다. 하지만 Immanuel Kant에 따르면, 당신이 그저 그에게 동정심을 느껴서 그를 돕는 것이라면, 그것은 전혀 도덕적인 행동이 아닐 것이다. 당신의 동정심은 당신의 행위의 도덕성과는 무관하다. 그것은 당신의 성품의 일부일 뿐, 옳고 그름과는 무관하다. Kant에게 도덕성이란, 그저 '무엇'을 하는가가 아닌, '왜' 그것을 하는가에 관한 것이다. 올바른 일을 하는 사람들은 단순히 자신이 느끼는 감정 때문에 올바른 일을 하는 것이 아니다. 그 결정은 이성에, 당신이 어떤 감정을 느끼게 되었든 관계없이 당신의 의무가 무엇인지를 알려 주는 바로 그 이성에 근거해야 한다.

어휘 injured 상처 입은 bleed 피를 흘리다 sympathy 연민 irrelevant 관계없는 morality 도덕성 reason 이성 regardless of ~와 관계없이 ethical 윤리적인

전략 06

전략 적용 연습

본서 p. 180

01 ② 02 ① 03 ④
04 ④ 05 ④

01 정답 ②

해설 글의 도입부에서 학생들의 통념을 언급한 뒤에 But을 통해 글의 주제, 즉 '무언가를 세상에 보여야' 중요한 사람들과 교류를 맺을 수 있다는 점을 주장하고 있다. 이후에는 But으로 또다시 주제를 강조하며, 당신이 '줄 수 있는 것'에 따라 사람들이 얼마나 당신을 위해줄지가 결정된다는 내용을 언급하고 있다. 특히, 좋은 인맥을 만들기 위해서는 인맥 전문가가 되기보다는 '어떤 일에' 전문가가 되면 된다는 점을 'It is not A but B'와 유사한 강조법을 통해 주장하고 있다. 마지막 문장에서도 명령문으로 통찰력과 결과물로 말하라는 주장으로 글을 마무리하고 있다. 이를 종합해 봤을 때, 글의 요지로 가장 적절한 것은 ② '좋은 인맥을 형성하는 것은 당신의 성과로부터 시작된다.'이다.
① 성공적인 커리어를 위해서 후원은 필수적이다.
③ 강력한 인맥은 당신의 성공을 위한 전제조건이다.
④ 당신이 인맥 형성의 전문가가 됨에 따라 당신의 통찰력과 결과는 성장한다.

해석 나의 학생들은 종종 그저 자신이 중요한 사람들을 더 많이 만나면 자신의 업적이 나아질 것이라고 믿는다. 하지만 이미 가치 있는 무언가를 세상에 내놓지 않은 한 그런 사람들과 교류하기는 매우 어렵다. 업적은 당신이 무언가를 가져갈 수 있다는 것뿐만 아니라, 무언가를 줄 수 있다는 것을 보여 준다. 인생에서 올바른 사람들을 아는 것은 확실히 도움이 된다. 하지만 그들이 당신을 얼마나 열심히 지지해 주고, 당신을 위해 얼마나 위험을 감수해 줄지는 당신이 무엇을 줄 수 있느냐에 달려 있다. 강력한 인맥을 구축하는 것은 당신이 인맥 형성에 전문가가 되는 것을 요구하지 않는다. 그것은 단지 당신이 어떤 일에 전문가가 되기를 요구한다. 훌륭한 인맥을 쌓으면, 그 인맥이 당신의 커리어를 발전시킬 수도 있다. 훌륭한 일을 한다면, 그 인맥들을 쌓기가 더 쉬워질 것이다. 명함이 아닌 통찰력과 결과물로 말하라.

어휘 remarkably 매우 engage with ~와 교류하다 achievement 업적 go to bat for ~을 지지하다 stick one's neck out 위험을 감수하다 insight 통찰력 output 결과, 생산량 accomplishment 성과 prerequisite 전제조건

02 정답 ①

해설 'S + V + that' 구조와 'It is not A but B' 구문을 통해 이 글의 주제, 즉 웃음은 다른 사람에게 쾌활한 기분이 들게 한다는 점을 소개하고 있다. 이후에는 이 현상의 생물 사회학적 기능을 소개하며 그 중요성을 기술하고 있다. 따라서 글의 주제로 가장 적절한 것은 ① '웃음이 다른 사람에게 미치는 영향'이다.
② 뇌 회로를 활성화시키는 것의 이점
③ 활동을 조정하기 위한 전략
④ 의사소통에 있어서 그룹으로 나누는 것의 중요성

해석 최근 연구자들이 웃음의 목적이 어떤 사람이 쾌활한 상태에 있다는 것을 전달하려는 것뿐만 아니라, 실제로 이런 상태를 다른 사람들에게서도 유도해 내려는 것이라는 점을 보여 주었다. 이 관점에 따르면 웃음의 특유한 소리는 듣는 사람에게 직접적인 영향을 끼쳐서, 아마도 어떤 특수한 뇌 회로를 활성화시킴으로써 웃는 사람의 감정 상태와 흡사한 긍정적인 감정적 자극을 유도해 낸다. 이런 식으로 웃음은 어떤 집단의 구성원들의 긍정적 감정을 결합시키고, 그렇게 함으로써 그들의 활동을 조화시키는 중요한 생물 사회학적 기능을 수행하는지도 모른다. 이것은 웃음이 왜 그렇게 전염성이 있는지를 설명해 줄 것이다. 우리가 누군가가 웃는 것을 들을 때 유쾌한 기분을 느끼고 함께 웃기 시작하지 않는 것은 거의 불가능하다.

어휘 playful 쾌활한 peculiar 특유한 induce 유도하다 activate 활성화하다 biosocial 생물 사회적인 infectious 전염성 있는

03 정답 ④

해설 빈칸 뒤 문장에서 비교급을 통해 서술한, 다른 사람들을 신뢰하는 것의 중요성이 글의 주제임을 알 수 있다. 이어서 업무 만족도와 혼자서 업무를 알아서 처리할 수 있는 권한 간의 '직접적인 상관관계'가 있다고 말한 것과, 마지막에서 'not only A but B' 구문을 통해 다른 이에게 책임을 맡길 필요성을 주장하였다. 따라서 이 글은 다른 사람의 업무에 자율성을 부여하는 것과 관련됨을 알 수 있다. 따라서 빈칸에 들어갈 말로 가장 적절한 것은 ④ '자율성'이다.
① 일 ② 보상 ③ 제한

해석 점점 더 많은 리더들이 원격으로 일하거나, 컨설턴트와 프리랜서뿐만 아니라 전국이나 전 세계에 흩어져 있는 팀과 함께 일하면서, 그들에게 더 많은 자율성을 주어야 할 것이다. 당신이 더 많은 신뢰를 줄수록, 다른 사람들은 당신을 더 신뢰한다. 나는 직무 만족과 누군가 모든 단계마다 따라다니지 않고도 직무를 완전히 수행할 수 있는 권한을 부여받는 정도 사이에 직접적인 상관관계가 있다고 확신한다. 당신이 신뢰하는 사람에게 책임을 맡기는 것은 조직이 보다 원활하게 운영되도록 할 수 있을 뿐만 아니라 당신에게 더 많은 시간을 만들어 내어 더 큰 문제에 집중할 수 있도록 한다.

어휘 remotely 원격으로 scattered 흩어져 있는 bestow 주다 empower 권한을 주다 execute 수행하다 shadow 그림자처럼 따라다니다 free up (특정한 목적을 위해 시간이나 돈을) 만들어 내다

04 정답 ④

해설 필자는 첫 문장에서 but을 통해 돈이 그렇게는 중요하지 않다는 점을 강조한다. 이후에는 There is only one ~ and that involves ~라는 강조 표현을 통해 사회적 관계의 중요성을 역설하고 있으므로, 이것이 글의 주제임을 알 수 있다. 그다음에는 내면 과정(행복)과 대인 관계(타인과의 좋은 관계 형성) 간의 상관

관계가 '강하다'는 점을 언급하며 또다시 주제를 강조하고 있다. 따라서 글의 요지로 가장 적절한 것은 ④ '행복은 사회적 관계 없이는 좀처럼 찾아오지 않는다.'이다.

① 행복한 관계는 공유되는 가치에 토대를 둔다.
② 어떤 사람들은 고독 속에서 꽤 행복하게 살 수 있다.
③ 행복을 결정하는 많은 변수들이 있다.

해석 충분한 돈을 가진 사람들이 돈을 많이 갖지 않은 사람들보다 더 행복하지만, 그 차이는 매우 작다. 돈으로 행복을 살 수는 있지만, 그것을 그다지 많이 살 수는 없는 것처럼 보인다. 행복에 있어 큰 차이를 만드는 것으로 보여 온 단 하나의 객관적인 경우가 있는데, 그것은 사회적 관계와 관련이 있다. 이 세상에서 혼자인 사람들은 강력하고 풍부한 사회적 관계망을 가진 사람들보다 훨씬 덜 행복하다. 이 강력한 연관성은 이 경우에 행복이라는 내면의 과정이, 이 경우에 다른 사람들과 좋은 관계를 형성하고 유지하는 대인 관계와 연관되어 있다는 것을 나타낸다. 인간의 감정 시스템은 한 사람이 인생에서 혼자서는 행복하기가 지극히 어렵도록 설정되어 있다. 심지어 건강, 부상, 돈, 직업을 포함한 다른 모든 경우에 대해서 그 차이는 작다.

어휘 apparently 보아하니 objective 객관적인 circumstance 경우, 상황 interpersonal 대인 간의 solitude 고독 variable 변수 absence 부재

05 정답 ④

해설 글 도입부에서 One of A is B 표현이 나오면서 효율성이 최적화할 수 있는 분야는 노동력으로, 개인의 생산성 증가를 통해 가능하다는 점을 언급하고 있다. 따라서 노동 생산성 향상이 글의 소재임을 알 수 있다. 또한 글 중반부에서 콜론(:)을 통하여 멀티태스킹을 중단해야 생산성이 증가한다는 점을 강조하고 있으며, 뒤에서 S + V + (that) 구조로 여러 일을 동시에 하는 경우 업무 효율이 떨어진다는 연구 결과를 소개하고 있다. 따라서 이 글의 주제는 노동 생산성을 위해서는 멀티 태스킹을 하지 말아야 한다는 것이므로, 글의 제목으로 가장 적절한 것은 ④ '더 큰 효율성을 위해 한 번에 한 가지 일을 하라'이다.

① 인생에서 더 많은 선택지를 만드는 방법
② 일상적인 신체 기능을 향상하는 방법
③ 멀티태스킹은 더 나은 효율성을 위한 답이다

해석 효율성을 최적화할 수 있는 분야 중 하나는 노동력으로, 한 직원이 주어진 시간 내에 처리하는 작업량(제품 생산량, 응대 고객 수)으로 정의되는 개인 생산성을 증가시키는 것을 통해 가능하다. 최적의 성과를 보장하기 위해 적절한 장비, 환경 및 교육에 투자했는지 확인하는 것과 더불어, 직원들이 현대의 에너지 고갈의 근원인 멀티태스킹을 중단하도록 장려함으로써 생산성을 높일 수 있다. 연구들은 동시에 다른 프로젝트들을 수행하려고 할 때 한 작업을 완료하는 데 25~40% 더 오래 걸린다는 것을 보여 준다. 컨설팅 회사 The Energy Project의 사업개발 부사장인 Andrew Deutscher는 더 생산적으로 되기 위해, "한 가지 일을 방해받지 않고 지속적인 기간 동안 하세요."라고 말한다.

어휘 optimize 최적화하다 optimal 최적의 staffer 직원 drain 고갈의 근원 simultaneously 동시에 vice 부(副) uninterrupted 방해받지 않는 sustained 지속된

전략 07

전략 적용 연습

본서 p. 188

01 ④ 02 ③ 03 ①

01 정답 ④

해설 ①은 동물의 공격적 행동의 영향, ②와 ④는 동물의 공격적 행동에 대한 원인, ③은 동물의 공격적 행동의 조절에 관한 내용이다. 네 선지 모두 동물의 공격적 행동에 관한 내용이므로, 이것이 글의 소재이다. 글에서 경쟁에 의해 동물들이 공격적 행동을 보인다고 했으므로, 이 글은 동물의 공격적 행동의 원인에 관한 내용임을 알 수 있다. 또한 그 원인을 '먹이'와 '서식지'로 특정하고 있으므로, 글의 요지로 가장 적절한 것은 ④ '자원과 공간이 동물의 공격성을 설명한다'이다.

① 동물의 공격적인 행동은 다른 동물이 그 지역을 떠나게 한다.
② 동물이 공격적인 행동을 보이는 경우에 대한 규칙은 없다.
③ 동물의 공격성은 훈련을 통해 통제할 수 있다.

해석 공격적인 행동은 주로 먹이와 서식지와 같은 자원이 부족하기 때문에 발생한다. 동물 개체 수가 증가하면 먹이와 영역을 차지하기 위한 경쟁이 치열해진다. 동물은 약한 개체군을 강제로 이주시키거나 아예 죽임으로써 경쟁자를 제거하여 증가하는 긴장감을 완화하기 위해 공격적인 행동을 한다. 개체 밀도가 감소함에 따라 공격적인 행동의 필요성도 감소한다. 자원이 풍부하거나 개체 밀도가 낮아 먹이나 서식지를 놓고 경쟁을 거의 하지 않는 동물 종은 공격적인 성향을 거의 나타내지 않는다.

어휘 aggressive 공격적인 scarcity 부족 shelter 주거지 territory 영역 engage in ~에 관여하다 relieve 완화하다 eliminate 제거하다 relocate 이주하다 density 밀도 seldom 거의 ~ 않는 abundance 풍부함 exhibit 나타내다 tendency 성향 account for ~을 설명하다

02 정답 ③

해설 ①은 계급이나 위계질서에 관한 내용이고, ②는 생태계의 다양성에 관한 것이며, ③은 서로가 서로에게 보험을 든, 즉 상생하는 관계에 관한 내용이다. 마지막으로 ④는 한쪽이 일방적으로 다른 한쪽에 기생하는 관계에 관한 선지이다. 본문에서는 어떤 박쥐든 특정한 밤에 확실히 먹이를 찾을 수 있다고 보장할 수 없으므로, 먹이를 구한 박쥐가 그렇지 못한 박쥐에게 자신이 수집한 피를 나눠 준다는 내용이다. 이러한 먹이의 공유는 서로 보험을 든 형태와 유사하므로, 빈칸에 들어갈 말로 가장 적절한 것은 ③ '상호보험 체계'이다.

① 복잡한 사회적 계급제도
② 생태계의 다양성
④ 기생관계

해석 10여 년에 걸친 전형적인 일련의 연구에서 생물학자 Gerald Wilkinson은 흡혈박쥐가 성공적인 야간 먹이 수집 후 공동의 둥지로 돌아오면, 그들은 빈번히 피를 토해내고 심지어 친족이 아닌 박쥐들도 포함하여 다른 둥지 식구들과 그것(피)을 공유한다는 것을 알아냈다. 그 이유는 피의 공유가 모든 박쥐의 생존 가능성을 크게 향상시키기 때문이라고 알려진다. 이틀 밤 동안

먹지 못한 박쥐는 죽을 가능성이 크다. Wilkinson은 피를 제공하는 박쥐가 일반적으로 그들의 잉여분을 공유하고 이를 통해 굶어 죽을 위기에 처한 먹이 수집에 실패한 박쥐들을 구한다고 밝혀냈다. 그래서 비용은 비교적 낮고 이익은 비교적 높아진다. 어떠한 박쥐도 어느 특정한 야간에 성공을 확신할 수 없기 때문에, 피를 제공하는 박쥐도 결국 어떤 둥지 식구로부터 도움을 필요로 할 것이다. 사실상 흡혈박쥐는 일종의 상호보험 체계를 만들어 낸 것이다.

어휘 classic 전형적인 communal 공동의 foraging 먹이 수집 non-relative 친족이 아닌 관계 surplus 잉여 forager 약탈자 starvation 굶주림 in effect 사실상 hierarchy 계급제도 ecological 생태계의 mutual 상호의 parasitic 기생의

03 정답 ①

해설 ①, ②, ③은 협상에 대한 조언이며, ④는 구체적으로 임금 협상에 대한 조언이므로, 모든 선지가 '협상에 대한 조언'과 관련됨을 알 수 있다. 따라서 이것이 글의 소재이다. 글을 살펴보면, 여러 협상 안건을 하나하나씩 제시하기보다는 여러 안건에 우선순위를 매긴 후 한꺼번에 제시하라고 조언하고 있다. 따라서 글의 요지로 가장 적절한 것은 ① '여러 문제를 연속적으로가 아닌 동시에 협상해라.'이다.
② 성공적인 협상을 위해 민감한 주제를 피해라.
③ 당신의 협상을 위해 적절한 시간을 골라라.
④ 급여를 협상할 때 너무 직설적으로 굴지 마라.

해석 만약 누군가가 당신에게 제안을 하고 당신이 정당하게 그것의 일부에 대해 걱정한다면, 당신은 보통 당신의 모든 변경 사항을 한꺼번에 제안하는 것이 더 낫다. "급여가 좀 적어요. 어떻게 좀 해주시겠어요?"라고 말하고 그녀가 그것을 처리하면 "고맙습니다. 이제 제가 원하는 다른 두 가지가 있는데..."라고 다시 말하지 마라. 처음에 당신이 한 가지만 요구한다면, 그녀는 그 하나를 들어주면 당신이 제안을 받아들일 (또는 적어도 결정을 내릴) 준비가 될 것으로 생각할 수 있다. 만약 당신이 계속해서 "그리고 한 가지 더..."라고 말한다면, 그녀는 관대하거나 이해심 있는 기분을 유지하지 않을 가능성이 크다. 더욱이, 하나보다 많은 요구 사항이 있다면, 당신이 원하는 그 모든 것들을 A, B, C, D로 단순히 언급하지 말고, 당신에게 있어 각각의 상대적 중요성을 표해라. 그렇지 않으면, 그녀는 당신이 가장 덜 중요하게 여기는 두 가지를 당신에게 주기 꽤 쉽다는 이유로 고르고 당신과 타협했다고 느낄지도 모른다.

어휘 legitimately 합법적으로, 정당하게 salary 급여 initially 처음에 generous 관대한 understanding 이해심 있는 signal 표하다 relative 상대적인 meet sb halfway ~와 타협하다 negotiate 협상하다 simultaneously 동시에 serially 연속적으로

전략 08

전략 적용 연습

본서 p. 195

01 ①	02 ②	03 ②
04 ④	05 ②	06 ④
07 ②		

01 정답 ①

해설 사회과학과 자연과학을 비교하는 글이다. 사회과학의 연구 대상은 상황에 따라 변하는 데 반해, 자연과학은 연구 대상의 불변성을 가정한다. ②, ④는 불규칙하며 변하기 쉬운 대상을 연구하는 사회과학에 해당하는 표현이며, ③도 측정할 수 없는 특성이라는 뜻이므로 자연과학보다는 사회과학에 가까운 표현임을 알 수 있다. 따라서 자연과학을 나타내는 표현으로서 빈칸에 들어갈 말로 가장 적절한 것은 ① '예측 가능한 속성'이다.
② 불규칙한 적용
③ 측정할 수 없는 특성
④ 변하기 쉬운 속성

해석 사회과학은 인간 행동 영역을 연구한다. 인간의 행동 유형은 장소에 따라 그리고 집단에 따라 달라진다. 그러나 자연과학은 좀 다르다. 화학자가 수소를 연구할 때, 하나의 수소 원자는 그것이 어디에서 발견되든 다른 수소원자와 매우 유사하며, 그것을 둘러싼 환경은 매우 정확하게 통제될 수 있다고 가정할 수 있다. 그것은 물리학자가 금속막대기를 측정하는 경우에도 마찬가지인데, 물리학자는 자연조건이 동일하다면 금속막대기의 길이가 늘어나거나 줄어들지 않을 것이라는 것을 확신할 수 있다. 자연과학은 연구 대상의 예측 가능한 속성 때문에 종종 "쉬운 과학"이라고 불린다.

어휘 vary 달라지다 somewhat 다소 hydrogen 수소 atom 원자 physicist 물리학자 shrink 줄어들다 unmeasurable 측정할 수 없는 property 속성

02 정답 ②

해설 처음 글을 읽을 때는 여러 대립 구도가 보이며, 여러 장르가 서로 대립되고 있기 때문에 + / -로 분류하기가 어려울 것이다. 그런데 글을 읽다 보면 however이 있는 문장 전후로 글의 맥락이 바뀌면서 이 글의 진짜 대립 구도가 '여러 분야 간 차이점 vs 공통점'이라는 것을 알게 된다. however 이전에서 나타난 대립 구도는 '여러 분야 간 차이점'에 해당하는데, 이 글은 결국 모든 분야에는 공통된 사고방식이 있음을 강조하는 글이므로, 선지들 중 이와 관련된 표현이 정답임을 알 수 있다. 따라서 글의 주제로 가장 적절한 것은 ② '창조 과정의 공통성'이다.
① 다양한 전문 직종의 구별되는 특징
③ 예술과 과학 사이의 차이점
④ 창의적인 사고의 방해물들

해석 사람들이 생산한 다양한 것들을 보고 그들의 차이점을 설명하는 것은 쉽다. 확실히 시는 수학적 공식이 아니며, 소설은 유전학의 실험이 아니다. 작곡가는 확실히 시각 예술가들의 언어와는 다른 언어를 사용하며, 화학자들은 극작가들이 하는(결합시키는)

것보다는 매우 다른 것들을 결합시킨다. 그러나 사람들을 그들이 만든 다양한 사물들로 특징화하는 것은 그들이 어떻게 창조하는가에 대한 보편성을 놓치는 것이다. 왜냐하면 창조 과정의 수준에서는 과학자, 예술가, 수학자, 작곡가, 작가 그리고 조각가는 소위 우리가 말하는 공통된 "사고의 도구"를 사용하는데, 그것에는 정서적 느낌, 시각적 이미지, 육체적 감각, 재생 가능한 패턴, 비유 등이 포함된다. 그리고 모든 창의적인 사상가들은 이런 주관적 사고 도구에서 생성된 아이디어를 대중적인 언어로 번역하여 자신의 통찰력을 표현하는 법을 배우고, 이는 다른 사람들의 정신에 새로운 사고를 불러일으킨다.

어휘 formula 공식 genetics 유전학 chemist 화학자 playwright 극작가 characterize 특징화하다 universality 보편성 sculptor 조각가 analogy 비유 subjective 주관적인 distinctive 구별되는, 독특한 commonality 공통성 obstacle 방해물

03 정답 ②

해설 글을 전체적으로 봤을 때, 생각과 감정을 통제하기를 강요한 고대 스파르타, 로마 공화정 시대, 빅토리아 시대와 그러한 능력이 오히려 이상하다고 여겨지는 오늘날의 시대가 대립되고 있다. (A)가 포함된 문장 앞에서 나온 문화에 대한 예시가 (A)가 포함된 문장에 나오므로, (A)에는 for example이, (B)에는 앞에 나온 시대와는 다른 오늘날의 내용이 이어지므로 역접의 연결사 however이 와야 한다.

해석 역사상 특정 시기에 사람이 생각과 느낌을 완벽히 제어하는 법을 배우지 못한다면 완전한 인간이 아니라는 것을 당연시하던 문화가 있었다. 예를 들어, 고대 스파르타 시대에서, 로마 공화정 시대에서, 빅토리아 시대의 영국 상류 계층들 사이에서는 사람들이 자신의 감정을 통제할 책임이 있었다. 너무 쉽게 화내는 사람은 공동체의 일원으로 받아들여질 권리를 박탈당했다. 그러나, 지금 우리가 살고 있는 것과 같은 역사의 다른 시기에는, 자신을 통제할 수 있는 능력이 항상 크게 존중받는 것만은 아니다. 이를 시도하는 사람들은 종종 이상하다고 여겨진다.

어휘 take sth for granted ~을 당연하게 생각하다 fully 충분히 upper 상류의 responsible 책임이 있는 lose one's temper 화내다 deprive A of B A에게서 B를 빼앗다 community 공동체 historical 역사의 attempt 시도하다

04 정답 ④

해설 이 글은 시각적 경험만 하는 경우와 청각적 경험이 시각적 경험에 동반되는 경우를 대비하고 있다. (A) 앞에서 시각적인 것 '이상의' 것, 즉 청각적 경험이 필요하다고 했으므로, 청각이 시각과 '일치하지 않는 한' 가상 경험은 산산조각 날 것이라는 맥락이 자연스럽다. 따라서 (A)에는 Unless가 들어가야 한다. 반면 (B) 뒤에서는 아직 청각을 설득력 있게 구현할 기술이 부족하다는 내용이 이어지므로, (B)에는 Unfortunately가 들어가는 것이 적절하다.

해석 오늘날 가상현실(VR) 경험의 시각적 구성요소를 만드는 기술은 널리 접근 가능하고 저렴하게 전환되고 있다. 그러나 강력하게 작동하기 위해서 가상현실은 시각적인 것 이상의 것이 필요하다. 당신이 '듣고 있는' 것이 확실하게 시각적인 것과 일치하지 않는 한, 가상 경험은 산산조각이 난다. 농구 경기를 예로 들어 보자. 만약 선수들, 코치들, 아나운서들, 그리고 관중들이 모두 코트 한가운데에 앉아 있는 것처럼 들린다면, 당신은 차라리 텔레비전으로 경기를 보는 것이 좋을 것이다. 당신은 그것으로 충분히 "그곳"에 있다는 느낌을 받을 것이다. 불행하게도, 오늘날의 오디오 장비와 널리 사용되는 녹음 및 재생 형식은 먼 행성의 전쟁터 소리, 코트의 농구 경기, 또는 위대한 공연장의 첫 번째 줄에서 들려오는 교향곡 소리를 설득력 있게 재현하는 임무에 전혀 적합하지 않다.

어휘 component 요소 accessible 접근이 쉬운 affordable 입수 가능한 convincingly 납득이 가도록 equipment 장비 inadequate 불충분한 symphony 교향곡

05 정답 ②

해설 이직을 자주 하며 그렇게 하는 데 큰 어려움을 겪지 않는 젊은 노동자와, 반대로 이직을 잘 하지 않으며 이직에 어려움이 있는 나이 든 노동자가 대조되고 있다. ② 앞에서는 젊은 노동자에 관한 설명이, ② 뒤에서는 나이 든 노동자에 관한 설명이 이어지므로 ② 뒤의 They는 주어진 문장의 Older workers임을 알 수 있다. 따라서 주어진 문장이 들어가기에 가장 적절한 곳은 ②이다.

해석 젊은 노동자들은 좀 더 보편적인 기술을 가지고 있어서 그들의 기술이 가장 잘 사용될 곳에 대해서는 확신이 덜한 경향이 있다. 그러므로 그들은 정기적으로 이 직장에서 저 직장으로 옮기는 경향이 있다. 그러나 그들이 이전 직장을 떠날 때, 그들은 새 직장을 찾는 데 거의 어려움을 겪지 않는다. 대조적으로, 나이 든 노동자들은 좀 더 자주 그들이 현재 고용되어 있는 산업이나 회사에 맞는 매우 특수한 기술들을 가지고 있다. 그들은 이미 최선의 고용 조건을 알고 있으며, 이 직장에서 저 직장으로 옮겨 다니려 하지 않는다. 그러나 그들이 이직을 하려 하더라도 그들의 정밀한 기술과 잘 어울리는 직책을 찾기가 종종 어렵고 시간이 든다. 그래서, 젊은 노동자에게는 성가신 일인 실직이 숙련 노동자에게는 타격을 주고 재정적으로 고갈시키는 경험이 될 수 있다.

어휘 specific 특수한 industry 산업 employ 고용하다 general 일반적인 put A to use A를 이용하다 on a regular basis 정기적으로 be inclined to ~할 의향이 있다 precise 정밀한 unemployment 실업 financially 재정적으로 drain 고갈시키다 mature 숙련된

06 정답 ④

해설 글의 서두에서 강한 결속으로 인해 의견 불일치가 없어진다면 성과가 둔화될 것이라고 하였다. 즉, 강한 결속은 의견 불일치 및 성과와 음(-)의 상관관계인 동시에, 의견 불일치는 성과와 양(+)의 상관관계에 있다는 점을 유추할 수 있다. 따라서 이러한 상관관계를 서술하는 ①, ②, ③은 자연스러운 반면, ④는 결속과 성과 간의 양(+)의 상관관계를 서술하고 있으므로 글의 흐름에 반대된다. 따라서 글의 흐름상 어색한 문장은 ④이다.

해석 집단 구성원들 사이의 사교적인 결속력과 애정의 역할에 관련된 다음(문장)이 의미하는 바를 생각해 보라. 만약 강력한 결속이 작은 불일치일지라도 그것이 생기는 게 덜 가능하게 만든다면, 집단과 단체의 성과는 손해를 입을 것이다. 투자 클럽에 대한 한

연구는 최악의 성과를 보이는 클럽은 애정적인 유대관계를 토대로 조직되었고 주로 사교적인 반면에, 최고의 성과를 내는 클럽은 사교적인 관계를 제한했고 돈을 버는 데 집중했다는 것을 보여 주었다. 의견 불일치는 높은 성과를 보여 주는 클럽에서 훨씬 더 빈번했다. 결정을 내려야 했을 때, 낮은 성취를 보여 주는 사람들은 보통 만장일치로 투표를 했고 공개적인 토론은 거의 가지지 않았다. (이 연구에서 보이는 것처럼, 높은 성과를 이룬 사람들은 낮은 성과를 이룬 사람들보다 사교적인 결속력에 더 큰 중요성을 두었으며, 그 결과 그들의 높은 성공률에 이르렀다.) 중심적인 문제는 낮은 성취를 이룬 집단들의 투표자들이 가장 높은 수익을 만들어내기보다는 사교적인 응집성을 구축하려고 했다는 것이다.

어휘 following 다음의 implication 의미, 함의 bond 결속력 affection 애정 institution 단체 impair 손상시키다 affective 애정적인 tie 유대 primarily 주로 unanimously 만장일치로 open debate 공개적인 토론 result in 결국 ~되다[하다] cohesion 응집성 returns 수익

07 정답 ②

해설 일반인의 입장과 이익을 대변하는 것처럼 보이기 위한 선전 기법에 관한 글이다. 글을 보면 일반인은 blue-collar audience, the crowd, folks에 해당하며, 선전가들은 politician, labor leaders ~ advertisers에 해당함을 알 수 있다. 빈칸에는 선전가들이 보이고자 하는 모습이 나와야 하므로 일반 대중과 관련된 표현이 와야 한다. 따라서 빈칸에 들어갈 말로 가장 적절한 것은 ② '우리 같은 평범한 사람들'이다. 참고로, ①에서 '화려한 추상어'는 선전가가 일반 대중을 대변하는 것으로 보이기 위한 방법이므로 이를 '넘어선' 것은 정답이 될 수 없다.
① 화려한 추상어를 넘어선
③ 남들과는 다른 무언가
④ 대중보다 더 잘 교육받은

해석 가장 자주 사용되는 선전 기법 중 하나는 선전가의 견해가 일반인의 견해를 반영하고 있으며 자신이 그들의 최선의 이익을 위해 일하고 있다는 것을 대중에게 확신시키는 것이다. 블루칼라 청중에게 말하는 정치인은 소매를 걷어붙이고 넥타이를 풀고 대중의 특정 관용구를 사용하려고 시도할 수 있다. 그는 심지어 자신이 "그 사람들 중 한 명일 뿐"이라는 인상을 주기 위해 일부러 언어를 잘못 사용할 수도 있다. 이 기법은 또한 보통 정치가의 견해가 연설을 듣는 대중의 견해와 같다는 인상을 주기 위해 화려한 추상어를 이용한다. 노조 간부들, 사업가들, 장관들, 교육자들, 그리고 광고주들은 우리 같은 평범한 사람들인 것처럼 보임으로써 우리의 신뢰를 얻기 위해 이 기법을 사용해 왔다.

어휘 propaganda 선전 blue-collar 블루칼라[육체노동자]의 sleeve 소매 undo 풀다, 벗기다 idiom 관용구, 표현 양식 on purpose 일부러 folks 사람들 minister 장관 confidence 신뢰 plain 평범한

전략 09

전략 적용 연습

본서 p. 204

01 ③	02 ②	03 ①
04 ④	05 ②	06 ②

01 정답 ③

해설 정서적 민감성은 중요한 변화만을 감지하게 되어 있으며, 어느 시점까지는 많이 감지하는 것이 좋지만, 그 시점을 넘어서면 해롭다는 것이 이 글의 요지이다. ①은 '감지'가 아닌 '표현'에 관한 내용이므로 주제와 관계없으며, ②는 '최대한 빨리' '모든' 변화를 감지해야 한다는 내용인데, 이는 변화 감지를 많이 할수록 좋다는 뉘앙스이므로 옳지 않다. ④ 역시 과거까지도 고려해야 한다는 뜻이므로 중요한 변화만을 감지하는 것이 좋다는 글의 맥락에서 벗어난다. 따라서 사소한 것에는 무관심해야 한다는 내용의 ③이 유일한 정답이 되므로, 빈칸에 들어갈 말로 가장 적절한 것은 ③ '별 의미가 없는 것들에 대해 무관심할'이다.
① 분별 있는 방식으로 당신의 감정을 표현할
② 가능한 한 빨리 모든 변화를 감지할
④ 과거의 사건뿐만 아니라 현재의 사건에 집중할

해석 글자 그대로의 의미에서 민감성은 주로 변화 탐지기이다. 즉 그것은 보통 특정한 감정으로 표현된다. 도난 경보기처럼, 정서적 민감성은 주의를 요하는 어떤 것의 존재를 가리킨다. 정서적 민감성의 최적 성질은 그 시스템이 더 민감할수록 그것이 더 많은 변화를 감지할 것이고, 그리하여 그것의 임무를 더 잘 완수할 것이라는 점이다. 비록 정서적 민감성의 임무가 변화를 탐지하는 것일지라도, 그것은 우리의 정서적인 관심사에 의미 있는 것들인 중요한 변화만을 탐지하도록 의도된다. 무차별적으로 민감한 것은 재빨리 무관하고 심지어 해로운 소음으로 시스템에 과부하가 걸리게 할 것이므로 역효과를 낳을 수 있다. 정서적 민감성에 관한 한 어느 시점까지는 '많을수록 좋지만' 그 이후에 더 많은 변화를 감지하는 것은 과하다는 것이 흔한 경우이다. 따라서 당신의 정서적 건강을 위해 당신이 별 의미가 없는 것들에 대해 무관심할 필요가 있다.

어휘 sensitivity 민감성 literal 글자 그대로 detector 탐지기 burglar alarm 도난 경보기 optimal 최적의 fulfill 완수하다 indiscriminately 무차별적으로 counterproductive 역효과를 낳는 overload 과부하 걸리게 하다 irrelevant 무관한

02 정답 ②

해설 선지를 보면 ①, ③, ④ 모두 MAP과 직관의 관계를 양(+)으로 보지만, ②는 직관을 '지연시킨다'는 의미로 유일하게 음(-)의 관계로 본다. 따라서 ②가 정답이 될 수밖에 없다. 설명을 부연하자면, 이 글은 직감에 기반하는 의사 결정을 연기하는 것을 목표로 하는 MAP이라는 접근 방식에 관한 것으로, 글의 중반부부터 해당 소재가 나오고 있다. 마지막 문장에서 개별적인 분석을 한 뒤에 전체적인 판단을 해야 한다고 덧붙인 것을 보아, 전체적인 판단을 바로 내리지 않고 개별적인 분석을 모두 마치기까지 판단을 '미뤄야' 하는 것을 유추할 수 있다. 따라서 빈칸에 들어갈 말로 가장 적절한 것은 ② '지연시키다'이다.

① 개선하다
③ 소유하다
④ 용이하게 하다

해석 노벨상 수상자인 심리학자 Daniel Kahneman은 인간이 이성적인 의사 결정자라는 개념을 뒤집으면서, 세계가 경제학에 대해 생각하는 방식을 바꾸었다. 그 과정에서, 그의 학문 분야를 초월하는 영향은 의사들이 의학적 결정을 내리고 투자자들이 월가의 위험을 평가하는 방식을 변화시켰다. 한 논문에서, Kahneman과 그의 동료들은 큰 전략적 결정을 내리는 과정을 개략적으로 설명한다. Mediating Assessment Protocol 또는 MAP으로 명명된 그들의 제안된 접근방법은 다음과 같은 간단한 목표를 가지고 있다. 여러 가지 개별적인 요인에 의해 선택이 정보에 기반한 것이 될 수 있을 때까지 직감 기반 의사결정을 연기하는 것이다. Kahneman은 최근 '포스트'와의 인터뷰에서 "MAP의 본질적인 목적 중 하나는 기본적으로 직관을 지연시키는 것"이라고 말했다. 구조화된 프로세스는 이전에 선택된 6~7개의 속성을 바탕으로 결정을 분석하고, 각각에 대해 별도로 논의하고, 상대적 백분위수 점수를 할당하며, 마지막으로 그러한 점수를 사용하여 전체적인 판단을 내리는 것을 요구한다.

어휘 upend 뒤집다 notion 개념 rational 이성적인 alter 바꾸다, 고치다 evaluate 평가하다 outline 개요를 서술하다 intuition 직관 attribute 속성; ~의 결과로 보다 percentile 백분위수 holistic 전체적인, 전체론의

03 정답 ①

해설 과학 및 지식의 발전과 그것이 세상에서 어떻게 쓰이는 지는 별개이며, 지식 자체는 그것의 사회적 또는 도덕적 적용과는 관계없다는 주장을 하는 글이다. 따라서 '지식의 발전'과 '가치 실현'이 대조되고 있는 것을 알 수 있다. 빈칸 앞에서 지식이 사회악을 치유하지 못했다는 것에 실망하는 것은 타당하다고 말했는데, 이후 but을 통해 맥락을 뒤집어 필자의 주장을 말할 것임을 유추할 수 있다. 따라서 빈칸에 들어갈 말로 가장 적절한 것은 ① '이것을 지식의 진보와 혼동하는 것은 터무니없다'이다. ②, ③, ④는 모두 '지식의 발전'과 '가치 실현'을 동일하게 보고 있으므로 필자의 생각과 반대되는 선지이다.
② 지식의 특성을 아는 것은 그것의 도덕적 가치를 실행하는 것이다
③ 사회적 불평등을 제거하는 것은 지식의 내재적 목적이다
④ 지식을 축적하는 것은 그것의 사회적 적용을 확대하는 것이다

해석 내 친구는 과학적인 발전이 전쟁과 기아를 없애서 세상의 병폐를 치유하지 못했다는 것과, 엄청난 인간 불평등이 아직도 널리 퍼져 있으며, 행복이 보편적이지 않다는 것에 실망했다. 내 친구는 흔한 실수, 즉 지식의 본질에 대해서 기본적인 오해를 했다. 지식은 도덕과 관계가 없으며, 비도덕적인 것이 아니라 도덕 중립적인 것이다. 그것은 어떤 목적으로든 사용될 수 있지만, 많은 사람은 그것이 사회를 위해 '그들이' 선호하는 희망을 증진하는 데 사용될 것이라고 가정하는데, 이것이 근본적으로 잘못된 점이다. 세상의 지식과 그 사용은 별개의 문제이다. 이해에 있어서의 진보가 세계의 사회적인 불행을 치유하지 못해 왔다는 것에 실망하는 것은 타당한 견해이지만, 이것을 지식의 진보와 혼동하는 것은 터무니없다. 아프리카나 중동의 갈등 때문에 지식이 진보하지 않는다고 주장하는 것은 요점에서 벗어난다. 지식에는 구체적인 사회적 또는 도덕적 적용을 지시하는 그 어떤 것도 내재되어 있지 않다.

어휘 amoral 도덕과 관계없는 immoral 부도덕한 assume 가정하다 further 증진하다 legitimate 타당한 inherent 내재적인 dictate 지시하다, 좌우하다 absurd 터무니없는

04 정답 ④

해설 ①, ②, ③은 모두 두 생각의 관계를 보완적으로 보고 있으므로, 선지만 봐도 ④를 정답으로 고를 수 있다. 설명을 덧붙이자면, 이 글에서는 '자신을 정당화하는 생각'과 빈칸 앞에서 언급된 '우리에게 잘못이 있을 수 있다는 생각'이 대비되고 있는데, 결국 자기 합리화적 생각은 우리의 본성이라고 말하고 있다. 따라서 우리가 틀렸을지도 모른다는 생각은 자기를 정당화하는 생각에 질 것이라고 유추할 수 있으므로, 빈칸에 들어갈 말로 가장 적절한 것은 ④ '압도된'이다.
① 인정받은 ② 밝혀진 ③ 강화된

해석 우리가 비합리적으로 행동할 때, 대개 우리의 행동이 우리에게는 합리적인 것처럼 보인다. 문제 제기를 받으면, 마음속으로 "왜 이 사람들은 나를 힘들게 하는 걸까? 나는 이치에 맞는 일을 하고 있을 뿐인데. 합리적인 사람이면 누구나 그걸 알 텐데!"라고 말한다. 요컨대, 우리는 자연스럽게 우리의 사고가 완전히 정당하다고 생각한다. 우리가 아는 한, 우리는 옳고 타당하고 합리적인 일을 하고 있을 뿐이다. 우리에게 잘못이 있을지도 모름을 내비치는 어떠한 순간적인 생각도 보통 "나는 해를 끼치려는 의도는 없어. 나는 정당해! 나는 공정해! 틀린 것은 다른 사람들이야!"처럼 자기 정당화하는 더 강력한 생각에 의해 압도된다. 이러한 인간 마음의 본성을 자연적인 상태로 인지하는 것이 중요하다. 다시 말해, 인간은 자기 정당화적이고, 이기적이고, 자기 기만적인 사고와 행동을 배울 필요가 없다. 이러한 양상은 우리 모두에게 있어 타고난 것이다.

어휘 irrationally 비합리적으로 reasonable 합리적인 challenge 이의를 제기하다 make sense 이치에 맞다 justified 정당한 proper 타당한, 정당한 fleeting 순간의 at fault 잘못한, 죄가 있는 state 상태 self-serving 이기적인 self-deceptive 자기 기만적인 innate 타고난

05 정답 ②

해설 ①, ③, ④는 전부 '터무니없는, 상상도 할 수 없는'이라는 뜻의 유의어이므로 정답이 되기 어렵다는 것을 알 수 있다. 따라서 자동으로 ②를 정답으로 고를 수 있는 문제이다. 글을 살펴보면, 고급 식당에서는 높은 가격에 상응하는 고급의 서비스가 요구되는데, 서비스의 효율성을 높이는 데는 한계가 있다고 말한다. 따라서 효율성을 높이기보다는 가격을 높이는 것이 현실적인 방법이므로, 가격을 높이는 것은 '불가피하다'는 결론이 나온다. 따라서 빈칸에 들어갈 말로 가장 적절한 것은 ② '불가피한'이다.
① 터무니없는 ③ 터무니없는 ④ 상상도 할 수 없는

해석 고급 식당은 가격이 높게 청구될 수밖에 없기 때문에 탁월함이 절대적인 전제 조건이다. 경영자는 식당을 효율적으로 만들기 위해 가능한 모든 것을 할지도 모르지만, 손님들은 여전히 정성

들인 개개인을 위한 서비스, 즉 매우 숙련된 요리사에 의해 주문 받을 준비가 되어 있으며 전문 서버가 전달하는 음식을 기대한다. 이 서비스는 말 그대로 수작업이기 때문에 생산성에 있어서 미미한 개선만이 가능하다. 예를 들어, 요리사, 서버, 또는 바텐더가 빨리 움직이는 데는 인간 수행 능력에 한계가 있다. 따라서 향상된 효율성을 통해서는 약간의 절약만이 가능하고, 이는 가격 상승을 불가피하게 만든다. (가격이 오를수록 소비자들이 더 까다로워진다는 것은 경제학의 자명한 이치다.) 따라서, 고급 식당의 손님들은 탁월함을 기대하고, 요구하며, 그것을 위해 기꺼이 비용을 지불한다.

어휘 prerequisite 전제 조건 fine dining 고급 식당 marginal 미미한, 근소한 moderate 중간의, 적당한 escalation 상승 axiom 자명한 이치 discriminating 식별력 있는, 차별하는 clientele 고객들

06 정답 ②

해설 이 글은 요리에 과학적 원리가 적용되기는 하지만, 요리는 형식과학이나 현대 과학 방식이 등장하기 훨씬 이전부터 존재했다는 내용의 글이다. 따라서 요리와 과학은 '다르다'는 맥락이 와야 하는데, 빈칸 앞에 'wrong'에 유의한다면 빈칸에는 둘이 '같다'는 말이 와야 한다. ①은 '과학'과 '철학'의 관계를 논하므로 바로 소거할 수 있으며, ③, ④는 요리와 과학이 다르다는 내용이므로 빈칸에 올 수 없다. 그렇게 된다면 ②만 남는다. 이때 '기술'은 뜬금없어 보일 수 있으나, 글의 마지막 2번째 문장에서 '요리의 기술'이라는 언급을 통해 필자는 '요리'와 '기술'을 동일 선상에 놓고 있음을 알 수 있다. 따라서 빈칸에 들어갈 말로 가장 적절한 것은 ② '기술이 단지 과학적 사고를 적용한 것이다'이다.

① 과학은 철학과 관계가 없다
③ 요리는 형식과학으로부터 언제나 독립적이었다
④ 요리는 구조화된 과학적 분석의 직접적인 결과가 아니다

해석 우리의 부엌은 과학의 훌륭함의 덕을 많이 보고 있고, 스토브에서 혼합 재료로 실험하는 요리사는 흔히 실험실에 있는 화학자와 크게 다르지 않다. 우리는 색을 유지하기 위해 적양배추에 식초를 첨가하고 케이크에 있는 레몬의 산성을 중화하기 위해 베이킹 소다를 사용한다. 그러나 기술이 단지 과학적 사고를 적용한 것이라고 생각하는 것은 잘못이다. 그것은 이보다 더 기초적이고 더 오래된 무언가이다. 모든 문화가 기원전 4세기에 Aristotle에게서 시작된 우주에 관한 체계화된 지식의 형태인 형식과학을 가지고 있지는 않았다. 실험이 가설, 실험법, 그리고 분석의 구조화된 체계의 일부를 형성하는 현대 과학 방식은 17세기인 최근의 일이고, 요리의 문제 해결 기술은 수천 년 전으로 거슬러 간다. 최초 석기 시대 인간이 날카롭게 만든 부싯돌로 날것의 음식물을 잘랐던 이래로, 우리는 항상 우리 자신을 먹여 살리는 더 나은 방법을 고안하기 위해 발명을 사용해 왔다.

어휘 brilliance 훌륭함 vinegar 식초 counteract 중화하다 acidity 산성 hypothesis 가설 flint 부싯돌

전략 10

전략 적용 연습

본서 p. 213

01 ④	02 ②	03 ①
04 ②	05 ②	

01 정답 ④

해설 주어진 문장은 이와 동일한 생각(The same thinking)이 여러 목표에 적용될 수 있다며, 직장에서의 성과를 한 예로 들고 있다. 따라서 이 문장 앞에는 '동일한 생각'에 상응하는 개념이 나와야 하며, 뒤에는 직장에서 성과를 거두는 것과 관련된 내용이 와야 한다. ④ 앞까지 장기적인 목표를 달성하기 위해서는 단기 목표를 세우는 것이 중요하다고 말하며, 다이어트가 그 예시로 나온다. 그런데 ④ 뒤에서는 우리의 직업에 대한 내용이 나오므로 문맥이 끊긴다. 따라서 주어진 문장이 ④에 들어가서, ④ 앞과 동일한 생각이 직장 생활에도 적용될 수 있다는 맥락이 만들어진 후, 뒤에 이에 관한 부연이 이어지는 것이 자연스럽다. 따라서 주어진 문장이 들어갈 위치로 가장 적절한 곳은 ④이다.

해석 행복한 두뇌는 단기간에 집중하는 경향이 있다. 사정이 그렇다면 결국 장기적인 목표를 달성하도록 이끌게 될 어떤 단기적인 목표를 달성할 수 있을지 생각해 보는 것이 좋다. 예를 들어, 만약 당신이 6개월 안에 30파운드를 감량하고 싶다면, 당신은 어떤 단기적인 목표를, 거기에 도달하게 해줄 더 작은 체중의 증가분 감량과 연관시킬 수 있을까? 아마도 그것은 매주 2파운드를 감량할 때마다 당신 스스로에게 보상하는 것만큼 간단한 일일 것이다. 직장에서의 성과를 향상시키는 것과 같은 많은 목표에도 이와 동일한 생각이 적용될 수 있다. 전체적인 목표를 더 작고 단기적인 부분으로 나누면, 우리는 직업에서 목표의 거대함에 압도되는 대신 점진적인 성취에 초점을 맞출 수 있다.

어휘 any number of 많은 accomplish 성취하다 associate 연관 짓다 increment 증가 overall 전반적인 overwhelmed 압도된 enormity 막대함 profession 직업

02 정답 ②

해설 (B)의 they는 주어진 문장의 Some researchers를 가리키는 대명사임을 알 수 있으며, 주어진 문장 뒤에는 이 연구진들이 새롭게 알아낸 것에 대한 내용이 이어져야 하므로 (B)가 주어진 문장 다음에 와야 한다. 그리고 (B)에서 언급한 네 가지 요소 중 하나가 (A)에서 예로 드는 '경영진에 대한 신뢰'이므로 (B) 다음에 (A)가 와야 한다. 마지막으로, (A)에서 새로운 상사로 인해 경영진에 대한 신뢰가 약간 상승한 경우를 예시로 들었는데, 이 약간의 신뢰 상승을 that small increase in trust로 받아, 그것이 임금이 36퍼센트 인상된 것과 동일한 가치가 있다고 설명하는 (C)가 이어져야 한다. 따라서 글의 순서로 가장 적절한 것은 ② '(B) - (A) - (C)'이다.

해석 매년, 우리는 같은 말을 듣는다. 당신이 삶에서 행복하기를 원한다면 직장에서 행복해야 한다는 것이다. 좋다. 하지만 직장에서 어떤 것이 나를 행복하게 만들 것인가? 몇몇 연구진들은 외관상 계량화할 수 없는 것을 계량화할 수 있는 흥미로운 방식을 생각

해 냈다. (B) 직업 만족에 필요한 네 가지 핵심 요소들을 고려하는 생활 만족도 조사를 분석함으로써, 그들은 각 요소가 임금 인상과 비교해 어느 정도의 가치가 있는지 알아냈다. (A) 예를 들어, 단연코 직무 만족에 있어서 가장 큰 요소인 경영진에 대한 신뢰는 전반적인 행복에 있어 상당한 임금 인상만큼이나 매우 가치 있다. 가령 새로운 상사가 오고서 직장 경영진에 대한 당신의 신뢰가 약간 상승했다고 해보자. (C) 연구진들이 계산한 바에 의하면, 신뢰의 그 작은 증가분조차 36퍼센트의 임금 인상과 같다. 다시 말해, 그것은 36퍼센트의 임금 인상과 거의 같은 정도로 전반적인 삶의 만족도를 상승시킬 것이다.

어휘 year after year 해마다 come up with ~을 생각해 내다 quantify 수량화하다 seemingly 외관상 unquantifiable 수량화할 수 없는 management 경영진 component 구성 요소 satisfaction 만족 overall 전반적인 substantial 상당한 raise 인상 workplace 직장 figure out 계산해 내다 calculate 계산하다

03 정답 ①

해설 주어진 문장을 보고 건강 모니터링 및 추적 장치가 글의 소재임을 알 수 있다. 모든 연령층에 이 장치가 인기를 얻고 있다는 내용 다음에는 이 현상을 This로 받아 특히(particularly) 노년층에게는 더욱 그러하다며 그 이유를 설명하는 (B)가 오는 것이 자연스럽다. 다음으로 For example을 통해 노년층에게 도움이 되는 낙상 경보의 실례를 언급하는 (A)가 와야 하며, 마지막으로 그 낙상 경보를 This simple technology로 받아, 그 작동 원리를 서술하는 (C)가 와야 한다. 따라서 글의 순서로 가장 적절한 것은 ① '(B) - (A) - (C)'이다.

해석 당신의 건강을 감시하고 추적하는 도구들은 모든 연령대에서 점점 더 인기를 얻고 있다. (B) 특히 노년층에게는 이러한 기술이 생명을 구할 수 있기 때문에 더욱 그렇다[인기 있다]. (A) 예를 들어 낙상은 65세 이상 성인들에게 있어서 주요한 사망 원인이다. 낙상 경보는 노인을 위한 인기 있는 양로 기술로, 수년 동안 있어 왔으며 최근에 개선된 것이다. (C) 이 간단한 기술은 노인이 넘어지는 순간 자동적으로 911이나 가까운 가족에게 경보를 알린다.

어휘 track 추적하다 fall 낙상, 넘어짐 lifesaving 생명을 구하는

04 정답 ②

해설 주어진 글에서 이 글의 소재가 우울증에 관한 통계임을 알 수 있다. 주어진 글 다음에는 우울증 통계에 대한 부연 설명으로, 여성과 남성의 우울증 통계를 제시하는 (B)가 오는 것이 자연스럽다. 그다음으로는, 이중 후자, 즉 남성의 우울증 통계를 the latter number로 받아, 그러나(But) 몇몇 연구자들은 그 수치에 이의를 제기한다는 내용을 언급하는 (C)가 와야 한다. 마지막으로, (C)에서 이야기한 '남자가 여자보다 정신과 치료를 덜 받는 경향'을 This로 받아 그 이유를 설명하는 (A)가 와야 한다. 따라서 글의 순서로 가장 적절한 것은 ② '(B) - (C) - (A)'이다.

해석 우울증은 어떠한 시점에서든 미국에 사는 1,900만 명 이상의 사람들을 괴롭히고, 일생동안 거의 5명 중 1명을 괴롭힌다. (B) 통계에 따르면, 모든 여성의 대략 20%가 우울증으로 고통받으며, 남자는 약 10%가 그렇다. (C) 하지만 몇몇의 연구자들은 후자의 숫자에 대하여 이의를 제기한다. "일반적으로 남자는 여자보다 정신과 치료를 덜 찾는 경향이 있다."라고 Clark 대학의 심리학 조교수인 Michael Addis는 말했다. (A) 이것은 남자들이 도움을 구하기보다는 어려움을 참고 견디는 성향이 있기 때문이다. 이것은 이 자주 인용되는 통계 수치에 오해의 소지가 있다고 전문가들이 믿는 여러 가지 이유 중 하나이다.

어휘 depression 우울증 afflict 괴롭히다 tough it out 어려움을 참고 견디다 often-quoted 자주 인용되는 statistics 통계 misleading 오해의 소지가 있는 approximately 대략 latter 후자의 assistant professor 조교수

05 정답 ②

해설 이 글은 컴퓨터의 발명이 고등교육에 미친 영향에 대해 서술하고 있다. 주어진 글 마지막 부분에 언급된 여러 가지 발명품에 대한 한 가지 예시(One recent modern invention)로 (B)에서 컴퓨터를 소개하므로 주어진 글 바로 다음에는 (B)가 오는 것이 적절하다. (B)에서는 컴퓨터 기술이 특히 교육을 발전시켰다고 말하며, 그중 한 중요한 영향(One important effect)인 '강의에 대한 접근성'을 언급하는데, 이 내용은 (C)의 첫 문장과 자연스럽게 연결된다. 마지막으로 (A)에서는 컴퓨터가 교육에 주는 또 다른 이점을 In addition을 통해 추가로 제시하고 있다. 따라서 글의 순서로 가장 적절한 것은 ② '(B) - (C) - (A)'이다.

해석 여러 시대를 거쳐, 부지런한 사람들은 삶을 더 편하게 만들기 위해 편리함을 지속적으로 창조해 왔다. 바퀴부터 전구의 발명까지, 발명품들은 사회를 발전시켜 나아갔다. (B) 최근의 현대 발명품 중 하나는 컴퓨터인데, 그것은 사람들의 삶의 많은 측면을 개선시켰다. 이는 교육 분야에서 더욱 그렇다. 고등교육에 있어서 컴퓨터 기술의 한 가지 중요한 영향은 강의의 이용 가능성이다. (C) 컴퓨터 네트워크 발달의 결과로, 학생들은 실시간으로 다양한 대학의 강의를 들을 수 있다. 그들은 이제 디지털 스크린 앞에 앉아 다른 대학에서 제공되는 강의를 들을 수 있다. (A) 게다가, 대화형 미디어가 강사에게 질문하거나 다른 학생들과 이메일로 의견을 나누기 위해 사용될 수 있다. 그러한 컴퓨터화된 강의들은 학생들에게 전에는 이용할 수 없었던 지식에 대한 접근을 제공한다.

어휘 industrious 부지런한, 근면한 propel 나아가게 하다 higher education 고등교육 availability 이용 가능성, 유용성

전략 11

전략 적용 연습

본서 p. 220

01 ④　　02 ②　　03 ④

01 정답 ④

해설 주어진 문장은 식민지 전역에 더 영구적인 주택들이 생겨났다는 내용이므로 이 문장 앞에는 비교 대상이 될 수 있는 덜 영구적인 거주지가 (임시방편으로) 존재했었다는 내용이 있어야 한다. ④ 앞까지는 동굴을 이용한 임시 거주지에 대한 내용이며 ④ 뒤부

터는 주어진 문장에서 언급한 더 영구적인 거주지에 대한 부연 설명이 이어지므로, 주어진 문장이 들어갈 위치로 가장 적절한 곳은 ④이다.

해석 당신은 미국 내의 초기 유럽 정착민들이 동굴에 살았던 것을 알고 있었는가? 그것은 사실이다. 이 초기에 도착한 사람들은 뭔가 더 나은 것을 지을 시간도 도구도 가지고 있지 않았다. 겨울 날씨가 사나운 New England 지역에서는 특히 그랬다. 어떠한 형태의 즉각적인 은신처가 필요했고, 동굴은 이런 목적에 적합했다. 이 강건한 식민지 개척자들은 그래서 벼랑 끝을 따라 동굴을 팠고 버팀목으로 지지된 나무껍질로 만든 지붕을 만들었으며, 이제 적어도 한동안은 자신들만의 공간이라고 부를 수 있는 곳이 생겼다. 상황이 나아지면서, 보다 영구적인 주택이 식민지 전역에 나타나기 시작했다. 그 식민지의 각 지역들은, 즉시 쓸 수 있는 재료나 기후에 의한, 그들만의 고정된 형태의 주택을 발달시켰다.

어휘 dwelling 주택, 주거지 emerge 나타나다 settler 정착민 harsh 혹독한 immediate 즉각의 shelter 은신처 hardy 강건한 colonist 식민지 개척자 cliff 절벽 at hand 가까이에 (있는)

02 정답 ②

해설 주어진 글은 화자가 빵을 몰래 가져가는 상황을 서술하고 있는데, 그 빵을 셔츠 안으로 밀어 넣었다고 말한 것을 보아 뒤에는 그 빵의 열기가 피부에 타들어 갔다는 내용의 (B)가 이어지는 것이 자연스럽다. 그다음으로, (B)에서 언급된 the loaves를 them으로 받아 그 덩어리들을 식탁 위에 떨어뜨렸을 때 여동생이 그것을 찢으려 손을 뻗었다는 내용의 (A)가 이어져야 한다. 마지막으로, 화자가 그 빵을 자른 후 함께 한 덩어리를 모두 먹었다는 내용의 (C)가 와야 한다. 따라서 글의 순서로 가장 적절한 것은 ② '(B) - (A) - (C)'이다.

해석 다른 사람이 무슨 일이 있었는지 목격할 수 있기도 전에 나는 그 빵 덩이들을 셔츠 안으로 밀어 넣고 헌팅 재킷으로 날 단단히 감싸고 재빨리 걸어 나갔다. (B) 그 빵의 열기가 내 피부에 타들어 갔지만 난 생명에 매달리듯 그 빵을 더 꽉 움켜쥐었다. 집에 도착했을 때 그 빵 덩이들은 어느 정도 식었지만 속은 여전히 따뜻했다. (A) 식탁에 그것들을 떨어뜨리자, 여동생의 손이 한 덩어리를 떼어내려 뻗어 나갔지만, 나는 그녀를 앉히고 어머니가 우리와 식탁에서 함께하도록 한 후 따뜻한 차를 따랐다. (C) 나는 그 빵을 잘랐다. 우리는 한 조각씩 빵 한 덩이를 모두 먹었다. 그것은 건포도와 견과류가 가득 들어 있는 맛있고 따뜻한 빵이었다.

어휘 witness 목격하다 shove 밀어 넣다 wrap 감싸다 swiftly 재빨리 tear off 떼어내다 chunk 덩어리 clutch 꽉 움켜쥐다 cling 매달리다, 집착하다 hearty 따뜻한 raisin 건포도

03 정답 ④

해설 서두에서 한 화학자가 바닥에 유리 플라스크를 떨어뜨렸는데, 그것은 놀랍게도 깨지지 않았다는 내용이 나온다. ② 뒤에서는 콜로디온 용액으로 인한 필름 코팅이 그 이유였다고 설명한 뒤, 이를 this unusual phenomenon이라고 말한다. 이후 그 화학자가 앞 유리창이 날아와서 다친 사람들에 대해 읽었다고 언급되는데, 이 유리창은 주어진 문장에서도 나오는 것을 알 수 있다. 또한 주어진 문장에서는 '특별한 코팅'이 언급되는데, 이는 앞서 나온 '콜로디온 용액 필름 코팅'을 의미하므로, 주어진 문장은 ③이나 ④에 와야 한다. 이때 주어진 문장의 then이 ④ 앞에 나온 several weeks later를 가리키는 것을 알 수 있으며, 그가 상상을 한 이후에 얼마 지나지 않아 세계 최초의 안전유리를 제작하는 데 성공했다는 ④ 뒤 내용이 주어진 문장에 이어지는 것이 자연스러우므로, 주어진 문장이 들어갈 위치로 가장 적절한 곳은 ④이다.

해석 1903년 프랑스의 화학자 Edouard Benedictus는 어느 날 단단한 바닥에 유리 플라스크를 떨어뜨려 깨뜨렸다. 그러나, 놀랍게도 플라스크는 산산조각이 나지 않고, 여전히 원래의 모양 대부분을 유지하고 있었다. 그가 플라스크를 검사했을 때 그 안에 필름 코팅이 있는 것을 발견했는데, 그것은 플라스크가 함유하고 있던 콜로디온 용액에서 남은 잔여물이었다. 그는 이런 특이한 현상을 메모했지만, 몇 주 후에 자동차 사고에서 앞 유리창이 날아와 심하게 다친 사람들에 대한 이야기를 신문에서 읽기 전까진 더 이상 생각하지 않았다. 그가 유리 플라스크에 대한 자신의 경험을 떠올린 것이 그때였고, 곧바로, 앞 유리창이 깨지지 않도록 특별한 코팅이 씌워질 수도 있겠다는 상상을 했다. 그 후 얼마 지나지 않아 그는 세계 최초의 안전유리를 제작하는 데 성공했다.

어휘 apply 바르다, 도포하다 windshield (자동차) 전면 유리 shatter 산산조각 나다 astonishment 깜짝 놀람 retain 유지하다, 보유하다 residue 잔여물 solution 용액 phenomenon 현상

전략 12

전략 적용 연습

본서 p. 225

01 ③	02 ①	03 ①
04 ④	05 ②	06 ②

01 정답 ③

해설 '문제점-원인-해결책' 구조의 글이다. 주어진 글은 빈번한 스트레스가 심혈관 질환의 위험 요소가 될 수 있다는 내용으로, '문제점'에 해당한다. (C)에서 One source of frequent stress로 그러한 심리적 스트레스에 대한 구체적인 예인 운전(driving)을 소개하고 있으므로 (C) 역시 문제점에 관한 내용이다. 이후 (A)에서 이에 대한 해결책이 있는지에 대한 질문이 나오므로 (A) 다음에는 해결책의 여부가 언급될 것을 알 수 있다. 이후 (B)에서 그 해결책이 있다는 점을 there is로 제시한 후에 ('의문문 + 그 대답' 형식), 운전하면서 받는 스트레스를 완화하는 방법을 설명하고 있다. 따라서 글의 순서로 가장 적절한 것은 ③ '(C) - (A) - (B)'이다.

해석 과거의 연구는 빈번한 심리적 스트레스를 경험하는 것이 심혈관 질환의 중요한 위험 요인이 될 수 있다는 것을 보여 주었는데, 이것은 미국의 20세 이상 사람들 중 거의 절반에 영향을 미치는 질환이다. (C) 잦은 스트레스의 한 가지 요인은 운전인데, 이는 교통체증과 관련된 스트레스 요인이나 미숙한 운전자들에게 흔히 동반되는 불안감 때문이다. (A) 하지만 이것은 매일 운전하

는 사람들이 심장 질환에 걸릴 것을 의미하는 것인가, 아니면 운전의 스트레스를 완화할 수 있는 간단한 방법이 있는가? (B) 새로운 연구에 따르면, 있다. 연구원들은 운전하면서 음악을 듣는 것이 심장 건강에 영향을 미치는 스트레스를 해소하는 데 도움이 된다고 언급했다.

어휘 cardiovascular 심혈관의 ease 완화시키다 stressor 스트레스 요인 accompany 동반하다

02 정답 ①

해설 '문제점-해결책' 구조의 글이다. 손실을 영원히 피할 수는 없다는 문제점이 제시된 뒤에, 손실에 맞설 방법(portfolio approach)을 해결책으로 제시하고 있다. 빈칸에서는 이 해결 방안을 수용한 결과가 나와야 하므로, 반드시 긍정적인 표현이 와야 한다. 빈칸 뒤에서 그것들이 큰 그림의 작은 부분임을 알게 된다고 했으므로, 문맥상 빈칸에는 손실에 너무 매몰되지 않게 된다는 내용이 와야 자연스럽다. 따라서 빈칸에 들어갈 말로 가장 적절한 것은 ① '개별적인 손실에 대해 덜 생각하게'이다.
② 당신의 투자에 흥미를 덜 가지게
③ 손실에 더 취약하게
④ 주식 시장의 변동에 더욱 민감하게

해석 손실에 대한 두려움은 인간으로서의 기본적인 부분이다. 뇌에 있어서, 손실은 위협이며 우리는 자연적으로 손실을 피하기 위한 조치를 취한다. 그러나 우리는 손실을 언제까지나 피할 수는 없다. 손실에 맞설 한 가지 방법은 주식을 거래하는 사람의 관점으로 바라보는 것이다. (주식) 거래자는 게임의 끝이 아닌, 게임의 일부로 손실의 가능성을 받아들인다. 이러한 사고방식을 이끄는 것이 포트폴리오 접근법이다. 즉, 이익과 손실은 모두 발생하지만, 가장 중요한 것은 결과의 전체적인 포트폴리오라는 것이다. 당신이 포트폴리오 접근 방식을 수용한다면, 그것(개별적인 손실)은 훨씬 더 큰 그림의 작은 부분이라는 것을 알기 때문에 개별적인 손실에 대해 덜 생각하게 될 것이다.

어휘 take measures 조치를 취하다 dwell on ~에 대해 숙고하다 vulnerable 취약한 fluctuation 변동

03 정답 ①

해설 '문제점1-원인-문제점2-해결책'의 다소 복잡한 구조의 글이다. 위험을 과대평가한 나머지 사람들이 서로 교류하기를 꺼리는 문제를 지적한 후에, 이에 대한 해결책으로 관계 형성을 통해 두려움을 극복하는 것을 제시하는 글이다. 주어진 글은 사람들이 가지는 여러 두려움에 대한 생각에 관한 내용으로, 이러한 생각을 These로 받아 그것들이 정당한 걱정거리지만 실제는 아니라고 말하는 (B)가 와야 한다. 이후에는 TV 뉴스를 많이 보는 사람들이 위협을 과대평가하는 것에 대한 의문을 'Why?'로 던진 후에, It's because로 이에 대한 답을 제시하는 (A)가 와야 한다. 그 다음에는 사람들이 교류하지 않는 문제로 인한 결과를 Thus를 통해 제시하는 (C)가 뒤에 이어져, 마지막에 해결책을 제시하는 것으로 글이 마무리되는 것이 자연스럽다. 따라서 글의 순서로 가장 적절한 것은 ① '(B) - (A) - (C)'이다.

해석 당신은 건강을 잃을까 봐 걱정하는가? 범죄, 전쟁, 테러 공격이 경제와 당신의 안전을 해칠까 봐 두려워하는가? (B) 이것들은 많은 이들이 공감하는 정당한 걱정거리이다. 우리는 힘들고 불확실한 시대에 살고 있다. 하지만 이러한 공포가 실제인가? 연구에 따르면 TV 뉴스를 많이 시청하는 사람들은 자신의 행복에 대한 위협을 과대평가한다고 한다. 이유는 무엇인가? (A) 이는 텔레비전이 세상을 실제보다 더 위험한 곳처럼 보이게 하는 뉴스에 집중하기 때문이다. TV에서 묘사되는 세상에 두려워하며 사람들은 가까운 가족과 집에서 머무르고 이웃과의 유대를 쌓지 않는다. (C) 따라서 그들은 더 약해진다. 그러나 우리 자신을 공포의 벽으로 둘러싸는 것이 해답은 아니다. 이 문제를 극복하는 유일한 방법은 다른 사람들과 좀 더 관계를 맺는 것이며, 이러한 관계는 공포와 고립을 줄일 것이다.

어휘 terrorist attack 테러 공격 bond 유대, 결속 legitimate 정당한 overestimate 과대평가하다 vulnerable 연약한

04 정답 ④

해설 문제점, 원인, 해결책이 번갈아 가며 제시되는 구조의 글이다. 달걀을 위생적으로 다루지 않을 때, 그리고 계란을 덜 익힐 때 살모넬라균으로 인한 식중독이 발생하므로, 달걀에 대한 올바른 취급법을 준수해야 한다는 점이 글의 핵심이다. 따라서 글의 주제로 가장 적절한 것은 ④ '살모넬라균 감염 예방을 위한 달걀의 안전한 취급법'이다.
① 계란 섭취가 면역 체계에 미치는 이점
② 살모넬라균 감염에 대한 다양한 종류의 치료법
③ 따뜻한 온도에서 살모넬라균의 수명

해석 식품의약품안전처는 음식을 조리하거나 기구를 사용하기 전에 달걀을 만지고 손 씻는 것을 소홀히 하는 교차오염으로 인해 식중독이 발생하는 사례가 생기고 있다고 경고했다. 이러한 위험을 줄이기 위해 안전처는 달걀을 냉장 보관하고 노른자와 흰자가 모두 단단해질 때까지 완전히 익힐 것을 권고했다. 지난 5년 동안 무려 7,400명의 사람이 살모넬라균으로 인한 식중독을 경험했다. 살모넬라균은 섭씨 약 37도가 최적의 성장 조건으로, 따뜻한 온도에서 번성한다. 날계란 또는 덜 익힌 계란 섭취와 날음식과 익힌 음식을 분리하지 못하는 것이 살모넬라균 감염의 가장 흔한 원인으로 밝혀졌다. 살모넬라 관련 질병의 위험을 최소화하기 위해서는 식품 안전 조치를 우선시하고 올바른 조리 방법을 준수하는 것이 매우 중요하다.

어휘 ministry 부처 food poisoning 식중독 cross-contamination 교차 오염 neglect 소홀히 하다 utensil 기구 mitigate 줄이다 yolk 노른자 staggering 충격적인, 무려 thrive 번성하다 optimal 최적의 identify 밝히다 infection 감염 prioritize 우선시하다 measure 조치 adhere to ~을 준수하다 minimize 최소화하다 immune system 면역 체계 life span 수명 handling 취급, 다루기

05 정답 ②

해설 약물을 잘못 처방하는 문제와 그 원인에 관한 글이다. 해결책은 제시되지 않았으므로, 문제점과 원인이 글의 주제임을 알 수 있다. 따라서 글의 주제로 가장 적절한 것은 ② '약물 치료 과오의 유형과 원인들'이다.
① 약물 치료 실수를 줄이는 방법

③ 의료 기록 공유의 중요성
④ 의료 보험 혜택 확대의 필요성

해석 약물 치료는 의료인이 그것을 환자들에게 안전하고 적절하게 처방하여 제공한다면 축복이다. 하지만 의료인은 인간이고, 그렇기에 실수를 할 수 있다. 그들의 전문지식과 우수성에 대한 그들의 맹세에도 불구하고, 실수와 약물 치료의 다른 부작용이 일어나고 때때로 인간의 고통을 유발한다. 잘못된 약, 잘못된 강도, 잘못된 양을 처방하는 것, 비슷하게 보이거나 비슷하게 들리는 약의 이름을 다른 약과 혼동하는 것, 의료 장비를 잘못 사용하는 것, 컴퓨터 화면에서 틀린 환자를 선택하는 것과 같이 최선의 노력에도 불구하고 이런 일들은 모든 의료 환경에서 모든 종류의 사람에게 매일 발생한다. 복잡한 치료 전략을 필요로 하는 건강 상태를 가진 고령 인구가 늘어나면서 그런 것처럼, 매년 도입되는 신약과 기술의 많은 수량이 약물 치료 사용을 한층 더 복잡하게 만들고 그것이 의료 과실로 이어진다.

어휘 medication 약물 치료 health care provider 의료인 prescribe 처방하다 appropriately 적절하게 fallible 실수를 할 수 있는 commitment 약속, 헌신 look-alike 비슷하게 보이는 setting 환경

06 정답 ②

해설 아이들의 유능함을 칭찬하는 것의 문제점과 그것이 문제가 되는 이유를 설명하는 글이다. 노력보다 지능으로 칭찬받은 아이들은 실패가 곧 멍청함이라고 받아들여 끈기와 즐거움을 잃고 덜 노력하게 되는 등 부정적인 영향을 받았다고 말하고 있다. 이에 대한 해결책은 제시되지 않았으므로, 문제점과 그 원인이 글의 주제이다. 따라서 글의 요지로 가장 적절한 것은 ② '지능을 칭찬하는 것은 아이들에게 부정적인 영향을 준다.'이다.
① 잦은 칭찬이 아이들의 자존감을 키운다.
③ 아이는 성공을 통해 실패에 대한 두려움을 극복해야 한다.
④ 부모들은 과정보다 결과에 집중해야 한다.

해석 많은 부모가 자녀의 자존감을 형성하는 방법은 자녀가 어떤 것을 얼마나 잘하는지 알려주는 것이라고 말해 온 '자존감 운동'에 의해 잘못 인도되어 왔다. 안타깝게도, 인생은 아이들에게 성공과 실패를 통해 그들이 실제로 얼마나 유능하거나 무능한지를 명백히 알려주는 법이기에, 아이들에게 그들의 능력을 납득시키려는 것은 실패할 가능성이 크다. 연구는 자녀를 칭찬하는 방식이 자녀의 발달에 강력한 영향을 미친다는 것을 보여 준다. 일부 연구자들은 노력보다는 지능으로 칭찬받은 아이들이 결과에 지나치게 집중하게 된다는 것을 발견했다. 이같은 아이들은 실패 이후 덜 끈기 있고, 덜 즐거워하고, 실패를 능력이 부족한 탓으로 돌리고, 향후 성취를 위한 노력에서 저조한 성과를 보였다. 아이들을 지능으로 칭찬하는 것이 그들로 하여금 어려움을 두려워하게 만들었는데, 이는 그들이 실패를 멍청함과 동일시하기 시작했기 때문이다.

어휘 misguide 잘못 인도하다 self-esteem 자존감 convince 납득시키다 competence 능력 unequivocally 명백히 capable 유능한 praise 칭찬하다; 칭찬 influence 영향 intelligence 지능 overly 지나치게 persist 끈질기게 계속하다 attribute ~의 탓으로 돌리다 achievement 성취 equate 동일시하다 stupidity 멍청함 frequent 잦은 overcome 극복하다 outcome 결과

전략 13

전략 적용 연습

본서 p. 233

01 ③ 02 ① 03 ③

01 정답 ③

해설 훈련된 심리학자는 사진만 봐도 가짜 미소와 진짜 미소를 구별할 수 있다는 주어진 글 다음에는, 그 기술을 this skill로 받아 연구자들이 실제 대학 졸업 앨범 사진 속의 미소를 구별해 보았다는 내용의 (C)가 이어져야 한다. 이때 (C)의 내용을 보면, 이 실험의 전제는 미소의 '진정성' 여부와 관련됨을 알 수 있다. 이후 (C)에서 언급된 141명의 여성을 All the women으로 받아, 그들이 오랜 기간에 걸쳐 몇 차례 질문을 받았다고 말하는 (A)가 와야 한다. 다음으로, 실험 결과를 Astonishingly로 제시하는 (B)로 글이 마무리되는 것이 자연스럽다. 따라서 글의 순서로 가장 적절한 것은 ③ '(C) - (A) - (B)'이다.

해석 훈련된 심리학자는 사진첩을 훑어보면 가식적인 미소와 진짜 미소를 한 눈에 구별할 수 있다. (C) 캘리포니아 대학의 Dacher Keltner와 LeeAnne Harker는 Mills 대학의 1960년 졸업 앨범에서 141장의 졸업반 사진을 연구했을 때 이 기술을 보였다. 그들에 따르면 3명을 제외한 모든 여성이 미소를 짓고 있었는데, 그중의 절반이 진짜 미소를 짓고 있었다. (A) 그 여성들은 27, 43, 52세 때 연락을 받아 결혼 생활 및 삶의 만족도에 대한 질문을 받았다. (B) 매우 놀랍게도, 진짜 미소를 지은 여성들은 그 후 30년에 걸쳐서 결혼하고, 기혼 상태를 유지하고, 더 개인적인 행복을 누렸을 가능성이 대체로 더 높았다.

어휘 look through ~을 빠르게 훑어보다 at a glance 힐끗 보면 genuine 진짜[진심]의 astonishingly 놀랍게도 demonstrate 입증하다 analyze 분석하다 senior-class 졸업반의 yearbook 졸업 앨범

02 정답 ①

해설 사람들이 자신과 비슷한 복장의 타인에게 더 긍정적으로 반응한다는 것을 두 실험을 예로 들어 설명하는 글이다. 두 실험의 전제는 모두 실험자가 피험자와 비슷한 복장을 했는지의 여부와 관련되며, 두 실험에서 모두 피험자는 자신과 비슷하게 입은 실험자를 더 잘 도와주었다. 따라서 글의 요지로 가장 적절한 것은 ① '사람들은 그들처럼 입는 사람들을 도울 가능성이 더 크다.'이다.
② 정장을 하는 것은 탄원서 서명의 가능성을 높인다.
③ 전화를 거는 것은 다른 학생들과 교제하는 효율적인 방법이다.
④ 1970년대 초반의 대학생들은 독특한 패션으로 동경 받았다.

해석 젊은이들이 "히피"나 "스트레이트" 패션으로 입는 경향이 있던 1970년대 초에 행해진 한 연구에서, 실험자들은 히피나 스트레이트 복장을 하고 캠퍼스에 있는 대학생들에게 전화를 걸기 위한 10센트짜리 동전을 요구했다. 실험자가 학생과 동일하게 입

PART 3 독해

었을 때, 그 요청은 3분의 2 이상의 경우 수락되었고, 학생과 요청자가 서로 다르게 입었을 때, 10센트짜리 동전은 절반 미만의 경우에 제공되었다. 또 다른 실험은 비슷한 타인에 대한 우리의 긍정적인 반응이 얼마나 자동적인지를 보여 주었다. 반전 시위에 참여한 시위자들은 비슷한 복장을 한 요청자의 탄원서에 서명할 가능성이 더 크고, 그것을 우선 읽어 보려 하지도 않고 서명할 가능성이 더 컸던 것으로 밝혀졌다.

어휘 attire 복장 dime 10센트 grant 허락하다 marcher 행진 참가자, 시위자 demonstration 시위 petition 탄원(서)

03 정답 ③

해설 Norman Triplett의 연구에서 전제는 자전거를 어떤 환경에서 타는지와 관련되며, 그 결과는 홀로 달릴 때보다 다른 선수들과 함께 달릴 때 기록이 단축된다는 것이다. 따라서 빈칸에 들어갈 말로 가장 적절한 것은 ③ '다른 사람들과 함께 있을 때 일을 더 잘 해낸다'이다.

① 자신이 관찰된다는 것을 알았을 때 노력을 덜 기울인다
② 집단의 공통 목표를 달성하기 위해 협력한다
④ 혼자 일할 때 스스로 일을 잘 해낸다

해석 사회 심리학 분야에서 수행된 아마도 역사상 최초의 실험이었을 한 연구는 인간은 다른 사람들과 함께 있을 때 일을 더 잘 해낸다는 것을 시사한다. 1890년대 후반 Indiana 대학에서 수행된 그 연구는 바로 자전거광이자 스포츠 애호가였던 Norman Triplett의 아이디어였다. 수십 번의 실험에서 그는 자전거 선수들에게 고정된 자전거에서 최대한 빨리 달리도록 독려했다. 이때 자전거 선수들이 아무런 방해도 받지 않도록 실험실에 혼자 남겨둔 경우도 있었고, 모터로 작동하는 자전거에 속도를 맞추게 하는 경우도 있었으며, 다른 자전거 선수들이 있는 곳에서 달리게 하는 경우도 있었다. 그의 관찰을 통해, Triplett은 다른 자전거 선수들이 옆에서 타고 있을 때 선수들이 더 빠르게 달리는 경향이 있음을 발견했다. 한 자전거 선수의 경우 혼자 있을 때 1마일을 2분 49초에 주파한 반면, 네 명의 다른 자전거 선수들이 옆에서 달리고 있을 때는 같은 마일을 2분 37초 만에 주파하는 것을 해냈다. 마찬가지로, 그는 혼자 있을 때 10마일을 달리는 데 33분 17초가 걸렸지만, 여럿이 함께 달릴 때는 2분 더 빨리 같은 거리를 달렸다.

어휘 conduct 시행하다 brainchild 아이디어, 독창적인 생각 enthusiast 광신자 dozens of 수십의, 아주 많은 stationary 고정된 pace 보조를 맞추다 manage to 해내다 robustly 왕성하게, 강경하게

PART 4 생활영어

전략 01

전략 적용 연습

본서 p. 240

01 ④ 02 ③ 03 ②

01 정답 ④

해설 A와 B는 구내식당 메뉴가 바뀐 것과 새로운 음식 공급업체를 구한 것에 대해 이야기하고 있다. 빈칸 뒤에서, B가 디저트 종류와 샌드위치 종류가 바뀐 점에 대해 말해 주고 있으므로 빈칸에는 메뉴가 어떻게 바뀌었는지를 물어보는 내용이 들어가야 함을 알 수 있다. 따라서 빈칸에 들어갈 말로 가장 적절한 것은 ④ '저번 메뉴와 다른 점이 뭐야'이다.

① 네가 가장 좋아하는 디저트는 뭐야
② 그들의 사무실이 어디 있는지 아니
③ 메뉴에 대한 내 도움이 필요하니

해석 A: 대학 구내식당 메뉴가 바뀌었다고 들었어.
B: 맞아. 내가 방금 확인했어.
A: 그리고 식당은 새로운 음식 공급업체를 구했어.
B: 맞아, Sam's Catering이야.
A: 저번 메뉴와 다른 점이 뭐야?
B: 디저트 종류가 더 있어. 또, 샌드위치 몇 종류가 사라졌어.

어휘 check out 확인하다 caterer 음식 공급업체

02 정답 ③

해설 B가 휴대전화를 잃어버려 찾고 있는 상황이다. 빈칸은 지하철 분실물 센터에 문의해 봤는지 묻는 A에 대한 대답이다. 이를 듣자, A가 자신이라면 먼저 그렇게 하겠다고 했으므로, B는 아직 문의해 보지 않은 것으로 추측할 수 있다. 따라서 빈칸에 들어갈 말로 적절한 것은 ③ '사실은 아직 안 해봤어'이다.

① 휴대전화에 관해 문의하러 그곳에 갔어요
② 오늘 아침에 사무실에 들렀어요
④ 모든 곳을 다 찾아봤어요

해석 A: 휴대전화 찾았어?
B: 아쉽게도 못 찾았어. 아직 찾는 중이야.
A: 지하철 분실물 센터에 연락해 봤어?
B: 사실은 아직 안 해봤어.
A: 나라면 먼저 그렇게 하겠어.
B: 응, 네 말이 맞네. 새 휴대전화를 사기 전에 분실물 센터에 문의해 볼게.

어휘 lost and found office 분실물 센터 stop by 들르다

03 정답 ②

해설 빈칸 이후에 스팸 이메일을 막을 수 있는 필터 설정에 관한 B의 대답이 이어지므로, A는 스팸 이메일을 막을 수 있는 방법을 물었을 것으로 유추할 수 있다. 따라서 빈칸에 들어갈 말로 가장 적절한 것은 ② '우리가 할 수 있는 일이 없을까'이다.

① 이메일 자주 쓰니
③ 이 훌륭한 필터를 어떻게 만들었어
④ 이메일 계정을 개설하는 것 좀 도와줄래

해석 A: 아, 또야! 스팸 이메일이 너무 많아!
B: 그러니까, 나는 하루에 10개도 넘는 스팸 이메일을 받아.
A: 스팸 이메일이 오는 걸 막을 수 있을까?
B: 그것들을 완전히 차단하는 것은 가능한 것 같지 않아.
A: 우리가 할 수 있는 일이 없을까?
B: 음, 설정에서 필터를 설정할 수 있어.
A: 필터?
B: 응. 필터가 스팸 이메일 중 일부를 걸러 낼 수 있어.

어휘 junk email 스팸 이메일 block 차단하다 weed out 걸러 내다 account 계정

전략 02

전략 적용 연습

본서 p. 244

01 ③ 02 ① 03 ③

01 정답 ③

해설 스웨터를 찾고 있는 B를 A가 도와주고 있는 상황이다. 빈칸 앞에서 B가 마음에 들어 하는 최신 스타일의 스웨터 가격이 120달러라고 했는데, 빈칸 뒤에서 A가 50달러로 세일 중인 다른 스웨터를 추천하고 있다. 따라서 문맥상 B는 최신 스타일의 스웨터를 '가격 때문에' 살 수 없다는 내용이 들어가야 함을 유추할 수 있으므로, 빈칸에 들어갈 말로 가장 적절한 것은 ③ '제 가격대를 조금 벗어나네요'이다.

① 거기에 어울리는 바지 한 벌도 필요해요
② 그 재킷은 저에게 완벽한 선물이에요
④ 토요일엔 오후 7시까지 영업합니다

해석 A: 안녕하세요. 무엇을 도와드릴까요?
B: 네, 스웨터를 찾고 있어요.
A: 음, 이것은 가을 컬렉션으로 나온 최신 스타일입니다. 어떠세요?
B: 멋져요. 얼마인가요?
A: 가격 확인해 드릴게요. 120달러예요.
B: 제 가격대를 조금 벗어나네요.
A: 그럼 이 스웨터는 어떠세요? 지난 시즌에 나온 건데, 50달러로 세일 중이에요.
B: 완벽해요! 입어 볼게요.

어휘 gorgeous 아주 멋진 on sale (할인) 판매 중인 price range 가격대

02 정답 ①

해설 어젯밤 마감 근무를 하며 주방 청소를 깨끗이 하지 않은 B에게 A가 주의를 주는 상황이다. 따라서 B가 사과의 말과 함께 할, 빈칸에 들어갈 말로 가장 적절한 것은 ① '다시는 그런 일 없도록 하겠습니다.'이다.

② 지금 계산해 드릴까요?
③ 그래서 제가 어제 그걸 잊은 거예요.

④ 올바른 주문을 받으실 수 있도록 하겠습니다.

해석 A: 어젯밤에 여기 있었나요?
B: 네. 제가 마감 근무를 했어요. 무슨 일인가요?
A: 오늘 아침 주방이 엉망이었어요. 조리기 위에 음식물이 튀어 있었고, 제빙 그릇이 냉동실 안에 있지 않았어요.
B: 제가 청소 체크리스트를 점검하는 걸 잊었나 봐요.
A: 깨끗한 주방이 얼마나 중요한지 알잖아요.
B: 죄송합니다. 다시는 그런 일 없도록 하겠습니다.

어휘 shift (교대제의) 근무 시간 mess 엉망인 상태 spatter 튀기다, 튀다 go over ~을 점검하다 bill 계산서

03 정답 ③

해설 빈칸 이후에 호텔 직원 A가 디럭스 룸과 럭셔리 스위트 룸의 차이점을 설명하고 있으므로, 빈칸에는 이 두 가지 룸의 차이점을 물어보는 내용이 들어가야 한다. 따라서 빈칸에 들어갈 말로 가장 적절한 것은 ③ '둘의 차이점은 무엇인가요?'이다.
① 더 필요한 것 있으세요
② 방 번호를 알려주시겠습니까
④ 객실에 애완동물이 허용되나요

해석 A: 로얄 포인트 호텔 예약부에 전화해 주셔서 감사합니다. 저는 Sam입니다. 무엇을 도와드릴까요?
B: 안녕하세요, 방을 하나 예약하고 싶은데요.
A: 방은 두 종류, 디럭스 룸과 럭셔리 스위트 룸이 있습니다.
B: 둘의 차이점은 무엇인가요?
A: 우선, 스위트룸은 매우 넓습니다. 침실 외에도 부엌, 거실, 식사하는 방이 있습니다.
B: 비쌀 것 같은데요.
A: 음, 1박에 200달러가 추가됩니다.
B: 그렇다면, 디럭스 룸으로 할게요.

어휘 in that case 그렇다면 go with (제의를) 받아들이다

전략 03

전략 적용 연습

본서 p. 247

01 ④ **02** ④ **03** ②

01 정답 ④

해설 A가 항공편을 예약하는 상황이다. 선호하는 좌석이 있는지 묻는 질문에 대한 대답이 빈칸에 들어가야 하므로, 빈칸에 들어갈 말로 가장 적절한 것은 ④ '네. 통로 쪽 자리를 원합니다.'이다.
① 네. 비즈니스석으로 업그레이드하고 싶습니다.
② 아니오. 편도권으로 하겠습니다.
③ 아니오. 짐은 없습니다.

해석 A: 안녕하세요. 서울에서 오클랜드로 가는 항공편을 예약하고 싶습니다.
B: 알겠습니다. 염두에 두고 계신 특정 날짜가 있으신가요?
A: 네. 5월 2일에 출발해서 5월 14일에 돌아올 계획입니다.
B: 알겠습니다, 고객님 일정에 맞는 항공편을 하나 찾았습니다. 어떤 좌석 등급으로 예약하시겠어요?
A: 이코노미석이면 됩니다.
B: 선호하시는 자리가 있으신가요?
A: 네. 통로 쪽 자리를 원합니다.
B: 좋습니다. 고객님의 항공편이 지금 예약되었습니다.

어휘 flight 항공편 specific 특정한 one-way 편도의 luggage 수화물 aisle 통로

02 정답 ④

해설 세미나 참가비가 비싼 이유를 듣고 Pete는 그만한 값어치를 하는 것 같다고 말하였다. 이에 Brad가 빈칸 내용을 언급하자 Pete가 서둘러야겠다고 했으므로, 빨리 등록해야 하는 상황임을 알 수 있다. 따라서 빈칸에 들어갈 말로 가장 적절한 것은 ④ '자리가 많이 남지 않았어요.'이다.
① 그 세미나는 초대받은 사람들만 참석할 수 있나요?
② 아쉽지만, 세미나는 끝났어요.
③ 케이터링 업체가 어디인지 잘 모르겠어요.

해석 Brad: Pete, 이번 주말 세미나에 오시나요?
Pete: 아직 결정하지 못했어요. 기조 연설자가 누구인가요?
Brad: Gary Jenson이에요. 그는 서울 투자 은행의 중역이에요.
Pete: 그건 놓치고 싶지 않을 것 같은데요. 근데 세미나 (참가비)가 너무 비싸요.
Brad: 아마 케이터링 점심을 무료로 제공해서 그런 것 같아요.
Pete: 이해가 되네요. 그만한 값어치를 하는 것 같네요.
Brad: 자리가 많이 남지 않았어요.
Pete: 정말요? 그럼 서둘러야겠네요. 알려 줘서 고마워요.

어휘 make up one's mind 결정하다 keynote speaker 기조 연설자 senior executive 최고 중역, 전무 catered 케이터링(음식 공급 업체)을 통한 by invitation only 초대 대상자만이 참석 가능한

03 정답 ②

해설 Celina가 빈칸 내용을 말하자 Kate는 일정을 바꾸지 말라며 자신이 혼자서 하겠다고 말하였다. 따라서 빈칸에서 Celina는 자신의 휴가 일정을 바꾸겠다는 말을 한 것을 알 수 있으므로, 빈칸에 들어갈 말로 가장 적절한 것은 ② '제 휴가를 변경해도 돼요.'이다.
① 병가를 내야 할 것 같아요.
③ 제 계획을 간략하게 알려 드릴까요?
④ 회의 안건이 아직 확정되지 않았어요.

해석 Kate: Celina, 다음 주 수요일에 시간 있어요?
Celina: 그날은 쉬는 날이에요. 왜요?
Kate: 아쉽네요. 제 출장에 같이 가 주실 수 있는지 궁금해서요.
Celina: 도움이 필요하신 일이 있나요?
Kate: 네, 몇 가지 후속 작업을 처리해 주셨으면 해서요. 사장님은 허락하셨는데 당신이 수요일에 쉰다는 사실을 잊으셨나 봐요.
Celina: 제 휴가를 변경해도 돼요.
Kate: 아니에요, 일정을 바꾸지 않으셨으면 좋겠어요. 제가 혼자서 할게요. 고마워요.

어휘 day off 쉬는 날, 휴가 accompany 동반하다 handle 처리하다 follow-up 후속의 approve 허락하다 call in sick 병가를 내다 brief 간략하게 알려주다 agenda 안건

실전 모의고사

본서 p. 252

01 ②	02 ②	03 ②	04 ③	05 ①
06 ③	07 ④	08 ④	09 ③	10 ②
11 ③	12 ②	13 ③	14 ④	15 ④
16 ④	17 ②	18 ①	19 ③	20 ③

01 정답 ②

해설 제한적인 자금과 엄격한 규제 요건을 포함하는 것으로, 이것에도 '불구하고' 과학자들은 놀라운 업적을 달성해 냈다고 말하고 있다. 따라서 빈칸에 들어갈 말로 가장 적절한 것은 ② 'constraints(제약)'이다.
① 실수 ③ 기회 ④ 특성

해석 과학자들은 제한적인 자금과 엄격한 규제 요건을 포함한 여러 제약에 직면했지만, 놀라운 업적을 달성해 냈다.

어휘 strict 엄격한 regulatory 규제의 requirement 요건 manage to RV ~을 해내다 remarkable 놀라운

02 정답 ②

해설 VIP 라운지 이용은 일등석 승객만 이용할 수 있다고 했으므로, 빈칸에 들어갈 말로 가장 적절한 것은 ② 'exclusive(전용의)'이다.
① 공공의 ③ 금지된 ④ 무료의

해석 공항의 VIP 전용 라운지는 오직 일등석 승객만 이용할 수 있다.

어휘 access 이용하다 passenger 승객

03 정답 ②

해설 빈칸은 동사 자리로, 안전 규약을 실행하는 것이 작업장 안전을 강화할 것으로 '기대하는' 것이 아니라 '기대되는' 것이므로 수동의 is expected가 적절하다. has expected와 will be expecting은 모두 능동을 나타내므로 정답이 될 수 없다. 참고로 advanced는 safety protocols를 꾸며주는 과거분사형 형용사이다.

해석 발전된 안전 규약의 실행은 제조 공장 직원들의 작업장 안전을 강화할 것으로 기대된다.

어휘 implementation 실행, 이행 advance 발전하다 protocol 규약 enhance 강화하다 security 안전 manufacturing 제조업 plant 공장

04 정답 ③

해설 (which → where 또는 in which) 관계대명사 which 뒤에는 불완전한 문장이 와야 하는데 여기서는 완전한 문장이 오고 있다. 따라서 which를 장소 명사 a million-dollar industry를 선행사로 받으면서 완전한 문장을 이끌 수 있는 관계부사 where로 고치거나, which 앞에 전치사 in을 더해 '전치사 + 관계대명사'로 만들어야 한다.
① 뒤에 each year라는 시간 부사구가 나왔고 주어인 Hundreds of self-help books가 '출판하는' 것이 아니라 '출판되는' 것이므로, 현재시제와 수동태가 적절하게 쓰였다.
② get이 2형식 동사로 쓰여 뒤에 형용사 보어 rich가 온 것은 적절하다.
④ for는 전치사이므로 뒤에 명사(구)가 와야 한다. 따라서 some goal을 목적어로 취하는 동명사 attaining의 쓰임은 적절하다.

해석 매년 수백 권의 자기계발서가 출판된다. 그 주제는 부자가 되는 것에서부터 금연, 관계 살리기에 이르기까지 다양하다. 그것은 저자가 자신의 개인적인 경험을 바탕으로 어떠한 목표를 달성하기 위한 해결책을 제공하는 백만 달러 규모의 산업이다.

어휘 self-help book 자기계발서 publish 출판하다 range from A to B (범위가) A에서부터 B에 이르다 attain 달성하다

05 정답 ①

해설 (continue → continues) 문장의 주어는 단수 명사인 The surge이므로, 단수 동사 continues를 써야 한다.
② 기간을 나타내는 in recent years가 나왔으므로, 현재완료시제 has even banned는 적절하게 쓰였다.
③ leave는 5형식으로 쓰일 때 'O를 OC 상태로 남기다'를 뜻하는데, 이때 목적격 보어로 형용사를 취할 수 있으므로 과거분사형 형용사 divided가 온 것은 적절하다.
④ 부대 상황을 나타내는 'with + O + OC'의 분사구문이 사용되었다. 여기서는 뒤에 목적어인 that절이 있고 많은 사람들이 '주장하는' 것이므로, 능동의 현재분사 arguing은 옳게 쓰였다.

해석 최근 몇 년 사이 전통 스포츠인 여우 사냥까지도 금지한 영국을 비롯해 전 세계 여러 지역에서 동물의 권리를 옹호하는 움직임의 급증이 계속해서 나타나고 있다. 그러나, 많은 사람들이 더 시급한 관심을 필요로 하는 인권의 측면들이 있다는 점을 주장하면서, 이 문제는 사회를 분열시킨다.

어휘 surge 급증 advocate 옹호하다 right 권리 emerge 나타나다 ban 금지하다 divide 분열시키다 urgent 시급한 attention 관심

06 정답 ③

해설 Tiffany가 자기가 보낸 이메일에 회의 안건 초안을 첨부했다고 하자, Jesse가 빈칸 내용을 언급하였다. 이에 Tiffany는 그것을 실수로 빠뜨린 것 같다며 다시 보내겠다고 말한 것을 보아, Jesse는 그 첨부 파일을 받지 못했던 것으로 추측할 수 있다. 따라서 빈칸에 들어갈 말로 가장 적절한 것은 ③ '지금 살펴보고 있는데, 아무 첨부 파일도 안 보여요.'이다.
① 다음 회의에는 안건이 필요하지 않아요.
② 작성하신 안건 초안은 이대로 완벽해 보여요.
④ 팀 전체에 그것을 전달한 건 좋은 선택이었어요.

해석 Jesse: Tiffany, 다음 회의 안건 초안 작성은 완료했나요?

Tiffany: 네, 조금 전에 보내 드린 이메일에 첨부했습니다.
Jesse: 지금 살펴보고 있는데, 아무 첨부 파일도 안 보여요.
Tiffany: 아, 실수로 빠뜨렸나 봐요. 죄송해요, 다시 보내 드릴게요.
Jesse: 별일 아니에요. 내일까지 피드백 줄게요.
Tiffany: 감사합니다.

어휘 draft 초안을 작성하다 agenda 안건 attach 첨부하다 accidentally 실수로 leave out 빼다 forward (우편, 이메일 등을) 보내다 entire 전체의 attachment 첨부 파일

07 정답 ④

해설 A에 물음에 B는 다박 숙박 시에는 무료 저녁 서비스를 제공하고 있다고 안내하고 있으므로, 빈칸에서 A는 장기간 묵을 경우에 혜택이 있는지 물었을 것으로 추측할 수 있다. 따라서 빈칸에 들어갈 말로 가장 적절한 것은 ④ '장기 숙박 예약 시 특별 혜택이 있을까요?'이다.
① 보증금을 온라인으로 결제해야 하나요?
② 제가 어떤 전망을 보게 될지 알려주실 수 있나요?
③ 방을 예약할 수 있게 되면 연락을 주실 수 있나요?

해석 A: 안녕하세요, 4월 7일부터 13일까지 일주일간 객실을 예약하려고 전화했어요. 빈 객실이 있나요?
B: 네, 정원 전망 디럭스 룸에서 숙박하실 수 있습니다.
A: 좋습니다. 얼마일까요?
B: 총 840달러입니다. 예약을 확정하시려면 50달러의 보증금이 필요합니다.
A: 알겠습니다. 그리고 궁금한 게 있는데, 장기 숙박 예약 시 특별 혜택이 있을까요?
B: 네, 방금 말씀드리려던 참이었어요. 저희는 다박 예약 시 무료 저녁 식사 서비스를 제공합니다. 저녁 식사 두 번과 와인 한 병을 준비해 드리는 건 어떨까요?
A: 너무 좋아요. 감사합니다.
B: 제가 감사드립니다. 곧 결제 정보를 보내 드리겠습니다.

어휘 book 예약하다 vacancy 빈 객실 accommodate (숙박) 공간을 제공하다 deposit 보증금 secure 확정[확보]하다 reservation 예약 treat 대접하다 available 얻을 수 있는

08 정답 ④

해설 글 초반부에서 알 수 있듯, 글쓴이는 다문화 가정 학생을 위한 무료 한국어 수업 개설을 요청하고 있다. 따라서 글의 목적으로 가장 적절한 것은 ④ '다문화 가정 학생들을 위한 무료 한국어 수업 개설을 요청하려고'이다.

09 정답 ③

해설 재정 상황과 관계없이 모든 다문화 학생이 한국어를 배울 기회를 마련해달라고 요청하는 글이다. 맥락상 status는 '상황'이라는 뜻으로 쓰였으므로, 이와 의미가 가장 가까운 것은 ③ 'situation(상황)'이다.
① 가치 ② 권리 ④ 중요성

08-09 해석 수신: 인천 교육청
발신: Minhee Kim
날짜: 5월 19일
제목: 다문화 가정을 위한 발전

관련자분께,

저는 더 건실하고 통합된 인천을 만들기 위해 저와 같은 다문화 가정 출신 학생들을 위한 무료 한국어 수업을 시에서 개설할 것을 제안합니다.

저는 자라면서 종종 주로 언어 장벽으로 인해 지역 사회에 완전히 통합되기 어렵다고 느꼈습니다. 아쉽게도, 한국어 수업은 비싸기 때문에 많은 사람들, 특히 저소득층 가정에서 한국어를 배우지 못합니다.

저는 인천시가 무료 한국어 수업을 제공함으로써 다양한 배경을 가진 학생들이 재정 상황과 관계없이 한국어를 배울 동등한 기회를 줄 수 있다고 생각합니다. 이러한 수업은 우리의 언어 능력 향상뿐만 아니라 한국 사회에 동화되는 데에도 큰 도움이 될 것입니다.

저는 이 사업이 인천 지역사회를 더 포용적이고 활기차게 발전시킬 것이라고 확신합니다. 귀하의 시간과 숙고에 감사드립니다.

진심을 담아,
Minhee Kim 드림

어휘 unified 통합된 integrate 통합시키다 barrier 장벽 diverse 다양한 regardless of ~와 관계없이 aid 돕다 assimilation 동화 initiative 사업, 계획 foster 발전시키다 inclusive 포용적인 vibrant 활기찬 consideration 고려

10 정답 ②

해설 글의 초반부에서 인구 고령화, 저출생을 비롯한 서울시 인구 경향 변화에 관한 대책 공모를 안내하는 글임을 알 수 있다. 따라서 글의 제목으로 가장 적절한 것은 ② '서울시 인구 문제에 대한 당신의 해결책을 제시해 주세요'이다.
① 서울시 청년 지원 정책에 대해 알고 싶으신가요?
③ 서울시 인구 고령화 문제에 관한 세미나에 참석하세요
④ 서울시 인구조사에 참여하고 선물을 받아 가세요

11 정답 ③

해설 글 중후반부에서 팀 단위의 제안은 허용되지 않는다고 언급되므로, 글의 내용과 일치하지 않는 것은 ③ '개인이나 팀 단위로 참가할 수 있다.'이다.

① 서울 시민을 대상으로 한다. → 글의 초반부에서 언급된 내용이다.
② 주제는 인구 고령화, 저출생, 이민에 한정된다. → 글의 중반부에서 언급된 내용이다.
④ 모든 상금은 세금이 면제된다. → 글의 후반부에서 언급된 내용이다.

10-11 해석 서울시 인구 문제에 대한 당신의 해결책을 제시해 주세요

서울은 노인 인구 증가와 출생률 감소 등 복잡한 인구구조 변화에 직면해 있습니다. 인구 정책 아이디어 공모전은 서울 시민들에게 현재 서울시가 직면한 인구학적 문제를 효과적으로 해결할 수 있는 혁신적인 아이디어와 참신한 시각을 기여해 주시기를 청합니다.

참여하기 위해 제안서는 다음 세 가지 주요 분야 중 하나에 관한 것이어야 합니다.

- **인구 고령화**: 노동력 부족 문제를 다루고 안전한 은퇴를 보장하는 제안
- **출생률 감소**: 가정에서 더 많은 자녀들을 갖도록 장려하는 제안
- **이주**: 학식 있고 전문적인 이민자를 유치하고 이민자들이 사회적으로 통합되도록 촉진하기 위한 아이디어

제출은 개인 제안으로 제한되며 팀 응모는 허용되지 않습니다. 제안서는 10페이지 이내로 작성하세요. 제출 마감일은 2024년 6월 22일 오후 6시입니다.

상금:
1등: 500만원
2등: 300만원
3등: 100만원
※ 모든 상금에는 세금이 면제됩니다.

자세한 내용은 다음 연락처로 문의하세요.
이메일: Seouloffice@seoulmysoul.com
전화: (02) 11-0000

어휘 complex 복잡한 demographic 인구의 elderly 연세가 드신 decline 감소하다 birth rate 출생률 resident 거주민 contribute 기여하다 innovative 혁신적인 perspective 관점 address 다루다 labor 노동력 shortage 부족 ensure 보장하다 secure 안정된 retirement 은퇴 policy 정책 immigrant 이민자 foster 조성하다 migrant 이주하는 submission 제출(안) entry 출품작 deadline 마감일 tax-free 면세의

12 정답 ②

해설 5번째 문장에서 문제를 신속하게 해결하기 위해 알맞은 부서로 문제가 전달된다고 언급되므로, 글의 내용과 일치하는 것은 ② '이곳은 문제를 적합한 부서로 이관한다.'이다.
① 이곳은 주말에 1시간 이내에 보고서를 읽는다. → 4번째 문장에서 영업일에만 1시간 이내에 검토된다고 언급되므로 옳지 않다.
③ 이곳은 모든 주민에게 개인 정보 제공을 요구한다. → 마지막 2번째 문장에서 익명으로 남기를 원하는 경우 개인 정보를 제공하지 않아도 된다고 언급되므로 옳지 않다.
④ 이곳은 불법 행위와 관련된 문제를 직접 처리한다. → 마지막 문장에서 법 위반 관련 문제는 경찰에 연락하라고 언급되므로 옳지 않다.

해석 저희 애버딘시 정부는 주민 여러분을 지원하기 위해 곁에 있습니다. 신고할 문제가 있으신 경우에는 아래 양식을 작성해 주세요. 저희에게 신고하셔야 하는 문제에는 도시 도로, 전기 및 가스 서비스, 전력선, 신호등 관련 이슈가 포함됩니다. 모든 신고는 게시된 후 1시간 이내에 검토됩니다(영업일에만 해당). 가능한 한 신속하게 문제를 해결하기 위해 알맞은 부서로 문제가 전달됩니다. 자세한 내용을 위해 연락할 수 있도록 성함과 전화번호 또는 이메일 주소를 남겨 주세요. 익명으로 남기를 원하시는 분은 어떠한 개인정보도 제공하지 않으셔도 됩니다. 법 위반과 관련된 사안의 경우 지역 경찰에 연락하시기 바랍니다.

어휘 resident 주민 traffic light 신호등 post 게시하다 business day 영업일 forward 전달하다 proper 적절한 department 부서 resolve 해결하다 swiftly 빠르게 anonymous 익명의 violation 위반 transfer 이관하다 appropriate 적절한 illegal 불법의

13 정답 ③

해설 4번째 문장에서 세무 전문가와의 일대일 상담을 통한 온라인 맞춤형 조언을 제공한다고 언급되므로, 글의 내용과 일치하지 않는 것은 ③ '온라인으로는 맞춤형 가이드를 제공하지 않는다.'이다.
① 소상공인을 위해 설계되었다. → 첫 문장에서 언급된 내용이다.
② 사용자가 세금 납부를 준비하는 데 도움을 준다. → 2번째 문장에서 언급된 내용이다.
④ 사용자의 민감한 정보를 보호한다. → 마지막 3번째 문장에서 언급된 내용이다.

해석 무료 TaxCare 프로그램으로 세금 신고를 간소화하세요

중소기업청(SBA)이 소상공인을 위한 새로운 무료 세금 지원 프로그램을 출시했습니다. 이것은 사용이 편리하고, 안전하고, 효율적이며, 세금 준비 및 세금 (법) 준수를 돕습니다. 이 프로그램은 단계별 가이드, 체크리스트, 템플릿과 함께 직관적인 온라인 포털 사이트를 제공합니다. 소상공인은 세무 전문가와의 일대일 상담을 통해 온라인 맞춤형 조언을 받을 수 있습니다. 최첨단 보안 조치로 민감한 정보를 보호하며, 이를 통해 소상공인은 안심하고 세금에 대한 준비를 할 수 있습니다. 등록을 위해서나 더 자세히 알기 위해서는 중소기업청 웹사이트를 방문하시거나 가까운 중소기업청 사무소에 문의하세요. 저희는 여러분이 가장 잘하는 일인 사업을 운영하는 것에 집중할 수 있도록 돕겠습니다.

어휘 tax filing 세금 신고 Small Business Administration 중소기업청 launch 출시하다 user-friendly 사용이 편리한 secure 안전한 compliance (법·명령 등의) 준수 intuitive 직관적인 step-by-step 단계별 personalized 맞춤형인 one-on-one 일대일 consultation 상담 professional 전문가 state-of-the-art 최첨단의 measure 조치 enroll 등록하다 local 지역의 run 운영하다 customized 맞춤형인

14 정답 ④

해설 수백 시간의 촬영 장면 중 어떤 장면을 보여줄 것인지는 결국 제작자의 의도에 따라 선택되기에, 다큐멘터리 영화 안에서도 현실이 특정 방향으로 재구성된다는 내용의 글이다. 따라서 글의

주제로 가장 적절한 것은 ④ '현실을 재구성한 표현으로서의 다큐멘터리'이다.

① 다큐멘터리 영화의 공감을 불러일으키는 능력 → 특정 인물에게 공감을 불러일으키고자 장면을 선별한다는 내용은 다큐멘터리가 현실을 재구성하는 측면을 나타내기 위한 예시에 불과하다.

② 다큐멘터리 영화 속 객관적 현실의 반영 → 제작자의 의도에 따라 현실이 재구성된다는 것이 글의 요지이므로 적절하지 않다.

③ 다큐멘터리에 대한 관객 수요의 결정 요인 → 관객 수요에 관해서는 언급되지 않았다.

해석 다큐멘터리는 실제 사건들을 보여주고 실제 사람들과의 인터뷰를 담고 있지만, 어떤 장면을 넣고 그것을 어떻게 관객에게 보여줄지 결정하는 것은 다큐멘터리 영화 제작자의 몫이다. 다큐멘터리 영화 제작자들은 보통 수백 시간의 장면을 촬영하는데, 이 장면들은 이후 장편 영화 길이로 편집되고 특정한 방법으로 배열된다. 영화 제작자들이 관객들에게 보여주고자 선택하는 장면은 관객들이 주제에 어떻게 반응할 것인가에 강하게 영향을 미친다. 예컨대, 다큐멘터리 영화 제작자는 관객이 영화 속 어느 한 인물에게 공감하기를 원할 수도 있고, 그래서 그들은 그 사람이 부정적으로 비치도록 행동하고 말하는 장면을 보여주지 않기로 할 수도 있다.

어휘 up to ~의 몫인 footage 장면 feature film 장편 영화 sympathize with ~에 공감하다 evoke (감정 등을) 불러일으키다 determinant 결정 요인 reconstruct 재구성하다 representation 표현, 묘사

15 정답 ④

해설 이 글은 영국 식민지 통치자들의 지배 방식이 인도 사회에서 여전히 막강한 영향력을 발휘하고 있는 오늘날의 카스트 제도를 형성했다는 점을 서술하고 있으므로, 글의 요지로 가장 적절한 것은 ④ '오늘날의 카스트 제도를 형성한 것은 영국 식민지 통치자들이었다.'이다.

① 카스트 제도는 오랫동안 인도인들의 삶을 파괴했다. → 이를 암시하는 언급은 있으나 이는 카스트 제도가 영국 식민지 통치자들에 의해 만들어진 것이라는 글의 중심 내용을 서술하기 위한 서론에 불과하다.

② 영국 식민지 통치자들은 카스트 제도에 의해 영향을 받았다. → 영국 식민지 통치자들은 카스트 제도에 의해 영향을 받은 것이 아니라 카스트 제도를 세운 주체이므로 적절하지 않다.

③ 영국은 인도에서 카스트 제도를 없애는 데 기여했다. → 오히려 카스트 제도를 만든 사람들이 영국 식민지 통치자들이었다고 언급되므로 반대된다.

해석 수 세기 동안, 카스트 제도는 힌두교의 종교 생활과 사회생활의 거의 모든 측면을 좌우해 왔으며, 각 집단은 이 복잡한 계급제에서 특정한 위치를 차지하고 있다. 종종 부당하고 퇴행적이라는 비판을 받음에도, 그것(카스트 제도)은 수 세기 동안 사실상 바뀌지 않은 채, 벗어나기가 거의 불가능한 고정된 사회 질서 안에 사람들을 가두어 왔다. 그러나 역사가들은, 18세기까지 카스트 제도의 공식적인 구분은 인도인들에게 제한적인 의미를 가졌고, 사회적 정체성은 훨씬 더 유연했으며, 사람들이 한 카스트에서 다른 카스트로 쉽게 이동할 수 있었다고 말한다. 새로운 연구에 따르면 견고한 경계는 영국 식민지 통치자들에 의해 세워진 것인데, 이들은 카스트 제도가 인도의 결정적인 사회적 특징이 되도록 만들었다. 사실, 그들은 관습법으로 쉽게 통치될 수 있는 단일 사회를 만들기 위해 최선을 다했던 것이다.

어휘 caste 카스트 제도 dictate 영향을 끼치다, 결정하다 religious 종교적인 occupy 차지하다 hierarchy 계급(제) unjust 부당한 regressive 퇴행적인 virtually 사실상 trap 가두다, 옥죄다 social order 사회질서 escape 벗어나다, 빠져나오다 distinction 차이, 구분 identity 정체성 flexible 유연한 colonial 식민(지)의 defining 결정적인 govern 통치하다 eradicate 없애다

16 정답 ④

해설 연구 프로젝트를 완수하는 데 한 사람의 지식과 기술만으로는 턱없이 부족하기에 협동 작업이 필요하다는 내용의 글이다. 글에서 언급된 인간 게놈 프로젝트는 협동 작업이 필수적으로 요구되는 대규모 연구 프로젝트 사례로 소개되었을 뿐, 과학 지식의 진위를 다루는 글이 아니다. 따라서 글의 흐름상 어색한 문장은 과학 지식이 가장 확실한 지식이라고 가정하는 것이 잘못되었다고 이야기하는 내용의 ④이다.

해석 협동 작업은 실질적으로 연구 프로젝트를 완수하는 데 필요한 일이 어떤 한 사람이 혼자 완수하기에는 그야말로 너무 많기 때문에 필요하다. 예를 들어, 목적이 인간 DNA에서 30억 개 이상의 화학 단위를 식별하고 배열 순서를 밝히는 것이었던 인간 게놈 프로젝트를 생각해 보라. 이 대규모 협력 프로젝트는 시작부터 완수까지 약 15년이 걸렸고 미국, 유럽, 아시아의 20개 대학의 연구팀을 참여시켰다. 그것을 완수하는 데 필요한 일의 순전한 양은 협력 체제를 필요로 했다. (솔깃하지만 잘못된 한 가지 가정은 과학 지식이 우리가 가진 가장 확실한 지식의 형태라는 것이다.) 한 개인이 관련된 모든 전문 지식과 기술을 가지고 있었다고 할지라도, 그 사람이 한 생애 동안 이 모든 일을 완수하는 것은 불가능했을 것이다.

어휘 practically 현실적으로, 실제로 on one's own 혼자서 identify 식별하다 sequence 배열 순서를 밝히다 massively 거대하게 inception 시작, 개시 sheer 순전한 necessitate 필요로 하다 set-up 구성 (방식), 체제 tempting 솔깃한 assumption 가정 possess 소유하다 expertise 전문 지식

17 정답 ②

해설 농업의 산업화는 농부들의 수확량을 증가시키는 데 도움이 되었지만, 그로 인해 생겨난 화합물이 환경과 인간에게 부작용을 일으켰다는 내용의 글이다. However로 시작하는 주어진 문장은 그것들(they)이 환경에 해롭고 인간이 섭취하기에 건강하지 않다고 했으므로, 주어진 문장 앞에는 반대로 그것들의 긍정적인 측면이 나와야 함을 유추할 수 있다. 한편, ② 앞에서 비료와 농약이 저렴하고 효과적이라는 긍정적인 내용이 나왔는데, ② 뒤에서 갑자기 부정적인 영향들에 관해 이야기하고 있으므로 문맥이 단절된다. 그러므로 주어진 문장이 ②에 들어가야 문맥이 자연스럽게 이어지며, 주어진 문장의 they는 ② 앞 문장에 나온 These fertilizers and pesticides를 지칭하는 것을 알 수 있다. 따라서 주어진 문장이 들어갈 위치로 가장 적절한 것은 ②이다.

해석 농업의 산업화는 농부들의 수확량을 엄청나게 증가시키는 데 도움이 되는 다양한 기술의 개발을 가져왔다. 화합물은 토양을 비옥하게 하고 곤충과 그러한 다른 해충으로부터 농작물을 보호하기 위해 사용된다. 이러한 비료와 농약은 저렴하고 효과적이다. 하지만, 그것들은 환경에 상당히 해로울 수 있고, 인간이 섭취하기에 건강하지 않을 수도 있다. 농장의 유출수가 상수도로 유입되면서 물고기와 다른 해양생물들이 병에 걸리게 하고 생태계를 교란한다. 인간은 이러한 화학물질로 처리된 음식을 취급하거나 먹는 것에서 심각한 문제가 생기는 것으로 알려져 있다. 예를 들어, 농약 사용은 농장 노동자들 사이에서 태어난 아기들의 선천적 결함과 관련이 있다.

어휘 harmful 해로운 ingest 섭취하다 industrialization 산업화 a multitude of 다수의 yield 수확량 immensely 엄청나게 chemical compound 화합물 fertilize 비옥하게 하다 crop 농작물 pest 해충 pesticide 농약, 살충제 runoff (땅 위를) 흐르는 물 water supply 상수도 disrupt 교란하다, 방해하다 defect 결함

18 정답 ①

해설 가상현실 기술의 장점을 서술하는 동시에 이를 이용하는 데 있어서 주의할 점에 대해 논하는 글이다. 가상현실이 우리 삶을 개선하고 혁신하는 강력한 도구가 될 수 있다는 내용의 주어진 글 다음에는, virtual reality를 it으로 받아 그것이 이미 많은 분야에서 사용되고 있다는 내용의 (B)가 와야 한다. 그다음으로, (A)에서 However를 통해 맥락이 반전되면서 그러한 이점(these benefits)에도 불구하고 우리가 그것을 지나치게 이용한다면 가상현실 기술(it)은 여러 문제점을 일으킬 수 있다는 내용이 이어져야 한다. 마지막으로, 그러므로(Hence) 우리가 가상현실을 적당히 이용하며 현실 세계와의 균형을 유지하는 것이 중요하다고 주장하는 (C)로 글이 마무리되는 것이 자연스럽다. 따라서 글의 순서로 가장 적절한 것은 ① '(B) - (A) - (C)'이다.

해석 가상현실은 올바르게 사용될 때 우리의 삶을 더 나은 것으로 바꾸고 우리가 일상생활에서 여러 일을 하는 방식을 혁신하는 강력한 도구가 될 수 있다. (B) 실은, 그것은 사용자들에게 더 개인화되고 직관적인 경험을 제공하고 전 세계 사람들을 연결하기 위해 이미 많은 분야에 관여되고 있다. (A) 하지만 이러한 모든 이점에도 불구하고, 우리가 이것을 지나치게 이용한다면 고립감과 현실감 상실과 같은 문제가 발생할 수 있다. (C) 따라서 가상현실을 적당히 이용하고 현실 세계의 상호작용과 건강한 균형을 유지하여 부정적인 결과를 겪지 않고도 가상 현실의 이점을 거두도록 하는 것이 중요하다.

어휘 virtual reality 가상현실 revolutionize 혁신을 일으키다 go about ~을 하다 ordinary 일상적인 personalize 개인화하다, 개인의 필요에 맞추다 isolation 고립 go overboard with ~을 지나치게 하다 intuitive 직관적인, 사용하기 쉬운 in moderation 적당히 interaction 상호작용 ensure 보장하다 reap 거두다, 수확하다 suffer 겪다, 시달리다 consequence 결과

19 정답 ③

해설 이 글의 요지는 이슬람교도들에게 요구되는 엄격한 생활 방식에 관한 것이다. 빈칸 앞에서 규율에 무심한 사람들은 이슬람교도가 되기 힘들다는 점을 서술하고 있고, 그 뒤에서는 이슬람교도들에게 요구되는 많은 책무에 관해서 서술하고 있다. 따라서 빈칸에 들어갈 말로 가장 적절한 것은 ③ '굉장한 노력과 절제력'이다.

① 배우려는 의지 → 무언가를 배우려는 의지에 관해서는 언급되지 않았다.

② 가난한 이를 위한 연민 → 이슬람교도들이 지켜야 하는 교리 중 일부만을 서술하는 선지이다.

④ 내면의 평화와 용서 → 내면의 평화를 유지해야 한다는 내용이나 누군가를 용서하는 마음을 가져야 한다는 내용은 언급되지 않았다.

해석 급속한 확산에도 불구하고, 이슬람교는 규정을 가볍게 여기는 이들을 위한 종교는 아니다. 오히려, 이슬람교의 교리를 준수하기 위해서는 굉장한 노력과 절제력이 필요하다. 이슬람교도는 동이 트기 전에 일어나 매일 요구되는 다섯 번의 기도 중 첫 번째 기도를 하는 교리를 지켜야 하고, 다섯 번의 기도 중 어느 한 기도도 먼저 의식에 따라 몸을 씻지 않고서는 할 수가 없다. 수면, 노동, 오락 활동은 기도 다음으로 우선순위가 밀려난다. 라마단 한 달 동안 금식하기, 일생에 적어도 한 번은 메카를 순례하기, 이슬람교를 믿는 가난한 사람들을 구호하기 위해 세금 내기, 그리고 이슬람 교리를 받아들이는 것은 진지하고, 힘든 헌신을 요구한다. 대체로 전 세계 대다수의 이슬람교도는 실제로 이러한 교리들을 지킨다.

어휘 casual 무심한, 건성의 regulation 규정 adhere to ~을 고수하다 observe 지키다 prayer 기도 ritually 의식에 따라 cleanse 씻다 recreational 오락의 take second place to ~ 다음으로 우선순위가 밀려나다 fasting 단식, 금식 pilgrimage 순례 relief 구호 creed (종교적) 교리, 신념 energetic 힘든 commitment 헌신 on the whole 대체로 vast majority 대다수 tenet 교리 sympathy 연민 discipline 절제력

20 정답 ③

해설 이 글은 영화 속에 등장하는 악당에 관해 서술하는 글로, 가학성과 이기주의를 그 특징으로 소개하고 있다. 이후 글 중후반부의 But으로 시작하는 문장에서 그중 '가학성'이 악당의 본질임을 주장하고 있다. 이 글에서 '가학성'을 희생자를 다치게 하는 것을 즐기는 특성이라 설명하고 있으므로, 악당의 본질을 나타내는 표현으로 빈칸에 들어갈 말로 가장 적절한 것은 ③ '해를 입히는 것에서 즐거움을 얻다'이다.

① 자기들만의 법칙을 만들다 → 악당은 단순히 법을 어기며 자기 멋대로 행동하는 것을 넘어서, 해를 끼치는 행위 자체에서 쾌락을 느낀다는 것이 이 글의 핵심이므로 적절하지 않다.

② 보거나 듣기에 재미있다 → 악당의 본질에 관한 내용이 빈칸에 들어가야 하는데, 이 선지는 악당이 나오는 영화를 보는 관객의 입장을 서술하고 있으므로 적절하지 않다.

④ 과신 때문에 결국 패배하다 → '과신'보다는 '가학성'이 악당의 본질이라고 언급했으며, 악당이 결국에는 패배한다는 점을 강조하는 글도 아니다.

해석 악당은 공포 영화에만 국한되지 않는다. 액션 영화는 나쁜 놈들로 가득 차 있다. 보통, 악당들은 돈이나 권력에 대한 탐욕에 의해 동기를 부여받는다. 이러한 동기는 많은 상세한 말 없이도 제시되는 경향이 있다. 두 가지 추가적인 특징이 흔한데, 그것은 가학성과 자기중심성이다. 영화 속 악당들 다수는 단순히 희생자들을 다치게 하기 위해 그렇게 하는 것을 즐기는 것처럼 보이고, 그들은 자기 자신에 대해 매우 높게 생각하는 경향이 있다. 사실, 그들의 자신감은 흔히 치명적인 결함으로 드러나는데, 왜냐하면 그들의 과신은 영웅에게 그들의 손아귀에서 벗어나 그들을 물리칠 기회를 주기 때문이다. 그러나 가학성 부분은 악당의 본질이다. 영화 속 악당에 관한 텔레비전 특집 방송에서, 전국적으로 유명한 영화 비평가인 Siskel과 Ebert는 이러한 일반적인 점을 강조했다. "악한 존재가 되는 것을 즐기는 것은 모든 성공적인 악당의 핵심이다." 그들은 이것은 '가장 중요한 특징'이라고 덧붙였다. 그러므로 악당을 정의하는 것은 단지 해로운 행동을 하는 것이 아니며, 진정으로 악한 악당은 해를 입히는 것에서 즐거움을 얻는다.

어휘 villain 악당 confine 국한시키다 greed 탐욕 elaboration 상술, 정교함 feature 특징 sadism 가학성 egotism 자기중심성 for the sake of ~을 위해서 exalted 높은 fatal 치명적인 flaw 결함 overconfidence 과신 clutch 손아귀, 움켜쥠 prominent 유명한 emphasize 강조하다 derive 끌어내다 inflict (괴로움 등을) 가하다 ultimately 결국

교재 내용 문의 및 무료 학습 자료 다운로드
http://cafe.naver.com/shimson2000

2025
공무원 영어 대비
필수 전략서

2025 출제 기조 전환 완벽 반영
미리 보는 신유형 출제 예상 문제 수록
심우철 선생님만의 구문·문법·독해·생활영어 전략 수록
암기 노트로 학습하는 핵심 문법 포인트/실무 중심 어휘/생활영어 표현